H. Webster Johnson
Professor of Marketing
Wayne State University

SOUTH-WESTERN PUBLISHING COMPANY

Cincinnati　　　　　　Chicago　　　　　　　Dallas
　　Burlingame, Calif.　　　New Rochelle, N. Y.
S90

CREATIVE SELLING

PREFACE

For the person seriously considering a career in selling, this book is indispensable. It has been prepared for the exacting demands of the individual preparing for a successful sales future. The contents emphasize those elements of selling that the salesman must use constantly. The presentation is factual, precise, and direct. Numerous examples make the text more realistic to the reader. The purpose is to develop sound sales strategy in such a way that the customer is convinced of the integrity of the salesman and his product.

Much of the material consists of fundamental sales information presented in a vivid manner that will hold the attention of the reader. The forceful presentation will also aid the reader in selecting from the material valuable ideas that are applicable to each prospect. The effectiveness of this material has been tested in the author's sales training classes.

Part I treats selling as a career. The many opportunities and rewards of a sales career are outlined.

Part II stresses the importance of personal preparation for effective selling through the salesman's understanding himself, his product or service, and his customer.

Part III presents in detail the process of completing a sale. Information and illustrations are interwoven to give an integrated approach which can be used every day in real selling situations.

Part IV blends the old and the new in selling. The salesman is instructed in how to use new, refreshing selling techniques and methods that will get affirmative action. He is also given valuable suggestions on how to reuse effectively some old techniques and methods and to integrate them with the new to get a favorable customer response. This part is packed with suggestions, ideas, and approaches that will be invaluable to any salesman.

This book will appeal to many people, but the author has directed the text primarily to the following specific groups:

(1) The business school student who wants thorough sales training that will prepare him for a lucrative selling career;

(2) The collegiate terminal student who is preparing for a career in the marketing field;

(3) The adult who enrolls in a special class to get practical selling information in minimum time;

(4) The employed salesman who wishes to sharpen his selling skills.

For instructional purposes, the material is blended to meet different approaches. Those interested in a rapid survey course will find the text material complete and adequate. Those desiring a more thorough approach will discover that answering the questions and solving the problems will fortify them with an improved understanding of the material. Those who seek a thorough and comprehensive grasp of the material will not only answer questions and solve problems but also will work on case solving. These cases range from relatively simple situations to very complex ones which will require imagination, ability, and concentration to reach satisfactory solutions.

The author wishes to express thanks to the many students and salesmen who have contributed to the contents of this text directly or indirectly. To name them all is impossible.

Some people stand out as deserving special recognition: My three brothers, all of whom are or have been outstanding salesmen, for their aid and counsel, and my sister who has shown me the value of patience; Ken Bement of the Burroughs Corporation for suggestions and ideas; John Malseed of the Pepsi Cola Company who has encouraged the author by his application of selling concepts developed in numerous discussions; and Don David of Campbell-Ewald Company who in his keen, penetrating way made suggestions that forced the author to reevaluate some of his thinking.

Appreciation is also expressed to Roger Peterson for his assistance in the preparation of illustrative material; to Edward Sharples, Jr. for his critical evaluation of the manuscript; and to Mrs. Sharyl Diegel for the patience she showed in typing the manuscript. To my wife, Josephine, a sincere thanks for suggestions and encouragement.

H. WEBSTER JOHNSON

CONTENTS

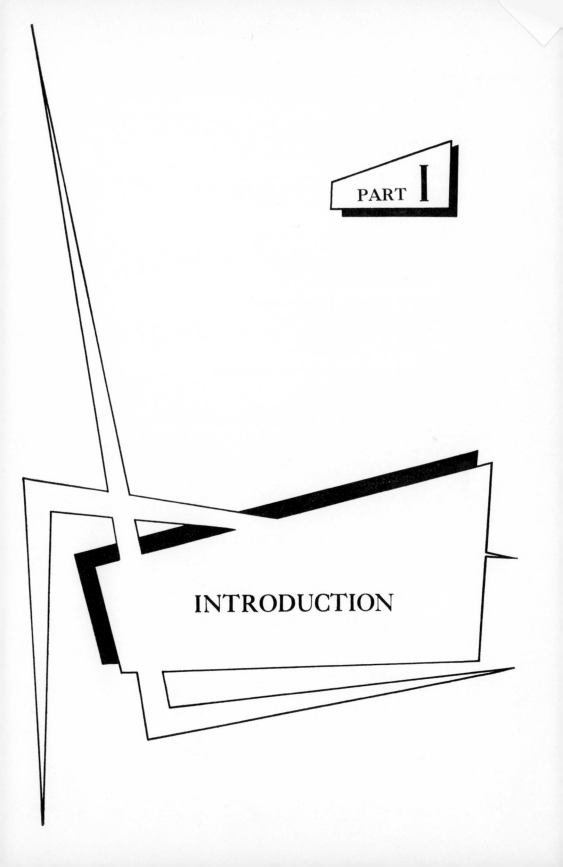

PART I

INTRODUCTION

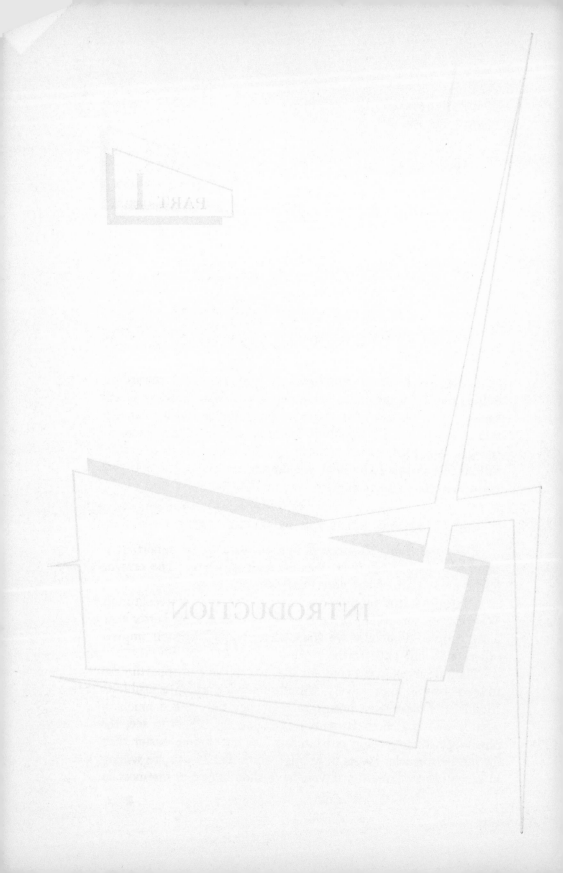

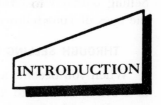

Selling as a Career

Selling as a career can be most promising and rewarding. Selling can be a means of achieving a satisfying position in our society. The person who wants respect and authority can use selling to gain such recognition. Selling leads the field in financial reward. But most of all, selling can be the road to a greater fulfillment of the individual within society. It is one job that multiplies your effectiveness to your fellowman.

SELLING HELPS YOU TO SECURE STATUS

Everyone wants to succeed. We all want to be important in some way to our relatives, friends, and associates. The craving for status is part of our very existence.

Securing status requires performance worthy of recognition. We must do something or be something that is a bit better than most people. Somehow we must show traits that will impress others with our real worth.

The salesman, in his complex life, has numerous opportunities to serve people impressively. Unselfish service which is visible to friends and associates brings early recognition. Since much of what a salesman does is readily available for others to see, the possibility of appearing outstanding becomes much easier than for the person who labors in relative obscurity. If you are willing to serve others honestly, if you have their interests foremost in mind, you can achieve your status and be the envy of others. Selling is that wonderful tool that permits you to rise or fall in the eyes of your fellowman.

THROUGH SELLING YOU GAIN A POSITION OF AUTHORITY

When you become a salesman, you have walked the first step in a series leading to a position of authority. You have placed yourself on "the firing line." As a salesman, you can enjoy dealing with people, satisfying wants, meeting requests. At this level you gain a foundation of knowledge of people, of products, of services. This can be the beginning of a fascinating career in which you progress step by step on solid achievement. You progress and advance slowly but steadily up that inclined path to greater opportunities. Schooled in the discipline of experience and work, your advancement to higher positions will be solidly based because you have gone forward a step at a time.

Authority may seem to be a privilege, but it is also responsibility. As you advance in an orderly way from beginning salesman to supervisor, to district manager, to regional manager, and finally to sales manager, your authority increases correspondingly—and so do your responsibilities. Your authority will give satisfaction; your increased responsibilities, concern. You will be confident you can handle your duties because your business experience has been one of growth. More and more, the highest positions in business are filled by men who have traveled the sales route.

SELLING PERMITS YOU TO SHOW YOUR REAL WORTH

Make no mistake; selling is not easy. People looking for easy ways to get ahead should not choose selling as a career. Which is the easy way to get ahead? There is none.

Choose selling as a means to demonstrate your real worth because you are confident of your own ability, proud of your ambition, and sure of your potential for success. Through selling, you can show your true strength and demonstrate traits of character that would not be brought out in other jobs. Just as in football a coach is measured by a winning team, a salesman is measured by profitable sales.

Success in selling can be measured by sales volume, sales profits, balanced performance, customer satisfaction, few complaints, special services, and a host of other activities. Your real worth can be shown in many ways through a wide spectrum of services.

SELLING CAN INCREASE YOUR CONTRIBUTION TO SOCIETY

Each one of us wants to do something worthwhile, something that will make this world a better place in which to live. Some people express themselves in lodge or club activities; some work extensively in charity projects; some find expression through church work; and still others use various ways to show kindness to their fellowman.

In selling you need not overlook such opportunities for expressing yourself. However, you have one additional way to express yourself—through selling products and services that will enrich the lives of others. Many a person living a drab existence has had his life enriched by becoming acquainted with and using a new product or service. Think how lives have been enriched through the availability of books and other reading materials made available by technology but sold by salesmen. Consider the contribution of radio and television, also developed by technology, but again brought within range of the masses by concentrated selling.

Invention and technology develop thousands of new products each year, but selling brings them to people. When selling falls down on the job, products disappear. Many worthwhile products have failed because selling was done inadequately. Many products have succeeded because selling was carefully planned and brilliantly executed when failure seemed imminent.

Our lives today are infinitely richer because salesmen have done a superior job of convincing people to buy more products and services. As more of each were sold, greater production permitted a decrease in price. This, in turn, broadened the market until most of our people now consider as necessities products unknown ten years ago or products so expensive that only the wealthy could buy them.

FINANCIAL REWARDS ARE GREATER IN SELLING

You will earn more in selling than you can in any other activity of comparable effort. Year after year, effective salesmen are among the nation's top earners. When you become a successful salesman, you need never fear being without a job. Employers will flock to you with lucrative offers, personnel men will constantly tempt you with new opportunities, and you will be besieged by individuals who want to go into business with you.

You can write your own program of advancement. You may choose to remain a salesman and reap rich rewards from your individual efforts. You may choose a career in selling administration and multiply your effectiveness through a corps of well-trained, highly effective salesmen. You may choose to sell franchises and increase your earnings through a well-chosen group of distributors. You may become a sales trainer to develop men for selling. You may become a top executive and head a sales-minded corporation which becomes more successful through your sales direction. Your progress will depend on your own ability; you will be unshackled by the weaknesses of others. As your limitations are your own and what you choose to make of them, so are your financial rewards your own.

SELLING MAKES YOU A WELL-ROUNDED MAN

The successful salesman has many desirable qualities. If he did not have them when he began selling, he had to acquire them along the way. He has rubbed shoulders with many people, and the rubbing process has smoothed him to a finer person. The further the salesman progresses, the finer becomes his perception.

A selling job forces the salesman to meet the public. Like it or not, he must meet people in order to sell. In the process of selling, he frequently bumps people. Bumping either removes rough edges of weaknesses or gouges holes in us which we must carefully rebuild. Every salesman's roughness is battered. He either gets rid of these rough spots, or he ceases as a salesman. But the other quality, that of rebuilding damaged spots, requires skill, perseverance, ability, and a willingness to learn. Failure to rebuild will soon force one out of selling.

This constant adjustment of self, ever responsive to customer wishes, develops a person so that he learns to sense what is proper and avoid the offensive. He becomes considerate of others without giving up his own individuality. He conforms with the conventional but remains original and persuasive on important things. He expresses his views in such a way that he gains agreement without antagonizing. He gains friends by being friendly; he gains sales by serving customers' interests; he gains success through constructive, balanced, planned application of principles of selling.

TYPES OF SELLING JOBS

To each of you selling may represent a particular job. But selling actually consists of a number of duties ranging from jobs with little selling to jobs in which selling is primary. Some selling may be done from the home, the office, or in the store. Some salesmen live at home and sell in the area. Others travel extensively, covering large territories and interesting assignments. Selling is not an opportunity; it is a wide range of opportunities that presents a variety of interesting work.

Direct Selling

Either as a part-time or full-time job, direct selling furnishes thousands of people a chance to work in a rewarding position. Several well-known companies sell almost entirely through the house-to-house approach. Others use the party system in which groups gather in homes.

Mail-Order Selling

An extensive selling area is the mail order. While we may think that area is monopolized by a few large mail-order houses, actually there are thousands of small firms and individuals carrying on lucrative selling entirely by mail. Careful preparation is essential because selling by mail has special techniques which must be adapted to particular needs.

Telephone Selling

Many types of merchandise and services are sold successfully by telephone. The housewife may sell directly from her home. Stores and small business firms conduct extensive selling by telephone. Many large firms use telephone selling. Frequently, however, the telephone is used as an aid in selling, in discovering likely prospects, in arranging appointments, and in setting up demonstrations.

Retail Selling

Retailing employs several million sales people. Retailing covers a wide range of products and requires people with varying skills. Retailing runs from the simplest type of selling in which a salesclerk takes the customer's money and hands out merchandise to very sophisticated selling in which a salesman may plan home interiors, help choose pianos for particular needs, suggest gowns for formal receptions, or select automobiles to meet specific requirements. Some may feel that the retail salesman is unimportant, but there are many retail positions that demand exacting requirements which are suitably rewarded. At the lower end of the scale, retail salesmen may get only a few thousand dollars a year in salary; at the upper end, incomes of ten thousand dollars a year and more are common.

Wholesale Selling

Selling for wholesalers can be most interesting and challenging. You deal with a tangible product. Much of what you sell is repeat business with customers you know. A part of your selling is relatively easy. Yet, to be successful, the wholesaler's salesman must aggressively sell new items and those which the buyer feels may not move readily. Wholesale selling is an area in which an average salesman who willingly puts forth effort can be successful, and in which the superior salesman can progress to management positions.

Selling for Manufacturers

Selling for a manufacturing firm is what some consider real selling. Many are employed in such work and many become amazingly successful. As in many other types of work, selling for manufacturers can be routine, consisting of giving services, making displays, and stocking merchandise. It can also be the most intricate selling, calling for laying out buildings, specifying equipment, making bids, and, above all, handling people skillfully.

Selling convenience items such as bread, cigarettes, and soap does not require great skill. But selling locomotives, machinery, and various types of specialized equipment requires skill, education, years of training and experience. For such a range of ability, the rewards are equally far ranging from five thousand dollars a year at the bottom to well over a hundred thousand dollars a year at the top. This can be an exciting field. You may enter at various points; and your progress is limited only by your ability, education, interest, and willingness to work hard. Goals in this area are virtually unlimited. Success depends on you, for the opportunities are there.

Selling Intangibles

Interesting, difficult, challenging—these terms may well describe the selling of intangibles. Insurance is one of the outstanding intangibles sold by thousands of salesmen to millions of customers. Many salesmen fail or are mediocre in selling insurance, but some are phenomenally successful. Much of their success can be attributed to careful preparation, intensive training, attention to details, and perseverance. If you are willing to work hard and are ready to accept training and instructions, your job can be appealing and satisfying. Most who want selling careers in the intangibles area can be successful if they are willing to follow the road outlined. Many salesmen selling securities—stock, bonds, mutual funds—have learned to follow prescribed patterns to secure the best sales.

Selling Services

As our economy expands, more of our income is being spent on services. Laundry, dry cleaning, beauty salon operations, janitor services, window cleaning, repair services—these are a few of the thousands of services used every day. If you doubt the term, "thousands of services," go through the classified telephone directory and you will be amazed at the number listed.

In industry, many services are available and most of them are unfamiliar to the average person. Examples are chrome plating and tumbling of metal parts; cutters in the garment trade; measured portions in the restaurant trade.

Selling jobs are expanding rapidly in services which not only give sales opportunities but also permit many to graduate from employee salesmen to salesmen owning their own business.

Manufacturers' Representatives

A manufacturer's representative is an independent salesman selling on commission in a specified territory at prices established by the manufacturer. He frequently represents several manufacturers in one territory and sells noncompetitive products to the same buyers. This group of salesmen frequently has outstanding salesmen who depend on their own ability to pioneer and sell. Financial returns are high, and the jobs are at the top rank in selling.

Broker Selling

A broker brings buyer and seller together. He is instrumental in developing sales and is paid a commission for each sale. A food broker may take on the character of a manufacturer's representative and become very successful since performance is limited only by ability.

Specialty Selling

Specialty selling embraces a wide area and covers many of the types of selling mentioned in the preceding paragraphs. A specialty man usually has a limited line, such as silver flatware in the jewelry store line, children's shoes in footwear, or industrial paints for a paint manufacturer. He becomes an expert in his narrow line of merchandise and handles larger orders as well as new accounts. Often a specialty salesman has gone through rigorous training for several years before he becomes productive in selling.

LOOK AHEAD

The following chapters will arouse your interest and quicken your emotions. They can unlock information and instruction that will change your life. You are on the threshold of opportunity and success beyond your fondest dreams. Here you have the key to unlock the door to financial security. You will see how you can forge ahead by developing yourself. You are the one who determines how far you will go. There is no restraining hand unless you choose to place one on yourself.

Whether you are a young man or woman starting your working career, an experienced person who still has not succeeded, or one who chooses to increase his effectiveness through part-time selling, to all of you the mastery of this material can be the first step to a successful sales career that leads to the fulfillment of your hopes and aspirations.

PART II

SELLING PREPARATION

CHAPTER 1

You

You are starting out as a salesman. Shyness, doubt, fear—what crowds into your mind as you wonder what the job will offer? Your problem is simple: Have you really mastered YOU?

Do you know yourself? Have you learned to control yourself, to discipline yourself so that you will act correctly? Let us start by molding you in a pattern that will make you an effective, successful, happy salesman.

HOW DO YOU APPEAR IN THE EYES OF THE CUSTOMER?

Consider your appearance. What do others see when they look at you? There are many features that cannot be changed or controlled; your features are individual and peculiarly yours. Starting with the raw material, how can you become an attractive, appealing individual to the customer?

Outward Appearance

First, concentrate on outward appearance. Your body should be clean, including fingernails, teeth, and hair. Your suit should be conservative, clean, and pressed; your shirt and tie appropriate; your socks a proper shade, matching your suit; your shoes shined and suitable for the occasion. If the weather is hot, rainy, cold, or otherwise unseasonable, you may have to freshen up several times during the day. Remember, the customer you are facing sees you as you are now, not as you were this morning or as you usually appear. Do you wear a hat? If it is your custom, continue to do so. If you do not wear a hat, find out what is the custom in your line of selling. If most of the salesmen wear hats, probably you should wear one. Sometimes it matters and sometimes it does not, but if you are in doubt, follow the accepted practice.

Do not walk into a customer's office with a pipe, cigar, or cigarette in your mouth unless you know him well. If he dislikes smoking, you will already have set up a barrier. Men who habitually smoke may be unaware of the resentment that smoking provokes in the nonsmoker. Not only does he resent the actual smoking, but he loses respect for the man who cannot control his appetite when he should be concentrating on selling. A man would not think of walking into a customer's office munching on a hot dog with mustard oozing out around the edge. Yet, the same man might walk calmly into an office, blow smoke in a person's face, and grind a cigarette butt on the floor. When approaching a customer, remember: at 23 feet he sees you; at 13 feet he hears you; at 3 feet he smells you. And when you shake hands, he feels you. Out of the five senses, seeing, hearing, feeling, smelling, and tasting, your customer has experienced four of them about you. Impressive? Important? You decide.[1]

Voice and Vocabulary

You open your mouth to speak and what comes out? Do you have a pleasant, well-modulated voice? Do you enunciate clearly, or do you mumble, speak with your mouth almost closed, and make indistinct sounds? Do you make an effort to be understood, to speak clearly, and to pronounce names correctly? Does your voice lack many desirable qualities? If so, do not despair. Voice training can accomplish wonders. All of us need to be conscious of our voices to prevent slurring and careless speech, but some may need to be more alert than others to overcome particularly bad voice habits.

---

[1] If you wonder whether you need a bath, you probably do; if you wonder whether you need a shave, you probably do; if you wonder whether you need a haircut, you probably do; if you wonder whether your shoes need shining, they probably do.

In selling, your voice is the primary means of communication. As such, keep it in the best possible condition and supply it with suitable words. At all times use words the customer understands. You can use a number of simple words to express differing shades of meaning. Instead of saying, "I had a swell time," one can use "delightful time," "pleasant time," "interesting evening," "entertaining evening," "a memorable occasion." Instead of an article having a "fine" color, one can use an "appropriate" color, "bright" color, a color "well shaded," a "harmonizing" color, or any number of words more adequately describing exact meaning. Enriching your vocabulary will make your communication more appealing, especially when you couple it with a carefully developed voice that is pleasant in tone, rich in quality, and clear in enunciation.

Poise

The next attribute to be stressed is poise, that particular aura or radiation about you that conveys a feeling about your presence, your power, your control, your assurance. We all know people who are commanding in appearance and influence; conversely, we have all heard the expression, "He's a mouse." Most of us are somewhere in between; but the greater your poise, the more effective you will be. Poise comes through hard work, thorough preparation, knowledge of product or service, careful approach, and intelligent practice. When you are poised, you control yourself, avoid showing irritation, impatience, or temper. You accept praise or criticism with no great outward display. Your attitude conveys to the customer proper respect at the same time that you show faith and confidence in yourself, your company, and your product. Looking at it from another viewpoint, poise shows a lack of fear, minimum traces of nervousness, little hesitation, and absence of failure traits. Failure traits show themselves in different ways. One individual may give an impression of failure through hesitation, stammering, downward looks, and fear; a second individual unconsciously shows failure by an unkempt appearance; a third individual may seek to disguise failure by being noisy, speaking in a loud tone, or by rudeness. Under a trying situation when you are attempting to answer a question or evolve a plan, be as calm as possible on the surface.

Smile

A ready smile goes far toward creating a friendly feeling. People instinctively respond to a smile and are rebuffed by a frown. Smiling can be cultivated. Many who do not smile easily can practice until it becomes natural. A pleasant smile should reflect an inward kindness or warmth which may not otherwise be visible. If you have not learned to smile readily, practice until your smile reveals you as you are to yourself and as you want to be to others. Incidentally, if you are not a friendly person by nature, it would be well to practice those habit-forming traits that will help you to be a friendly, likable person.

Mannerisms

Many people unconsciously develop little quirks or traits which become habits that are often annoying to another person. All of us are familiar with the scene of a little boy reciting for the first time in school before an audience of parents and friends, nervously shuffling his feet on the platform, tugging at his coat, fidgeting with his hands, tweaking his nose, or scratching his ear. Amusing in this situation and at this age, these same habits in the salesman become deadly. Most of us know people who exhibit one or more annoying habits. These mannerisms become particularly dangerous if carried over into speech. (The author remembers well one speaker who had a most unfortunate habit of making an unusual noise about every fifteen seconds of his speech.) Unfortunately, some of these little oddities creep up on us unaware; and while children are corrected by adults who notice such behavior, the average adult or salesman can offend indefinitely because most people are too polite to say anything. Even such a little thing as keeping your hands in your pockets may be offensive at times. Most salesmen appear far better to customers with their hands in a natural position, not in their pockets. "The Case of the Hidden Hands" is often a sign of weakness or nervousness which indicates lack of poise.

Overall Appearance

A commanding appearance, a crisp incisiveness, a brisk walk, a cultivated smile, a well-modulated voice, a look of strength and determination—all these are produced most effectively when a person has excellent health. The many activities of a salesman are physically exhausting and require stamina that must be renewed daily by careful attention to the requirements of the body. Adequate rest, sufficient sleep, attention to details of the body are a necessity if your body, which carries you to success or failure, is to function properly. Just as the mechanic of a racing car tunes it to proper pitch through careful attention to detail, so must the salesman engaged in the everyday activity of pitting himself against other salesmen, buyers, and a host of problems be physically sharp so that he can focus his attention on the required tasks knowing that he is well-equipped to do his best. Physical hindrances which lessen his capabilities and force him to extraordinary effort to overcome some contingencies can be very costly.

TRAITS THAT AFFECT YOUR PERFORMANCE

The following traits are important to success. Some may be more important than others, particularly in specific situations. You already have some of them in great measure; others must be developed. Just because you are strong in one does not mean you may neglect others. No attempt is made here to tell you which are the most important because the individual situation often determines qualities needed most. However, if you are strong in some and weak in others, the combination may be sufficient to pull you along until you remedy certain weak areas. Do not neglect self-development because, at the moment, you seem adequate in that regard. Ours is a complex, ever-changing world, and your adequacy today may leave you woefully inadequate tomorrow if you are unwilling to work toward improving yourself constantly.

Personality

Personality is that complex of characteristics which distinguishes you, sets you apart, makes you YOU. Many of the traits to be discussed are inseparable parts of your personality. The following is a preview of you, inspecting, probing, judging, evaluating to see if the buyer's measurement fits YOU.

Will your product or service measure up to the buyer's needs as he sees them from your presentation? Are your words, expressions, motions, and word tones of the right caliber to make him act favorably toward your proposition? Do your hands aid in presenting your ideas eloquently, or are they awkwardly stuffed in your pockets? Are you so deeply engrossed in your work that some of your enthusiasm rubs off on the customer? These are positive points.

Looking at personality negatively, do you reflect indifference, laziness, carelessness, indecision? Is your attitude one of disbelief or indifference in what you are saying? Do you appear disinterested in the customer, the sale, the immediate situation? Do you show boredom, impatience, even disdain? It was said of one man that he would never become a successful salesman because he showed his contempt for the customer. If you feel superior to the customer and have a patronizing air, it is no wonder you frighten, offend, or anger him. These traits of unpleasantness do rub off on the customer. Study the list of traits to be discussed and see how you measure up, how you fit, how your personality incorporates factors that others consider desirable.

Sociability

To start with, recognize that the terms "extrovert" and "introvert" do not apply literally and absolutely. Unquestionably, there are those who dislike meeting people and detest mixing to such an extent that they would not entertain the idea of being salesmen. At the other extreme are those who are so extroverted they would dislike settling down to a solid application of selling. Extroverts may enjoy conversation but dislike reading. They may be delighted to be with a group but shun filling out sales reports at home or in the hotel in the evening. They would enjoy a friendly conversation with a buyer but would not want to prepare a detailed presentation which required grueling work. In between are most men who, if they are willing, can be trained to sell adequately. The ones who are introverted can be taught and motivated to become more friendly; the ones who are extroverted can be taught to tone down their native exuberance and develop traits more in line with the requirements of successful selling. All of us have experienced misgivings at times because of feelings of inadequacy, but once we have tried to improve our techniques, the results have usually been gratifying.

We all recognize that some people make friends more easily than others. To make friends, be friendly. Be the first to hold out your hand, to say cheerfully "Good morning," and to make a pleasant remark. Force yourself to strike up a conversation. Practice talking on a variety of topics. Like so many other attributes, interesting conversation comes through patient practice.

Social graces are highly desirable. Good manners, politeness, tact, thoughtfulness, courtesy, kindliness, and an innate sense of propriety are always welcome in a salesman. That does not make him superior, aloof, or a snob; rather, it sets him apart as one you would enjoy knowing and being with. Be well-groomed physically, mentally, and socially, for all these qualities make the man the well-rounded, *wanted* salesman who puts customer interest before his own. He instinctively learns to please others and, through this, achieves success.

Dependability

Are you dependable? Do you keep your promises? Can a customer rely on what you say, what you do, what you sell? Your product need not be the best there is so long as it lives up to the qualities you describe, but it should do what you say it will.

Do you carry out big, important jobs well but neglect small, seemingly insignificant ones? Can you be trusted to do your part even when no one can actually check up on you and when no one but yourself will ever know the difference?

If, so far, you have had a record of little dependability, that need not follow you all your life. Bad habits that previously caused you to neglect things can, in the future, be overcome by your conscious effort. Note the phrase "conscious effort" because improvements result from intelligent practice and determination to overcome faults. You must prevent lapses or deviation from a self-prescribed, self-approved procedure. Marked improvement and significant advances in dependability will not come easily. It is going to take sustained, zealous, and conscientiously devoted effort.

Honesty

Are you honest to others and to yourself? Dependability and honesty go hand in hand. Honesty is an attitude of mind shown by word and action; dependability is usually shown as you carry out certain activities. Many times, one never learns whether a person is honest or not because there is no occasion to check on him; but over a period of time, honesty will eventually show. Actually there may be little need to define the word "honest," for most of us know its meaning well enough.

To many of us, the opposite of honesty is dishonesty or lying. But another aspect of honesty is a reflection of ourselves. Being dishonest with yourself is consciously or perhaps unconsciously attributing certain qualities to your character which, on sober reflection, you know you do not have. Maybe it is a form of daydreaming, wishful thinking, or hopeful expectation which, in small measure, may be flattering and not harmful if indulged in occasionally. But when you are working as a salesman, do not let it cloud your real self so that you delude yourself into thinking that you are someone else. Unconsciously, some of us who try to be honest with others may be dishonest with ourselves by fostering pleasant illusions.

Sincerity

The sincere individual is anxious to please, to be helpful, honest, kind, thoughtful, unmistakably zealous in furthering some desirable end, and trustworthy. The sincere person is usually what we term a fine person. We enjoy being with him because he inspires confidence and promotes a relaxed attitude. At times, of course, he may make others uncomfortable by stepping on toes or antagonizing people who are particularly reluctant to act. He may try to "fire up" others to get action. He may be a "go-getter," upsetting indolent people who are happy to leave things as they are. Some buyers dislike a sincere salesman. The buyer may be dishonest, careless, or weak. He may be working deliberately against the best interests of his firm. This situation probably is infrequent, but there are times when such conditions exist and must be handled by the salesman.

Sincerity gains respect which, in turn, can foster confidence resulting in a signed order. When the salesman is sincere in the best sense of the word, the buyer may be assured that the salesman is working in the interests of both firms but primarily in the interest of the customer's firm.

Loyalty

"Don't bite the hand that feeds you" is an old quotation with ever-fresh meaning. Loyalty to family, friends, group, boss, firm, church, and country is a desirable trait. Yet, there comes a time when our loyalty may be flagging, weakening, or low. Sometimes, through mistreatment, either real or fancied, loyalty to our employer may reach a low ebb. Loyalty shows when we work for the best interests of our employer. Usually when we divide our loyalty, working for ourselves first and our firm second, the results are questionable in the long run. Of course, the relationship should be set up originally so that the best interests of salesmen and employer are one, but that is not always possible. In such cases, it is necessary to work to further the aims of the company, even though temporarily you do not get the best treatment. For the best interests of the firm as a whole, it does not follow that the interests of each person in the firm can always be maximized. We must recognize this and be willing to bend our efforts toward the development of the whole. Eventually, we should benefit through improvement of the company and better working conditions. Even if this does not hold true in the firm we work for, the training we get will serve us well when we transfer to some other employer.

When you call on a customer who criticizes your company and the way you do business, you may have to accept it whether it is just or unjust. But if you start to pick your company apart in front of him, he will lose respect for you. Would it not sound silly for you, a thoughtful adult, to work for a badly managed firm? And when you constantly find fault with your employer in front of a customer, he obviously wonders what is wrong with you. If you showed a spark of initiative, you would not be working for such a firm. Criticism of your firm, your boss, or your product before a customer is essentially self-criticism. By implication, something is wrong with you, too; otherwise, you would not be working for an inferior company. If you do lose respect for your company's management, products, or policies, resign. You cannot be an effective company salesman if you have lost respect for your employer.

Integrity

Webster's dictionary defines integrity as "an uncompromising adherence to a code of moral, artistic, or other values." Positively defined, it indicates a sense of values that gives priority to truth, quality, and reliability. Defined in another way, it is the absence of deceit, shiftiness, broken promises, unfulfilled obligations. Integrity is exhibited in frankness and openness of operation, in readiness to do certain acts which will help others even to the detriment of the salesman, in scrupulously fulfilling obligations and promises, in going beyond the original agreement to do a good job.

The person with integrity can be depended on to carry out duties punctually, even though unwatched and unrewarded. He does not give grudgingly when called on to fulfill a promise, nor will he compromise and try to substitute something inferior to prevent a loss on his part. He does not find fault, criticize the work of others, or carry tales of difficulties and problems that may injure people. He does not imply weaknesses in competitors through subtle criticisms, nor does he give others the impression he is deliberately trying to discredit competition.

Integrity should be much sought after, treasured when acquired, and used wisely. Integrity can be strengthened through conscious exercise of your facilities toward genuine improvement and an awareness of its meaning to your customer. You work to build integrity. You recognize that it will help you to become a better person. You know that it will improve your relationship with customers.

Morality

There should be no reason for your morals as a salesman to be different from those of an office worker, a truck driver, a farmer, or a teacher. The difference, if any, lies in temptations, time away from home, and observation of some cases which are not typical. Traveling salesmen often come in contact with questionable or undesirable forms of behavior. Some people act quite differently away from home than they do at home. If you think someone gets away with something, follow his progress, and you will eventually think otherwise. As time goes on, the one who bases his morals on weakness and indulgence finds life becoming increasingly difficult and frustrating. The one who follows accepted codes of behavior finds that time develops respect for him in the eyes of others. The two ways—the one questionable, the other reflecting high standards—start from the same point, then diverge over the years. The first pattern becomes increasingly distasteful and difficult; the second gathers strength and confidence. Too often immediate gratification, though not immoral, prevents later long-range realization of worthy goals.

Maturity

If the salesman exhibits immaturity in the selling environment, he becomes the object of amusement, pity, scorn, derision, or even disgust. The customer may rightfully say, "Take your marbles and play elsewhere."

A mature man does not exhibit unusual ways of dressing, nor does he talk childishly and have tantrums. During the sales presentation there is no time to be irked outwardly, to show impatience with a customer, or to be upset easily.

The maturity of the individual shows primarily in his understanding. He meets a customer's indecision with composure and assurance. Do not confuse maturity with sluggishness, however. While certain types of exuberance are not customary in an adult, neither should one be intolerant, gloomy, overly critical, or morose. Serenity, control, understanding, moderation, consistency of behavior—in such ways is maturity displayed.

The mature person has dignity and poise that should come with age. One should become more settled, less easily swayed, given to calmness and reason. Disturbances are anticipated and the unexpected prepared for. One important trait is that of not noticing when others flare up over some indignity, real or fancied. When mature, you think logically about the problems of men and women facing life.

Intelligence

What about intelligence? Will the brilliant man become a top salesman? At times, the answer is yes and at others, no. Does the man with average intelligence make a capable salesman? He can. Could the man with below-average intelligence develop into a satisfactory salesman? Occasionally, yes.

Naturally, there are times when the selling is so technical or so difficult that it takes men with the highest intelligence to perform the job. Such occasions are not nearly as frequent as one might think. Very often the man with average intelligence can learn to do as well as, or even better than, the brilliant salesman. Fortunately for many of us, there appears to be little correlation between successful selling and intelligence as long as the person is at least an average individual. By average we mean a salesman is not at the top in intelligence, but neither is he stupid. He is not a brilliant conversationalist, but neither is he tongue-tied in a group. He is not the best dressed in a group, but neither is he dressed shabbily. He does not live in a wealthy neighborhood, but neither does he live in the slums. He does not drive a new $5,000 car, but neither does he drive an old battered wreck. Through repetition, even the salesman of average intelligence learns far more about his product and what it can do and understands it better than most buyers who are exposed to it for the first time or who must consider briefly the product or service. Frequently, the salesman succeeds if he presents his material slowly and simply enough so that the buyer can follow. High intelligence is not a barrier to selling. In most instances it is very helpful. If you are of average intelligence, however, you may have to work harder to accomplish the same results as the salesman does who has a higher intelligence. If you are unfortunate enough to have a lower intelligence, do not despair. Choose a sales area that is less demanding intellectually. Choose products or services you can explain. There are many people like you who will appreciate you and what you say, particularly when you show warmth, kindness, and understanding.

Mental Agility

An agile person is a nimble one who can handle his body well, who can bend, twist, turn, change direction, or exhibit dexterity in other ways. So, in mental agility we recognize an ability to think quickly, to handle or parry questions, and to respond readily with a sound answer.

The agile thinker has many facts at his fingertips and can use them to handle customers' questions. Frequently, customers need information in order to understand some feature of a product. Sometimes they ask a difficult question to see if the salesman knows what he is talking about. At times, a customer might ask an embarrassing question which might trap or upset the salesman because it is irrelevant or because no correct answer is possible.

You must be an opportunist. During an interview, conversation will open up opportunities on which to capitalize, just as dangerous periods will arise that require you to skirt certain areas or to change the line of conversation. To think quickly is worth intense training; with time and application you can improve. You simply cannot keep saying, "Why didn't I think of that during the interview?" as you go over your lost sales later on. Practice, study, careful preparation, and experience should enable you to provide the right answers at the proper moment.

Courage

Courage is a "must" if you are to succeed. From the very beginning the salesman must take the initiative to find customers, to persuade people, and to ask for orders. He must be the first to hold out his hand, to break the ice of silence, to overcome the awkwardness of a situation, or to open a conversation in a group that seems lost in finding a common meeting ground.

With courage, you can take refusals graciously, return repeatedly if you think the business is worthwhile, find new approaches to a problem, or continue a campaign that may not, at the moment, appear promising. Stay with a problem until it is solved, for the problem that looms like a mountain may almost disappear if you meet it in a sensible fashion. Most successful people have had many problems, but they also have had the courage to stick with them until the problems were solved. Some measure success by their ability to solve problems. Others measure success by their courage. Recognizing their inability to conquer certain difficulties, they learn to live with them and minimize their limitations.

Cheerfulness

Leave your troubles at home or in the office, but do not take them to your customer. Aren't we all anxious to meet the happy, contented, cheerful person, the one who inspires, the one who makes the world look brighter? At the same time, do we not tend to avoid the other extreme—the one who finds fault, is disgruntled, unhappy, talks only of unpleasant events, always drags up problems, gossips, and spreads half truths?

The cheerful salesman is optimistic. Problems seem less formidable to him because he looks at life in a cheerful frame of mind. He analyzes his problems, exposes them to the light of reason, and solves them logically. Today's cheerful salesman need not have solved every personal and professional problem; instead, he should meet his difficulties one at a time.

With cheerfulness we associate the ready smile, the warmth of a human being, the kindly attitude, the thoughtfulness of understanding. Consider a clergyman. All in the same day he may call on a hopelessly sick person in a hospital, may officiate at a funeral, conduct a wedding, baptize a child, counsel with a broken family, speak at a fund-raising dinner. It would be a mixed day that would exhaust the emotions, and yet he is expected to take it all cheerfully. If you have cheerfulness within, it will appear outwardly in your attitude, your optimism, your zest in life. Be cheerful in your dealings with others; be optimistic and give others renewed strength to overcome life's many irritating incidents.

Control

Two words we can readily associate are "discipline" and "control." When we speak of control, we almost always assume that a certain amount of discipline is present. When you discipline yourself, you plan your activities and you follow your plan. Discipline says when it is time to write a letter, you write it; when it is time to make a call, you make it; when it is time to write reports, you write them. Control guides your efforts in a planned way and helps you to carry out prescribed procedures meticulously. Control implies steady application toward set goals. Plan your course, and then use enough self-control to carry it out.

"Anger is a luxury few of us can afford," is a statement many should remember. Seldom is there occasion to show anger in selling. Anger is upsetting. It disturbs the customer as well as the salesman. It may bring out undesirable qualities and cause you to make statements that you regret. If a customer gets you angry, he has a decided advantage. Your reasoning power becomes warped. You are unable to think logically. You are filled with emotion. You lose an objective approach. You forget your primary purpose. Just as you learn to control your body by avoiding excesses that would prevent maximum effort and efficiency, you should also avoid psychological excesses that might contribute nothing to success and give meager self-satisfaction. Why take chances of offending when with a bit of forethought and discretion, you avoid all possibility of offense?

Respect

Respect a customer for what he is. You may not agree with him or enjoy his company, yet in the business world he is entitled to the respect that his position demands.

Too many of us are inclined to underrate someone because we may not like him, what he believes, how he acts, what he proposes. From this lack of compatibility may arise unwarranted disrespect. Often we judge too hastily and learn long after of the actual conditions that accounted for the individual's erratic behavior. If we learn to tolerate others' foibles, we can respect men as beings who cannot be perfect.

Lack of respect may be a dangerous fault. We may not respect the other person because he has had little formal education, he holds an inferior job, he may not dress properly, his diction is faulty, or his behavior uncouth. Even more dangerous, we may act superior and belittle him and his accomplishments. Such an attitude is instinctively communicated and obviously resented. By properly respecting the individual, you show appreciation and good judgment. He will be impressed with your good sense and will, in turn, have a much greater appreciation for you and what you sell.

Too often, a new salesman shows disrespect for a secretary or office girl in the buyer's office. True, she cannot sign the order, but she can help you, and she can hinder you. She might keep you waiting overly long for an appointment, be slow in mailing an order or a payment, handle your correspondence carelessly, and prejudice her employer by dropping slanted remarks.

Imagination

Some people are strictly unimaginative. Prosaic, down-to-earth, solid, plodding citizens, they do what they are told to do, and they do it well. Yet, ask them for an original idea and you draw a blank. A salesman must be creative and possess imagination to be successful on the higher rungs of selling. The run-of-the-mill salesman can take orders, follow directions explicitly, and carry out routine work; but ask him to do something out of the ordinary and he becomes lost.

An imaginative salesman is one who can see new possibilities for his customers. He can develop new uses for his product or new ways of displaying it to make it more attractive. The imaginative salesman thinks in terms of the customer. The customer who is confined to his own locale frequently depends on his salesman for new developments and for information for adapting them to fit his needs.

You must be able to discern relationships, to assess new developments to fit customers' needs, to take segments of ideas and fit them together into new patterns. Intensive application, careful thinking, constant searching, and mental alertness are necessary to meet this challenge successfully. The salesman who gets an idea now and then will not qualify. The imaginative person is alive with ideas, many impractical, some not applicable, others not pertinent, but some will be useful. It is necessary to have a flow of ideas to aid customers who might use your product. Suggest the ones that appear feasible or the ones that can become applicable with some change.

Determination

How many salesmen give up after half trying? How many salesmen lack the will to hurdle obstacles? Why do some men trip over pebbles, while others leap over great stones with ease? Some have determination; others lack it. Intelligent determination is in the one who strides after an objective enthusiastically even though he knows that obstacles will slow him, that difficult problems will appear, and that efforts might be made to thwart his progress.

Determination keeps one going when sales are slow. It is the inspiration which pushes one forward as he works constantly to achieve what can be done. It is an objective that one sets himself, an objective that can be reached because others have already done it. Determination is a vehicle that can push one onward, give him greater staying power, and change goals to accomplishments.

Initiative

Oftentimes initiative goes hand in hand with resourcefulness. With both qualities used adequately, progress can be steady and measurable. Lack of initiative describes the salesman with routine characteristics; he is content to follow instructions, but he does not exceed expectations because he is afraid of mistakes or because of laziness.

The salesman with initiative always looks for new ways, new ideas, new methods, and new applications. He can take present plans and rearrange them to create new possibilities; he can take existing methods and adjust them so that their impact strengthens. He can put vision into concrete applications. He is willing to try and is willing to make mistakes in the hope that some of these attempts will bring about successful developments. He weighs alternative approaches and, while not minimizing risks, is still willing to go ahead. He has faith that better ways remain to be discovered, studied, tried, adjusted, reworked, and applied.

Initiative suggests many new methods; some are rejected, others are refined, and a few will be effective as they were originally conceived. The salesman with initiative helps the grocer rearrange his stock so that it sells better, convinces the druggist to stock a new product, helps the hardware dealer to secure a line of chemicals for swimming pools, tells the factory owner how to reduce scrap, sells the dry cleaner on renting shirts, or shows his customer how to use less of his product by making it go further. He constantly thinks in terms of the customer, customer benefits, and customer successes.

Interest

Are you an interesting person? You will be interesting to others if you are interested in them. Do not have a small inquisitive interest, but a genuine interest, a concern for others' problems. Give attention to their needs and sympathize in their problems. When your customer accomplishes something worthwhile that gives him recognition, congratulate him because he has achieved a worthy goal. When you learn of sorrows and griefs, extend sympathy and even more tangible symbols when appropriate. Your thoughtfulness indicates interest that your customer will soon detect.

If you are interested in the sale only for a bigger commission or to benefit yourself primarily, yours is not the interest of selling success. A selfish interest excludes the needs of the customer who instinctively feels this and shuns you. One salesman selling kitchen equipment reported that when he first started to sell, results were mediocre because he concentrated on selling new kitchens that would be profitable to him as a salesman. Later, he changed his attitude and became interested in the customer's welfare, concentrating on providing each potential customer with the finest kitchen possible. As soon as he changed his interest from himself to the customer, his sales rose rapidly.

Confidence

Confidence is the belief in yourself that makes others believe in you. It is won through reliability that gets things done.

Confidence in yourself comes through a feeling of adequacy, a feeling that you know how to do something, when to do it, the best way to do it. Usually, it comes from a series of acts successfully completed to the satisfaction of others. When you have tried and succeeded, you develop a tested confidence that will be revealed as you carry out new assignments.

Inspiring confidence in a customer goes far toward making him loyal. If he feels secure in your able performance, he will come to you for advice because he knows that he can depend upon you for helpful ideas.

Do not underrate yourself. Lack of self-confidence can be harmful to your well-being. How hopeless is the individual who has lost all confidence in himself. He can accomplish nothing because he believes he is incapable of doing anything. Others may lose confidence in you, but do not lose confidence in yourself. Instead, reassess your ability in terms of your successes and failures. Simply because you fail once, do not go from all-confidence to no-confidence. While you were not good enough to justify the former, neither are you so weak as to settle for the latter.

Perseverance

Salesmen often give up too easily. They lack the quality that will enable them to stick to a job until it is finished. They strike out too soon by taking the first or second "no" as the final "no." Actually, trying a bit harder, attempting one more close, or giving one more demonstration may be all that is needed to change the last "no" into a final "yes." The weak salesman is the individual who fails to follow up, to persevere in the face of refusal, because he feels that continued effort would only result in failure. He does not realize that persistent, careful selling can often turn some of those refusals into sales.

Remember that it is too easy to give up, to be too tired to make that extra call, to consider it futile to make another demonstration, to think that it is useless to try some other way. You have heard others say that a salesman should not quit until he has exhausted every possibility, but it may be that he exhausts his few possibilities too quickly. He may have equipped himself with so little ammunition that he soon runs out and has nothing left with which to persevere. Possibly, lack of perseverance is not lack of inclination but lack of preparation. If you are properly prepared, if you have the determination to succeed and have confidence in yourself, you will usually persevere until you successfully conclude the sale.

Enthusiasm

Enthusiasm, the priceless ingredient in every sale, is also the basic equipment of every salesman. Enthusiasm quickens the spirit, enlivens the person, increases tempo, and stimulates people to act. All of us are familiar with the boy who is too tired to do any work after dinner, and yet he bounces with energy as soon as a ball game is announced. This same energy pervades us when we get sufficiently aroused. Our tired feeling disappears, and we zestfully look forward to the approaching period because our entire self has been revitalized.

To make a sale, arouse the customer's enthusiasm. Low-pitched interest in the salesman will create the same effect in the customer; but high-pitched enthusiasm in the salesman will, in turn, affect the customer favorably. Sincerely believing in your product or service and convinced that the customer should have it—and that if he does not buy, he will suffer—should help you generate such enthusiasm that it becomes contagious and changes your customer from a potential to a real customer.

SUMMARY OF YOUR THOUGHTS

After looking at YOU through the eyes of this chapter, how do you rate? Are you encouraged? Disappointed? Scared? Hopeful? Now that we have looked at YOU, what is the next step? Are you going ahead as a salesman, or do you feel that it is not the life for you?

Just like you, other salesmen have, in varying degrees, qualities that we have discussed. All are strong in some, deficient in others. Your job is to develop the weak qualities. Strive to improve by setting up a pattern for improvement and by rigorously following it until you can change your present rating. *Believe in yourself, and many things become possible.*

CHECKLIST

Rate yourself honestly on these qualities. Do not worry if you are low on some. That is to be expected and will give you a chance to improve. For each trait listed below, give yourself 4 points if you are A, 3 points for B, 2 points for C, and 1 point for D.

RATINGS

Sales Traits	A Outstanding	B Successful	C Average	D Need Improvement
PERSONALITY				
SOCIABILITY				
DEPENDABILITY				
HONESTY				
SINCERITY				
LOYALTY				
INTEGRITY				
MORALITY				
MATURITY				
INTELLIGENCE				
MENTAL AGILITY				
COURAGE				
CHEERFULNESS				
CONTROL				
RESPECT				
IMAGINATION				
DETERMINATION				
INITIATIVE				
INTEREST				
CONFIDENCE				
PERSEVERANCE				
ENTHUSIASM				
Total				

HERE IS YOUR GRADE

Range

22 – 43	Not good enough
44 – 65	Room for improvement
66 – 77	Could be better
Over 77	Excellent

QUESTIONS AND PROBLEMS

1. Why is it important to be careful about your personal appearance?
2. How can one overcome a voice weakness?
3. "You are judged by the words you use." Explain that statement.
4. Why is it necessary to retain poise in a selling situation?
5. Many people are offended by mannerisms. What are the two possible dangers involved?
6. From the customer's viewpoint, does a salesman's personality set him apart?
7. Salesmen are inclined to belittle social graces. Is this particularly harmful?
8. Are there many opportunities to test a salesman's honesty?
9. Is the sincere person a better salesman? Can sincerity be a hindrance?
10. Give five examples of loyalty, using a different illustration for each.
11. "I like his integrity," the purchasing agent said about a salesman. Give various meanings that can be attached to that statement.
12. How do salesmen show immaturity?
13. How important is intelligence in selling? Is there a direct relationship between intelligence and selling ability?
14. Why must the salesman be a quick thinker?
15. Should a salesman be cheerful with all customers? If not, when ought he avoid cheerfulness?
16. Many sales managers say that salesmen must learn self-discipline. Why is this important?
17. Imagination is indispensable in a successful salesman. To what extent does this statement hold true?
18. Give several examples in which determination had a commanding role.
19. "Every successful salesman must have initiative. Without initiative he will fail." Explain.
20. Why must a salesman be interested in his customers?
21. Can we say that when a salesman loses confidence, he loses sales? Discuss in various applications.
22. Most people fail because they lack perseverance. What steps would you suggest to develop greater perseverance?
23. Prepare a 200-word paper on "Enthusiasm."
24. "Who am I?" Prepare a list of 25 answers to this question. This will require careful thought and a searching analysis of yourself.

CASES

1-1: AMERICAN DRUG WHOLESALE COMPANY

The American Drug Wholesale Company, a full-line drug wholesaler located in Brestwood, a city of 500,000 inhabitants, employs 12 salesmen. Two of their salesmen have resigned to take better positions. Two sales trainees of the firm have been assigned as salesmen to the two territories left vacant. Now the sales manager must hire two men to become trainees for future sales positions.

Each year the sales manager replaces about three salesmen. Some quit, some are fired. Most trainees advanced to salesmen have been in training from 6 months to 12 months.

To get applicants for the two trainee positions the sales manager inserted an advertisement in the Sunday edition of The Brestwood Journal. Twenty-one applications were received by mail. Only mailed applications were received since the advertisement did not carry the company name, and all inquiries were to be sent to Box No. 6. After a rapid examination, 16 applications were rejected as being not suitable. Five applicants were interviewed, and the following information recorded for each.

Jack Keane

Jack Keane, 21 years old, has just graduated from the business school of Brestwood University. He is not married and lives with his parents. His marks in college were average. He was active in school affairs, belonged to a fraternity, and had many college friends. He is 5 feet 10 inches, weighs 165 pounds, has light hair and blue eyes. He makes a nice appearance and speaks well.

Jack is a church member and sings in the choir. As a boy he was active in boy scouts. He enjoys sports and attended social activities in high school regularly. He never tried out for any athletic team.

During high school he worked at various summer jobs, such as mowing lawns, delivering circulars, and caddying at a golf club. When he entered college, he worked at the post office each Christmas vacation. One summer he was a counselor at a YMCA camp. The second summer he did manual labor for a cement contractor. The third summer he sold encyclopedias house-to-house. Jack is interested in a sales career and is willing to work at a starting salary of $100 a week.

Oscar Lindman

Oscar Lindman is 24 years old, married, with one 2-year-old son. He is buying a modest home in a suburb of Brestwood. His wife takes care of the home and has no outside employment.

Oscar graduated from high school when he was 18. His grades in high school were average. He played on the high school football team but was not an outstanding player. He met his wife when both were students. Three years after his graduation they were married.

Shortly after graduation Oscar got a job driving a delivery truck for a local department store. A year later he became a salesman in the automotive section of this store. Oscar enjoyed selling, but not in a retail store.

When he was 21 years of age, he left the store and became salesman for an automotive jobber. His income increased each year and he was happy with his work. After he had sold for the automotive jobber for three years, the owner died, and the business was liquidated. Oscar was out of a job.

He has applied for the position of sales trainee because he feels the job would soon lead to one that was similar to the one he had. Oscar could have gone to work for another automotive jobber in Arcadia, but then it would have been necessary to sell his home and move to Arcadia, 300 miles away. Both Oscar and his wife prefer living in Brestwood. On checking references, it was determined that Oscar had been fairly successful in selling and had built up a friendly clientele. Oscar wants $125 a week as starting salary.

William Savage

William Savage, age 28, finished high school but never attended college. He is married, has two children, and lives in an apartment. Physically, he is below average height, weights 150 pounds, has dark hair and brown eyes. When you first meet William, you are not impressed. But after you talk with him awhile, you recognize him as being somewhat unusual. His work history reveals several jobs, such as store clerk, house-to-house salesman, apprentice toolmaker, and insurance salesman. He did not stick to any job over three years. Checking with former employers revealed that his work had been satisfactory on each job, but as soon as he got to know the job, he became bored and quit. His poorest work had been as a toolmaker. His income has provided an adequate living for his family, and he drives a medium-priced car, one year old.

He was still selling insurance when he applied for the position as sales trainee. When asked why he wished to change jobs, he replied that he had finally made up his mind to be a wholesale salesman which would give security with opportunity for advancement financially as a star salesman or as an administrator. He stated that he could sell insurance, but preferred a job selling tangibles. The interviewer commented that William was a convincing speaker and showed traits of courage and perseverance. The starting salary would be $130 a week.

Samuel Pickens

Samuel Pickens, age 35, is a bachelor. He drives a big car, is well dressed, and gives the impression of being a free spender. He had lived at home with his parents until he was 30 years of age. Then he moved to Brestwood when he took a sales analysis job for a local manufacturing firm. Sam, as his friends call him, has a bachelor apartment, plays golf in the summer, and skis in the winter. He usually spends his vacations in Florida in January. Sam is friendly, well-liked, and generous. His job performance is satisfactory. He is six feet tall, blonde complexioned, and weighs 190 pounds. He has a pleasant voice.

Sam had graduated from a small church-related college. Immediately after graduation he went to work for the Tidewater Company, a manufacturer of pumps. He worked at a number of jobs in the office for this company; when he left, he was supervisor of the adjustment department.

Sam left Tidewater and his hometown because he realized he was in a rut. Life was pleasant, but he was getting nowhere. When he took the job as sales analyst in Brestwood, he soon became acquainted with the activities of the sales department of the large pharmaceutical house he worked for. After several years on various "desk jobs," he concluded that ultimately he would like to be in sales administration. To get this type of job he would have to do some selling. He had suggested to the sales manager that he would like to sell, but the sales manager told him that he would be far more successful working in the sales department in the office.

Determined to gain selling experience, Sam applied for the job of sales trainee. When interviewed, he stated frankly that he knew he could sell and was willing to start out as a sales trainee which is a lesser job than he now has. His present salary is $150 a week, but he is willing to start as trainee at $130 a week. He stated he was confident that in five years he would be in a sales administrative position with The American Drug Wholesale Company.

Fred Meyer

Fred Meyer, age 40, is married, has 3 children, owns his own home, almost paid for, in a nice suburb of Brestwood, and drives a medium-priced car.

Fred completed high school and started to work at 18 years of age. His first job was as stock boy in a supermarket. After one year, he became cashier. Six months later he became head of the produce department, and a year later he was made assistant manager. In spite of his retail background, Fred did not like store work, so he resigned and started to work in the warehouse of a grocery wholesaler. He enjoyed the work with this establishment but concluded his future would be limited there. So when his friend Arnold Coulter invited him to work for a drug wholesaler, he was glad to leave the grocery area. After a year's experience in the warehouse and office of the drug wholesaler, he became a salesman with his own territory. His success as salesman, though not outstanding, was sufficient to give him an increasing income each year. Fred had every intention of staying with this firm, making this his life's work.

Six months ago the owner of the firm retired, leaving management to three sons. Almost immediately dissension arose. The brothers were constantly bickering with one another. Morale declined, and sales suffered. Because of the turmoil created, Fred decided he would have to seek other employment.

When he saw the advertisement for a sales trainee in wholesale drugs, he applied. He suspected that it was The American Drug Wholesale Company that wanted these trainees. When interviewed for the position, he stated frankly the reason for wanting to change. He said he would be willing to start for $140 a week, even though now he was making $160 a week. He said that he anticipated a very short training period. He felt that within six months he would be out in his own territory. He was convinced he would be back at his former income within a year. He said he would be glad to work for the American Drug Wholesale Company since it had a fine reputation. The sales manager of American Drug knew of Fred and knew that he had the reputation of being a steady salesman and a consistent producer.

Questions

1. Should you draw up a job description before you decide whom to hire ?
2. Which two applicants should be hired?
3. Rate the five applicants in order of preference.
4. How might you handle the applicants you do not hire?

1-2: OAKLER COMPANY

The Oakler Company sells high-fashion shoes. It is one of the largest women's retail shoe chains in the world. Their 1964 sales were over $147 million. They sell shoes in every price range. The inexpensive shoes are sold under one brand name, and the more expensive shoes under another. They also sell handbags, polish, and bows to match the various styles of shoes. These accessories bring a wide margin of profit. The company chooses its salesmen carefully.

Glen Oaks Shopping Plaza is the location of one of the Oakler Company's best stores. This store is called Cooker's. At Cooker's the price range of shoes is from $4 for the flat-heeled shoes to $8 for the high-heeled shoes. Since the dollar profit on their shoes is small, Cooker depends on a high sales volume.

One of their main policies is called "all at once." They insist that each salesman present to the customer four pairs of shoes. The first pair should be the one the customer asked for, the second and third pair being similar to the first, and the fourth should be completely different from the first three pairs. The salesmen also are required to show two or three handbags, three bows, and the proper polish to each customer. The company feels that the only way to sell something is to show it.

Dave Gray is one of the salesmen working in Cooker's at Glen Oaks Shopping Plaza. He has worked there for three years full time and two years part time. He attended business college for two years. For the last three years he has been the top seller of shoes in the store. In 1963 he sold more shoes than anyone in the district. He has a good outward appearance and is neatly dressed. He has a great deal of confidence, sometimes overconfident, perhaps. The company, although pleased with his high volume of sales of shoes, is not pleased with his volume of accessories. One week he sold $2,000 in shoes and only $20 in handbags. The company believes that each salesman should sell ten percent in handbags of his shoe volume. The manager of the store has told him many times to follow the "all at once" policy, but Dave pays little attention.

Dave has a good sales volume in shoes because he waits on three or four customers at a time and rushes the customers in and out of the store. He is also well acquainted with the stock. To most of the customers, he shows only one pair of shoes, the one the customer asks for. He shows a handbag only if it matches the shoes perfectly. Most other bags he sells are at the customer's request to see them. He will ask the customer if she wants the matching polish, rather than bring it out and demonstrate its use. His conversation is limited and consists of fashion comments to the customer, such as, "This shoe is made of genuine leather. It has the new set-back heel which is so popular now. You have probably seen this in *Vogue* or *Seventeen*." Customers seem impressed with these remarks, and most of his customers usually walk away with a shoe purchase.

Another fault of Dave's is that if a customer does not like the first pair or the second, he will give up on this customer and say, "I'm sorry, but this is all we have in your size right now." Dave believes that volume of shoes sold to the customer is the most important thing to the company and to him. Upon insistence of the manager, Dave will work on "all at once" for a few hours, but then he gives up on it when the boss is busy.

Jim Devine is another salesman in the store. He is almost the complete opposite of Dave Gray. However, he is very neat. He does not rush any of his customers. He waits on not more than two at a time. He has a fine personality and is liked by most customers as well as by his fellow workers. He has many call customers. In fact, many customers will come up to the manager and compliment him on Mr.

Devine. Jim has a ready smile and almost never becomes angered at a customer. He has a great deal of poise and is enthusiastic over the product he sells, no matter if it is polish or shoes. He has one big fault—spending too much time with the customer. While Dave Gray rushes the customer in and out of the store, Jim spends up to a half hour with a customer. At the end of an average week Dave sells $400 more in shoes than Jim. However, Jim has ten percent in handbags and three percent in findings (bows and polish) of his shoe sales. He talks to customers not only about the latest shoe fashions, but also about the weather, politics, movies, etc. The manager has told Jim about this unnecessary conversation many times, but it is hard for Jim to break the habit. Jim also has confidence in himself, as does Dave, and most of the people he sells believe him. Customers appreciate Jim telling them if he does not like particular types of shoes on their feet. He greets each customer with "Hello, how are you today?" When they are about to leave, he says, "Thank you very much, and please ask for Jim Devine next time."

Bud Hanson is another salesman at Cooker's. He is a company man all the way. Of the three salesmen, he is the only one who follows "all at once" to every customer. He does exactly what the company tells him to do. The company has a set of instructions on how to present shoes, handbags, and accessories to the customer, and Bud follows this method step by step. Of the three salesmen, he has the lowest shoe sales, and the second lowest accessories sales, next to Dave who has the lowest. He is loyal to the company. He gets to work on time, puts up stock when he needs it, trims windows, and takes inventory. These jobs are done when he could be selling. He is courteous and well mannered to the customer. He is not easily upset or annoyed. He has infinite patience, but he seems to lack confidence. When he speaks, he sounds like a poor advertisement for his company.

The customers seem to run him, and he is more like a clerk than a salesman. One good feature about Bud Hanson is that he never gives up on a customer, even if it seems that the customer is not going to buy. Bud never admits defeat and does not give up until the customer has left.

The manager, trying to help these three men to become better salesmen, wrote a dialogue showing how each of the three men sell. He took a typical customer and showed how each salesman would handle her.

Dave Gray—Dialogue A

CUSTOMER: Please show me style 11026, the white silk pump to be dyed.

DAVE: Please have a seat in my section over there. I'll be with you in a couple of seconds. (Dave returns with the one shoe and tries it on the customer's foot.)

CUSTOMER: It feels a little tight.

DAVE: This is the way the shoe fits at first, but it will stretch out. Here, let me take it back and put it on the stretching machine. (Dave goes in the back and uses the broom to stretch it out.)

DAVE: That should feel much better. I hope I didn't stretch it too much.

CUSTOMER: It does feel a little looser.

DAVE: This shoe has the new hourglass heel. It is very stylish. Excuse me for a second while I take care of my other customers. (Dave returns in one minute.) Have you decided yet?

CUSTOMER: Yes, I'll take this shoe. Are you sure you can have it dyed in two days?

DAVE: Yes, I'm positive. Well, thank you very much. Please take the shoes up to the counter and the lady will help you.

CUSTOMER: Do you have a matching bag for this?

DAVE: Right now, we are out of the matching bag, but we have other dyeable bags up there. Why don't you take a look up at the counter, and maybe you will find something you will like. If you find something, please bring it back to me so I can get credit for it. By the way, do you have the spray polish for these shoes?

CUSTOMER: Yes, I do. Thank you.

DAVE: Thank you. Don't forget that we have our sale coming up in December. Stop in and see me.

Jim Devine—Dialogue B

JIM: Hi, how are you today? It sure is cold out.

CUSTOMER: It sure is. I nearly froze walking from the parking lot.

JIM: Can I help you with something?

CUSTOMER: Yes, could you show me 11026, the silk pump? I want it dyed.

JIM: You came to the right place. I'll be with you in one minute. (Jim returns with three shoes.) Sorry, I took so long, but yesterday I sprained my foot playing basketball, and it takes me a little while getting up and down the stairs.

CUSTOMER: Oh, that's too bad. Did you put some kind of liniment on it?

JIM: No, but that's a good idea. Well, now, let me try the shoe on your foot. How does it feel?

CUSTOMER: It feels a little tight.

JIM: Maybe it's the last on the shoe. It might not fit you right. Let's try on this other shoe. The last is different. In the first shoe the last is two A's narrower in the heel than the toe. In the second it is only one A narrower than the toe. How does this one feel?

CUSTOMER: This feels much better. I don't know if I like this one as much though.

JIM: This is a matter of opinion. They are both stylish. My sister just bought the one you have on. I have a twenty-five year old sister. She likes it and says it's very comfortable. Let me come back in a few minutes to give you time to decide. (A few minutes later) I bet you thought I'd never come back. Well, what's your decision?

CUSTOMER: I'd like to take a look around and see if I can find another pair that might fit. Please hold these out. I will be back in fifteen minutes if I want these. Thank you very much for being so considerate. I need a lot of shoes for my new spring wardrobe.

JIM: Good, please ask for Jim Devine when you come in. We are getting a beautiful spring line with matching bags and bows for your shoes. Don't forget to ask for me, Jim Devine.

Bud Hanson—Dialogue C

BUD: Hello, May I help you please?

CUSTOMER: Yes, could you show me 11026? It is a silk pump to be dyed.

BUD: Yes, will you please have a seat in my section and I will bring you a fine selection to choose from.

A couple of minutes later.

CUSTOMER: Gee, I only asked for one shoe. You have four there.

BUD: Well, it's the company policy to show four pairs of shoes. In this way you will have more than one shoe to choose from. I'll put one shoe on one foot and the shoe you asked to see on the other foot so you can compare. In this third box I have another shoe that is similar to the other two, and in the fourth box I have a shoe that is completely different. It is something in a flat shoe to wear around the house.

CUSTOMER: Now, I'm really confused. I like this flat shoe also. Maybe you could bring out some more flats so I can compare them.

BUD: Okay, I'll be back in a second. (Bud returns with three pairs of flats.) I also brought out three bows. Try this one on your silk shoe. It makes the one shoe into two shoes at almost the same price. (Bud leaves her and returns with three bags.) Here are the matching bags for the shoes you have out here. Step up to the mirror and take a look at the way the shoe, bow, and bag complement your outfit. I also brought the matching polish for your shoes. Let me demonstrate it. (Bud demonstrates the polish.) I'll be back in a few minutes.

CUSTOMER: Okay.

A few minutes later.

BUD: Well, have you decided about any of the shoes?

CUSTOMER: I'm not sure about the silk shoes. They all seem tight, but I am interested in that flat on the rack there. I like it better than the ones you have here. Could you bring it to me?

BUD: Yes, I will be back in a moment.

A job promotion as assistant manager is in line for one of the three men. Each of the three feels he has a good chance.

Questions

1. Evaluate each man as a salesman.
2. Evaluate each man as a potential assistant manager.
3. How does each man measure up to the YOU concept?

CHAPTER 2

Your Customer

When you turn the car key in the ignition switch, you expect the car to start. When you turn on a water faucet, you expect water to run. But when you call on a customer, you are never sure exactly what will happen. Why? Customers are human beings; they are predictable as a group, but each one varies as an individual.

Yes, the customer is a most valuable friend, and you must never take him for granted. Just as you are subjected to pressures which make you one person today and another tomorrow, so does the customer go through similar moods. The quiet, meditative type whom you see on Monday afternoon may be a roaring lion Tuesday morning. Thus, you cannot predict your reception in any man's office.

Ambitious attempts have been made to catalog customers by types, but to differentiate accurately among various buyers is relatively impossible. You may be able to separate customers by types and develop a pattern for handling each type, but to the average salesman this procedure is too difficult. Even if the best distinctions are made, there could always be some conditions that would cause the customer to react unusually. Use broad outlines to categorize the customer, and then, during the interview, adjust yourself to his mood at the moment.

43

Since the customer is the salesman's most important asset, the salesman should guard him zealously. That salesmen fail to do so is frequently evidenced by their superiority or by their belief that customers are meekly submissive. If the overly confident salesman could look into the buyer's mind, he would often be shocked. The salesman who thinks that he is the master of situations can, to the customer, be a pest, crackpot, bully; he can be unmannerly, incredibly stupid, offensive, rude, ignorant, naive, and overbearing.

Will these differences between salesman and buyer ever be resolved? No, they cannot be. New salesmen are constantly coming on the scene, and they have to learn as much as possible (and learn it as quickly as possible) about workable techniques of salesmanship. Sales training is an ever-continuing job because men are always entering the field, and experienced men need refresher training to get new ideas and new inspirations for new situations.

How do we discuss customer knowledge? If you have tried to eat an orange by peeling and then stuffing the whole fruit into your mouth, you soon learned that the orange was too large. But if you separate the orange into sections, it becomes relatively easy to eat. We propose to separate customer knowledge into its sections, so that you can cover each portion adequately. Let's start with facts.

FACTUAL INFORMATION ABOUT CUSTOMERS

Most salesmen know far too little about their customers. They are content to know the names and some general facts about their buyers but then neglect the more personal (hence, the more important) facts. To be certain you have the necessary information about each buyer, develop an organized method of obtaining and recording such information and have it readily available. Some men use a pocket notebook with a space reserved for each customer. Some use index cards with carefully cataloged data. Whichever way you choose, be sure that it is all inclusive and easy to find when you need it. Having decided on the approach to use, let us detail some useful information.

Hundreds of facts are available on most customers, and the type and variety that you need will depend largely on your particular customers and what you sell. A housewife purchasing from a door-to-door salesman, a retail customer buying in a store, a store owner buying from a wholesale salesman, a contractor buying building materials, a farmer buying seed, a family buying a home, a businessman buying a store or factory, a man buying a cottage, boat, or gun, a woman shopping for a wedding dress, a committee buying school equipment, a coach buying football equipment, a doctor buying medical equipment, a department store buyer ordering fashion items, professional purchasing agents buying for manufacturing plants and other industries, a buyer of ships costing millions of dollars, an individual buying remedies or patent medicines for personal aches and pains—in such a bewildering complex of situations, it is obviously not feasible to set up one group of criteria that will be applicable in each case. Rather, develop an overall set of instructions which will cover most of your situations, including your customers.

Customer Facts of a Personal Nature and How to Handle Them

Name. Any individual is proud and sensitive of his name. Pronounce it correctly, spell it properly, and know the first name or initials. Some people use a first initial with their middle and last names; most use the first name and a middle initial; some have compound first names; some have three names and use all of them; some have no given name at all, but merely initials. Thus, the following combinations are possible: Frank Smith; Frank A. Smith; A. Frank Smith; A. F. Smith; A F Smith; Frank A. B. Smith; Frank Elliott Smith; Frank Elliott Smith, Jr.; Frank Elliott Smith, Sr.; Frank A. Smith, II. In handling foreigners, many complicated name factors can emerge. Each country may have significant variations which the salesman ought to know so that the customer will not be offended. Pronunciations of a name may vary so that what is acceptable in one section of the country or for one family may be wrong for another. Listen carefully when a customer introduces himself, for *his* pronunciation of *his* name is the only right pronunciation. If you do not know the correct pronunciation, ask the buyer's secretary before you enter his office.

Address and Telephone Number. A correct address is a simple item that is frequently neglected. Beware of abbreviations, know if the customer lives on a "street," "road," or an "avenue," and use the zip code. If the customer gives you an unlisted telephone number, guard it carefully! Some firms have multiple addresses; some telephone numbers represent several firms; and some offices have several tenants. When selling to a store, find out the headquarters of leased departments if there is occasion to contact people in such an arrangement.

Important Dates. Record birthdays, wedding anniversaries, and other special dates; appropriate remembrances can build goodwill. Know the customer's age as well as his birthday, so that you are best able to offer the most suitable gifts, remembrances, and best wishes. Be on the lookout for marriages within a firm or between members of firms; remembering anniversary dates can then become a problem.

Nationality. In our mixed American culture, nationality plays an important role. Our backgrounds may still reflect our fathers' and grandfathers' nationalities. The effect may not be too strong, but there may be lingering traces which, if properly touched, arouse the customer's pride; improperly used, it develops antagonism. If a customer uses substandard grammar, syntax, or diction, do not fall into the same idiom as you try to make him feel at ease. He may resent it if he recognizes that you have noticed one of his weaknesses.

Family. Most customers are proud of their families. A man's wife may have faults, but it is never the salesman's function to make disparaging remarks about her. Whatever a man's children might be or do, they are still the major sources of pride. Not only should you be familiar with the family—ages, birthdays, accomplishments, outstanding characteristics—but you should also listen intently enough to learn the buyer's attitude toward each member of his family. How pleased a father is when you bring in a newspaper clipping in which a son or daughter has been praised for work in school, church, scouts, or summer camp.

Education. Knowledge of the buyer's education enables you to speak without offense. If he has a college degree, you can point out how pleasant it is to deal with a person who readily understands you and your proposition. If the buyer should be relatively uneducated, he will probably be the first to mention it after you have come to know him. In that case, point out the advantages of having graduated from the "college of hard knocks." Do not act superior to him because he does not have a college degree. Even with little formal education, he still will feel that he knows as much as anyone else.[1]

Financial Status. If you are to sell a product to a homeowner or to a family, you must know if the buyer can pay for the item. To make a sale and then to learn that the individual cannot pay is wasted effort and frustrating to both. For example, a man buys a car on time, promising to make regular monthly payments. Later, the car dealer discovers the man has so many obligations that he cannot make the car payments. The same holds true if you make a sale to a businessman and later have the order rejected by your credit department.

Job. At times, a customer's job may be a determining factor in whether or not he will purchase. Even though he can afford the purchase, he may not go through with it because of his position in the business world. For example, a bank president likely would not buy stock in a gambling casino. His job may interfere with the use of the product; it might cause him to have to join a group that is unsuitable for some reason. Thus, it is unwise for a family to buy season tickets with a group to a series of concerts when the husband's work will prevent his participation most of the time. On the other hand, when you learn of the position a buyer holds, his job may be an increased reason for buying your product or service. For example, he may need protective garments because he must make physical inspections in factories.

Social Qualities. The customer's life after working hours may govern many personal purchases. Even if the purchases are for business, his buying may be governed somewhat by his social attachments, thereby inhibiting his buying from you if you are outside his circle of friends. Learn about his social likes and dislikes since they may influence what he buys as well as from whom he buys.[2]

---

[1] An advertising executive told an amusing story of a vice president of a major firm who would start his remarks by pointing out how little formal education he had and how inexperienced he was in advertising. But in the next breath, he would start criticizing the advertisement the advertising executive brought in for inspection before running it in a magazine. He would pick the advertisement apart and find many faults, even though experts had prepared it. As a result, the advertisement would be redone, incorporating the vice president's suggestion, even though the result was to worsen it.

[2] In a large city, members of a group of firms held regular monthly "social" luncheons in which they discussed buying from one another. The main qualification seemed to be to buy from your friends.

Organizations. Is the customer an ardent lodge man, a member of clubs, or a participant in fraternal activities? Is he active in boy scouts, church, or civic groups? Does he aspire to lead his groups? What positions does he now hold? What are his particular interests in such activities? Does he belong because he enjoys the work, or is he dragged into it because of his position in the community? Is he active in politics? If so, you should know so that you can make appropriate and timely remarks.

Religion. When you know your customer's religion, you can praise judiciously as you learn of activities outstanding in his church. Also, by knowing his religion, you can avoid antagonizing him. Why, for example, would you deplore the weaknesses of parochial education if you are talking with a Roman Catholic or Lutheran who has children in a church school?

Hobbies. Most people have hobbies. A man might hunt, fish, or bowl; and a woman might sew, make scrapbooks, or cook unique dishes. A salesman who is interested in his customer's hobby soon establishes a common bond. Actually, the salesman need only express an interest in the pastime; from there, the customer will take over and eagerly talk about it.

Recreation. To most of us, the difference between recreation and a hobby might be hair-splitting, but it can also be a meaningful difference to some. A customer might derive recreation from immersing himself in a group activity, or he might excel in bridge. Incidentally, you must widen your knowledge and read in order to converse intelligently on a number of recreational pursuits. You need not be an expert, but you should have a speaking knowledge of them.

Customer Disapproval. Most customers have particular ideas of what is wrong or bad. Much of this may be conditioned by background and training. One customer may have many more taboos than another, but all customers have some. Recognizing this, it becomes desirable for the salesman to uncover such areas or learn about them early, primarily to avoid them or to be prepared to handle them. A customer might be highly biased in some ways and totally wrong in others, but correcting such a person will have little lasting effect and will often kill your sale.

Motivation. Everyone has a vulnerable ego which drives him. If you can tap this trait, your success in selling a customer is increased immensely.

A customer has specific ideas about his strengths; if you recognize them, he will admire your exceptional judgment. He feels that he has made a favorable impression on you; and, consequently, you recognize his importance in the area in which he wishes to excel. Although a person with an incredible ego may be only slightly stimulated, he will probably visualize himself as highly motivated. When selling to such a man, do not simply equate ego with drive. Ego may direct motivation, but the amount of ego may surpass the amount of motivation.

Customer Facts of a Business Nature and What to Do About Them

When dealing with purchasing agents of firms, the salesman should know certain basic facts before he calls. To sell those who will be rejected by the credit department is a waste of time. To sell those who clearly do not need your product is only a temporary victory, for you will probably never again sell to those people when they have considered their purchase. Before approaching a customer, know as much as possible about the information outlined below.

Company Name and Address. You must know the company's correct name and address. This may appear simple, but there are numerous companies that have names so nearly alike that they can be confused. If you look in the Detroit telephone directory, for example, you could find listed: Acme Press; Acme Printers, Inc.; Acme Printing Ink Co.

A firm's address might be in the city or in a suburb. The street name, for example, might extend through city and suburb, but 2000 Main Street, Bloomsdale, and 2000 Main Street, Rockhurst, can, even when Bloomsdale and Rockhurst are neighbors, be ten miles apart. Fiftieth Street, East, and Fiftieth Street, West, would be miles apart in Cleveland, but in another city those addresses might be separated by no more than the width of one street.

Volume of Business. A salesman mentioned calling on a high school science teacher who said that he had the complete confidence of the board of education of the county and that he could buy anything up to $25. You, too, may find a buyer whose purchasing power is quite limited, or an insignificant company with an imposing name. Is your product purchased centrally in a large firm, or are there independent buyers for each subsidiary? What is the potential volume of business available to you?

Products. Closely tied to volume is the nature of products manufactured by a firm. Or, if you are selling to a service industry, what particular types of supplies does it use? Is there a possibility that more of your material can be used if it could be substituted for a competitor's product?

Markets and Users. Discover the potential market for your customer's products. The more you learn about his problems, the better you may be able to help him. In giving this help, you may increase sales for your product or service. The alert salesman is always trying to help his customer by seeing the customer's operations through the customer's eyes.

Company Credit Rating. Learn at the outset the credit rating of your customer. Perhaps you will not wish to sell him when you find out he is financially shaky. Or, you may find him very honest, but not a good businessman. In that case, you may extend limited credit, but be particularly watchful to see that he doesn't get too involved. His credit rating will determine the size of orders you can sell and the length of time you can give him in paying. It just makes good sense to work with a customer so that he keeps himself financially solvent. It is a must for both of you.

Organization and Men. Familiarize yourself with the organization of the buyer's firm. This is particularly important if you sell major equipment. Frequently, the key man in purchasing is not in the purchasing department. Some firms have strong purchasing departments that handle most major and all minor decisions; other purchasing departments are rubber-stamp operations in which buyers make only minor decisions.

Type of Operation. If you are selling to a manufacturing firm, is it mostly an assembly operation, or does the firm buy raw material and do most of its own fabricating? Is the operation seasonal, cyclical, or regular? Is it a simple operation in a highly competitive industry, or is it a highly complicated manufacturing operation? Can the outside salesman help the buying firm, and does the buyer look for advice? If you sell to a wholesaler, how much does he help his customers, and how can you help solve his selling problems?

Previous Relationship to Your Firm. Has your relationship been one of long standing and mutual trust, or is the buying firm new to you? Have you had any outstanding difficulties with this firm before? What has been the history of the relationship between your firm and the purchasing department of the customer's firm? What has been the pattern of buying, and what type of people have been contacted in the buying firm? Has the relationship been a seesaw one, or has it been steady most of the time? Is the customer prone to take every advantage he can and try to gain on every sale?

Future Growth. Is the future bright for your customer? Is the industry growing, stagnant, or dying? Will imminent changes materially change the industry? What is his position within the industry, and what will he likely do in the coming periods? Does the leadership in the firm have a progressive attitude?

Frequency of Call. The potential of some customers merits frequent calls, while others need be visited but a few times a year. By assessing the sales possibilities, you can partially fix the number of calls in a period. Also, because some buyers prefer to be called on more often than others, you frequently have to respect their wishes and call more often than seems justified. Eventually, you can make provisions to handle the business in some other way.

Receptionist and Secretary. When calling on a buyer, you might first meet a receptionist; then, in a large firm, there may also be a secretary. Usually one or more office girls stand between you and the buyer. While she may not seem important, she has the power to get you in fast or keep you cooling your heels, waiting and wasting valuable time. By all means, cultivate these girls so that they get to know you and like you. A box of candy or some flowers sent to the secretary's home on a birthday or anniversary may do much to keep a friendly relationship.

Customer Facts of a General Nature. Certain types of information may have general bearing on the customer, even though the specific effects may be tenuous. Such information may slightly affect a customer, or it may tend to steer other firms away from doing business. On the other hand, certain information could be quite favorable to a customer and enhance his prestige. Occasionally, the customer's neighborhood may indicate certain degrees of progressiveness, or the customer's reputation in the area may be important to your sale. Labor relations of a firm may have some effects on its growth and may affect purchases. Know whether a firm is widely owned or family controlled. Is the firm paternalistic to its employees? Is it considered fair to its employees? Is it considered a good place to work? Selling to a firm that is well entrenched in its field and to one that has a fine reputation in the city may be quite different from selling to one that is weak, constantly beset by labor troubles, and ill-regarded in the community. Miscellaneous information about a company may be gathered from many sources, and it can add valuable overall assistance to the salesman.

WHERE TO SECURE CUSTOMER INFORMATION

To get information on a customer who is buying for his family, you can use your company's records, information supplied by relatives, friends, and neighbors, and from other companies doing business with this individual. Also, the person's bank and credit agencies can be used. In a large metropolitan area there are several agencies that specialize in credit information. Some have data on over a million families filed on cards readily accessible. In a matter of minutes, such an agency can give you the credit history of an individual for a period of years. The data includes where he has made credit purchases, how much he has owed at any one time, and a history of how he pays his accounts.

When securing information on a company and its buyer, salesmen serving the same account with different products often have valuable tips. Trade associations, rating agencies, banks, trade directories, trade magazines, and other periodicals also may be used. Official and legal records often prove helpful. In industry, credit men have a national organization which compiles and makes available pertinent credit information on businesses within the United States. Banks furnish helpful information on credit of companies in other countries. Rating agencies, both general and special ones such as those in the furniture trade, lumber trade, and jewelry trade, maintain active files of credit information.

TYPES OF CUSTOMERS

When a salesman first meets a potential customer, he "sizes him up" by appraising him and determining the best way to handle him. Customers do the same thing with salesmen, and professional buyers sometimes have their own systematic approaches. A snap decision is dangerous because you cannot know a customer until you have been with him several times and have seen him in his various moods. At times, if we judge hastily, we can make some serious errors in our approach.

Common sense tells us that we cannot handle everyone alike; nor can we set up a standard approach and use it always in the same way. (Do not confuse "standard approach" with "standard presentation" which will be discussed in a later chapter.) Although all people are alike in many ways, they are also individualistic in many others. In any kind of differentiation, we must realize that we cannot neatly pigeonhole people; to do so would require too many categories with too many fine distinctions.

To avoid probing too deeply and making serious errors of judgment, be content to study each customer when you meet him for the first time and fit him into some simple pattern you have developed. Later, if you discover that you have misplaced him, you can then shift him into another group that more accurately reflects his characteristics. Many systems and steps have been developed for cataloging by salesmen; some are relatively simple, while others are highly complex. As a new salesman, use a system like the following. As you grow more experienced, you may vary this pattern to fit your needs and abilities. Remember that the following points are only a guide; no one can give you the perfect, all-inclusive system.

Talkative

Some people like to hear themselves talk. Seemingly, they are experts on every topic, and they freely volunteer significant and insignificant information. You will find it difficult to slow down a continuous talker; only by interjecting complimentary remarks will you be able to catch him, slow him, and switch his train of thought. Just as a railroad train may be switched from one track to another, so you can introduce your own topic, gradually bringing the customer to your topic, and direct his conversation and yours toward the object of your sale.

Since he really believes his words are golden, you do not contradict a customer or get in an argument with him. Yet, it is essential that you halt his flow of words, that you get him to concentrate on the product or service you are selling so that the two of you will be in empathy, directing yourselves to the end result—the sale. He may be a tiresome bore who is naive and incredibly egotistical; yet he is a customer, and through your skillful leading, he can be sold. Somewhere along the way you must take firm control of the situation, change the monologue to a dialogue, and arouse his interest in your proposition.

Silent

One of the most difficult people to handle is someone who refuses to talk. Some buyers are reticent, talk little, and communicate practically nothing. In some way you must communicate so that the customer will respond to your proposition with other than a curt "No" or a shake of the head. One salesman spent 15 minutes trying to get a buyer to talk. After a monologue which seemed interminable, the buyer finally said a few words but never became talkative.

Sometimes a buyer may be silent through ignorance or because he has nothing to say. Other times, he may use silence to disconcert a salesman, upset his calm, and make him more vulnerable in bargaining. One way that is frequently successful with a silent customer is to ply him with questions that call for answers, questions that cannot be successfully answered with a mere "Yes" or "No." This tends to open him up; with skillful guidance you soon have a normal conversation in progress.

Another way is to begin your conversation in your usual way and, getting no response, ask a question. Then remain silent until the customer does something. Sit quietly; do not fidget; do not become disturbed. What may seem an interminable time to you is perhaps half a minute or a minute. Sometimes, a salesman has remained silent as long as five minutes, neither he nor the customer saying a word. What may seem a long time to you may not be long to the customer who is thoughtfully considering what you have said. If he is a slow thinker, he will not resent the silent treatment. If he is deliberately using the tactic to disturb you, he will soon learn that you are familiar with it and will resume his normal approach. As long as you are selling a worthwhile product which will benefit this individual, have no fear of what he thinks or says. Yours is an honest, legitimate effort, worthy of every skill you can command.

Customer Who Stalls

We are all familiar with the person who seemingly cannot make up his mind. Of course, a person might be constitutionally weak, or he might be stalling the salesman. When you encounter such a person, firmly influence the customer to accept your proposition. Now you can use a number of selling techniques which have successfully moved such individuals to action.

If the customer procrastinates, determine the cause and apply the correct procedure. If he doubts the quality of your product, talk construction; if he doubts its durability, talk performance and use testimonials; if he is worried about financing the product, suggest easy-payment plans.

People hesitate, however, to buy for many other reasons. They may be slow buyers, or they might think that, by prolonging the conversation, you will add a sales inducement. Many techniques are available for handling such people. You can stimulate the sale by making a better offer, such as the car salesman who will add floor mats without charge. You can stress the importance of getting the item immediately. For example, "Buy the electric fan now and be prepared for the hot weather coming our way tomorrow." If delivery is slow, you can point out that now you have the item in stock that he needs, but you cannot get another for a month. You can show the customer a factory release that states prices will be advanced next month. Tell the customer that tickets are selling rapidly and that if he wants a good seat, he will have to buy now. The resourceful salesman can easily find other approaches.

Disagreeable

Many people are disagreeable from time to time. Just as in any activity—for example, taking a trip, you may encounter dust, heat, rain, mosquitoes, detours, and other hindrances, so in selling you must expect disagreeable situations. It is all too easy to shrink from disagreeable customers; avoiding them labels you a weak-kneed salesman who is unwilling to face the reality of successful selling. Permit your customer to carry on, but do not become upset even if he should be insulting, cruel, nasty, or sarcastic. Yours is a professional relationship; do not honor his attitude by responding to his slurs and accusations. Very little is accomplished by taking issue with such an individual. At worst, it may irritate him; at best, it will do little to soothe his feelings.

Listen patiently to his diatribes. Do not disagree and do not argue; as soon as possible redirect the conversation until it is concentrated on your product. If the approach leads to an interesting conversation, he might soon forget his personal gripes. Once you have penetrated his exterior, you may find him an excellent customer, a valuable friend, and a wonderful individual in spite of his crusty exterior.

Customers Who Lack Confidence

The customer who lacks confidence is afraid to commit himself. Most of us have such periods of timidity, but, here we are concerned with the one who is characteristically of this nature.

Such a person needs guidance, assurance, and support. By your manner of speaking and the way you exude confidence, you can build him up. If timidity is caused by financial problems, help him work out a solution. If he fears something new, mention the names of people known to him who have already used this product. If the quantity appears too great, point out how long it can be expected to last. If the color does not seem quite right, indicate how others have adjusted themselves to it. If the price and value received appear equal, indicate that even a short period of comparative comfort is worth the expenditure. A person buying an electric fan the last week in August possibly could get along without it for a week or two until cooler weather arrives. But why deny himself now this present comfort which can make him happier? Next year and thereafter he can enjoy the fan during every hot spell.

Sometimes a person hesitates because he does not completely understand the proposition, and it may be necessary only to detail it again carefully so that he knows what is being offered. Properly presented to an interested customer, an article can be sold if you know how to nudge in the right spots.

Superior Customer

Some buyers consistently act superior. They create the impression, in a condescending way, that they will listen to your explanation. Of course, they already know the answers, or they want you to feel that they are well-versed in your area. They speak casually of quality, big orders, special considerations. They toss well-known names around with familiarity. Inwardly, you may have an amused tolerance; but outwardly, show an avid interest and be suitably impressed by what they say. Do not fear such customers, for it is unlikely that they will ever know as much about your area as you do. They will not, that is, if you are as well prepared as you ought to be.

Once you have gained the confidence of such an individual, recognized his ability to his own satisfaction, and given him free play to demonstrate his capacity, then you are in a position to move in because you have established rapport. He will listen to what you say and be favorably impressed. What else can he do since he has already cataloged you as a wise individual? His ego has been recognized, inflated, and soothed. He will listen.

Sarcastic or Pleasantly Disagreeable Customer

You might say that it is impossible to be pleasantly disagreeable, and yet a sarcastic customer with his pointed barbs may make you mighty uncomfortable if you have not learned to parry such thrusts. The skillful salesman is the one who can take negative remarks and return them pleasantly to the customer and do it with a positive emphasis. For example, if the buyer should say the blanket is too thin to be warm, you might reply, "True, in a single thickness it will be adequate only in moderate temperatures. However, we find two such blankets together are much more useful under varying situations than one heavy blanket warm enough to meet the most penetrating cold."

Or, if he says, "This truck is too big for my needs," you can reply: "In some instances it is more than adequate for your needs; however, study has revealed that for people in your situation, there is frequent enough demand for this larger truck to warrant your purchase. Actually, when you stretch the price differences over the life of the vehicle, this truck's added cost becomes relatively insignificant. The redeeming feature, of course, is that you are adequately prepared to handle your most exacting needs without going elsewhere to secure a truck for those special occasions."

Some people take great pride in their ability to be sarcastic. They have not learned that such an attribute is undesirable, but it is not your duty to set them right. Whatever your personal feeling, never forget that your primary job is to sell customers and not to reform them. When you really know these people, you understand their strengths and weaknesses and ignore their "digs," which may not be meant to be too personal.

Pleasant Customers

Let us now consider what we term the normal customer. He represents what we would like to be, under the same circumstances. He is usually pleasant, somewhat conservative, open-minded, and willing to give attention. All that is necessary is to observe the common courtesies of behavior, remembering, however, that the two of you may not look upon these common courtesies alike.

Some of you have heard the story about the person who was asked to reconcile two friends who had become estranged. In this situation, the neutral individual went to each of the others, made each agree not to go half way but two thirds of the way to effect the reconciliation. This was necessary because what one person thought was two thirds of the way was, in the other's opinion, barely half way. Understandably, then, such is the case when $2/3 + 2/3 = 1$.

Usually, you will find consistent success with the pleasant customer. If you are properly equipped, trained, and experienced, your sales to such people will be satisfactory. Do not forget, however, that "difficult" people may be so because of irritating salesmen who have such little finesse that they do not even observe the ordinary social amenities. Only too often we find ill-equipped salesmen desperately bucking their way forward against almost insurmountable odds. Their formula for success is a compound of brute force, overbearing manners, and sheer awkwardness. The blunt force of a clumsy weapon never equals the cutting effect of a sharp knife honed to perfection. A figure of speech, perhaps, but you should be like that knife; be as skillfully perfected as possible and easily cut through difficult problems until you have accomplished your goal.

UNDERSTANDING CUSTOMERS

We may easily be able to catalog customers into specific types, and we may have much information on each customer; but until we understand people and know what motivates them, our success as salesmen will be limited. As individuals, we learn to get along with our wives or husbands, our parents, our in-laws, our children. One learns how far he can go in kidding at home, what spots are sensitive in members of the family, and when "silence is golden."

In dealing with others, we soon recognize individuals with traits and peculiarities which need our special care if we are to get along with them. At home, discussion is a give-and-take proposition with dad doing his share. But when facing customers, dad is the conciliator, the diplomat, the soother of aroused feelings. He must, in fact, be able to lead the customer to be receptive to the proposition. So, it is essential that the salesman learn about people.

Learn about customers' motives and their attitudes toward different ideas. Know their likes and dislikes, their loves, hatreds, aversions. Learn how they will react under varying situations so that you can guide interviews accordingly. Seek out the many facets of their lives, and use this information to develop your approach. Accept the fact that these persons are governed not only by your competitors' sales presentations but also by heredity, environment, education, financial status, and many other fast-changing conditions. Simply stated, you must learn much about your customers so that you can meet them intelligently.

CUSTOMER BEHAVIOR

Various ways may be used to describe and interpret customer behavior. We can list rational and emotional motives of the customer and discuss each. We may distinguish between motives and talking points; people have motives, but our product or service has talking points. We may catalog primary and secondary motives, human instincts, social drives, and other attributes common to the individual and assign different definitions to each.

However we make these differentiations and whatever methods we use, we still come back to the simple fact that we must learn what makes a customer "tick." Having learned what he is, we can work on him and with him to gain our end. Let us now examine some traits of customer behavior.

Behavior in the Past

Undoubtedly, the best way to study a customer in the present is to find out what he has done and how he has behaved in the past. Most of us usually do not change rapidly, and habits and customs that we have practiced for years will probably persist in the future. People's eating habits give us one example of predictable behavior. Although we vow to diet, to change our pattern of food intake, and to cut our weight, most of us never fulfill the resolution. After a few half-hearted attempts, we go back to old habits unless illness forces us to change.

Real Reason Versus Reason Given

Commonly, a person questioned about doing something will give a reasonable answer, an answer that sounds appropriate or an answer that is believable, but not necessarily the most significant one. We are prone to do this because we are, in many ways, engrossed in picayune details, in low thoughts, and in unworthy ideas. Frankly, we are "small" in many ways, and we do not want others to find out about it. "A penny for your thoughts," someone says; and if we really told what we were thinking, we might be ashamed of ourselves. Have these thoughts ever run through your mind? "How can I get the biggest steak for dinner?" "Do I need to take a bath tonight?" "Why didn't I get the chance instead of my brother?" "What reason must I dream up to explain the expensive shoes I bought?" "How can I get my friend's girl?" "Who will get stuck for the bill when we go out for dinner tonight?" "I must not forget to get a haircut tomorrow." Yes, our thoughts are usually mundane. Yet, it is well to have some idea of what runs through the mind of the customer so that you can address him intelligently.

Does Not Know Why He Buys

All of us occasionally buy something only to wonder, later, why we did it. Some may buy in this fashion most of the time by acting impulsively with fleeting, at-the-moment reasons predominating.

Price Conscious

Many people are quite price conscious; others appear to be but actually are not. Distinguish between these customers because appeals must differ in selling. One person's price consciousness might be directed toward low sales prices, but not particularly toward the item's quality. Another person might buy more expensive goods if he is convinced that the quality is high. Price can refer to cash or to extended payments. Price can be too high, not because the individual cannot afford it, but because he does not see the value. With a professional buyer, cost can spell the difference between profit or loss. In retailing, the buyer who makes advantageous deals can sell at a lower price and still reap his necessary profit. In industry, shaving a fraction of a cent on many items results in major savings over the life of the manufactured product. Price components include time periods, discounts, allowances, returns, and special inducements.

Service

In talking with your customer, you may discover that his interest in service is paramount. Many people buy new cars regularly to avoid breakdowns and repair bills. Purchasing agents frequently buy items because the manufacturer offers fine service. Many people who live in small towns avoid buying foreign cars because of poor service. People will patronize one establishment rather than another because of convenient service hours. "Install it and forget it" means a lot to certain people. They might be buying a gas water heater for the home, a television set with an outside aerial, a roof that is guaranteed to last twenty years, or equipment with hermetically sealed motors that are trouble free. You can add many more examples where service is the main criterion in a sale.

Loyalty

Some people are intensely loyal. When dealing with such an individual, mention his loyalty whenever possible. Loyalty to family, religion, college, lodge, fraternity, and nationality, or brand of car, suit, shoes, and washing powder—all become powerful levers to sway the buyer's decision.

Prestige

Some customers worship prestige. How frequently we hear such remarks as these: "My brother is manager of the plant." "My cousin is assistant to the president." "My boss drives an Exter convertible." "Prominent people in town belong to this group." "The head of the women's club has her hair done here." "I always buy my furs at Dittrich's and hats at Judson's." Many people are hero worshipers, blind followers of some prominent individual who endorses a product. Yes, that is the way they are; and if your customer is a great believer in testimonials by prominent figures, satisfy his craving for them.

Ego

In some ways, prestige goes hand in hand with ego. Everyone wants to excel, to be important in some way, and to gain recognition. Most people welcome praise, and hunger for some kind word that points to their exceptional qualities. At an expensive boys' summer camp, enough contests were held so that everyone took home some ribbon or prize. In certain instances, it was almost impossible to devise a contest in which certain boys might excel above all others. Many a customer has been lost because you neglected to give him the attention he craved, and someone else did. Winning a prize or getting his name or picture in the newspaper can be your customer's way of advertising his superior qualities.

How much praise or adulation can you heap on a person without sickening him and becoming sickened yourself? Occasionally, you may overdo, but far more frequently your praise will be inadequate. Skillfully worded praise, justified praise, warms your customer. Imitation is a terrific compliment because it is a form of praise. The person being imitated is flattered to know others see his fine qualities.

Pride

Many a person is proud, and few are sincerely humble. Since pride is characteristic of the individual, you should find sources of pride of your customer and bring them out in the open. There may be so-called false pride as well as pride that is thoroughly justified. Do not pass judgment on the merit of the deed that your customer is proud of. Let the customer be the judge of its worthiness. Pride is connected not only with self-achievement but also in the accomplishments of other members of the family, relatives, and friends. At the other extreme, the salesman should be aware of those ideas that arouse *jealousy* or *envy* because these thoughts arouse negative feeling which can hinder the sale.

Status

Each of us wishes to achieve status. You can recognize this desire for status by pointing out to your customer that position in his community or organization makes him a leader. Status is assured the customer once you indicate that you appreciate his leadership qualities.

Emulation

"If I only could be like him," we often hear someone say. Your customer is like that, too, wishing that he could emulate a successful man. You can soon learn what your customer's secret desires are and gently point out his qualities which are similar to the one he admires. Show him how he is approaching his goal by pointing out those qualities. All of us have secret ambitions, and we are willing to sacrifice if we can fulfill them.

Comfort

Life is a series of "ups and downs" for most of us, but through them all we try to secure comfort for ourselves and our family. We strive for happiness and try to escape physical pain. We also want to avoid tension and mental disturbance, or any conditions that are disturbing. If we understand our customer, we can avoid distractions or words that reduce his comfortable status unless our selling theme deliberately makes him uncomfortable. Making a customer uncomfortable usually disturbs him and withdraws him from a buying mood.

Effort—Laziness

Is your customer habitually industrious, or is he lazy and careless? You are concerned with traits he possesses. You should know which ones predominate so that your approach is correct. To handle both the industrious and the lazy persons alike would be hazardous, for you would slow down the industrious person who felt that you were too lackadaisical, and the indolent type would resent being pushed. Even the lazy person resents being considered lazy; rather, he calls himself cautious, deliberate, or careful.

Personal Finance Control

Some people go deeply into debt to satisfy their wants. Others are careful in their spending and buy only what they can afford. On the one hand, you may be dealing with a spendthrift; on the other, with a frugal individual. In order to sell, you must convince the buyer that he can afford what you have to offer, that the price is reasonable, that the satisfaction from the purchase will be greater than from any other similar expenditure. Otherwise, he might buy something else.

Personal finance is odd because one's attitude toward it varies greatly from person to person. One person may worry about his inadequate reserves and be loath to part with a nickel lest he be in want, while another in far poorer circumstances may blithely obligate himself far beyond prudent limits. While you must be satisfied that the customer can pay for what he buys, you can work with him in developing a pattern for handling the purchase.

Belief in Reciprocity

Some people are firmly convinced that reciprocity is an ideal way to do business; others want nothing to do with it. If your customer happens to believe in the slogan, "You scratch my back, and I'll scratch yours," use reciprocity whenever possible with him. There are some dangerous points in this philosophy, but carefully handled, reciprocity can be useful. The trouble in reciprocity arises because frequently inferior merchandise or poor service is substituted for quality merchandise and superior service. If you are involved in a reciprocity deal, you are unable to protest at shoddy treatment, for your own company may be guilty of giving inferior merchandise to customers who must buy from you. The "all things being equal" slogan, so often mentioned as a part of reciprocity, only too often becomes empty words. Substandard merchandise and poor service must be tolerated even though costs rise.

Recreation, Hobbies

One of the most successful ways of becoming friendly with a customer is to learn about his hobbies and recreation. These are areas in which he is vitally interested, and he often pursues them more avidly than his business. While you do not need too much knowledge about his particular hobbies, you should know enough about them to ask intelligent questions and to be able to praise him on his success. Sometimes his work and hobby are closely connected. If the owner of a sporting goods store is an ardent hunter or fisherman, he becomes familiar with his products as a businessman and also as a user. While many participate in active sports, others may be content to be spectators, getting enjoyment through the effort of other people.

Just as it is important to know what the buyer enjoys, it is also important to know what he dislikes. Do not discuss football if the buyer thinks it is a brutal game which brings out the worst in people. Do not talk about hunting if he thinks it cruel to shoot animals. Do not bring up cards and gambling if he regards a game of cards as sinful. Again, let me repeat, utilize this area to the fullest because people are particularly susceptible when you discuss a topic which is highly pleasant to them.

Beautiful Things

Whether it be a beautiful home, a handsome man, a lovely girl, an outstanding painting, or an unusually fine dog, people are proud of possessing, being in contact with, or having access to anything or anyone which arouses admiration. By your comments you demonstrate that you, too, recognize the unusual. If nothing more than as a conversation piece, the reference to something beautiful opens up interesting flows of thought which later can be channeled to your objective. (You will note, as we continue, that we are opening up many methods to help you influence people favorably. Too often, the salesman equipped with only baseball information finds it hard to interest buyers. Do not underestimate your customers as having one-track minds; once you get to know them, you will find them interesting in many ways.)

Romance

On many occasions, romance is a dominant factor in making a sale. Little need be said about its obvious characteristics with which we are all familiar—dating, love, and marriage. The wedding itself involves high costs. Romance may be instrumental in causing sales of clothing, cosmetics, flowers, candy, and jewelry. Romance is a factor that eventually leads to buying homes, furniture, and appliances. And we must not overlook summer vacations, South Sea trips, world cruises, and other attractions which outwardly have reasons easily explained, but inwardly have romantic tinges. The same could be said for many sports and types of recreation. Be aware of the importance of attaching romantic urges to various age levels. These instincts are more powerful at some ages than at others; yet, one should not eliminate any person from this urge because environment can often be a controlling factor. For example, youth is often considered the time for marriage. Yet, older people do get married for various reasons, one of which is romance. Age in adults may be a deterrent in romance but not a barrier.

The Crowd

Some people are so sensitive about what others are doing that they are almost fearful of exercising independent action. They make a fetish out of following the crowd and are lost if their dress, action, and even thoughts are not synchronized with the group. Such people, of course, are easily susceptible to testimonials and can be led readily by telling them what is the current practice. They do little thinking for themselves and blindly follow the leadership of well-known figures. This trait is far more influential at certain ages in a person's life. Thus, the high school girl would not wear a blue jacket if her friends all had red jackets. Many a woman has foregone a party because she did not have the right clothes. Some people stay away from church because they do not have Sunday clothes. Some people attend concerts so that others can see them there. Once a neighborhood has a certain number of families with clothes dryers (someone has said eight percent), the rest of the housewives must buy clothes dryers.

Health

Everyone is vitally concerned about his health. Some customers will talk indefinitely about their ills. To handle such customers, gradually wean them from their aches and pains to your product. Health is a fundamental topic which can create empathy between salesman and buyer. The salesman must never start a health discussion by mentioning his aches and pains. Many buyers will not be sympathetic.

Search for Something New or Different

The newest, the latest, the unusual, the spectacular—yes, having that which sets one apart appeals to many people. Just as some prefer to buy only that which has been proved in service, so others always want to be first with the latest car, dress, boat, machine, food, education, and, for some, even religion. Perhaps it is the spirit of adventure which motivates these people to exhibit such a need for the unusual, or it may be a desire to conform to a group.

Another group is more cautious in its approach but still wants to take advantage of something better. The desire for something new is characteristic of many people in varying intensities. In one sale, it may be the dominant approach to use, while in another situation, its attraction may be so slight as not to warrant pushing.

Sense of Justice

You have often heard the statement, "Don't strike below the belt." If you criticize someone who cannot defend himself, your customer might resent the unfair advantage that you are taking. People instinctively resent abuse of an animal, manhandling of children, unfair use of authority, and stepping on the toes of the weak. Most people have a strong enough feeling of right and wrong that you can use it to strengthen your position whether you sell a farm, collect money for a worthy project, push for certain reforms, or develop new areas of interest.

Fear

Using fear may be a negative approach, but it is a powerful tool for influencing people. Fear is a healthy trait that is essential for survival. The brave, but foolhardy, individual finds life insecure. He may take chances that cause accidents or death. He risks losing his job by coming in late to work, by spending work time on outside projects, or by turning in late reports.

Modern warfare goes back to the Indians who believed in using all types of protection and concealment to win. Senseless exposure may draw outward admiration but inward contempt. One of the most lucrative sales areas counteracts fear. We buy insurance because we fear fire or death; we invest in safety features because we fear accidents. We are fearful about job security, and we are concerned about our families' health and life itself. Yes, fear is a sharp spur that drives us toward self-preservation. As a salesman who has raised the specter of a particular fear, you then suggest that it can be removed with the assistance of your product or service.

Power

Power satisfies most egos and ought not to be condemned unless it becomes overbearing or excessive. Frequently, power is more apparent than real. An authoritarian often thinks he is stronger than he actually is. As a result, he deludes himself that he is influential, impressive, and important. Once you understand him, you can talk him into believing that both of you are aiming for the same objective. Powerful people consider themselves "big shots." Treat them in the right fashion, and they will be putty in your hands.

Guilt

Guilt can be another strong emotion in your customer. Guilt may be openly admitted or secretly kept; yet, it frequently exists. Even though a wrong has been corrected, the customer might still feel remorseful. From a selling standpoint, one might arouse a feeling of guilt both by the sin of commission as well as the sin of omission. If you can make one feel guilty because of what he is unwilling to do, you might successfully change his mind. Guilt and fear are basic human traits and are powerful tools to use in selling. As they can be most effective when correctly used, so can they also backfire viciously when improperly applied.

Examples of the guilt complex are legion—buying a power lawnmower for a small lawn, justifying it by comparing it to your wife's vacuum cleaner; buying an expensive gun with the money you saved by not taking a vacation (neither did the family get a vacation); justifying a larger, more expensive car because you must be comfortable on long business trips; buying a new home when you and your wife convince yourselves your children each need a bedroom, while actually you both want to live in a more fashionable neighborhood; taking out a family golf membership which really gives you more opportunity to play. The more direct you can make the association, the more likely can you improve selling effectiveness. These examples of guilt association which might prevent a sale can be overcome by rationalization to the point where the individual justifies his purchase.

Independent Thinkers

Many people pride themselves on their independent thinking. They want to reason constructively and base their buying decisions on facts. Such people may be deliberate thinkers who want to discriminate between purchases. If such a customer genuinely needs your product or service, he will welcome your intelligent approach without the use of gimmicks. He appreciates a straightforward presentation and can justify buying on merit.

QUESTIONS AND PROBLEMS

1. Why is it unlikely that a salesman will be able to catalog customers by types?

2. There are always new salesmen that must be trained to handle customers. Is this true of all salesmen you hire?

3. Is there a standard list of information a salesman should have about each customer? Why might such lists vary?

4. Prepare an outline of information a salesman needs on a customer he calls on weekly. Would this outline be different if the salesman made monthly calls? Semiannual calls?

5. What are some of the mistakes salesmen make when they lack relevant information about their customers?

6. Why is it important to speak at the customer's level?

7. "You can determine the type of customer he is by his hobbies and recreation." Explain.

8. A salesman who has not qualified his customer properly may get into serious trouble. Indicate what difficulties might arise.

9. How can your company lose money on a steady customer even though there has never been any previous trouble?

10. Prepare a list of sources of customer information. Use your library freely to fill in your list.

11. When you expect to sell a customer who talks constantly, what advance preparation is necessary?

12. Is there any sure way to get the silent customer talking? Should one use rough tactics if necessary to get him to respond? Is it preferable to risk dubious methods to get him to talk? Should you give up if he does not respond to a reasonable approach?

13. When dealing with an unpleasant person, to what extent should you put up with his discourtesy?

14. How can you change a timid person to a customer? How far should you enter into his personal affairs in order to get buying action?

15. Some customers like to feel important. How do you handle such customers?

16. Usually what does one accomplish through the use of sarcasm?

17. Why is it essential for you to understand each of your customers? Why should you bother to work this hard?

18. Why can we predict future behavior on past behavior? Do people frequently change? When do they change and to what extent?

19. Frequently, one finds it almost impossible to get to the real reason for a customer's actions. Why is this situation so common? Can we take steps to overcome such behavior?

tinguish between the price-conscious customer and the one ho appears price conscious. Can you sell both equally well? To what extent can you depend on customer loyalty? What should a loyal customer expect of you?

22. From your own experience, give examples of prestige buyers.

23. How can you use a customer's pride to increase your sales? Is this approach proper?

24. Name several examples of buying because of emulation. Is this really hero worship?

25. Is the appeal to comfort a basic appeal? Is it more effective at different age levels? What conditions favor the comfort appeal?

26. "Do not underestimate the interests of your customer." Illustrate what is meant by that statement.

27. Is it appropriate to use romance as a buying appeal? Can romance have a wide appeal? Does it have many facets?

28. Can the health appeal be effectively used to influence customers? Give examples.

29. Why must some people be the first to have a new car, the first to move into a new home, or the first to try a new boat? Can such persons be very profitable customers?

30. Fear is a desirable trait. It is often used and misused in selling. Give examples of using fear to induce a customer to buy and examples of using fear to meet the selfish ends of salesmen.

31. Can a customer be induced to buy because he wants to show his power? When is power simply ego?

32. Many people make purchases but afterwards have a guilty feeling. Are you justified in making a sale which brings on a guilt feeling and then helping your customer justify his purchase?

CASES

2-1: SYSTEMS INCORPORATED

Frank Bundy had just completed his call on the Imperial Tube Company. He had been invited by the purchasing agent Arnold Rivers who wanted to discuss some equipment Mr. Bundy's firm was to supply in six months.

Mr. Bundy had left his plant 500 miles away yesterday. He flew in last evening, spending the night in a local hotel. He had spent all morning with Mr. Rivers. When they completed their work, they had lunch together, and then Mr. Bundy left.

Mr. Bundy's plane did not leave until 5 p.m. Therefore, he decided to call on Odel Sorenson, purchasing agent for Systems Incorporated. He had learned that Systems Incorporated was contemplating using a type of equipment manufactured by Mr. Bundy's firm. On such an important call Mr. Bundy usually made an appointment, but in this case he felt he could stop in to see what was developing. Through previous calls he had become well acquainted with Sorenson.

Mr. Bundy entered the office of Systems Incorporated and exchanged pleasant greetings with a new receptionist. He said: "Will you tell Odel Sorenson that Frank Bundy is here to see him." "I'm sorry, but Mr. Sorenson told me explicitly that he would see no one this afternoon," she replied. "But I have come 500 miles, and I know Mr. Sorenson will see me if you tell him I'm here," Mr. Bundy said. "Sorry, but those were his strict orders," she said.

Question

How can Mr. Bundy see Mr. Sorenson this afternoon?

2-2: SCOTT MACHINE COMPANY

Harold McCormick, salesman for Scott Machine Company, has just entered the office of Warren Purvis, purchasing agent for Boor Manufacturing Company.

McCormick: Good morning, Warren.

Purvis: Hi, Hal. How are you?

McCormick: Fine, Warren, and you?

Purvis: Oh, not bad at all.

McCormick: Got your letter about coming down to clear up some details on our bid.

Purvis: Oh, yes, there were some things we weren't sure of. I thought if you came down, we could clear them up. By the way, your bid looks awfully good. The way it looks now, you're in. Big order too, $100,000. The boss sort of leans towards Gamble's machine, but I told him I thought yours was far superior.

McCormick: I'm sure glad to hear you say that, Warren. You can count on me to work with you. I know you're going to like our machine. It's new, but the firms who have bought it so far are happy.

Purvis: We've always had a fine relationship with your company, Hal, and I'm sure we will be satisfied with your new machine if we decide on it. Oh, by the way, Hal, did you say you came in last night?

McCormick: Yes, Warren, I arrived on the 6 o'clock plane, went directly to the hotel, had dinner there, and spent the evening in my room working on a bid.

Purvis: Hal, could I ask a favor of you? You know we've been friends for years.

McCormick: Sure, Warren, what is it?

Purvis: When you leave, could you drop in on the boss and say hello? And when you're there, you might drop a hint that I spent last evening with you in your hotel room discussing details of your bid.

McCORMICK: Warren, is anything wrong?

PURVIS: Yeah, Hal, I'm sort of in a jam. Got in a little game last night with the boys. Lost a lot of money. If the boss hears about it, he probably will fire me.

McCORMICK: You mean to say that your boss will fire you for playing cards on your own time in the evening?

PURVIS: Well, Hal, there's a bit more. It started out innocently about six months ago. I met some men downtown one evening, who invited me to the hotel for a friendly game of cards. Don't get me wrong. These men aren't gamblers, just a group of men enjoying life. Well, we got going pretty strong, and I guess I got in a little heavy financially. My wife got angry and told me that if I kept it up, she would tell the boss. Well, I guess I did let things get out of hand a bit, and as a result we had to skimp pretty badly at home to get along. To make a long story short, she did tell the boss and he blew his top. You know he's a strict "do-gooder" type. Frowns on this sort of thing. Anyway, he made me promise I'd quit it.

I stayed away for several months, but last night I went downtown and happened to bump into these men. They invited me to play, but I said 'thumbs down' because the boss threatened to fire me if I got caught again. But they assured me they were only going to play an hour or two for fun. No money of course. Well, you know how it is. We played a few hands. Things sort of got out of hand. They didn't keep their word, and I lost a lot of money. If this leaks out, I'm afraid I'll lose my job. Oh, yes, we played in a room in your hotel, so all you have to do is tell the boss you met me in the hotel last night and we spent the evening together in your room discussing details of your bid.

Question

What should Harold McCormick do?

CHAPTER 3

Your Product or Service

Because so much emphasis is placed on the salesman's selling techniques and his treatment of his customers, we may overlook the importance of the product and the company. When we go out for dinner, we talk about the restaurant's decor, service, and clientele, but we still expect the food to be appetizing and well prepared. The steak has to be right for our taste, or all else becomes insignificant. We can use this analogy in selling. No matter what approach or techniques you use and no matter how friendly your meeting with a customer may be, if the product or service does not meet the needs of the buyer, he will not be satisfied. You must know your product and what it can do for the buyer.

PRODUCT KNOWLEDGE IMPERATIVE

The salesman must be well-equipped to talk intelligently about his product and how it meets the customer's needs. Otherwise, he may recommend his product for uses for which it was never designed. Equally bad, he might overlook opportunities to introduce his product in new applications that are suitable for his customer.

Customers Demand Information

The housewife and the mother want to know how a garment wears or whether the bug bomb will kill flying ants. The technical buyer wants information about the cutting properties of tools, how to machine titanium, or how to speed up production. Between these illustrations of the housewife and the technical buyer are thousands of buyers with requests for information ranging from the very simple to the highly complex. The salesman's need for information varies with his customer, but all customers want to be satisfied. They come to the salesman for specific information; if the salesman does not know the answer, the customer becomes angered by such a (stupid) reply as: "It's better because it costs more," or "You get what you pay for." Both of these statements are highly inaccurate. In short, it is safe to say that you cannot be a successful salesman unless you can answer most of your customer's questions. You have to be able to assess the features of your product line and how it can meet his needs. Then formulate an answer that will give your customer the greatest satisfaction.

Facts Are Necessary to Meet Competition

You walk into a customer's office with your sales presentation. After a few minutes, the buyer begins questioning you about your product. He points out that Competitor A states that his product will perform in a certain way; Competitor B talks about the long life of his product; Competitor C points out the economy of his product even though it is higher priced; Competitor D undersells everyone else but guarantees that his product will perform satisfactorily. Then the buyer turns to you and asks, "What about your product?" Unless you have a comprehensive grasp of the field, you are at a loss to meet this question.

Handling questions of this nature demands wide product knowledge. A wide product knowledge means knowing not only your product but competing products. Just as a debater must know his opponent's points, so should you know competition's points. Put yourself in the competing salesmen's shoes and see how you would sell their products against yours. Usually, if your product or service is complex, it is doubtful that your product will excel competitors' products in all aspects. Probably, you will find that each competitor's product has strong points to which he ties his sales talk. Just as your products have strong as well as weak points, so, too, will your competitors. In your presentation, therefore, bring out the favorable features of your product and do not mention competition. If the buyer brings the competitor into the picture and asks about certain features mentioned by another salesman, you should be aware of these strong points and admit that any successful product has certain advantages. But you can point out that the other product has certain weaknesses that the competing salesman has not revealed, and that in evaluating a presentation, it is necessary to assess most of the features in order to come up with the one product that best meets the buyer's needs.

Buyer Confidence

Perhaps the key phrase is "customer satisfaction." Walking into a buyer's office with a calm, confident, self-assured air may immediately impress your prospect that you understand your business. But you have to follow this up with information that the buyer can trust. Sometimes, giving an honest appraisal may lose a sale because the buyer's needs may best be met by a competitor's product. In this case, the professional salesman is obliged to inform the buyer that he should buy elsewhere. This takes a good deal of courage, but in the long run it pays big dividends in customer loyalty and faith.

One salesman was given an order for almost 200 machines to be sent to various branch offices. He refused to take the order from the home office because he preferred to sell each branch manager on the merits of the machine. Doing this, he found that only 25 percent of the managers were willing to accept his product, and his sale was cut proportionately. In calling on the branch managers, however, he developed a presentation that showed how his machine was adapted to that particular business. That year he lost the sale of almost 150 machines. But the increased buyer confidence he cultivated enabled him to sell 300 machines to the firm within the next three years.

KNOW YOUR COMPANY

Building buyer confidence is a continuing effort. Under some circumstances, however, buyers are more interested in your company than they are in you and, to some measure, your product. This is particularly true when a buyer questions the ability of a particular company to provide the necessary services. It has happened, more than once, that a company was awarded a contract on the basis of a low bid before it was discovered that the firm did not have the technical ability to do the job.

Organization

Occasionally, a customer will be interested in a firm's organizational structure. This is largely a protective measure. It may seem a little farfetched to think that the way a company is organized is intimately linked to the customer. Yet, if a company shows weakness in this area, a customer may hesitate to place a large order because he fears a performance failure.

Personnel

Even more important than the organization is the staffing of management positions. As a salesman for your company, know who the strong leaders in your company are. Know what they have done for your company; and, if they have been associated with other firms, know their contributions to them as well. You must rely upon the people at the home office to see that orders are handled as promised. Understandably, your customer will be reluctant to deal with you if he has learned through experience that there is a troublesome clashing of personalities in your firm.

The reputations of the personnel involved and their willingness to stand behind their spoken, as well as written, word is of prime importance. Therefore, know how your firm operates and its reputation.

Policies

Most firms follow a definite set of policies or rules of action. Your reputation and your firm's reputation suffer if you make promises that cannot be fulfilled. Know exactly what your company can and cannot (and will and will not) do.

Some companies have an extensive list of policies; others have few. Some firms insist upon rigid adherence to policies, while others may permit deviations to fit the particular case. If you know your firm, you will know the latitude in judgment and leeway in promises that you can assume.

Procedures

Procedures are such working details of the company as prices, discounts, installations, guarantees, returns, and so forth. If you are not fully versed in these little details, you run the risk of making a sale that breaks down in such final details as delivering, collecting, and adjusting. Know thoroughly the meticulous details that your firm insists upon so that you can go through the final steps of the sale effortlessly.

The Past

We have not yet said anything about those magnificent, saintly graybeards who founded your firm seventy-five years ago. When you go into the field for the first time, you will probably be shocked to learn how unimportant they are to your customers. They are interested in what is happening now and in the reputation you have earned for dependability and extra effort in the last few years, not in ancient history.

KNOW YOUR PRODUCT

The most important words in this chapter are these: *Know your product.* Someday you may hear of a salesman who knows too much about his product, but the truth is that most salesmen know too little. The real reason for restricting product information is to hide undesirable features from salesmen or to prevent the salesman from talking too much. Product information, correctly used, is priceless.

Materials Used

The actual materials used in the construction of your product will often be important to your customers. Saying that your product is strong enough or will last long enough is not sufficient for the discriminating buyer. The equipment may be used for operation in which the materials are not compatible; or the materials themselves may work successfully, but the side effects may be disastrous. When a buyer of a tool asks how long it will last, you must have concrete information at hand. Product knowledge is important no matter what the materials are.

Manufacturing Processes

In some cases, describing manufacturing processes can be confusing to the buyer and add nothing to the presentation. But there are many situations in which the buyer will want to know exactly how the product is made. For example, manufacturers of high-quality clothing may be interested in the weaving and dyeing processes used on the cloth and how particular materials are interwoven for effect. It is quite possible that this information will be among the selling points used on the customer. A buyer may be interested to know that the product is made by a continuous manufacturing process, which could insure a uniform order rather than one from several batches. Color variations in some paints necessitate that lots be thoroughly mixed because slightly different shades could result if batches were applied separately.

Inspection features in manufacturing might have considerable significance to one who feels that high uniformity is essential. Most people feel the danger in quality deviation is necessarily downward; but if the equipment that uses your product is standardized, it can be equally dangerous if quality goes up. If some of the parts you furnish for further machining are made of a harder steel than requested, the tools might break. Or, through familiarity with food manufacturing processes, you may be able to assure a buyer that your table product cannot be contaminated in processing. Such knowledge can result in customer confidence.

Extent of Line

The number of items in your line, the variety of colors, and the range of sizes may be clinching arguments for a customer. It will be easier for the buyer if he can get all his needs from one source. This becomes even more important when duplicating lines, even though slightly different, can be eliminated. The salesman who has enough patterns, styles, sizes, strengths, and other features will probably sell the most. However, it is not wise for you to bring the entire offering of an extensive line to the potential customer's attention. It enables you, instead, to be highly selective in bringing an appropriate assortment to him. With a large selection, you can present not all, but more than the buyer wants. This permits him to choose from a desirable group, rather than from a group which is only slightly suited to his needs. With a large selection of tools, you can go from plant to plant with special groupings that are suitable for various uses. The weakness of a large selection, from a selling standpoint, is that a salesman may become overly fond of some specific items while neglecting others. This is dangerous; unintentionally, he may be narrowing himself to a particular type of customer and neglecting other customers who could be equally important.

Complementary Lines

Complementary lines can be varied. The coal company that delivers coal in the winter and ice in the summer is an example. The warehouse which stores different products at various seasons illustrates the optimum use of space. Many salesmen representing a firm with a narrow product range will take on other lines to round out their list of items. The same is true of many firms which try to develop a series of items to keep busy the year round, or store products for seasonal consumption. As an alert salesman, you should spot opportunities for introducing complementary lines to broaden existing operations. Your timely suggestion of complementary lines may so improve your customer's operation that his continued success will be largely dependent on your future additions.

Think of the word "complementary" as embodying a multitude of possibilities. Your new items might use the same manufacturing facilities, the same distribution facilities, the same raw materials; they might use by-products and waste products; they might use manpower more effectively or storage facilities more adequately. Never view complementary lines too narrowly and overlook potential expansion.

Brand Name

If your products are well-known brand items with wide advertising support, capitalize on this aid. Many people buy particular retail brands; the same is equally true in industry. That does not mean that the buyer cannot adopt an equally good, less-known, item. However, if a branded product has earned a reputation for good performance, the purchaser will have to be sold effectively on another product. Of the thousands of items purchased in industry, many are needed frequently. Once a standard source featuring brand name items has been established, many buyers continue purchasing them through inertia or because they do not know of suitable competing products.

Quite often a brand name item will be chosen even though it has a slightly higher price. Consider retail sugar sales. Some stores have purchased bulk sugar and packaged it in five-pound sacks. They discovered that the five-pound brand name sugar commanded a differential of 5 to 10 cents. At that time unbranded sugar sold well at the lower price. Since then, through improved packaging and because of rising cost of in-store packaging, the national brands have taken over almost entirely. Consumers generally feel that well-established brands are good insurance against disappointment—and they are usually right.

Two distinct approaches are used in creating brand names. One is the use of a family brand name, such as Heinz, in which you have Heinz catsup, pickles, relish, and related products. The other approach, used by Procter and Gamble, uses such distinctive brand names as Ivory, Tide, and Puffs, names which the public need not associate with the firm. Both approaches are successful. If you are associated with a firm in which you can capitalize on a family name, do not hesitate to do so. Although Frigidaire is a well-known brand name by itself, sales are also helped because it is associated with General Motors. A well-known brand name is a powerful selling tool.

PRODUCT PERFORMANCE

Often a salesman becomes confused when selling because he concentrates on the product rather than on what it will do.

What the Product Will Do

In buying a product, we are interested primarily in what it will do for us. Thus, in buying a three-horsepower motor for fishing and a 25-horsepower motor for water skiing, we are aware that both are similar motors, but we expect different results from each. A decision to buy a paint brush for one dollar or ten dollars might be based upon needs. Both these examples employ generic application. The motors are used to satisfy two distinct recreational needs. The only common factor is that both are water sports. The paint brushes are both used for the same purpose. In the one situation, however, an amateur is using the brush for occasional painting, while the professional painter uses the brush throughout the day in earning a living.

Speed is one performance factor that you may cite when a customer asks for performance data. A salesman once discussed a drying cycle for plastics with a foundry superintendent who indicated that he would like to find drying equipment that could reduce the cycle by only a fraction of a minute.

There are many types of performance questions that a prospect may ask. Will the car start in cold weather? Will the tennis shoe stand grueling punishment on a cement outdoor basketball court? Will the metal buckle under high temperature? There are many situations in which performance data is helpful.

How Long Will It Last?

The expected life of a product can be an important sales point. If the installation costs are high but one product far outlasts a competing one, original costs may be of minor importance. On the other hand, if a buyer needs something that he will seldom use or use under little stress, it would not be sensible to pay a high price for something designed for long use under severe conditions. In most cases, the industrial buyer wants a product that meets his needs at the lowest possible price. On the other hand, the debutante is not interested in an evening gown with exceptional wearing quality. The length of service from a product must be recognized as a relative term and incorporated with many other features to justify the asking price.

How It Should Be Used

Higher price does not necessarily mean a stronger or a more durable item. An ermine wrap is expensive and beautiful but not particularly strong or warm. A drill that is satisfactory for intermittent use might be inadequate for constant high-speed work. Thus, if you see two drills of the same size side by side, one selling for 20¢ and the other for $2.00, you are actually looking at two different products. Their use is quite different in application. The housewife can buy a home permanent to curl her hair; the professional beauty operator will also use a similar preparation. The beautician, however, can use materials which work more rapidly, but they might be unsafe for the amateur.

What to Avoid Using

Many people become unhappy when answering a bargain ad and find that the salesman tries to upgrade them to a more expensive product. "Bait Advertising" describes this approach. An individual paying a high price may protest even though it performs well. But one who buys an inadequate product, no matter what the price, may become furious when he finds it unsuitable for his needs. Sometimes a fly-by-night company will make extravagant claims, make a large number of sales at a handsome profit, and then disappear before angry users catch up with it. Extravagant promises are costly, expedient for the present, but disastrous for the future.

PRICES, DISCOUNTS, HANDLING, SHIPPING, LEASING

Price has many components: cash price, time payments, anticipation, advance dating, interest, position discount, quantity discount, and cumulative discount. In certain areas total price may be increased above base by special handling, by alternate methods of shipping, by preferential treatment, and in dozens of other ways. More and more, leasing is becoming common. Many who have purchased before now prefer to lease. This is especially true of the buyer who is short of capital. Leasing may be an ideal method for the buyer who would prefer to buy but, at the moment, lacks money. The combination method is often advantageous, for one can lease for a period with the right to buy and apply the lease payments to the final price. You are not completely familiar with your product until you understand all possible price variations that can be used.

INSTALLATION

Numerous products entail installation which may be simple or complex. If the product is inadequately installed, the operation may be defective, and you will have an unhappy customer on your hands. If it is important, you may insist upon doing the installation yourself with your own trained installation crew. This may be expensive to the customer, but may save him many future problems.

SERVICE

If what you sell requires expert service, customers should be well briefed on such service and thorough explanations made as to *why* it is necessary, thus preventing misunderstandings later.

Factory Service

If a product is intricate, it may be necessary to have factory-trained people service it. It is not uncommon to have purchasing firms have their own men handle the service. Yet, this may be questionable when experience dictates use of factory-trained personnel. If one buyer is large enough to require extensive servicing, his men might be trained at your plant. Otherwise, it may be better to insist that service be handled by your own technicians.

Guarantee

If specific guarantees are attached to your product, they may be validated only under specific circumstances. Certainly, this should be stressed to the buyer. Otherwise, he may assume that the product is covered under all circumstances. If your guarantee has time qualifications, be sure to indicate them. If it is governed by guarantee of replacement parts, that, too, should be indicated. Be sure to explain all the technicalities and limitations of the guarantee. Unless the purchaser understands all the restrictions and limitations of the guarantee, disagreements are sure to arise.

Often, firms guarantee a product for a period of time and make replacements without question even though product abuse is evident. Sometimes it is cheaper to make an unjustified ten-dollar adjustment than to refuse to do it and lose a sale.

Know how much discretion you are permitted to exercise in allowing returns. Some companies are extremely liberal in their return policy. Others are not. Know where *you* stand.

Customers frequently have little compunction in returning a product. One case history cites the example of a man who returned a dress shirt because the cuffs wore out after 3 years; another refers to a housewife who wanted an adjustment on a washing machine because the tub leaked after 19 years.

The whole area of returns and adjustments is frequently tied together because the buyer can often be persuaded to keep an inferior product if he is given an adjustment on the price. While most firms have a policy for handling returns and adjustments, the policies are seldom so rigid as to preclude exceptions.

Repair and Replacement Parts

Know what your company policy is on repair parts. Many times, a very profitable business can be established by selling repair and replacement parts. Included in this category can be equipment that is worn out through use: drills, sandpaper, brushes, and files. The aftermarket in the automobile industry is fantastically large. Each year millions of batteries and tires are sold for used cars. Millions of dollars each month are spent on automobile repairs. Accessory sales for automobiles account for sales of millions of dollars yearly. A hard snowstorm wipes out local inventories of tire chains and snow tires. Many times the aftersales may be more important than the original sales. Numerous wholesalers and distributors depend exclusively on sales in the aftermarket.

If a small part breaks, it must be replaced. The actual value of the part may be only a few cents, but, because of overhead costs, it might cost up to $3. Since a $3 bill for the replacement of an inexpensive part might make the customer angry, it could be preferable to give him the part free and to avoid all billing and accounting costs. Even if your firm is unwilling to do this, you might do so personally because the slight cost to you might be more than made up by the trouble it avoids.

KNOWLEDGE OF PRODUCT PROMOTION

The successful salesman seizes every opportunity to capitalize on his firm's promotion efforts. Sales tools provided to make work easier should be effectively employed. That is what they are for.

Advertising

Where advertising is used to presell a product, the salesman's selling activities are often at a minimum. And, of course, his financial return will not be great. In most instances, however, in sales with which we are concerned, advertising is only an introductory step to aid the salesman. As such, it may pave the way to an interview, create some interest, and arouse a little desire. The job of the salesman is to begin at that point and bring the sale to a successful conclusion. Advertising seldom can "write up the order," but it can be instrumental in furnishing leads. Insofar as possible, the advertising and sales presentation should be coordinated toward a common end.

Dealer Aids

In selling to retailers, whether hardware stores, department stores, or auto showrooms, dealer aids can be of great help. Brochures, displays, and point-of-purchase material can increase your effectiveness because the retailer is willing to buy products for resale when sales aids are included. These aids frequently presell the merchandise so effectively that the retailer has only to display the merchandise, collect money for the sale, and wrap the customer's purchase. The information conveyed by these media should be accurate and understandable. This relieves the salesman of a great deal of informative work and furnishes authentic data to the buyer. Too frequently, a salesman is inclined to neglect some of these aids because he regards them as ill-suited to his needs. However, the facts usually reveal that carefully prepared material is the consensus of the best thinking of the firm's sales executives and is superior to anything the salesman could provide.

Consumer Approaches

Various consumer approaches have been developed over the years which suit the needs of house-to-house and in-store salesmen best. Do not make the mistake that many inexperienced salesmen make and think that your own approach is superior. This is not usually the case. If the product cannot be sold the company way, it usually cannot be sold at all.

ORGANIZING PRODUCT INFORMATION

You may have a wide knowledge of your product, but your presentation may lack organization. You may jump from point to point and confuse rather than enlighten. Do not let them say: "He knows his subject, but he cannot express himself." Marshal your facts so that you can make a logical presentation.

In the logical approach you would ascertain the prospect's needs and give the facts to fit in with his thinking. Determine the approach he wants and develop your presentation accordingly. Step by step you must lead him from his present position to one where he sees the logic of your ideas and incorporates them into his thinking. A reasoned approach will appeal to the man who wants economy, a faster operation, or a more uniform product.

Organizing product information chronologically appeals to the prospect who likes to follow an orderly arrangement over a period of time. This approach precludes backtracking, jumping from feature to feature in a hit-and-miss fashion, and the omission of important points. Starting with an original premise, you go along tracing the development of the product. You show setbacks which forced your firm to retrace certain steps to meet particular problems. You show how each part was tried and tested before it was incorporated into the final product. You tell why some parts of your product differ from conventional ones. By the time you complete your presentation, the prospect has been given a complete story of the development, construction, applications, and advantages of your product. He knows what it can do for him.

An emotional approach is effective when the product is used for protection, to avoid accidents, or to prevent sickness. This approach would become emotional towards the close, but in the early part it could be factual, precise, and descriptive. A home presentation of a set of children's books would be factual, informative, and include examples of use in real situations. Once having covered the material, however, you could end with an emotional close dramatizing the help the books could give to the children in school. You could describe how the children's school grades would improve, how they would be called on to give class presentations, and how they could get on the staff of the school newspaper.

SOURCES OF PRODUCT KNOWLEDGE

The wise salesman knows where to get information. Frequently, valuable sources are overlooked because the salesman does not know or is too lazy to find them.

Company Supplies Information

Always look to your company as a primary source of information. It will usually have specific sources available. These sources include bulletins, brochures, advertisements, training manuals, parts lists, illustrations, and samples. A visit to the plant is one of the better ways of giving a customer current information of your firm.

Training Course

If you are a new salesman in a firm which has a training course, you should be adequately prepared to begin your sales tour when you leave the training program. In most training courses, the trainee must master each lesson before proceeding to the next. This procedure varies from secondary school and college courses which grade a student's performance within a specified time. No salesman can flunk his training course and continue on the payroll. If you have the opportunity to take a course of this nature, work hard; it is designed to help you.

Printed Literature—Factory Experience

Many firms which do not have formal training courses are still able to inform salesmen through brochures, pamphlets, and factory tours or work. If your company allows you to educate yourself in its matters in your own way, use as many reference sources as possible. In your conversations, take advantage of the knowledge of others; learn as soon as you can some of the ideas and facts that others may have needed years to master.

Library Sources

While most salesmen do not have the reputation of being well-read, you can become an exception by learning what your city or town library has to offer. Numerous books and periodicals are fruitful sources of data. Although you cannot expect every book or magazine to aid you explicitly in your work, you will often glean bits of useful information from your reading. The further you progress in your work, the more you will have to read in order to be well informed and to keep ahead of others who would like to have your position.

Personal Experience

As you advance in your sales career, your own experience will become valuable. At least you should profit by your own mistakes. Talking with buyers, with salesmen of noncompeting products, and with the public in general can make you better informed. Be a good listener; you seldom learn when you talk.

RETAIL PRODUCTS KNOWLEDGE

Usually, retail sales personnel do not need such depth of information as do men in other types of selling. Retail product knowledge is usually confined to a small area such as washing machines, men's furnishings, ladies' dresses or shoes. If you are in retail sales, you should familiarize yourself with necessary details to satisfy customers. For example, if you sell shotguns, you should know choke, barrel length, shell sizes, firing mechanisms, and safety features. If you sell fishing reels, you should be familiar with fly-casting reels, spinning reels, and casting reels. You should know the kinds of line to use on each reel under a variety of fishing conditions. Retail salesmanship is one of the weakest areas in product knowledge. Sometimes this is true because of faulty training, but all too often it must be blamed on the salesman's laziness. Retail salesmen who make over $10,000 a year (and there are many) train themselves in knowledge of their product and in handling customers.

SERVICE KNOWLEDGE

Much of what has been said about products applies to service as well because people buy articles to be used just as they buy services to be used. Those who sell services should thoroughly explain the benefits of their particular services. Many people are so "thing" conscious that they want most of their purchases to be tangible items. Yet, all who buy telephones, transportation, dry cleaning, and amusements are buying services. Many service companies have had excellent success in promoting extended use through sales presentation of customer benefits. Thus, the telephone company stresses the convenience of having several instruments in the home. It stresses the beauty of its telephones by presenting streamlined instruments in appealing colors. Many other services are sold through demonstrating various uses, such as private line, answering and recording equipment, automobile telephones, and low service rates during special hours at night and on weekends. You have tantalizing appeals to potential customers simply by explaining how your service will make their lives easier, more successful, or more enjoyable.

TO YOU . . . HOW DOES THIS FIT?

You probably appreciate some facets of selling a bit more now than when you started to read this chapter. Be on the safe side and read it again. By the time you have finished rereading, you should have a better grasp of what will be expected of you when you face your customers.

To be a successful salesman you must work hard to know yourself, your customers, your company, and your product. Always remember Francis Bacon's advice: "Knowledge is power."

QUESTIONS AND PROBLEMS

1. Explain how a salesman can help a customer through the use of product knowledge.

2. Why is it essential to know not only your own products but also products of competitors?

3. Is it wise to recommend a competitor's product if you feel it will meet the buyer's needs better than your product?

4. Why might a buyer be interested in the organization of your company?

5. Can the type of management personnel in a salesman's firm influence a buyer to give or refuse an order?

6. "Be sure you know your company's policies." Can this statement be significant in closing a sale?

7. Many mistakes are made through the purchase of wrong material. How do you guard against this danger?

8. Can material be too high in quality even though the price is acceptable?

9. A wide line of merchandise may eliminate duplicating lines of merchandise. Explain.

10. List several instances of complementary lines in:

    (a) manufacturing, (b) wholesaling, (c) retailing, (d) services.

11. A well-known branded product widely advertised is half-sold. Describe how a salesman finds such advertisements useful.

12. What are two distinct approaches in developing brand names?

13. Sometimes one buys identical products for different purposes. Before a buyer does this, what must he know?

14. Discuss durability of a product, pointing out advantages and disadvantages. Give examples where durability is a hindrance instead of an aid.

15. Why should a firm avoid "Bait Advertising"?

16. "Price has many facets." Examine this statement from ten points of view.

17. When should you insist that your own technicians install a machine you sold?

18. Under what conditions should factory service be used?

19. Guarantees are frequent sources of disputes. Why do such situations arise? Are these unpleasant occurrences inevitable?

20. "Sales in the aftermarket may be more important than original equipment sales." Discuss this statement, indicating why this is frequently true.

21. What is meant by "dealer aids"? How can a salesman take advantage of them?

22. What are the advantages of an original product information approach?
23. When can you use an emotional approach successfully? Can you justify such an approach?
24. Outline six sources of product knowledge.
25. Why is product knowledge weak in retailing?
26. "Service knowledge is the primary factor in service sales." True or untrue?

CASES

3-1: BREMER MANUFACTURING COMPANY

Jack Dane and Fred Briggs had just completed their training course at the Bremer Manufacturing Company. Both men were hired a month previously and both were started in the training course at the same time.

At the end of the training period, each man was assigned a territory, given final instructions, and sent out in his territory. Nothing of importance came to the attention of the home office during the next two weeks. Both men sent in a few small orders but nothing unusual. During the third week, orders from Jack Dane increased in size and number. No noticeable change occurred in Fred Briggs' territory.

At the end of six weeks, Jack Dane's territory was producing satisfactorily, but sales in Fred Briggs' territory continued disappointing. A supervisor was sent to work with Fred during the seventh week and orders increased. Apparently, the two salesmen working together were able to sell satisfactorily. The eighth week Fred worked alone, and sales fell.

The ninth week the supervisor went to Fred Briggs' territory and called on several buyers contacted the preceding week by Fred. The information the supervisor gathered was disturbing. In several situations Fred had been unable to supply buyers with adequate product information. He talked in generalities and avoided specific details. When asked to suggest new applications, Fred was unable to come up with intelligent answers.

On return to the home office, the supervisor reviewed the training of Fred and Jack. He discovered that in examinations Jack did well in all his work, but Fred was strong on personality traits and weak on product knowledge. When the teacher had pointed this out to Fred, he had brushed it aside with the comment that selling was mostly "getting the buyer to like you." The supervisor prepared a report on Fred Briggs and gave it to the sales manager. The sales manager studied the report and began to consider solutions to the problem. He knew that Fred Briggs' territory must produce more orders.

Questions

1. What are the problems facing the sales manager?
2. Name several alternatives open to the sales manager.
3. How would you handle this situation?

3-2: DRIED MILK COMPANY

The Dried Milk Company, an Ohio based firm, manufactured a complete line of milk and ice cream stabilizers. The company was organized in 1955 and had experienced a steady growth in sales through 1964. In the fall of 1964 a budget for the coming year was submitted to Mr. J. S. Oaks, president of the company. Included within the budget was a sales forecast of $950,000. After nine months of operation, the forecast was considered optimistic by management and subsequently reduced to $890,000. The 1965 sales volume was the first year that sales had not increased over the preceding period.

In 1964, Mr. Oaks completed "pilot" studies for a blender used in mixing stabilizers with raw milk. The blender was introduced into the market in August, 1964, with only moderate success. Mr. Oaks had personally directed the engineering effort and considered the blender "a potential high-profit item."

The Company and The Industry

Dried Milk Company competed in a market dominated by several national manufacturers of dairy foods. Sales of these companies were derived primarily from commercially prepared milks and ice creams. In addition to commercial sales, these companies were currently developing industrial markets, which included the manufacturing of stabilizers for resale to independent producers. Prior to 1965, Dried Milk had not considered this encroachment a real threat to sales.

Dried Milk's largest profit item was a powder stabilizer used in the manufacturing of milk. Stabilizers were used primarily to increase the butterfat and protein content of raw milk. The quantity used varied depending on the minimum state requirements governing these sales. The product consisted of non-fat dried milk, protein, "flaked" dried fat, and sugar. Dried Milk also produced an ice cream stabilizer. Stabilizers improved the texture of the product and also prevented shrinkage of ice creams when held in dealer freezer cabinets for long periods of time.

The blender was developed to reduce the time lag required to disperse the powdered stabilizer into raw milk. The design was similar to a positive displacement pump and reduced the time lag by approximately one third the normal mixing time. The powder was metered through an orifice and was controlled by the volume of milk passing through the pump.

The Sales Organization

The sales department was responsible for both marketing and sales activities. Prior to 1965, sales were handled exclusively by selling agents covering ten midwestern states. The agents, in most cases, carried other, noncompeting lines. The product lines represented most dairy supply companies with a complete assortment of equipment, cartons, cones, and flavors. In addition, agents offered assistance by periodically reviewing merchandising techniques, pricing procedures, and equipment replacement policies with their customers.

In January, 1965, a sales department was formally created and three salesmen hired. Mr. Oaks believed that sales—the blender in particular—were suffering because the agent's attention was diverted to other more profitable items. Also, future expansion could be better controlled through a company sales organization. At the time the sales staff was created, customers in less-populous areas were dropped. Mr. Oaks instructed his salesmen to concentrate effort on high-volume customers who were not presently using either the blender or stabilizers. The three salesmen hired were experienced in dairy sales, but only one had prior experience in dairy equipment sales. After a short training period, which included a demonstration of the blender, the salesmen were assigned territories.

Within the first six months, it became obvious that the salesmen were experiencing problems with the blender. Customers had complained that heat generated from the rotating blades caused the fat in the stabilizer to melt, clogging the orifice. Because of the difficulty, one large account and several smaller ones were lost. In reviewing the sales records, Mr. Oaks noticed that in each case the companies had indicated their satisfaction with the stabilizer, but were unhappy with the operation of the blender. Mr. Oaks felt that the salesman had not sold the blender properly. He recalled that during the four months that selling agents had carried the line, not one customer indicated a dissatisfaction with the blender.

Stabilizer sales were below 1964 figures. Mr. Oaks knew something had to be done, but he was not sure how he should approach the problem. He first considered holding a series of training sessions to acquaint the salesmen with the operation of the blender. While this approach seemed the best, he felt five or six weeks would be necessary and during this time additional customers might be lost. A second alternative would be to recall the blenders, but he felt this would be admitting inferior product quality.

Questions

1. How would you define Mr. Oaks' major problem?
2. Which of the two alternatives should Mr. Oaks employ?
3. Is there a better way to approach the problem?

PART **III**

SELLING TECHNIQUES
AND PROCEDURES

CHAPTER 4

Finding and Qualifying
Potential Customers

As a salesman, you should spend your time with potential customers rather than with people who are not in the market for your product. Since you cannot afford to waste time, look into an individual's background before you try to persuade him to buy. Assure yourself that he can use your product, and then see if he thinks that he needs it or not. If he does not need it consciously, is your product or service a part of his sublimated wish-fulfillment? Study your customer and his needs so that you squander neither his time nor yours.

FINDING POTENTIAL CUSTOMERS

Among the numerous ways of finding potential customers, some are general and may be used in many situations. Others are specialized and can be used only under particular circumstances.

Cold Canvassing

In cold canvassing you call on a large number of people and hope that some of them may be interested in your product or

95

service. In house-to-house canvassing, you call on every home, knock on every door. Sometimes car salesmen will use this method to get leads. They may do the canvassing themselves or hire others to make initial calls. By contacting hundreds of people, you often uncover a number of interested people. The same process can be used by men who sell landscaping, storm windows, home modernization, furnace repair, and laundry service. Once interest has been noticed, the interviewer passes along his information to another person who will do the actual selling in a second interview.

Magazine and book salesmen frequently use the cold canvass to get customers. In these cases the sale is attempted immediately to interested people. Wholesale salesmen will canvass stores they have never sold, hoping to gain the manager's interest and, if possible, an order. Real estate salesmen may use the cold canvass to get listings. Insurance salesmen must do a certain amount of cold canvassing to obtain prospects and to build up their lists of potential customers. Factory salesmen may call on purchasing agents to learn if these buyers can use the salesmen's products. On one occasion, a salesman was employed to contact buyers and engineering departments of manufacturers to determine if they had possible new uses for magnesium and titanium. Thus, while the cold canvass approach is often associated with house-to-house selling, it is effectively employed at both consumer and industrial levels.

When a person shows interest, prepare a prospect card or name and address file. Later, expand this information if the individual qualifies; discard the information if he seems to be an unlikely customer.

Influential People

In any community, some people are leaders. They may be clergymen, bankers, industrialists, coaches, or many other people in prominent positions. Many ladies exert strong influences in their community. Some set fashion trends, some are social leaders, and some are active in charities and civic enterprises. Many people emulate these leaders in dress, home, car, furniture, and even in the choice of vacation spots.

By building friendships with such people you will be able to use their recommendations for your product or service. The banker's recommendation could give you immeasurable assistance in selling insurance or real estate. If you operate a bookstore, you could be helped by a clergyman's casual statement that you carry certain books. The recommendation of a factory owner could help you sell industrial products, and his recommendation might give you access to the country club crowd. Not only can influential people recommend you, but they can also give you leads. Cultivate the friendship of influential people by belonging to the same country club, the same lodge, or the same luncheon club. Then you can meet people socially and gain their confidence by your talk and behavior.

Prominent women can be helpful in giving you leads. If such women associate with a salesman's wife, many useful tips will be dropped that an astute wife can convey to her husband. This can be particularly helpful to insurance salesmen who might get advance notice of family changes that could alter insurance needs.

Endless Chain and Referral

The endless chain technique merely means getting names from a present buyer. When you sell an insurance policy, you ask the policy owner for the names of friends who might need insurance. Usually, he will be glad to oblige. Since he has taken the wise step of buying insurance, he feels that it will be prudent for his friends to do likewise. If a housewife has purchased a vacuum cleaner, she will happily give the salesman names of her friends and neighbors. Very often, the sale of a car to one member of a family leads to sales to other members of the same family. The landscape gardener will find many people willing to recommend him to friends if he has done a good job for the original buyer.

In referrals, the person not only may give you names but may also give introductions which will make it easy for you to see these people. If an executive in a firm invests in a mutual fund, he may give you the names of other executives of the firm as well as names of managers on lower levels. The use of the executive's name alone can exert a powerful influence on lower levels of management if younger men are thinking of investing. College teachers are often asked to recommend students for jobs. Or, if a student with unusual qualifications appears, he may be recommended to a particular firm. In this case the product is the student, the sale is the job. Do not forget people who do you favors. Thank them and occasionally show appreciation in some tangible form, such as a gift, an invitation to dinner, or an invitation to a baseball game, concert, or an afternoon of golf.

Personal Alertness

Some salesmen's eyes and ears are open for business at all times. Other salesmen stumble over promising opportunities and seldom know what has tripped them.

You must be alert at all times to actions, conditions, and suggestions that might lead you to a potential customer. Each season of the year has its opportunities. Spring brings clothing sales and sales of recreational equipment. The farmer buys implements and seeds. The painter gets opportunities to redecorate homes. The real estate salesman finds renewed interest in property.

Vacations are common in the summer. Vacation equipment—clothing, sports equipment, cars, motel rental, cottage rental, resort hotel occupancy—these are only a few items among many. In the summer, people get outdoors, spend more freely, and look for ways of enjoying themselves at, out of, and away from home.

The fall requires back-to-school clothing, hunting equipment, fur coats, bowling equipment, and exterior house repairs. Football calls for specialized equipment. Families spend weekends traveling to college football games. This calls for traveling expenses, gasoline, blankets for the game, motel rooms for weekends, gowns for Saturday evening parties, dinners at fashionable restaurants. Parents leave extra money for Tom or Mary, who are students at college. Invariably, students are excellent consumers if they have the money. Halloween furnishes opportunities for selling special costumes, candy, and party favors. Thanksgiving stresses family living as well as travel.

Each new seasonal requirement furnishes salesmen with opportunities to make sales. The winter season calls for winter clothing, winter sports, trips to warm climates, and many indoor activities which call for specialized equipment. The TV repairman will find many opportunities to sell his services; the snow removal salesman can sell his services; and fuel salesmen find many customers. The pattern that fits the northern tier of states may not fit the southern states, and the pattern that fits the

United States may not fit Australia; but most countries and territories have seasonal patterns that can aid an alert salesman.

The wise salesman who finds he has busy seasons and off seasons may supplement his line to an all-year-round activity. Summer resorts in the summer can become winter ski resorts in winter. The men who sell ski clothing may sell bathing suits. With the use of complementary lines, the salesman can make his selling a year-round job.

Religious events and religious holidays may stimulate wants that salesmen can satisfy. Religious events are frequently accompanied by special foods. At Christmas, various ethnic groups have unusual types of food. At Easter, the use of Easter hams and Easter candies grows each year. Jewish religious holidays call for specially prepared foods. Some religious groups observe special diets during Lent. Specific types of clothing are often used for religious celebrations. Christenings, confirmations, marriages, and funerals usually require particular clothes for each occasion. Often, graduation from school becomes associated with religious celebrations which call for new clothes, dinner, gifts, travel, and entertainment. Sometimes, these activties are held in tents, stadiums, or halls which require chair service, janitor service, sound equipment service, photographer, and food service.

Holidays, whether religious or secular, furnish many possibilities for finding potential customers. Frequently, each holiday has a pattern of expenditures. Thus, Christmas is associated with gift giving; Valentine's Day, with candy and flowers; Easter, with special candies and toys; and Mother's Day, with gifts and dining out. Even Father's Day is developing to an occasion for gift-giving and dining out. Birthdays are important occasions for cakes, cards, gifts, and remembrances. Unlike holidays, birthdays are celebrated every day and so become a continuous source for sales. Other holidays have their special demands. Holidays cut the number of working days during a month and may reduce sales in some categories. When families go away for a holiday, the local food sales suffer. Attendance at activities in a city may decrease substantially in summer because many people are on vacation.

Our society thrives on different events in our lives—births, weddings, christenings, funerals, graduations, and change of dwelling. When someone purchases a home, he will probably become a new customer for the milkman, the dry cleaner, and the newspaper boy. In all probability, he will hire men with a van to move his belongings. Deaths and funerals sell caskets, cemetery lots, and flowers. The death of the husband may require a wife to learn to drive the family car, and someone will have to sell her driving lessons. Births provide sales potential for diaper service, photographs, and furniture. Graduations mean new clothes and possibly such gifts as a new car or a trip abroad. The thinking salesman finds many opportunities that he can cultivate for his own benefit.

Read the newspaper carefully. Many salesmen find the daily newspaper a gold mine for leads. The newspaper gives the story of life, of people, and of events. The broad coverage of a newspaper that aims at the interests of thousands of readers will often given you clues that you might not otherwise find. Besides such vital statistics as births, deaths, marriages, and divorces, each of which can have meaning to a salesman, newspapers list a variety of social events, meetings, concerts, and recreational activities. All of these must be supplied with products or services. Connected with these activities are individuals who need products and services. Although what you sell may not have a direct bearing on any of the above products or services, you may benefit by supplying the supplier of them. For example, if you sell greenhouse equipment and you sense that the demand for flowers and plants is increasing (or, better still, if you have some statistics to prove that it is increasing), you can go to a grower and urge him to double the size of his greenhouse. Listening to news on your car radio may provide you with information that gives you a time advantage over competition.

You must learn to recognize opportunities even though many are not clear at the moment. Some are embryonic opportunities that must be developed. You will hear of some indirectly. Thus, you may join a political party or a bridge club without having business in mind. In time, however, your social contacts will give you some of the raw material that goes into the finished product of selling.

Personal Solicitation by Assistants

To save time, salesmen often use assistants to uncover potential customers. Instead of the salesman calling many people in the hope of finding prospects, he hires less experienced assistants on a part-time basis to secure leads. Such people often work on a commission basis on the sales actually made to customers whom they have discovered. Sometimes, these assistants are junior salesmen employed by your firm in a training program. The type of selling, the product, or the service you sell will often require a special kind of person to assist you. Often, housewives with unlimited telephone service make thousands of calls in a systematic way from the telephone directory. In this way, they cover each neighborhood quite thoroughly and avoid overlapping.

Telephone

The telephone is a rapid means of finding prospects. A number of people can be contacted in a broad geographical area. Even though you may miss some good prospects because you cannot develop their interest adequately, do not become discouraged; the number of people you may call is practically unlimited. Often, lists can be purchased which give you a selective group of names to call. Such a list would presumably be people who could buy and would probably be interested in what you sell.

Mail

Direct mail is frequently used to discover potential customers. Mail pinpoints the people to whom you write—it covers wide territories inexpensively. Mail can be handled by unskilled clerical help. One car dealer stated that for every 50 cards mailed by one of his salesmen, he could count, on the average, on 10 replies which would lead to 5 demonstrations and 2 sales. He also said, however, that his greatest problem was to get salesmen to mail the cards.

Most salesmen find the use of direct mail effective. Not only can mail uncover potential customers for your original product, but, in the aftermarket, many people will buy your parts and equipment even though their original purchase was from a competitor. Both mail and telephone multiply your effectiveness because of the time that you save.

Old Customers

A satisfied customer is your best advertisement. If you have old customers, presumably you have sold them repeatedly. Thus, you have built an effective working relationship with a number of individuals. Their recommendations can help you to make contacts. Not only could such people mention you, but they might also boost your product. When you walk into an old customer's office, you can expect to be received graciously. At times, old customers may even get enthusiastic about you to their friends. If you sell house-to-house, you can safely ignore "no solicitors" signs because you have come with an invitation.

Service Personnel

Service personnel in your own firm can give you many leads. When they go to a home or factory to repair equipment, they can see the condition and age of the equipment and give you information which enables you to prepare a convincing presentation of the new item. Then, too, service personnel in other firms can also be helpful because of their contacts with the public. An automobile repairman in the gasoline station or private garage can give car salesmen many names. Driving schools can turn over a list of their graduates to car dealers, particularly if the dealer handles the same brand that the students have used. Be sure to compensate people who furnish you leads. Sometimes this may be done by a certain amount for each potential customer discovered. Other times, compensation is based on sales to such customers. You should share financial rewards generously.

Cultivate acquaintanceships with installers of new equipment. The man installing clothes washers may see opportunities to sell clothes dryers. The carpenter who modernizes and expands an office may tell his office equipment friend about the expansion. A house painter doing an interior job may notice that the carpets need cleaning, and he decides to call the carpet cleaner. He can notify the dry cleaner who may get a job cleaning drapes, or he can tell the drapery store because a new color scheme calls for new drapes. Almost any outside individual called to a home, commercial establishment, or factory to perform some service can gain ideas of additional needs for that individual or firm. In that way, a new prospect for additional products or services can be called.

Some firms are members of the "welcome wagon." As soon as a newcomer moves into a home, the "welcome wagon," usually a small truck or station wagon, comes to the housewife with a number of gifts from local businessmen. As the driver of the wagon presents the gifts to the housewife, the caller invites her to patronize the firms that have provided the gifts.

Lists and Directories

Let us say more now about the lists that have already been mentioned several times. You can purchase lists of names of people who might be your prospects. These lists are organized in many ways—occupation, income, race, ethnic groups, church membership, car owners, age, sex, education. By using lists and direct mail, or the telephone, you can concentrate on a group which should be interested in what you sell. Thus, you need not waste time with people who normally are not in your market.

There are special directories and general-purpose directories. The telephone directory and the city directory cover most of the people in a city. Use them to reach people if your product has broad application. Special directories are useful in reaching groups of people who are particularly interested in one area. There are hundreds of such directories pertaining to every industry, occupation, and activity.

The Yellow Pages of the telephone directory give firms that will sell a variety of mailing lists. R. L. Polk & Co., Detroit, Michigan, is representative of firms that sell mailing lists. Letter-mailing services sell lists of names.

Thousands of trade associations have directories of members. Clubs, lodges, churches, and business groups have membership rosters. You should be aware of the importance of a list or directory that gives you a selected group of people. You may find that 90 percent of your business comes from just such a group.

Bids

Building contracts are competitively awarded, as are furniture and equipment contracts. Much buying by government, municipalities, and institutions is through bids.

Many purchases come only from submitted bids, and much of *your* business may come through bidding. Although some requests for bids may come directly to you, most requests are published in newspapers, journals, or other printed media. Learn of any special publications in your area that carry such information. Often government publications—national, state, and city—carry requests for bids. Large cities have special newspapers of their own. Legal publications carry particular types of information. *Dodge Reports* gives information on the building industry.

Auctions

To a limited extent, auctions are a method of finding buyers. Art auctions bring art buyers together. Farm auctions bring groups of farmers to one location. Fruit auctions in cities draw numbers of wholesale buyers as well as buyers for chain stores. Tobacco auctions bring together buyers for tobacco firms. Cattle buyers come to cattle auctions. Used car dealers patronize car auctions. Whether or not you sell much of your product through auctions may not be important. The contacts secured may enable you to set up a channel of communications with potential customers. Those you meet at auctions may later become direct customers.

QUALIFYING POTENTIAL CUSTOMERS

How can you tell if someone is a potential customer? How can you tell that John Smithley is in the market for your product or service? That may depend on one or a combination of several factors discussed below.

Is Income Sufficient?

Many people may want to buy your product; not all can afford it. Many a car salesman learns that the interested prospect has no way of paying for a car. Many families tramp through new houses which are much too expensive for them to buy. People with a rowboat income will waste a salesman's time by discussing $35,000 yachts. Even when a person's income appears sufficient, he may have so many obligations that there is little money left to purchase your item. A person's income may fluctuate; even though his income today appears to be adequate, by the time he is ready to pay you, he might not have the money. An individual who seems to have adequate finances may have little discretionary money if his funds are tied up in trust or by a parent. The examples above are but a few of many that might be mentioned to illustrate the importance of qualifying a person financially.

Is Your Product a Necessity?

Most people would say that it should be relatively easy to sell necessities. But what is a necessity? Although most Americans consider more items necessary than do all other nationalities, even Americans agree that there are degrees of necessity. Food is necessary, but ground beef might serve the purpose as well as sirloin steak. A $10,000 home will fill the necessity for shelter, although it would not be as desirable as a $20,000 home. The $4,000 car would be nice to have, but the $2,000 car will also get you to destinations on time. It is easier to sell a liability automobile insurance policy than a life insurance policy. It is easier to sell a textbook to a student than it is to sell him another book that is not on his required reading list. When ill, people will usually call a doctor; when a tooth aches, they call a dentist. On the other hand, it is impossible to get some people to have checkups if they do not have discomfort. It is easier to sell a man a tire when one is flat on his car and he has no spare, than it is to sell him a rear view mirror for the outside of his car. A housewife may find that one new dress is a necessity, but a woman in society may find it necessary to get one new dress a week. The point is this: Do not construe necessity too narrowly. What is a necessity changes from year to year, according to income, station in life, and demands of society.

Does Your Product Fill an Emotional Need?

People buy things because they want to buy, not because they need them. Yet, they will rationalize such a purchase as a necessity, and, to them, it may be so. The housewife feels that she must have a clothes dryer because other women in the neighborhood have clothes dryers. The husband feels that he must have a bigger outboard motor because others in his group are buying bigger motors. The daughter gets a convertible for graduation because her girl friend got one. You give a substantial contribution to church so that your name gets on the bronze plaque. You join the country club because most of your friends belong to country clubs.

In many instances, emotions are controlling factors in determining purchases. Consequently, if you can qualify a person emotionally, he can be registered as a potential customer. To qualify a person emotionally, try to determine if he can be influenced by what his friends, relatives, or neighbors do. Thus, one family will send their daughter away to college because their neighbor's son went away to college even though there is a fine university in town. One family will rent a cottage by the seashore because a cousin's family spent a week at a lodge in the mountains. One wife buys a mink stole because a member of her bridge club bought a fur coat. Some people are very practical and not easily influenced. Others can be moved to buy at the slightest provocation. Most people at some time or other can be emotionally influenced.

Does Your Product Affect Health?

Most of us jealously guard our health. This is perhaps our most precious possession. Almost any sacrifice is not too great to preserve or regain health. Reducing foods, exercise equipment, prescriptions, and patent medicines all take large segments of people's incomes. Vacations and travel are sold because of their health benefits. People buy and sell homes and move from one part of the country to another for health reasons. Many types of clothing protect health. The health appeal is effective not only for the buyer but also for his loved ones and dependents.

Health appeals can be creative or preventative. Thus, you may buy athletic equipment for use in exercising your body to build a sound physique. You purchase protective clothing so you do not get wet in rain, or cold in a snowstorm. You buy food for children so they grow strong bodies. You vaccinate people to prevent illness. Sometimes, health may be used as a secondary appeal when the primary appeal may be ineffective.

Do not overlook appeals to mental health, e.g., baby-sitting services can ease the mother's physical and emotional strain. So, too, can diaper services. Many books are published on the themes of positive thinking and guides to relaxation. Counseling services are employed to improve mental health. Special groups may be formed to develop attitudes towards life's problems.

Does Your Product Give Protection?

Your product may have appealing protective features. It might protect against heat, cold, dust, sun, mildew, rust, spotting, discoloring, hunger, thirst, fire, water—the list is practically endless when considering numbers of products. Education can protect against joblessness. New clothes may help you to gain status and protect against snobbery. Personal care products protect your body. Many times, protection is a secondary reason for buying, but it can still be a significant reason.

Does Your Product Make Life More Pleasant?

Many people can be qualified as prospects merely because your product can enrich lives or make them happier. In selling art, music, sculpture, books, plays, and travel, one is often surprised by what he learns about people. Some items have status and class appeal, but others appeal universally. Music, for example, may appeal to rich and poor, young and old, native Americans and foreign born. With growing sophistication in our population, we find an increased interest in art. Paperbacks have enlarged the reading horizons of millions of people. Through advertising, television, radio, and newspaper, the tempo of adoption of new products has increased. Demand has been accelerated. Introduced one month, a product may be well accepted the following month because people want products that make life more pleasant.

Is Your Product a Luxury?

Perhaps your product is strictly a luxury item and must be sold that way. Perhaps the potential customer may qualify because of snob appeal. Qualify the prospect on the distinctiveness of the product. Availability in limited quantity appeals to some people. Some can be qualified because of the high price, and individuals will brag later about how much they have paid. Items limited in usefulness, but expensive, may appeal to some people because of the rarity of the product. Extreme luxury is purchased for a high price, and the best appeals must be developed to interest some individuals.

Is Your Product a Service Item?

Can you qualify a prospect through a service your product performs? Essentially, most products are purchased for use. Therefore, an individual has a choice of buying a product for use or choosing to hire someone to use that product. For example, whether a prospect buys snow removal service or buys equipment for snow removal may depend on such factors as amount of snow, frequency of use of equipment, whether prospect has money to buy equipment, and possibly the effectiveness of the person selling the snow removal service. Other prospects may have alternate choices which present a different qualifying problem. Thus, a retired couple may live in their home during the winter and contract for snow removal, or they can close their home and move South for the winter.

Is Your Product Educational?

Many people can be qualified by their desire and need for more education. Some people feel they should always be learning. Curiosity has a powerful effect on some individuals. Something new, different, or difficult challenges them. They want to conquer. Those seeking improvement in their way of life frequently turn to education to aid them. Men and women use educational facilities to help them gain status, social position, and leadership assignments. Parents and ministers respond to educational appeals for children. Young businessmen are quite vulnerable to an educational approach. Often, a product with one basic use may have a minor educational use that can motivate a prospect.

Does Your Product Furnish Recreation?

People of all ages crave recreation. Many are willing to spend freely for particular amusements. Groups of people can become interested in activities that require specific products. Enthusiasm and sparkle lead many to carry on activities to enrich their lives. Can your product be used for fun? Can it stimulate friendly rivalry? Does it get people together socially? Can it be used in a get-acquainted game at a party? Does it require teamwork? Does it have hidden appeals? Keep this in mind: Work for one person may be fun for another.

Does Your Product Fit an Age Bracket?

Some products appeal specifically to age groups, but age does not always refer to the number of years that someone has lived.

Thus, a married couple with young children will be interested in toys regardless of the age of the couple. Families that have little need for tangible possessions may be interested in services, entertainment, and travel. Certain products are definitely related to age—toys for children, bicycles for youths, records of popular music for teenagers, TV for all the family, rocking chair for Grandpa, knitting needles (but not exclusively) for Grandma. Age appeal can also be tied in with environment. The boy in town may want baseball equipment, while the farm boy wants fishing equipment. The man who loved tennis may change to golf as he grows older. The married couple that enjoyed dancing may join a bridge group. The man who pushed his hand lawnmower may be glad to change to a power mower. The interests of yesterday are replaced by a new pattern of interest today and again will change in years to come.

Will Your Product Increase Production?

In industry, people are qualified by showing them improvements. If what you sell can improve the lot of the industrialist, he will be interested. If you can show how he can reduce cost of operation, he will listen. If you have a means of lengthening life of equipment, he will let you explain. Tell him how your product can reduce labor costs, and he will ask for more details. Point out how he can increase profitable sales, and he will listen to your statements. Demonstrate how he can reduce inventory and speed up turnover, and he will ask you to submit more data. Present data on how you can lengthen the life of his equipment by using your product, and he will give you a chance to prove your statement. The heavier tire gives more mileage; the bigger truck requires fewer trips; the better paint needs only one coat; the brighter lights prevent accidents; the recreation program increases employee morale—these and many more reasons can influence a person to become a potential customer. The discerning salesman can—out of thousands of possibilities—discover numerous applications of his product that should appeal to potential buyers.

QUESTIONS AND PROBLEMS

1. Why is it important to concentrate only on genuine customers?
2. Describe the cold canvass method of finding potential customers,

3. Make a list of important people in a community who may influence buyers.
4. What is the theory used when you get a customer to suggest prospects?
5. "Nothing takes the place of being wide awake." How does this statement affect you?
6. How can the salesman find customers by taking advantage of the continuous parade of events in a community?
7. Why can holidays be doubly important to a salesman? What is the strength of buyer resistance for holiday merchandise?
8. What has the reading of newspapers to do with developing individual alertness?
9. List the advantages and disadvantages of using assistants or junior salesmen.
10. Suggest ways of using the telephone and mail to uncover potential customers. Can you determine the quality of such customers?
11. What advantages in gaining new customers come from suggestions of old customers?
12. Service personnel are in an enviable position in locating prospects. Why?
13. Explain the use of a "welcome wagon."
14. Use of special lists of names may enable you to pinpoint prospects. Explain.
15. Study ten directories and show how each can be used to aid you in finding prospects.
16. What is the purpose of using bids in buying?
17. To what extent may auctions be used to develop lasting customer relationships?
18. Are you wasting your time if you do not qualify a customer in advance?
19. Describe ten methods of qualifying potential customers.
20. Can you qualify a single customer under several categories?
21. What is meant by fitting an age bracket?
22. Would you qualify an industrial customer in the same way you qualify a customer buying for personal or family use?

CASES

4-1: HOME MODERNIZATION CO.

Otis Barnstable started the Home Modernization Co. two years ago. Previously, he had sold home modernization for five years in Arnoldsville, a city of 200,000 population. During the five-year period, Mr. Barnstable worked for two modernization firms.

Home Modernization Co. specialized in remodeling kitchens. For the first year, it had been largely a sales firm since all the actual remodeling was contracted to outside builders. By the second year, business had grown so that Mr. Barnstable was able to hire five men to do remodeling work. Mr. James, one of the five, acted as foreman and supervisor. If any job had a little left to do at the end of a day, he would go back the next day and personally finish it. The regular men would be assigned to new jobs. In this way, the regular men would not waste time finishing one job and traveling to another during working hours. Mr. James also completed jobs held up by material shortages. Such jobs might continue too long and waste time of the regular men.

At the end of two years, Mr. Barnstable found himself operating a successful modernization operation. Although most of their work had been remodeling kitchens, some work had been done in adding rooms, porches, and in attic remodeling. In the second year, two garages were built. Both had been profitable.

In assessing the opportunity to expand, Mr. Barnstable concluded that his firm should expand to a complete home modernization operation including construction of garages and fences. So far, Mr. Barnstable had done much of the selling himself. He had one salesman who was out constantly contacting prospective customers. The salesman's selling had been satisfactory.

With the more ambitious program in mind, Mr. Barnstable hired a man to manage the office, schedule work, and handle most of the operating detail, including financing and collection. He wanted to leave most of the operations to this man. Then, Mr. Barnstable could concentrate on selling. With the two of them selling full time, it was anticipated that the firm would grow rapidly.

One of the major problems in selling was to get qualified prospects. Advertisements in the newspaper had brought inquiries. Referrals from satisfied customers were contributing more leads each year. However, a certain amount of cold canvassing had been necessary. Mr. Barnstable felt that both he and his salesman would be more effective if they had a large number of qualified prospects to contact.

Questions

1. Outline a procedure to find potential customers.
2. How would you pay for this information?
3. Is there any one way to secure potential customers that is better than all others?

4-2: AADTA DRIVING SCHOOL

Aadta Driving School operates an automobile driver training school in Lansdowne, a city of 1,000,000 inhabitants. The school has been in operation three years.

The first year was a struggling operation in which Mr. Umster did the driver training in one car, while his wife took care of the office. The second year, business increased so that Mr. Umster kept busy on his driver training teaching all year. During the summer busy season, he hired a second driver on a second car he purchased.

In the third year, business increased so that Mr. Umster employed a driving teacher the year around. Mr. Umster did some driving, worked some in the office, and carried on promotional work. Through advertisements and referrals, business grew so that the third summer there were three full-time driving teachers plus Mr. Umster, who shared his time equally between the office and teaching.

With the return of autumn in the third year, business declined as usual. Yet, business was better than the autumn of the preceding year. To Mr. Umster, this seemed to be a turning point in his business. He felt that with proper promotion he should be able to keep two full-time teachers busy through the winter. As usual, Mr. Umster would take care of all classroom activities. He would spend more time in the office and more time in promotion work. He anticipated doing very little driver training teaching in cars.

For the past year, Mrs. Umster had been giving decreasing time to the business. She did handle the telephones and scheduling when Mr. Umster was out of the office. It was hoped that by the beginning of the fourth summer, Aadta could hire a full-time office girl, thus relieving Mrs. Umster entirely. To justify this expense, it would be necessary to have six to eight cars in operation during the summer busy season, going down to four in the off-winter season. When business increased to this extent, Aadta Driving School would be profitable.

Mr. Umster realized that to secure enough customers for the increased business would require additional methods of promotion. He realized he was attempting to accelerate his growth curve. His ambition was to build the school to the point where a twenty-car summer operation and a ten-car off season operation prevailed. The average sale was $50.

Questions

1. Outline approaches Mr. Umster might use to secure potential customers.
2. Could customers be qualified on the telephone?
3. Could customers be sold on the telephone?

CHAPTER 5

Beginning the Sale

You are ready to begin the sale. For a long time you have been making preparations by studying, working, and thinking. You wonder if you will take the right steps and make this first sale. It is important to prepare adequately for the beginning of the sale. So much depends on what you say, what you do, how you act, and how your behavior influences the customer that you cannot be too careful nor too ready to do the right thing.

PREPARING FOR THE INTERVIEW

To be sure that you are prepared to begin the sale, go over every step carefully to see that you make the best opening.

See the Right Person

Do not waste time trying to sell a person who does not have the authority to buy. It might be easy to meet an individual who is supposed to screen out salesmen. Nonetheless, it is pointless to spend much time with a powerless subordinate. In any sale, there is a right person or persons to contact. It may be an individual, several individuals, a committee, or even a group, but know that you are talking to the right person or persons. Before calling at the office, know the names of those who can close your sale.

Choose the Best Time

If the sale is important and the individual is often busy, phone ahead for an appointment or try to call when he will probably not be busy. Know if the buyer's most convenient times are in the morning, in the afternoon, or in the evening. Some buyers have hours during which they do not want to be disturbed. Should you walk into a buyer's office when the buyer cannot talk, excuse yourself and return later. If possible, ask about the best time to call to avoid coming in again at the wrong time.

Be Ready Physically

In an earlier chapter, we discussed how to prepare yourself physically to meet a customer. Keeping yourself physically fit is a constant job. Unless you are careful, you will become careless and, perhaps unconsciously, begin to slip. Even if you might not notice it, your customer will. Dress properly, have sufficient rest, and seem to be relaxed. Walk in with a firm step, a pleasant smile, and a composed appearance.

Be Ready Mentally

Not only must you look sharp, but you must be sharp. Be relaxed but alert. Sense the atmosphere, and be ready to adapt to the conversation. Perhaps you can comment on the new office furniture. Last night's newspaper may have featured a story on the buyer's firm. Some recent political event may have bearing on the firm's production. This is not the time to be sluggish or careless, nor is it the time to let precious moments go by while you grope desperately for the right thoughts and the words to express them. You must be ready to carry on a conversation with the customer facing you.

Equipment Must Be Immaculate

Walking into an office, many salesmen carry an equipment case, a model, or materials to present to the buyer. Frequently, a kit of samples or other pieces of equipment begin to show wear; or a salesman may have carelessly thrown his materials together when he left his last customer. Then, when the salesman meets a new buyer, he opens a jumbled kit and creates an unfavorable impression.

Any wear, any bruises, any checks, or any signs of disorder not only indicate the salesman's carelessness but also imply that the product itself might have inferior characteristics. If the salesman shows imperfect equipment, the buyer fears that the material shipped on an order would be carelessly handled and might not meet the specified quality. The writer remembers one firm which gave each salesman a kit of samples. These samples were wrapped in felt and carefully protected so that the salesman would show the customer nothing but the finest products. The samples were superb representations of the firm's fine equipment.

Equipment Must Operate

Particularly embarrassing incidents arise when the salesman demonstrates a product whose moving parts fail to operate.

If it is necessary to carry spare parts, have them readily available. Failures of electrical tubes, for example, should be planned on. Frequently, however, totally unforeseen events can damage a salesman's equipment. Consider what happened when one man simply assumed that all buildings are wired with alternating current. Unknowingly, he once found himself in a building with a direct current. As soon as he plugged in his film projector and sound equipment, a tube burned out. Since he had not prepared for this contingency, his demonstration and his visit were failures.

Plan of Interview

Do not walk into a buyer's office without a plan for the presentation. Do not be tempted to say, "I'll wait until I get in and be guided by circumstances." An old-timer who has spent years calling on buyers might take such a risk, but even he will probably feel better if he has a plan. A well-prepared plan gives direction to the salesman in making his approach, in making his presentation, and in carrying out necessary activities during the sales presentation. Unless he has a plan to follow, much of his thinking will be occupied in developing a plan as he goes.

The better the preparation, the easier it will be to turn your attention to those facets that are important at the moment. Avoid the danger of making your plan too general. A well-laid plan gets into specifics and covers product and price; it deals with closing the sale and other pertinent details.

GETTING THE INTERVIEW

Merely getting the interview may be almost as much of a selling job as making the sale itself because the prospective customer may not be anxious to see you. As a matter of fact, a salesman may be discouraged by the receptionist when he enters the office for an interview.

Handling the Receptionist

When you enter an office, you will meet someone in the outer office who will ask what you want. Whatever your attitude may be to this individual, remember that she is an employee of the firm you are calling on. As such, give her the respect and attention that you would to any other important employee. Yes, she is important because she can lock or unlock the door to the right person.

When you say "Good morning," she will ask who you are and whom you represent. Hand her your card or tell her your name, your firm's name, and, if necessary, the business you are in.[1] Cooperate with her and give her courteous attention.

Always try to know the name of the person whom you wish to see. Sometimes, however, you will go to a large firm that has a number of buyers. Then you must tell the receptionist the type of material you are selling, and she will refer you to the appropriate person. In this case, you must tell her clearly about your product or your line. There are times when she is not entirely certain about whom you should see, and your further explanation can often help her refer you to the right person. Whatever you say or do, be confident. Make her feel that you have something worthwhile for her company and that she would be making a mistake if she were to hinder you from seeing the right person. If you have some special device or material in your hands, that may help you gain admittance. Treat the receptionist graciously; treat her as a lady; treat her with the consideration that she deserves. Some salesmen hurt themselves by acting fresh or by kidding the receptionist before they know her.

---

[1] Many approaches can be used in addition to the one mentioned. Frequently, if you tell the secretary who you are and what your business is, she will then tell the boss and he can say that he is not interested. It is imperative that your introductory remarks arouse the interest or curiosity of the man you wish to see. Capable salesmen often give their names and addresses: "Just tell Mr. Smith that Paul Johnson of Muskegon is calling on him."

If you have difficulty in getting past the receptionist, or if you are getting too many refusals, improve your opening techniques and choice of sentences. A salesman once found that a secretary refused to let him see her boss because the boss told her that he would see no one that day. The salesman informed her that he was certain that the boss would see him if the boss knew who was there. When the girl even then refused, he stretched himself to his six foot height and said, "I have ten distinct ways of getting past secretaries to get to the boss. Now will you go and tell him I'm here, or must I use all ten of them?" He got to see the boss.

METHODS OF SECURING INTERVIEW

Instead of leaving you with these generalities about getting an interview, let us get into specifics and show how we can secure interviews by taking definite steps. Once you learn the various ways for getting interviews, you can use the ones that are most suitable for you or for the persons on whom you are calling.

Letter in Advance

If you are making a "cold" call, a letter in advance can pave the way. Make it a sales letter that will whet the prospect's appetite. A cold, prosaic, ordinary letter will hit the wastebasket. When you arrive, the buyer will have forgotten your weak letter, or if he vaguely remembers it, he will probably say that he is not interested. You can never afford to send a dull, uninteresting letter.

A letter of introduction need not be long. As a matter of fact, brevity is desirable. You are solely attempting to get an interview and to introduce your topic so that the prospect will have an inkling about the subject of your call and will welcome you when you arrive.

Telephone

Many salesmen have had great success in arranging appointments by telephone. An appointment is essential when your presentation is lengthy and when several people must be present. If you are selling life insurance to a professional man, arrange an appointment when he has sufficient time to give you the proper attention. If you are selling household items to a family, be sure that you get the husband and wife together and that you can have sufficient time to present your sales talk. In cases like these, the appointment becomes a necessity. Seldom can you walk in on people and get them in the right mood to sit down and listen to a long presentation.

There are various techniques for securing appointments on the telephone. Books on this topic are available. The main idea in working for an appointment is to use an approach that will interest the potential customer. Ask questions and try to intrigue him into setting an appointment for a later date.

Introductory Letter

If an introductory letter has preceded your call, it breaks the ice when you meet the buyer for the first time. A lot of trouble can be avoided and the way gently paved by writing such a letter. In a way, an introductory letter creates a bit of rapport between you and your prospect.

There are various ways of securing introductory letters. The executives of your own firm will gladly write a potential customer to indicate that you will be calling on him and that they would appreciate whatever courtesy he can extend. Sometimes one of your friends will be glad to write a letter of introduction to a prospect whom your friend knows.

An introductory letter can be a great help to any salesman who must set up an appointment for an interview which will take considerable time. A man is not likely to give you, a stranger, part of his busy day unless he feels there are genuine advantages. The letter preceding you can give sufficient information to make him curious. Bridge the gap of the unknown as rapidly as you can; remove "strangeritis" as soon as possible. A simple introductory note written on the back of a card may be all that is necessary to provide the opening, but if a friend of yours is writing, do not imply that his card endorses your product. You are, in a sense, trespassing on the good nature of your friend when you cultivate this impression. Through his letter or card of introduction, your friend merely wants you to have an easy access to your prospect and to present your proposition on its merits. Seldom is he endorsing your product unless he deliberately says so; by writing an introduction he is simply bridging the gap for you.

APPROACH TECHNIQUES

There are various ways of reaching a buyer, starting your conversation, and getting his interest.

Introducing Yourself

It is customary to introduce yourself as you walk into the buyer's office. Do not feel affronted if your prospect forgets your name or your company; try to repeat both during the conversation and give him your card when you introduce yourself. If you are calling for the first time, say something about yourself and your company during the introductory remarks. For example, you could say, "I have been representing my firm in floor coverings for ten years. I have not called previously, but other salesmen of our parent firm, Bantam Mills, Inc., have sold to your company for five years. My company, Fleury Corporation, is a subsidiary of Bantam Mills."

Customer Benefit

A salesman who can promise a buyer a new benefit is in an advantageous position. Picture these situations: You call on a housewife and say, "How would you like an automatic peeler?" You call on an outboard motor owner and say, "How would you like to insure easy starting?" You call on a gardener and say, "These seeds will grow every time." You call on a card player and say, "Would you like to know how to win 9 out of 10 times?" Perhaps these potential customers would view your opening remark with skepticism, but their interest would be aroused so that you can make your presentation.

Flattery

Most people are so hungry for flattery that any kind thing you say about them will meet with their approval. People are so used to being criticized that when someone says pleasant things to them, they are delighted. Particularly is this true when they can agree with you. The author knows of individuals who have deliberately flattered people to see how far they could go before the other persons tired of it. As a result of these experiences, the author suggests that you not worry about excessive flattery; perhaps once out of a hundred times you may anger a person, but the other 99 times, he will be pleased.

Surprise

A pleasant surprise is usually an effective device. You might lower the cost, promise reduced trouble of operation, or indicate that your equipment will ease certain types of work. The surprise approach must have something unusual or unexpected.

Testimonial

One of the most effective ways of securing attention is through the use of testimonials. When a potential customer hears that one of his friends or someone else whom he respects is already using the product and is finding it satisfactory, he will listen. The old adage that "the proof of the pudding is in the eating" holds true. If you can show the potential customer how others are enjoying the product, he will be encouraged to buy. Some of the most effective advertising in newspapers and magazines or on television and radio is the testimonial type. Most of us can recall advertisements showing a golf professional swinging a particular brand of clubs, a well-known fisherman casting with a particular brand of reel, an African hunter explaining why he used a particular gun, or a racing driver stating he always depends on a certain brand of tire. For years, patent medicines have been sold successfully through testimonial advertising. Industrial advertisers have also found testimonial advertising effective. Some of the most effective industrial advertisements show pictures of satisfied users. Such individuals explain in detail why particular machines helped them. These advertisements avoid generalities and specify precisely how the individual benefited.

Product

If you are able to carry a sample of your product or even a model of it, you are fortunate. The appeal to the senses is very strong, and the customer who can see a product, handle it, and admire it understands quickly how it might fit his needs. Many of us have heard a vivid description of some product and thought we might like to own it. As soon as we saw it, however, we knew that it was not for us. Why? The description did not disclose certain undesirable features about it.

Cut-away models are advantageous. If you cannot possibly carry the product itself, you might have illustrations or pictures with a series of overlays which give a piece-by-piece demonstration of the various components of the product. Some salesmen even describe such intangibles as insurance with charts, diagrams, or pictures.

Gift

Most of us are familiar with the sales device of a small token or gift. The Fuller Brush man, for example, leaves some small gift for or with the housewife. The house-to-house baked goods salesman may leave an introductory premium offer on an item which can be paid for over a period of time with other purchases. The cleaner salesman puts an imitation pocket handkerchief in a man's suit when he returns it.

At the opening of a filling station, people crowd to get free balloons or other tokens for buying gasoline. Evaluate the following gift offer: "Free candy and cake are as near as your 'phone—call now; this is the greatest offer yet; get your share of the sensational savings and delicious free gifts. You get both Longmarch candies and Ellen May cake absolutely free with any estimate. No purchase necessary—but hurry, the offer is limited." "Gifts make foolish the hearts of the wise," is a saying that applies as well now as in other eras.

Survey

A much-abused technique is the survey. We mention this particularly because it is so frequently abused that it interferes with the legitimate surveys that are being carried out in marketing research. Too many surveys connected with the sales approach are dubious devices; they have no merit for gathering information but are only methods of gaining entry.

People have been duped so frequently that they are suspicious when you mention "survey." This is particularly true when dealing with the housewife. Even the industrial buyer, however, is becoming suspicious when he learns that some of the so-called confidential surveys are not such at all but merely devices to gain information for further sales. When calling on a professional buyer with a legitimate survey, do not hesitate to show him your questionnaire or whatever you are using so that he can immediately see that there is justification for what you are doing.

Inquiring Mind

Many people have an inquiring mind. They are looking for something new and different, something that will give them a new lead or help them in their work. Curiosity seems to be an inborn trait and may be used by the alert salesman to secure attention and gain entry. Sometimes, to arouse this interest, the salesman will bring a product or an item which is not related to what he is selling. But it will be sufficient to interest a person and enable the salesman to strike up a conversation. Later, he will be able to switch to the topic that he wants to discuss. The inquiring buyer says, "Watch;" and if your product is designed to solve his problem, he will buy.

Future Payment

The idea of future payment is captivating to many buyers. The idea that you can enjoy it now and pay later has proven successful. Listen to this ad: "Use it free for eight full months. Why wait? Take advantage of Jones' most liberal credit plans. Anyone can enjoy the product now. All summer—and fall—and all winter. Only one cent down—don't pay anything else till spring." All of us know that we can buy houses, cars, and major appliances on time. But now it is fashionable to buy small items on time and pay for them at the end of a thirty-day period or even a longer period if desired. If it were not possible to buy now and pay later, most buyers would have to wait for months or years to get what they now can enjoy.

Promises

"If this new washing powder isn't better than any you've used before, bring it back and we'll refund double your money." "If you don't find that these ten gallons of gas will give you greater mileage than any other fuel you have used previously, come back and we will refund your money." "Use Dab-it complexion treatment for ten days, and if you are not completely satisfied, don't pay for it." Yes, we are all familiar with promises of various kinds —promises that will improve us, improve our status, make us healthier, wealthier, or wiser. A guarantee is nothing more than a promise for a future period. A bona fide promise is valuable because it removes uncertainty, gives certain protection, and removes fear of possible hazards involved in using the product.

Imitation

An imitative approach has certain values. If we can adopt the techniques and procedures of experts, we may benefit greatly. Proven methodology has much to warrant its use. Not only can it be a surefire method of success if it is properly used, but it saves the time of going through numerous trial-and-error methods to find successful ones.

The danger, however, is that the approach used by someone else may not fit you. In the hands of an expert, one type of approach may be magnificent, but the same one used by an amateur or an inexperienced professional might appear ludicrous. Do not hesitate to imitate successful people insofar as you are capable of using their techniques successfully. Beware that you do not go too far in mimicking people, trying to carry out gestures and facial and voice expressions, which are difficult to master.

Drama—Suspense—Mystery

Since emotion plays such an important part in selling, you may secure the attention of a potential buyer in a dramatic way. You may be able to create suspense that will arouse his curiosity. Since most of us must be moved in some way or another before we purchase, it is logical to assume that certain ways of arousing interest must be successful. Avoid a strange approach that becomes sensational and self-defeating. Suspense may prove intriguing to the buyer, but it is easily overworked. One salesman succeeded in having the buyers in his office sit on the floor and take apart plumbing accessories which had some new features. These buyers, however, were technical people who were interested in new developments.

Rewards

Most people work for some type of reward. A reward is a promise of something in the future for what we are now doing or hope to do. Dangling the carrot in front of the horse's nose, giving the performing seal the fish after he has completed his act, or paying the person for his work during the day—these are all tangible, immediate, and influential rewards. The same might be said of the buyer or any customer who is interested in making a purchase. Naturally, he says, "What's in it for me? What will

I get for my money, for my time invested?" Generally, the sooner a customer can benefit from a purchase, the more likely he will buy.

DO'S AND DON'TS TO REMEMBER

A number of selling points should be explored in detail so that you will understand when and how to use them. Their effectiveness may be measured by the way that they are used.

Use of Card

Should you use a calling card? Some salesmen use cards whenever possible, while others have found that they give little aid and prefer to say their names.

A calling card can be a detriment. Very often, a salesman walks into an office and hands his card to the receptionist. She carries it into the inner office but soon returns to say that the boss is not interested. A card used in this way tips your hand prematurely. In this situation it would be preferable for the salesman merely to give his name and perhaps the name of his firm.

Some salesmen use unusual types of calling cards to attract attention. Cards may be engraved in a special way or made out of materials that the salesman sells, such as aluminum, steel, or even plywood. Occasionally, a salesman will use a large card to attract attention. Many salesmen find that leaving a card at the end of an interview serves their purposes better than giving it at the beginning because it acts as a reminder to the man on whom you have called. If he later wants your product, he may refer to your card to secure the address.

The new salesman may believe that a beautiful card with his name and the name of his well-known firm will give him prestige and help him get an interview. Perhaps the young salesman is impressed, but the buyer cares little for this sort of gesture.

The effective use of a card also depends upon the type of selling you do. There may be industries in which the calling card is universally used. A card is typically used where the salesman of one manufacturer calls on the buyer of another manufacturer. The buyer expects salesmen to call and expects to receive them. When a salesman has an appointment, he can give his card to the receptionist to announce his arrival. There may be other situations in which a calling card is seldom used. A calling card would seldom be used at the beginning of an interview in a house-to-house sale. Keep in mind that your calling card is a sales aid that should be used effectively. It is not an end in itself, and should not be used if it might hinder your sale.

Prevent Early Dismissal

When a salesman gets an early dismissal, he has not developed an interesting presentation. You may call on a potential customer and know your product's general benefits, but if you concentrate solely on yourself and your product, you might forget the particular benefits that your item can give the user. Soon the potential user loses interest in what you are saying and says to himself, "I'm just wasting my time."

If you are salesman-benefit conscious, your stay will be short; if you are customer-benefit conscious, your stay will be longer and more interesting. Many times, it requires real ability to explain to a potential customer how he can derive the greatest benefit from your product.

To avoid early dismissal, pick out certain striking facts about your product. Headline your product by mentioning its most appealing features. Sprinkled with a few questions, such an approach should hold his attention.

Many early dismissals occur because the salesman knows too little about the customer and his problems. If the salesman takes time to study the customer's problems, his products, and his needs, the salesman could create interest at once and hold the buyer's attention for a considerable time. If the prospect has a genuine need for what you are selling and he gives you an early dismissal, the fault is largely your own. You have not convinced the buyer that your product or service could benefit him. He feels little relationship to you and less interest in your product.

Apologizing—Optimism

Too often, the beginning salesman enters an office with an apologetic air. His calls on housewives are hesitant and fearful; he feels that he is intruding and begging for attention. Do not feel like this. Presumably, you are selling a worthwhile product or service to one who can benefit from its use. As long as you are offering a real service, giving a person an opportunity to buy something at the right price and with a quality that meets his needs, you should not fear to see him. Rather than being apologetic, hesitant, and fearful, you should express optimism, pleasure, confidence, a sincere belief in your product, and a sincere feeling that you are giving the potential customer an opportunity that will benefit him.

A problem may arise when you, as a new salesman, call on a top executive. You may be reluctant to go on with the interview for fear that you are intruding. You might believe that you are not worthy of taking his time. Overcome such feelings. No matter who he might be, he must also buy certain products and secure certain services. Once you gain access to him, you will probably find him more likable and easier to talk to than many other prospects.

True, a man in an important position becomes irritated by a salesman who walks in unprepared or presents a product that is obviously unsuitable. Busy people object to having their time wasted by salesmen who have propositions which cannot appeal to or be useful to them. Frequently, executives and other important people are the best customers, however. They make the highest incomes and can buy the items that they want. They may be the most likely prospects for your product.

Pave Way for Call-Back

If, as the interview progresses, you sense that you are not getting attention or that the individual is busy and wants to dismiss you, ask him to set a convenient time for you to call back. It would be pointless to stay, waste his time, and irritate him. Although he may not care if you ever return, you must make specific plans to get together in the near future. Some potential customers have suggested that the salesman call back a year or two later; but when the salesman returned, he found that many things had happened between visits. His call-back could develop into nothing more than a short visit. Be specific; set a new time for a new meeting, and try to make the new date as soon as possible.

Even if your first interview was unrewarding because you did not make progress, do not begin the second call where you ended the first one. Have something new and inviting to talk about. To ask lamely whether or not your customer would be interested in what you suggested at the former meeting would only give him the opening which he was waiting for; he could then say that he had not changed his mind and that he was still not interested. All of us are familiar with the little boy who comes to the front door, knocks, and says to you, "I don't suppose you want to buy anything, do you?" You answer politely, "No." Do not invite a refusal on a call-back. After an interesting opening, go into a presentation that is similar to the original one. Since days or weeks will have elapsed between visits, your prospect will have forgotten most of what you said when you first met him. Vary it sufficiently, however, to maintain interest even if his memory is good.

Undivided Attention

Some busy executives continue to work at the desk while you are there. Even though they say, "Go ahead, I'm listening," you are wasting your time if you talk when you do not have undivided attention. Few people can give careful attention simultaneously to two things. By some pretext, you must make him stop what he is doing and pay attention to what you are saying.

One common way to get attention is to sit silently until the other person raises his head and says, "Well, go on." Then start your presentation again but immediately stop when he starts to do something else. In this way you tell him that you are not able to make your presentation adequately unless you have his attention. Do not worry about offending him. If you continue to talk while he works on another project, you are not reaching him anyway. Some buyers use this as a pretext to disconcert new salesmen. Others really are busy and, feeling that what you say probably is not very interesting, they choose to continue their work. Use discretion; give every individual the chance to be as courteous to you as you are being to him.

Develop your own methods of handling people who do not give you their attention. A little thought and planning before an interview begins can pay off during the interview itself. In your presentation select and develop interesting, attention-getting sections. Ask questions, show drawings, or have your prospect inspect a model to aid in understanding some of the features that you are explaining. Ask him what he thinks of certain operations or how he would improve something. Vary the strength and pitch of your voice, shuffle illustrations around, draw diagrams, operate little pieces of equipment; those are some of the many ways that you can use to attract and keep attention.

In opening an interview in which you are selling an object, point out the striking appearance which makes it so unusual. Is it extremely large? Is it extremely small? In this day of micro-equipment, he might be intrigued in seeing how a tiny article can do a big job. Perhaps your article has outstanding features of fastness, or it has resistance to abrasions or fatigue. Like some fishing lures, your product might have unusual action. It appears different in daylight than at night. It may sparkle in sunlight but be dull on a dark day.

You may be presenting a product that is doing an old job in an entirely new way. Many of us remember the heat indicators that were built into the radiator cap on cars of years ago. For many years this device was the only heat indicator used by automobile manufacturers. Today, of course, it has been super-seded. Each year new devices appear which do the jobs in different and more effective ways. Although sawmills seem to be a stable part of the wood industry, a recent article explains how a jet of water, instead of a saw, can cut lumber and logs. A thin jet of water cutting lumber will save a lot of wood which presently goes into sawdust.

At times, your product can be explained by the way it differs from other products on the market or how it utilizes different principles to accomplish the same objectives. Instead of selling the product on the basis of its similarity to present-day products, emphasize its unique aspects. Some products are effective only when used in a series or in conjunction with other items; yours might be one which can operate independently.

Create images about your product's operation. With word pictures you can develop the buyer's interest and make him eager to hear more of your story. Frequently, a news item or a current event can be used as part of your presentation. If you can take some important current event and weave it into the opening of your presentation, your listener may sense a connection between your product and this news item.

WHAT YOU MUST DO EARLY IN THE INTERVIEW

To be sure of obtaining a satisfactory interview and making a presentation which will eventually lead to a sale, you must accomplish certain things early in the interview. Unless you do them rapidly, your time will be wasted. Consider each of these steps separately.

Impress Buyer

When you open the interview, create the impression that you are selling something worthwhile. People are reluctant to give time to strangers unless they can see value for themselves. Even a professional buyer—whose job it is to meet and deal with salesmen—is loath to spend time with a salesman whose product or service does not interest him. When you first meet a potential customer, you can start talking about him, his problems, his interests; talk about anything that is pertinent to the buyer himself. The buyer will become interested in you and your product if he feels that your presentation bears upon his problems. As soon as you have created interest, you have established an opening. When you call later, it will be easier to talk with him.

Size Up Situation

Size up the situation as soon as you step into an office. Not only will you gain impressions when you meet the receptionist, but these impressions will be reinforced as you step into the buyer's office. Even the physical surroundings may give clues about what to expect. If the office is clean and bright, you may anticipate an alert buyer ready to talk with you. If you sense tension and discord in the outer office, you may find tension and confusion in the buyer's office. If you find a buyer seated in a large noisy office with many other workers surrounding him, you may anticipate a noisy interview. If you come into a dingy office in a small factory where the owner is also purchasing agent, you probably will have constant interruption and confusion.

As soon as you walk into the prospect's office, you will appraise and be appraised. Both of you will try inductively and deductively to get general impressions of each other. Some sales teachers and sales books suggest that you type the individual soon after you have first walked into his office. The idea is to treat him according to a prearranged plan. This may seem relatively easy, but it is far too simple an approach. To catalog an individual at once is a dangerous procedure since even the experts make many mistakes. In logical terms, it commits the fallacy of the hasty generalization. It is far better for you to "play it by ear" until you know the person better and learn how he acts, what motivates him, and what his interests are.

Once you have given some attention to the physical surroundings and to the individual to whom you will talk, determine quickly how you will hold his interest. This is not easy. In the short period between the time you enter the buyer's office and begin speaking you must make some quick decisions. You must judge not only the physical but also the psychological characteristics of the individual before you. Is the buyer old, young, or middle-aged? Is he large or small? Is he heavyset or thin? Does he appear relaxed or concerned? Does he seem preoccupied? Is he tired or fresh looking? Is he shouting to his secretary? Imagine how different your reception could be in a dirty, noisy factory office compared with that in the office of a cosmetic buyer. The buyer in the first office could be a man wearing old clothes; the buyer in the second, an immaculate smiling woman.

Create Interest

One of the first essentials for a successful interview is to create interest at the start. To hold the buyer's attention, encourage him to ask questions so that you can give explanations; try to establish a bond between both of you. Sometimes, advance information through a letter or brochure can be a fruitful way of gaining that interest because the buyer can already have gained some familiarity with your product and its performance.

Do not open the conversation with an insulting remark that you "just happen to be in the neighborhood" and called on him. Why give the impression that your call is an insignificant afterthought? Neither should you encourage the idea that you have so much free time that you can drop in on prospects haphazardly.

Some people say that the salesman should dominate the interview, but "dominate" is a rather harsh word that connotes an overbearing role. Instead of dominating, *direct* the interview. The wise use of a series of questions frequently puts the buyer in a talkative mood, arouses his interest, and makes him quite ready to carry on a conversation. In your conversation give the buyer interesting facts and bits of information, and make pertinent comments. Say things to arouse his curiosity and make him eager to see what else he can learn.

In your presentation be sure that the prospect is following you. The salesman becomes so well acquainted with his product and his line that he is inclined to pass rapidly over much material that becomes commonplace to him. To the buyer who is hearing it for the first time, the presentation becomes garbled, and the buyer cannot understand it because it comes so rapidly. If your material cannot be grasped when first stated, repeat it a second or third time. Better still, rework your presentation and slow it down so that it *can* be understood when first given.

A teacher once mentioned that a salesman for a calculator explained its operation very quickly because the salesman thought that the teacher would readily understand mathematical operations. As a matter of fact, what seemed elementary and simple to the salesman was, for the teacher, quite complicated. Though he nodded his head in agreement, he understood little.

Keep the buyer's self-interest in the foreground, and do not let thoughts of your benefits creep into your presentation. Such thoughts hamstring you by tying your thoughts to the wrong subject. You will be riding two horses at once—your interests and the buyer's interests. While they should be the same in the long run, in the short run they may differ. Point out how your product can save money or time and what its fringe benefits will be. Perhaps your product can be incorporated into his product to give greater trouble-free operation. Your product will save him money because he can use less to meet his needs. For example, one coat of your paint will do the same job as two coats of any competing paint. Your product will save time because it can shorten a cycle. For example, your glue dries in one hour instead of two hours and thus speeds up production, requires less space for storing the material glued, and cuts down the inventory. You can detail particular advantages such as ease of working material, consistency of quality, and response to temperature change. Few buyers will ignore pertinent information presented by alert, intelligent salesmen.

When you begin the interview, the important individual is the buyer. He knows it, and you should not only realize it as well, but you should also indicate to the buyer that you recognize his importance. Perhaps you can repeat some of the buyer's statements with which you agree. You may be able to tell him that he has pointed out some advantages which you are repeating.

How can he interrupt you or disagree with you if, in essence, he would be criticizing himself?

Listen eagerly to every word, and the buyer will be flattered. To add to a speaker's self-importance, listen with great interest. Now and then, interrupt to ask a question which will let the buyer enlarge even more on the subject.

Let us review what you should do in the very beginning of an interview. You must impress the buyer so that he will let you go on. You must size up the situation so that you can determine which approach you should use. Create sufficient interest so that the buyer will give you his undivided attention. All of these processes must be carried out rapidly in the first minute or two. The opening of an interview can be likened to the sharp blow of the bat that sends the ball into the playing field. A top batter has a batting average between .300 and .400. Even good batters sometimes have averages as low as .250. But in batting with your customers, you must have a batting average much higher than even .400. You cannot have many strikeouts or many foul balls. After all, a potential customer is not an opposing pitcher who is trying in every possible way to prevent you from hitting the ball. Rather, he is an interested individual who, if properly approached, will be glad to let you hit that ball over the fence.

CONDUCTING INTERVIEW

If you have carefully read the chapter to this point, you should have learned how to open the interview. Much has been said about what you should do and what you should avoid doing. Now we must discuss the major elements of the interview itself.

Entry

Let us assume you wish to buy a new house. You and your wife get into the car and drive around looking at new homes. Then you see an advertisement in the paper and decide to investigate. As you approach the section of the city in which the house is located, you look at the surroundings and note the area of the city. Is it a good area? Are the people the type with whom you would like to live? Is the house run down? Is it in a wealthy section? Is it well kept? A thousand and one thoughts flash into your mind. Then you approach the street and watch intently for the house number, studying homes as you drive along.

Shortly, you come to the house and appraise it from the outside. You look at the yard, at the paving, at the driveway. You look to see if there is a garage, if the house is newly painted, if there are awnings; you check its general condition. What impressions do you gain? If they are unfavorable, you would probably not appraise the interior of the home realistically because your first impressions are negative.

Now translate the same idea into entering the buyer's office. Just as you gain an impression of the firm through the office and just as you gain an impression of the buyer by looking at him, you must expect the buyer to get an impression of you as you walk into his office. You walk in, and the buyer looks up. What does he see? What do you look like? Did you make a firm entry? Did you open the door confidently, or are you a nervous milquetoast? Is a smile on your face? Are you well groomed, not overdressed or underdressed? Do you radiate health and confidence? Do you convey an air of friendliness?

No buyer is interested in a salesman who slouches in and is careless, indifferent, worried, and looks as if he had been pulled through a knothole. Each salesman has personal problems which must be left at home. The buyer may take his worries to his office and share them with you, but do not reciprocate. Neither carefree laughter nor grim determination may be appropriate for a salesman, but a ready smile conveys the warmth of friendliness.

Handshake

Do you or do you not use a handshake? It depends. This becomes part of sizing up the situation. Some buyers are always ready for a friendly handshake. Others are reluctant to do so. A few even resent shaking hands. If your offer to shake hands is refused, do not feel hurt. As a matter of fact, it might occasionally be preferable to wait a moment to see if the other person extends his hand. If he does not extend his hand, perhaps you ought not force the situation.

Avoid the limp handshake which indicates a lack of enthusiasm and physical weakness. Too hearty a handshake may crush the bones of the other person and leave him with an aching hand. Instinctively, the buyer feels that the crushing handshake will be followed by a resounding slap on the back which will jar his teeth. It is not pleasant.

Opening Conversation

The first few words can be such a standard opening as, "Good morning, Mr. Jones, I'm representing the Fishtail Bait Company. My name is Adam Smith." Immediately follow up with some constructive statement. At this point you are standing near the buyer, and he probably has not asked you to sit. Remain standing until he invites you to sit. Standing may seem awkward, but as long as you are standing and he is sitting, it is easier for you to control the interview.

Prepare several opening statements in advance for various situations. Use the one that is most appropriate at the moment. After many interviews, you will be able to check back on the various opening statements that you have used and discover that some have been more successful than others. Do not forget that your use of the statement is as important as the words themselves. One of your effective opening statements might not be successful for another salesman, and one that he uses very well might not be too suitable for you.

To this point we have been giving instructions—what you should do, how you should do it, and how you should deport yourself. By this time, though, running through your mind is the thought, "Why don't we get down to brass tacks and see exactly how to do it?" Here, then, are some practical examples of opening conversations.

You are a house-to-house salesman making cold calls, selling a book for children. You knock on the door; as the housewife opens it, you say, "Good afternoon, Ma'am. Would you like to see some material that will make your child's work in school much easier?" "Are you interested in helping your child get ahead in school?" "Mothers who have used our material say that their children's school work improved 25 percent."

You are an insurance salesman. As you open the interview you say, "Would you like to hear a way of guaranteeing enough money to secure your children's college education?" "No matter what happens to you, we can show you how to assure that your house payments will be continued or that your house will be paid up." "An income of $100 a week is awaiting you under our plan. Whether you are ill or injured in some accident, you still get the $100." "Our mutual fund is a safe, painless way of providing for your future."

The real estate salesman says, "This home not only will provide you with a delightful place in which to live, but it will remain a sound investment." "When you pay money in rent, it's gone. When you pay money on your own home, it remains with you." "Thousands of people have increased their income by investing wisely in real estate."

The salesman calling on the retail druggist opens with, "We've sold over a thousand clocks in the past month." "Several retailers made over $75 the first week they handled these clocks." "Once you've got a good customer, hold him. These clocks will help you do just that." "Let me show you some figures from other stores on what they're making in selling these clocks." "These greeting cards fill out the line you already have, and will keep people from going elsewhere to make purchases."

The salesman selling cleaning supplies may open: "Using our cleaning fluid, your janitor will be able to get the floor clean in half the time." "One application of our wax is guaranteed to outlast two applications of anyone else's." "With our cleaning solution, you don't have to rub nearly as hard." "Our patented applicator goes easily into every corner and cleans out cracks; when not in use, it fits easily in the corner cupboard."

The car salesman says: "Our wide, easy-opening doors let you slip into the driver's seat with ease." "To keep the car looking like new, simply give it an occasional wash." "See yourself riding carefree in this sporty convertible on the open road."

The retail clerk selling a sport shirt says: "These sleeves will not bind you when you swing your golf clubs." "This pattern came on the market for the first time this week." "This shirt not only looks smart but feels comfortable."

In selling memberships to a new country club, you may open: "Membership in this country club is a mark of distinction for the leaders of the community." "People in your station of life need a distinctive place for entertaining." "Exclusive, yes—but friendly. That's the motto for our new country club."

Whether you are selling cabbages or cemetery lots, landscaping or boats, summer cottages or encyclopedias—in each case, the first step is to arouse the interest of the potential customer. Try this: Sit down a moment and think about something you would like to buy. How could your interest be aroused immediately? Think about the possible angles or alternatives or ideas that you would like to know about this particular product. How would you respond to various approaches? Develop several, and ask yourself: "If someone came to me and opened the sale like this, what would I say? What would I do?" Keep in mind that your customers are no different from you or me—they have their likes, their dislikes, their hopes, their sorrows, and their ambitions.

We repeat over and over again that you do not sell products —you sell people. One woman wishes to be beautiful; another, prominent; still another, a leader. One man wishes to make a lot of money; a second wishes to gain status in the community; a third looks for honor. All have wants that can be satisfied. Discover those wants and learn how your product will satisfy them. A genuine customer needs your product. When you approach him, he may not know that he needs it, but your job is to show him that he does.

Problems of Interview

As soon as the salesman appears at the front door of a house or in the buyer's office, tension arises. Instinctively, the potential customer knows that the salesman is about to take some of his money. There is always a feeling of uncertainty because the customer has often bought items of little value. He may have been sold products which he did not need. Why should the customer exchange his money or go into debt for a product which he does not need?

All of us fear the unknown; in buying a product, there is always some uncertainty. In the dime store, we are not too concerned because if we pay 10 cents for an item and later find that it is not what we want, we have wasted only ten cents. When someone is selling us a new car, a new home, or some other expensive product, we carefully consider. In buying clothing or shoes, we do not want to buy only good looks but also a comfortable feeling and the assurance of good wearing qualities.

One serious problem is gaining the full attention of the customer. We have already discussed how to handle the individual who chooses to go ahead with his own work, while he says that he will listen to what you say. But what about the individual who stops what he is doing and does listen? If you notice that he is preoccupied or that you are not getting through to him, you have opened, but he has not. What shock treatment, startling statement, or process is necessary to wake him out of his lethargy and make him give you his undivided attention?

How do you handle an individual who is genuinely busy? You may approach a housewife at the wrong time of the day when she is wrapped up in her work. You may meet a store buyer when he is swamped with book work, or answering letters, or dealing with his help. You may arrive at a buyer's office when he has a desk full of papers that he must clear off rapidly. If the person is genuinely busy, arrange to meet him at another time. If he simulates being busy, it is up to you to say things that will make him curious enough to give you his attention. If you made a mistake and called on an individual who is not interested and will probably not become interested, terminate the interview promptly and thank him for his attention.

If you have prepared carefully before the interview, you should know that your customer ought to have a genuine interest in your product. If he does not, challenge him so that he will become curious. If you are speaking to one who should be interested but appears not to be, the problem is that you have not hit a responsive chord. Your job, then, is to highlight a number of points and watch carefully for a responsive glint in his eye to show you that you are on the right track. Making the best opening approach is like opening a bag that has been sewed shut or like unraveling a ball of twine. In opening a bag, the thread unravels if you start to work at the right side. Start at the wrong end and you will be faced with a series of futile steps that lead nowhere. Many of you have had the experience of unraveling the backlash on a fishing reel. If you start painstakingly and carefully pull in the right spots and slowly work out the kinks, it will not take long before the line flows off the spool freely. However, if you become exasperated and start jerking, forcing, and pressing, you only get a worse tangle.

THINKING FORWARD

What you have read in this chapter fits many selling situations. Since the author cannot see you individually, he must use a shotgun approach to fit all readers. Your job, however, is to use the rifle approach; sort out the particular material that fits your product or service, adapt it, and put it in a clear outline which will provide a pattern for beginning your sale.

QUESTIONS AND PROBLEMS

1. Why do we stress talking with the right person? Are there any advantages in sometimes talking to the "wrong" person?

2. Discuss the various problems of preparing for the interview. Show how failures at this point can hinder a sale.

3. Name ten reasons why you may not get to the buyer. Is it possible to anticipate these difficulties?

4. The receptionist is a key person in getting an interview. How can she help or hinder you?

5. Give the advantages and disadvantages of using a letter in advance to get an interview.

6. What is the proper use of the telephone in selling? Can sales be completed on the telephone?

7. Why is it desirable to open an interview with a customer benefit?

8. How often can you overdo flattery? Should flattery be sincere?

9. Do people enjoy pleasant surprises? Can you employ unpleasant surprises successfully?

10. Testimonial advertising has been successful for many products and services. Why do testimonials have so great an appeal?

11. Effective product display proves very successful in many instances. Discuss the various appeals that may be aroused by a product.

12. How can the appeal of a free item move many people to act even though the item can be purchased for a few cents?

13. "Nothing down; a year to pay" often is effective in producing sales. Why do people frequently bite on such an offer?

14. How does a guarantee differ from a promise in selling a product?

15. "Imitation flatters the one being imitated but may be dangerous for the one doing the imitating." Explain this statement.

16. What are the advantages and disadvantages of using suspense in selling?

17. Is a reward essential for top selling performance? Will people work without a reward in mind?

18. Point out successful uses of a calling card. When may a calling card be a hindrance?

19. When a buyer dismisses the salesman quickly, what may be the problem?

20. A salesman should not apologize for taking the time of a prospect or a professional buyer. Why? Under what situations ought a salesman apologize?

21. "To pave the way for a call-back, avoid an outright 'no'." What is the meaning of this statement?

22. Suggest expedients and methods for securing attention during the interview.

23. When you step into an office for the first time, how can you impress the receptionist?

24. Demonstrate the use of questions to create buyer interest.

25. What is the danger in assuming that the prospect is following your presentation? For what reasons might a buyer not understand you?

26. How should you walk into a buyer's office?

27. "You size up the buyer, and the buyer does the same with you." What is meant by the statement?

28. What are the suggestions for shaking hands with a prospect or buyer?

29. "If the buyer lets you stand after the introduction, you may be at an advantage or perhaps at a disadvantage." Explain.

30. Prepare a paper listing a different opening statement for 15 different products or services.

31. Throughout this book you will read again and again, "You do not sell products, you sell people." Why is this idea repeated so often?

32. Why do we say that the fear of the unknown hinders selling?

CASES

5-1: SALES TRAINING AND DEVELOPMENT CORPORATION

During a class in sales training on the topic of "Beginning a Sale," the discussion centered about the use of a standard opening versus an opening tailored to fit each buyer.

Several in the class felt that a standard opening was preferable. It would be uniform, challenging, and would not deviate from excellence. When using the standard opening, the salesman would have an opportunity to survey the situation and ready himself for the interview. He would have one less problem to meet.

Others in the class disagreed with the use of a standard opening. They said it would be stilted, would lack originality, and would not fit all situations. They even insisted that a standard opening might kill any possible sale.

Since there was such a diversity of opinion, the instructor felt each student should explore the problem further and bring in a written report on his point of view. Among other factors this report must cover:

a. Advantages and disadvantages of standard openings
b. Effects on salesman
c. Effects on customers
d. Advantages of training

5-2: TAPEX PAINT COMPANY

The Tapex Paint Company manufactures and sells paint in the United States, east of the Mississippi River. Several years ago the company developed a new type of shellac, compounded under modern technology, which resulted in a much purer and more uniform product. Since then, the company continued to improve the quality of the newly developed shellac and finally had a variety of types to offer for special uses.

Mr. Paul Raymond, the sales manager of Tapex, decided to introduce the new product to one of its leading customers—Forest Products Corporation, an important furniture manufacturer with its major plant in Grand Rapids, Michigan. Orders of the Forest Products Corporation are placed by a central purchasing department at that plant.

Mr. John Kingsley was assigned the task of introducing the new types of shellac to the Forest Products Corporation. He services accounts in Michigan. He has had this territory for six years.

Before introducing the shellac, Mr. Kingsley talked the situation over with his sales manager. They noted that the head of the central purchasing department of Forest Products Corporation is Mr. Alex Rodgers. Mr. Rodgers joined Forest Products ten years ago when it was a small firm. Since then it has undergone tremendous expansion. Rodgers' job has evolved from routine buyer to Director of Purchasing. Through the industry grapevine, they heard that Rodgers is under constant fire from top management to meet rising competition. Both men felt that if Rodgers is approached in the right way, he can be persuaded to sign a contract for the new type of shellac.

Mr. Kingsley made a special trip to Grand Rapids where the central purchasing department is located. He asked the receptionist to see the Purchasing Director. Mr. Kingsley was referred to Mr. Rodgers.

KINGSLEY: Good morning, Alex, how are you?

RODGERS: John, if you are here to talk about shellac, you could not have come at a worse time. I just had my weekly meeting with top management. They are really put out at our shellac suppliers, especially your company. First, your last carload of shellac arrived two days late, and we nearly had to shut down two of our plants waiting for your product. Secondly, our production people have been able to relate our recent shellac troubles to impurities.

KINGSLEY: It looks as if I came at the right time, Alex. My job is not only to sell but to help you satisfy the production people.

RODGERS: Well, I have the authority to buy from whichever company can give us the best price without top management's approval. However, if it is a new product, I must get their O.K. before making a purchase. But, in either case, I have to keep the plant people happy. This is the picture. Our other suppliers have plants within 175 miles of us. Your nearest plant is 400 miles away. Delivery from them is about four days, and from you, about eight days. When I am in a rush, I cannot afford to order from you.

KINGSLEY: What about the impurity problem?

RODGERS: Once again, you are in a jam, John. Remember those serious production problems I told you about last time? Well, they have been traced to shellac impurity. Your competitors' shellac averages 95 percent pure. Your purity, according to my figures, is consistently 94.5 percent. On the basis of delivery and purity, I cannot continue to give you a share of our business if I am going to meet my company's competition.

KINGSLEY: Now I am convinced that I came at the right time, Alex. I never mentioned this to you before, but my company has been developing a new type of shellac which is much clearer and more uniform than any existing shellac on the market. This product is finally ready for distribution. It is 99.9 percent pure, which is about five percentage points above your other suppliers. In fact, I have along with me a report prepared by a leading testing concern . . . (shows report) . . . which shows the superiority of our new product.

RODGERS: John, I'm not a technical expert. How can I be expected to understand this report if I cannot even read it? Why don't you leave it here. Then I'll take it to the next week's staff meeting. The Production Manager, Edward Davis, can read it over. Leave it here, John, and drop back in a couple of weeks. By then he will have had a chance to go over it.

KINGSLEY: Why don't you send it to him right now? Any questions he might have, I can get answers for today. Really, it is pretty open-and-shut proof of the quality, purity, and superiority of our new product. It should not take him more than twenty minutes to go over it.

RODGERS: Good idea. Davis gave me a rough time this morning. I would like to show him something good. (Turning to his secretary: Miss Smith, would you please take this report over to Mr. Davis and ask him to go over it right now. Tell him that I have the sales representative from the Tapex Paint Company here in the office, and I need his opinion.) You must realize, John, that no matter how superior your new product is, it does not mean a thing to me unless you get orders here on time.

KINGSLEY: I realize that our plant being 400 miles away places my company at a disadvantage to local suppliers. I have talked this matter over with the sales manager, and we have formulated a purchase program which will assure stock at all times.

RODGERS: You will have to convince me. Go on.

KINGSLEY: Alex, you use one carload of shellac twice a month?

RODGERS: That is right.

KINGSLEY: My company's delivery time is approximately eight days.

RODGERS: Not the last time, John. Remember, it took ten days.

KINGSLEY: You mentioned the last time I was here that when your supply of shellac gets down below half, the production department notifies you. Then you send out the order to one of your suppliers.

RODGERS: Correct. And they take four days and you need eight. If an unforeseen event occurs and your car is delayed a couple of days, we are in real trouble—like last month. If your idea is for us to order in advance, forget it. I cannot see why we should alter our way of doing business to make up for your tardiness.

KINGSLEY: Right, Alex; delivery is our problem. This is how we propose to handle it. We will keep one car of shellac on your rail siding at all times. When your supplies drop to the halfway mark, you send us an order as usual; then you are free to unload from the standby car when you need it.

RODGERS: What if you have a strike, fire, or some other catastrophe? Then I'm a dead duck.

KINGSLEY: That is correct, Alex, when you are dealing with small suppliers. But my company has three plants in three different states. If for some reason we had trouble at the plant that normally supplies you, there are two others ready to go into action.

RODGERS: That is a good point.

KINGSLEY: Do you think Davis is through with that report by now?

RODGERS: Good question. (Rodgers calls Davis: Hi, Ed, this is Alex again. What do you think of the report on Tapex's new product? . . . Thanks a lot, Ed, I will let him know. See you at coffee.) You are right, John. Davis was really impressed with that report.

KINGSLEY: Well, Alex, our new product will more than meet competition. The proposed purchase program will solve the delivery problem. Would you like to order immediately rather than waiting until next month?

RODGERS: John, you have convinced me, but there is one major drawback. As I mentioned to you earlier, top management must approve a new product. And they won't meet until next Tuesday. However, with my recommendation along with that of Ed Davis, I assure you approval will be automatic.

KINGSLEY: All right, I will stop by on Wednesday of next week. Then we can sign the contract.

RODGERS: Fine, I will be expecting you.

KINGSLEY: Good-bye, Alex.

QUESTIONS

1. Did the background information on Rodgers help Kingsley?
2. What is your reaction to Kingsley's method of opening his interview with Rodgers?
3. How could Kingsley's approach be improved?
4. What did Kingsley do well?

CHAPTER 6

Presenting Your Product
or Service

Having gained the prospect's attention, you next present your product or service in an interesting fashion. How to do this effectively is the subject of this chapter.

MOTIVATING FORCES OF PRESENTATION

To make a successful presentation, you must know how to carry on a conversation. The prospect is interested in his own needs, has his own desires, is absorbed in his own problems. His capacity to understand and appreciate what you say is limited by his background; remember that he does not necessarily know what you know and that he might be bored with your interests.

We can consider a prospect in different ways. What kind of an individual is he? What mood is he in? What is his environment? To be effective, adjust presentations to each new situation.

Customer Behavior

A customer may habitually be more rational than emotional, or he may be an even combination of both characteristics. Realize, however, that the corporation buyer may be quite reasonable when at work, and yet he might be highly emotional in the evening when he purchases a pleasure boat for himself. Most of us, even though we consider our buying highly rational, may be motivated emotionally under certain conditions. We may, for example, be swept along with the group consciousness when we attend a carnival with friends. Or we might act out of character when we go to some entertainment when we wish to be known as liberal, generous, and more than willing to carry our share. In one particular instance, two salesmen almost battled over a dinner check. Both insisted on paying. Both wanted to impress the guests who were potential customers.

Rational

The rational buyer carefully considers each move. His intelligent approach is based on facts and figures. He considers alternatives and weighs consequences. He is not likely to buy on the spur of the moment, or reach hasty decisions based on suggestions. When he buys, it will be after mature deliberation and careful consideration of aspects of the proposition.

Consider, for example, Mr. Green who is buying a new home. At the present time, Mr. and Mrs. Green and their two small children, a boy and a girl, are living in a rented apartment. They have been married five years. During that time, they have been able to buy furniture, start a family, and make some modest savings. Within two years, their oldest child will be attending school. Both children will be playing with youngsters in the neighborhood. The neighborhood, which has previously been relatively unimportant for the children, will take on greater significance as they grow older.

After searching for quite some time, the Greens have narrowed their choice to three possible houses in three different locations. The first house is a small one in a rather crowded neighborhood. There are many children in the area, the down payment is small, monthly payments are moderate, and there will be no particular strain on their budget. Both Mr. and Mrs. Green realize, however, that they would not expect to live in this neighborhood for more than five or ten years at the most. Then they would expect to sell and move into a new community.

The second house they are observing is in a growing new suburb. The cost will be $5,000 more than the first house. Financing can be arranged satisfactorily, but monthly payments will be considerably higher than in the first situation. As a matter of fact, unless substantial promotions and raises come through, it is likely that carrying the burden of this home will require prudent management. Yet, this home is likely to meet their future needs as well as their present ones. The environment is more to their liking, and the people in the neighborhood have backgrounds similar to their own. The school system is adequate, the grade school is located nearby, the high school is a mile away.

The third house they have been considering is in a more fashionable neighborhood. The lot is larger; the house is new and more commodious; several beautiful trees are growing on the lot. The house has just been completed, while the other two are ten years old. At the moment, the residents in this neighborhood have larger incomes than the Greens, but possibly in the next ten years, if promotions come along as hoped, Mr. Green will reach the financial status of the other men in the neighborhood. The Greens determine that House Number 3 costs $5,000 more than House Number 2 and $10,000 more than House Number 1.

The Greens recognize that living in House Number 3 will be more expensive. They will have to borrow from relatives to get an adequate down payment, and the monthly payments will be burdensome. On the other hand, it is likely that in a few years, salary increases could make the payments come more easily. Improvements can be added and permanent plans worked out with the assurance that this house will probably be the only one they will buy in their lifetime. If they buy House Number 1, it is an assured fact that within five to ten years they would move. If they buy House Number 2, they could live there satisfactorily at least 10 years. Beyond that, they do not know. Purchasing any one of these three homes would have disadvantages. The Greens should list each home's advantages and disadvantages on paper and carefully compare them. Then exercising their best judgment, they should choose the best home for this time. They both agree that the primary consideration in their decision will be the financial one.

Emotional

Many people base decisions on emotional criteria. They may try to rationalize; they may try to justify; they may try to explain; but, in the last analysis, one recognizes that emotional factors control. Here, practical considerations are often waved aside.

Let us illustrate by using the Greens again. They purchased House Number 3. They moved in and are scrimping along, trying their best to keep their "heads above water" financially. Everything goes along fairly well for the first year. Then one day Johnny pops in and says, "Did you notice? The neighbors got a new Cadillac." That night Johnny asks his father, "You see the new Cadillac the neighbors bought?" A few days later, the little boys are playing together and they begin talking about the cars their fathers own. The man next door has his new car. The man on the other side has a year-old Lincoln; the neighbor across the street has an Oldsmobile 98; down the street, the family with the two-year-old Chrysler has just purchased a Falcon as a second car. Most of the families in the neighborhood have one big car and one small car, both in good condition.

Mr. Green and his wife begin to talk about cars one evening. Mrs. Green says, "You know, I'm kind of ashamed of driving that seven-year-old Chevy." "Yes," her husband says, "and even my three-year-old Ford looks kind of shabby next to these big cars, doesn't it? If we're going to live in this neighborhood, I guess we've got to have the same kinds of cars as the rest of the people." And so the Greens start planning how they can work a new car into their budget even though both of their present cars are operating satisfactorily.

When they lived in the apartment, Mrs. Green used the landlord's washer and dryer in the basement, but now she has had to buy her own. In the old neighborhood, housewives sometimes hung their clothes on lines to dry, but in the new setting they are always dried automatically. Yes, "keeping up with the Joneses" is a powerful emotional appeal.

Combination of Rational and Emotional

Instead of deciding on any of the three houses mentioned previously, let us assume that the Greens kept looking and found a fourth house that pleased them. This home is in a new suburb in which many people their own age are living. The cost is $1,000 more than House Number 2. The grade school is located two blocks away; the high school is six blocks away. School will be within walking distance for the children. The house has a double garage, the lawn has been sodded, and the street is paved. There are no large trees, but they could plant some small ones immediately if they buy the house. Because this house will meet their needs and their budget, they buy.

They move in, and everything seems to be going smoothly. They soon notice, however, that people in the neighborhood are buying many new items. Previously, the Greens had been content to buy cautiously and to pay cash for most of their purchases. Now, however, they are in an environment where people spend freely, mortgaging their future. One or two families in the area pride themselves on having new cars every year. One neighbor has just bought a new boat and an outboard motor for water skiing. Another neighbor has built a pool in his backyard. Two others have cottages on a lake nearby. Looking at the pattern of living, it is evident that the Greens are hopelessly behind their neighbors. Though the Greens purchased wisely and rationally, they have become subjected to emotional pressures.

Why should they deny themselves pleasures that neighbors have? Why should their children not have the same opportunity that other children have in the neighborhood? Everybody else is buying on time. Aren't they behind the times? The Greens are rationalizing to do certain things against their better judgment. Their situation reminds one of the little girl who said, "Heads, I buy an ice cream cone; tails, I don't." She had to flip her coin six times before heads won.

Behavior is the result of many internal and external forces which interact and conflict with each other. At any given moment, these forces may blend together in a particular pattern that influences the prospect's actions. What we willingly do today, we might not think of doing tomorrow under a slightly different set of circumstances.

EFFECTS OF CUSTOMER BEHAVIOR

Each prospect—a product of his environment, background, and set of situations at the moment—will react in his own way under certain conditions. Yet, his reaction might be significantly altered if the salesman, planning carefully, would make his presentation properly.

Motives

We live in a complex world. Our pattern of living changes from day to day and is modified by conditions facing us at the moment. If the prospect decides to buy one item, he has to forego another. If he decides to take one action, another becomes impossible. The Green family must decide between a relaxing vacation or a new car. But who can say what constitutes a relaxing vacation for the Greens? To one family, it is time spent at the seashore; to another, a long auto trip; to a third, a plane trip plus a stop at a resort hotel for a few days. If we are motivated strongly enough (or if a salesman can develop a motive for us), we will try to gratify that desire. Regardless of how inane our reasons for doing something might appear to a disinterested observer, we assure ourselves that we are striving sensibly toward something attainable and beneficial.

Goals

Often, a prospect has a particular goal in mind for which he has carefully planned. Further consideration indicates possible alternative paths which will lead to the same end by different routes. For example, a prospect may want prestige. He may have determined that buying a certain new car will give it to him. The alert salesman can indicate alternative paths of achieving prestige. Instead of a new car, he could buy a boat, join a country club, remodel his house, take a vacation trip, or become a leader in a local organization.

Once having discovered a man's goal, the salesman can suggest various ways to satisfy it. Do not forget that we decide on the basis of available facts and information. Supplied with additional material or alternative procedures, our final decision can be quite different from the first one. Good salesmanship frequently redirects a prospect's thinking, modifies his present desires, and causes him to make new decisions which can be more satisfying than the original would have been.

Perceptions

A salesman must be aware of the prospect's perception. Ask three men what they think of a particular car. The first will say it has a powerful engine; the second will say it has reliability; the third will mention performance. Ask three men to look at a grove of trees. One will consider the beautiful shade they give; the second will think of the board feet of lumber; the third, a contractor, will wish that the trees were not there at all if he has to build houses on the property.

A salesman must recognize that the prospect will probably not understand the proposition as you see it. The customer does not see with your eyes; he sees with his eyes, his background, his thinking, his education, his reasoning. Both of you may be looking at the same object and see two entirely different things. The sooner that you learn to look at the product or service with the eyes of the prospect, the sooner you will be able to understand his reasoning and influence him in your direction. Time and again, you have heard disagreements about certain things and have later discovered that the debaters were not actually talking about the same thing. They only thought that they were.

When we see an object or hear a presentation, we relate it to our own backgrounds. It fits into a niche in our mind but may fit into a different niche in some other individual's mind. The salesman must not assume that he is right and the other person is wrong, or that the other person is not aware of the qualities of his product. The salesman must consider the same situation in different ways. If he feels the prospect is viewing it inadequately, it is the salesman's job to change this viewpoint by changing the prospect's frame of reference.

Attitudes of Customer

Combining emotional and rational factors, we end up with what we call attitude. An attitude is a characteristic of a person. Many of our attitudes are unconsciously received from others without our volition. If you are basically honest and someone asks you how you got that way, you might say after thinking a while, "Well, I guess it's just the way I am." Thus, you have one attitude that you apply to life, politics, education, religion, neighbors, and any number of situations.

We express our attitudes in words, actions, or deeds. We may have attitudes of disdain, disrespect, intolerance, generosity, attention, consideration. Once you have learned the attitudes of your prospects, you can generally adapt yourself to their approaches to problems. At least, you can judge how to avoid insulting your customer. If the attitude toward you and your product is unfavorable, handle your prospect with great tact. If friction exists, get to the source of it and determine whether or not conflicting attitudes can find a common meeting ground.

Salesman—Customer Interaction

As you present your story, certain influences will develop. Watch the prospect as you talk; alter your approach, your techniques, your wording when it seems desirable. What you say will affect him one way or another. In response, you will adjust to suit the need. This changing relationship will depend on the buyer's reactions, words, and looks. See if the "eyes light up," or if there is "pained surprise," a "look of disbelief," or of disappointment.

Most frustrating for the salesman is the prospect's failure to react. It is like talking to an empty room. In contrast, good interaction is like talking to a political rally in which everyone is on your side.

Role of the Salesman

In your presentation, you have to play a role in which you are trying to influence the prospect. What is the impact of your presentation on the prospect? To assess this, you must consider how effectively and how well you communicate. How can you measure communication? If you are communicating effectively, the end goal may be measured in sales. But in many types of selling in which negotiations are drawn out, measuring one particular interview is difficult. One way to determine the effectiveness of your communication is to probe occasionally—to ask questions—to see how much the prospect is gaining from your talk. When he asks questions, are they relevant or offbeat? Is his mind on what you say, or is it wandering? Are you holding his attention?

If the salesman is doing his job properly, he learns more about the prospect, more about his desires and his needs, more about ways of handling him, of interesting him. The salesman's role is that of communicating with and studying his prospect to see how effectively his message registers. Your prospect is a living, vibrant, dynamic, impatient, selfish individual, intent on bettering himself, intent on gaining his ends. The better you understand him—his likes and dislikes—the better you will meet his desires and present your product or service in a way that will influence him to purchase.

TECHNIQUES OF PRESENTATION

Many useful techniques of presentation are available to the wide-awake salesman. These cannot be used indiscriminately, however, but must be tailored to meet specific objectives and situations.

Logical Approach

It is often wise to use the logical approach when you deal with the "average" individual and with the professional buyer. Most of us are usually level-headed. Even when we become highly enthusiastic, we still retain caution that is grounded in what we consider sensible prudence.

Reasoning Approach

When you use a reasoning approach, you appeal to the common sense and the intelligence of the buyer. Your presentation can be geared to factual, informative, and appropriate data that has practical significance.

Point out recognizable (and, if possible, verifiable) advantages. Extol economies. Indicate applications to his field. Within the capacity of the prospect, you can sit down and work out significant ideas. You can go into detail, explaining why your product will be superior in his applications. You can indicate specifically why he would be better off by using your product. Recognize, however, that a limiting factor in this approach is the mental ability—the educational background as well as the innate quickness to grasp new ideas—of your prospect. Going beyond his capacity will only confuse him and make him fearful. It is useless and wasteful to spend time developing ideas or applications not pertinent to the prospect.

Case Histories

A logical way to give the buyer information is to use illustrations. Case histories are excellent because they bring practice to his attention. The prospect can read or see how a particular application has been made and how well it has succeeded. However skeptical he may be of a salesman's statements, the prospect will be more impressed if the salesman uses actual case histories which can be proved. Furthermore, the realistic approach becomes even more significant when using a case history with the name of the firm and the individuals concerned, the situation that was handled, the problems that were encountered and solved, and the ultimate results and improvements. If you are fortunate enough to have a variety of case histories available, you have one of the most significant, believable, and impressive sales tools.

Demonstrations

At this point, we merely mention that a well-executed demonstration is an impressive method of influencing a prospect. Properly done, it is part of the logical approach. The next chapter will cover demonstrations in detail.

Research

Our rapidly expanding technology rests more and more on research. Most major corporations are successful because their research departments are outstanding. Many of you have probably heard that over half the sales of some of today's large corporations are in products that were unknown ten years ago. With this in mind, it is imperative that the salesman use the many research facilities that are applicable to his product or service. Much of this information may come from his company, but information is even more convincing when the salesman can get it from publications or sources other than his firm. Seemingly, outside sources modify bias.

An excellent source of material is from independent research organizations. Whatever the nature of the data, whether it be in development of products or in marketing information, as long as there is some applicability to your product, such information can be most helpful.

The words of a third party who is not present during the interview and who would have nothing at stake in the possible sale would be given much greater authenticity than the same information by the salesman. In one situation an automobile salesman was trying to sell a customer a particular color of car. As far as the customer was concerned, the interior seemed to clash with the exterior. Since the salesman had only the one car to sell, he had no other choice but to convince the prospect that the colors were harmonious. Eloquent as he was, he was not able to convince the prospect until a passerby stopped, looked at the new car, and remarked about its beautiful interior. Within a few minutes, the car was sold. In other cases, buyers of securities have followed the advice of the shoeshine boy or the bellboy rather than that of brokers.

Suggestion

Many of us are delighted when a salesman paints an exquisite word picture in which he joins us with the subject. He describes our feelings as we drive the red convertible on a warm June evening or as we push the boat through frothy waters with spray splashing in our faces. In a French restaurant we are hosting friends; the group's attention is focused on us as deferring waiters skillfully handle our guests. Yes, suggestion is powerful.

There are many kinds of suggestions, and their effects can be quite different. You can get the prospect to do something by suggestion. He can drive the car, row the boat, taste the food, play the musical instrument, operate the tool. Even handing him a pen and a completed order blank, suggesting that he sign as indicated, is an expression of action. One salesman who sold a wall map tried to stimulate action from prospects by having them feel the paper. Often, if the prospect can perform some little favor for the salesman, it expresses an interest which may be developed.

A happy situation develops when suggestions occur to the prospect himself. Through your skillful presentation and conversation, the prospect may see possibilities he had not recognized before. Recognize and encourage your customer's expressions by saying, "You see, Mr. Prospect, you, yourself, have indicated how useful this product may be," or "You've pointed out a use that I never thought of," or "Your contributions to this discussion have been extremely valuable." This pleases the prospect and makes him feel important. How often do men go to a car dealer just to look around and end up buying a car? How frequently have you heard, "I have no intention of buying"?

Planting ideas and developing motives will become everyday occurrences for you. A salesman has many possibilities to make suggestions which will strike responsive chords in prospects. Many people, for example, are hero-worshippers. If a famous person uses a product, that is enough for some prospects; they, too, must have it. Seldom do people inquire about the authenticity of the endorsement or whether or not the individual who makes the endorsement has actually used the product. It is believable to them, and that is all that matters. When a prestige suggestion appears useful, do not hesitate to use it.

Usually, positive suggestions are most effective. Occasionally, however, the use of a negative suggestion might bring action. A negative suggestion could be a warning of danger. Thus, the suggestion, "You wouldn't want to be caught without car insurance, would you?" would be a powerful stimulus to drivers whose insurance is about to expire. You could paint a picture of dire events that could happen if you were the cause of an automobile accident. You could cite examples of court judgments that crippled families financially. You could name specific cases where excessive hospital and medical bills handicapped families for years. "You wouldn't like to go out in a boat without life preservers, would you?" would be a real reason for securing them, particularly if the lake was rough. "Aren't you afraid of running out of gas?" could prod you to put an extra can of gas in the boat if you are going on an all-day trip. Even in selling cemetery lots, one or two well-timed negative suggestions can cause the individual to think a minute, and say, "Well, I'd better prepare for this contingency." As soon as your prospect has responded to a negative suggestion, offer positive suggestions which tell him how to avoid misfortune. After all, you do not want him to be depressed when he leaves you.

OBJECTIVES OF PRESENTATION

As we discuss the entire sale, it must be apparent that we are dividing it into a series of steps. Each step is not clearly and sharply differentiated; instead, it blends into the next one. Only to simplify the entire discussion do we use a series of steps and emphasize what each is intended to do. In the objectives of the presentation, we must accomplish several things.

Make Customer Unhappy

Did you every try to change or influence an individual who is happy, contented, who has no worries, no apparent trouble? He is a pleasant chap, agreeable, and easy to get along with. Why shouldn't he be? As far as he's concerned, he does not have a care in the world. Until now, he has lived happily without your product or service. He has never had it, never missed it; he does not want it because he does not think that he needs it. Your job is to convince him that he could be even happier if he were to use your product. To do that, you are going to make him slightly unhappy. The big frog dominating the little puddle is perfectly happy as long as he does not know that there are bigger puddles. The big fish, the king of the lake, does not know that there are oceans of water in which he would be just a little fry. In so many illustrations, people appear to be perfectly contented because they do not know of anything better. As you enter this picture with a product which is definitely superior to the one now being used or with a product which is built upon a new concept, you have to stimulate your prospect to recognize that his present position is not what it could be. The man with the used car can be stimulated so that he is unhappy until he gets a new car. The housewife with the old comfortable furniture can be made unhappy because it is out of date. The factory owner, in his profitable small factory with wooden floors can be made unhappy by comparing it with his competitors' concrete-floored buildings. Skillful salesmen can make a prospect feel that he's outgrown his old clothes, his old car, his old home.

Do not think that making the prospect unhappy is bad. He may be happy because he has a limited horizon and is restricting himself to such narrow fields that he is only partially living and profiting. As you open broader horizons, he sees the many things he is missing, the interesting life he might lead, the possibilities that could be his. Discontent leads to progress because the discontented man tries to remedy his situation.

There are at least two types of gripers; one gripes and does nothing about it; the other gripes but takes positive action to better whatever is undesirable. You can see the plan that we are now developing. Once you get a prospect unhappy, the next step follows naturally.

Solution of Customer Unhappiness

Our prospect is discontented. We have convinced him that his previous happiness was contentment at a low level. There was nothing particularly wrong about it; he was simply missing a lot of life because of his ignorance. Millions of people miss some of the good things of life because they do not know about them. Let us assume that you have painted a picture so clearly that he recognizes one facet of his life that needs improvement. What do you do now?

His mind starts casting about for possible solutions to remedy his unhappiness. Of course, you are not sadistic; you do not make people unhappy just for the pleasure of doing it. You have a reason for it. As you see it, this man has a type of illness which you have diagnosed in understandable terms. Your prescription is that he purchase your product or service.

Perhaps we seem to be a little extreme, but think about how much more pleasurable, how much more meaningful your life has become because of some product that has been sold to you. How would you like to have a home without an electric refrigerator, without a TV set, without a radio, without running water, or without a furnace? How would you like to live without car insurance, without fire insurance, without life insurance? How would you like to live without a car, without a bus, without an elevator, without airplanes, without trains? Do you see what we mean? All of these things are important to us, and yet a salesman has had to convince us of the need for each one. Somewhere, sometime, each of the products mentioned has been resisted. At first they were resisted through ignorance or superstition. Later, some were resisted because they were imperfect and in many cases were dangerous to use. At one time, vaccination to prevent disease was fought bitterly. Currently, water fluoridation is creating much antagonism

Doesn't it make sense to you, MR. SALESMAN, to recognize how important you are? All of these modern products and services have, at one time or another, been new on the market. They have been sold by enterprising salesmen who have convinced people that their old way of living was unsatisfactory, and that the addition of a product or service would make life far more meaningful and enjoyable.

Complete Understanding

The purpose of the presentation is not to tell as little as possible about your product, but to tell as much as possible within the needs of the listener. There can be such a thing as talking too much, but usually there is too little information given rather than too much. To make a thorough presentation of a product, you have to know the product. You must know the product not only in general terms, but in specific terms.

When we say specific terms, we mean applications to the prospect's needs. Thus, it is not uncommon to sell a product for several purposes, many of which are unlike. Let us say that you are selling a water system to a small community. Water is used for drinking and for washing; it is used for sprinkling the lawn and for putting out fires. Water is used for steam heat; as a coolant, it is ice for the refrigerant. You can swim in it, row a boat in it, skate on it, sail on it, catch fish in it, irrigate with it; there are thousands of uses for water. Yet, in one particular situation, you pick out and emphasize the applications suitable for the prospect.

Standard Talk

The standard talk or presentation, sometimes called the "canned talk," has many uses. Prepared in advance by experts who know the product in every way, the standard presentation is a coherent, clear, understandable, and organized approach. The salesman should know that a well-given standard presentation is the work of thousands of people over a period of time. Every possibility has been combed, every approach considered, every idea weighed. Much material has been assembled, many talks have been prepared, reams of data have been studied and worked over. With this welter of material, experts have put together the best possible approach that they can think of. Is it not often presumptuous of you to think that you can do better? As a matter of fact, you can often forget important points if you draft your own talk on an intricate idea. You will start and stop at odd places. Many of your approaches might not be the most suitable ones to use. People who use their own approaches have often been studied. Their presentations have been recorded, and they have been amazed to hear what they said. Most salesmen think that they vary each talk to fit the customer. The truth is that they do not. Over a period of time, most salesmen fall into a comfortable rut that might not be nearly so direct as the standard presentation.

At times, the difficulty may not be so much in the presentations. It is in the delivery. Having used the same talk over and over again, you may deliver it in a singsong fashion, a routine and repetitious way that is devoid of enthusiasm and lacks sparkle, spontaneity, and individuality. When you next find fault with a well-developed "canned" or standard presentation, think about the actor who does not write his lines but merely repeats what someone else has written for him. His success as an actor comes from his delivery of the lines and his individualized expression of them. He gives life to what a less successful actor could only mouth.

Take a standard presentation, and make it come alive. Even if it sounds repetitious to you because you have said it over and over again, think of the buyer or the prospect who has never heard it before. It cannot be repetitious to him, and it should not bore him because it is new. Neither does he know whether you are using a standard presentation or developing a presentation of your own.

In some types of selling, the salesman must give a standard presentation as it has been written out, word for word, from beginning to end. This is particularly true when you call on new customers who have never heard the story before or on housewives or homeowners to whom you are presenting a new idea or a new product. Before they can make a decision or understand what you are trying to do, they must get the complete picture. For example, an encyclopedia salesman has the husband and wife sit on each side of him so that he can thumb through an illustrated loose-leaf notebook which carries the presentation in a perfectly directed and coordinated appeal from the need for home reference material to the edition that they can afford.

When you sell professional buyers, watch the reaction of the prospect as he listens to your presentation. If certain sections seem to be repetitious or boring, proceed to other sections which are more interesting. In some situations, it is essential that you start at the beginning of the presentation and go through it methodically but with enthusiasm and sparkle. In other types of selling, you can use the standard presentation but select sections that are appropriate for the immediate prospect.

Organized Talk

All presentations should be well organized. Whether memorized or extemporaneous, they should be given in an orderly fashion. To do this, you must study your product and know its features and its talking points. Before seeing your customer, you must develop a complete catalog of information about your product or service and how it can be used in any particular situation. Then, list the information in an orderly sequence. Finally, present it in a coherent, understandable, and interesting way that fits the prospect.

The organized talk employs a good deal of memorization. It need not be word for word, but thoughts must follow a logical pattern if you are to give your prospect all of the pertinent information that he needs for a good decision. It is easy to digress and miss salient points and features, skip important sections, and thereby leave blanks in the listener's information.

Prepared Presentation

The successful salesman approaches his customer with a prepared presentation. It will be organized carefully and it will cover those features that will contribute to the prospect's knowledge of the product. Irrelevant material will be omitted.

Even if the salesman with the prepared talk does not use the standard presentation, he will have the important facts assembled. Just as you choose carefully when going through a cafeteria line, so the salesman who gives a well-prepared talk chooses wisely from the complete facts. But you do not sample everything in the cafeteria selection, and the salesman does not present all of the information that he has. Both your meal and your presentation should be balanced. Remember, too, that each meal during the day is different from the other two. If we continue to use our analogy, each presentation during the day may well be different from the others. Each meal fulfills a particular need, and each prepared talk can meet the particular requirements of a new prospect.

Remember the erector set that we had as children? It was made up of screws, bolts, and pieces of metal of many sizes and shapes. With it came a book illustrating different types of machines, equipment, and buildings we could construct. Similarly, in selling you have a great many parts in your catalog of information. Some sales will need only a few pieces of information. Others will require many bits of knowledge before they can be completed. A customer may be so backward (or so thorough) that you will have to use all the pieces to convince him.

Your prospects will vary widely in intelligence, knowledge, and background. You may start at the same point for all prospects, but some can be brought along more rapidly than others. Whatever distance you traverse, and whatever time is involved, the result should be the same—securing the sale.

To this point, you have been given suggestions, advice, approaches, and techniques, most of which are useful to you. Individually, you cannot use all that has been covered at any one time, but a group of salesmen will be able to use the material over a period of time. At this point, however, let's get down to the actual presentation.

Get Going

This is no time for hesitation, for "beating about the bush," social conversation, or other distractions. You are with the prospect for a purpose—that purpose is to make a sale. You know it and the prospect knows it. Time is passing; you must maintain the interest that you created with your opening statements.

Use of Words

Words are the tools to fashion our ideas. Just as the master carpenter has an adequate selection of tools; the pro golfer, a bag full of clubs; the dentist, his array of drills, so you should have a well-stocked cache of words. A poor vocabulary causes you to work a few words to death. You become monotonous, worrisome, uninteresting. You have heard someone say that a pianist "can make the piano come alive." In a similar way, your words should make your presentation come alive. An adequate choice of words, coupled with enthusiasm, sincerity, and knowledge, can make a presentation irresistible.

In speaking of a religious man, you might say that "He is a good man," but the word "good" can be replaced by such words as devoted, reverent, devout, eminent, earnest, zealous, consecrated, faithful. A "fine" person may be "reliable," "dependable," "safe," "never-failing." Vary your sentences through word choices so that you need not repeat the same words over and over again. Also, a variety of words gives the fine distinction of meaning so that you convey your exact ideas. Practice constantly to make your conversation more interesting. Filling in crossword puzzles or sending away for "Home Study Courses in English" is not enough. You must not only expand your vocabulary; you must also know how to use it. If we could define "synonyms" as "words which mean the same thing," we must see that synonyms do not exist; no two words mean *exactly* the same thing. Every word has a slightly different connotation from all other similar words; every word is unique. Which would you rather be: drunk, inebriated, or soused? Would you rather be an "intellectual" or an "egghead?" Words, then, are not enough. They are only as good as our use of them. Make it a practice to be reading something worthwhile at all times. Follow the best-seller list, and subscribe to at least one magazine that has literary merit. Do not saturate yourself with journals that publish everything in one style or those that use business or technical jargon instead of standard English.

Remember this: To read well is to think well; to think well is to prime yourself for business success.

Speed of Delivery

Sometimes a salesman talks too fast. On the other hand, some men are so earnest, slow, and careful that they bore the prospects. Probably we can say that few rates of delivery would be too fast or too slow; they are merely too fast or too slow for a particular prospect. Gauge your speed of delivery to fit the prospect. You can acquire this ability by watching many prospects as you talk and seeing how well they pick up what you say. Also, you can determine how well your story is being received by the questions they ask, by the responses they give, or even by their lack of response.

Repetition of the same story may make a salesman wonder why everyone does not completely and quickly comprehend. And yet, his material may be quite complicated and unintelligible to the listener. If the product is complex, the salesman must keep that complexity in mind. If his product is relatively simple, he can talk along easily at a conversational rate, without stopping or hesitating, knowing that the customer is able to follow. If the presentation is easy to understand, it should be given at a normal rate of speed. If the product is complex, he must gauge the individual to whom he is speaking. If the person seems to comprehend rapidly, the salesman can talk rapidly; but if the person seems to catch on slowly, the salesman must talk slowly, and possibly repeat himself.

Speed is also governed by the salesman's diction and enunciation. If his voice is clear, loud, and readily understandable, he can speak much faster than the one who speaks in low tones and slurs words. If you are the latter kind of salesman, improve your speech. Listen to yourself after you have read into a tape recorder. Ask friends for an honest evaluation of your speech patterns. You might even take a speech course at a local college or university.

Conversation

Too often we think of the presentation as a monologue. Actually, it should be a dialogue. Do not talk your prospect to death. Be careful when you fire off facts, descriptions, testimony, and a host of ideas that you think are excellent ammunition in gaining your end. When you shoot with a shotgun, most of the pellets are wasted; when you hit your target with a rifle bullet, there is no waste.

As you continue your presentation, test now and then to see whether you are registering with the listener. Ask questions which require answers, or invite his comments; give him opportunities to break into your talk. Make it a conversation. As he talks, he may reveal facts or ideas which help you. You will begin to see his interests. As he asks questions, you can tell what direction to take. You can also judge if he is a slow thinker or a slow speaker, if he thinks before he speaks, likes to hear his own voice, and what seems to affect him most.

In the interchange between you and the prospect, new ideas crop up. New angles are exposed; new possibilities uncovered. Just as a river may have many channels, so may a presentation have many approaches. In the river, you take soundings to determine which channel is the main one. In a similar fashion, you may have to probe in a discussion for the right approach in selling.

Headlining

When we pick up the newspaper, we glance at the headlines to get an idea of what is in it. In presenting your product to a prospect, you should headline benefits, advantages, and possibilities for improvement. As you go along, you will bring up one fact after another. Watch for the prospect's signals which indicate interest. This does not mean that he may have only one interest. Several headlines in the newspaper may interest us, but we read the article whose headline has interested us most; then we read a second one and a third one in descending order of interest.

Watch a child eat the frosting off the cake, pick the raisins out of the pastry, or eat the chocolate off an ice cream bar. This is similar to what a prospect does when faced with a buying situation. He may have several pressing needs for your product, or he may have a few very weak needs for it. Or his needs may vary from several important ones to one or two which are relatively unimportant. If you can highlight the one that looms most important to him and close the sale without using any others, that is what you should do. Do not hesitate to use more ammunition if necessary, but do not waste it after you have made the sale. Inadvertently, you might undo what you have already accomplished.

Practicing Your Presentation

Your first presentation will probably not go too smoothly. In all probability, little improvement will appear in even the second, third, fourth, and the fifth presentations. That is why it is wise to practice a sales presentation several times before using it. First, be sure that you have a good presentation. Then, practice it on your wife, your friends, or your neighbors. Practice it in an empty room before a mirror as you watch yourself talk. The best actors and the biggest shows have many rehearsals before a play is given. The difference between the first and the tenth presentation is astounding.

What are some of the weaknesses in your presentation that can be eliminated by practice? In the beginning, your choice of words may not be too appropriate. Your gestures might be ineffective or your tone unpleasant. Perhaps your technical explanations sound garbled, or your strong reasons for buying sound unconvincing to the buyer. Whenever we do anything for the first time, we are clumsy. We make false starts and are not very convincing. We are naive and unrealistic, unused to the environment. We press on too rapidly or too slowly, take things for granted, make statements detrimental to our position. You must never forget that the job of presentation is to convince the customer that he is not in the best possible situation and that your product will remedy the deficiency. You must be convinced that what you sell will make his life more pleasant, worthwhile, or better; it is your job to tell him so convincingly that he will feel the same way about it.

Individuals are similar in many ways but different in others. When we have covered the main points of a product, we must follow with the details of interest to the individual. This will build a mutual understanding between the salesman and the prospect. These facts must be kept in mind when we practice because we must not only sharpen our presentation but also sharpen it so that it becomes more effective with our prospects. We do not make presentations to people but to particular people. In any sales situation, there may be a number of obstacles purposely or inadvertently thrown in. Many are beyond the control of the salesman, but he must practice to learn to cope with them.

Interruption

At times, the salesman barely starts his presentation when the phone rings. A few minutes later, a colleague comes in and wants to talk to the buyer. Later, an old friend walks by and shakes hands. These interruptions are probably beyond the control of either party, but there are other interruptions which the buyer may deliberately stage to confuse the salesman. He may excuse himself and leave the room for a few minutes. He may say that he has a conference in 15 minutes, or he might give any number of other excuses. In a store, a presentation can be interrupted when a customer wants service, the telephone rings, merchandise is delivered, or a visitor drops in. In a home presentation, the telephone rings, the husband goes to the kitchen for a drink of water, or the kids burst in. These are but a few of the distracting interruptions a salesman must learn to handle.

How difficult it will be to continue the presentation after an interruption will depend upon the length of the interruption, the complexity of the product, and the interest of the prospect. If a prospect is keenly interested in what the salesman is saying and is closely following the presentation, he will be anxious to continue. In such cases, the prospect has resented the intrusion and welcomes the opportunity to hear more. Then the salesman should recapitulate in a sentence or two before he introduces the new material. The salesman may say: "As you remember, Mrs. Brown, we were discussing the binding on the books." "As you recall, Mr. Green, we were just beginning to discuss the electrical requirements of this equipment." But if the prospect is mildly interested or not interested at all, the salesman must go over some of the material again before continuing the presentation so that the buyer has a clear picture of the entire story. It might be necessary to restate briefly most of what you have already said.

If your presentation was not particularly effective before the interruption, this may be an opportunity to introduce another idea or two which may have greater appeal. In any event, you must present enough material so that the buyer clearly understands your proposition. If interruptions continue during the presentation and you sense that the buyer is irritated by them and interested in what you are saying, suggest that you both go to another room or that you take a coffee break so that you can get away from the office. If it is near lunchtime, invite him to lunch so that you can have an hour of uninterrupted conversation. Be careful, however, since some buyers do not wish to discuss business matters over the lunch table.

When major sales are involved, you can invite the buyer to your office where you can talk without interruption. Occasionally, a buyer will be invited to a "neutral" place or to a city that is some distance from both offices to insure uninterrupted conversation. A favorite pretext for getting the buyer away from his office is to invite him to see an installation that you sold another firm. Whatever you do, do not tell the buyer that you are arranging the interview so that you can do a better job, but rather that you are arranging a meeting away from his office so that he has a better opportunity to exercise his judgment.

If interview interruptions are continual and the presentation is faltering badly, close the interview as rapidly as possible and arrange for another at a more convenient time. If a buyer is constantly being interrupted during his regular working periods, find out if he has hours early in the morning or later in the evening, or if he has some more convenient time when he is alone. He may be willing to grant you some of this time so that you can talk without interruption.

You may be vexed time and again when talking to buyers who have constant interruptions. Some potential prospects are very difficult to talk with because they are so busy. It will not do much good to bewail the fact that you can never talk to particular buyers without interruption. If a buyer is important, it is your job to find a way to get to him when he is not so busy.

Most salesmen can make a standard presentation in a commendable way under ideal situations. It is in difficult situations that one can separate the topnotch salesman from the average. In one case, a salesman asked a buyer when he would be able to see him. The buyer said, "See me at 6 a.m. tomorrow." The salesman was there at 6 a.m. and got his interview. In this case, the prospect started to work at 6 in the morning, and he had to be sold before job problems arose.

Many an executive can be reached after 5 p.m., when most of the office staff has gone home. Some executives prefer to sit around for an hour or so after work to discuss the day's problems. Particularly may this be true in a crowded city, where the period from 5 p.m. to 6 p.m. is difficult to travel.

A salesman making repeat calls on the same customer should soon learn what periods of the day are the most productive. Many times, he can arrange his schedule to get to customers when they have the most free time. Obviously, following suggestions of this nature means that you must be willing to work—

to work hard, and to be inconvenienced so that your time fits the time that your customer has available.

Lack of Attention

You hear a speaker and, when you return home, someone says, "Well, what did he talk about?" Perhaps little of what he said remains with you. Or after class you remember little of what the teacher said. All of us are familiar with such situations that show a lack of attention or interest. If a person is vitally interested in a subject, he will remember most of the material from a talk.

To illustrate attention, one sales instructor has frequently used the dollar-bill approach. He takes a dollar bill from his pocket, holds it up before the class and says, "Are you interested in this?" Try it sometime. Immediately, every eye is glued on the dollar bill. Then continue, "Are you interested in having some of these? Are you interested in having many dollars? If so, listen carefully to what I say."

Some people believe that a person will not read a long advertisement about a product. Therefore, advertisements should be composed of illustrations, diagrams, big headlines, and little copy. However, did you ever have a severe backache during the day, come home, sit down in an easy chair, and open up the newspaper to see a full-page advertisement with a big headline, "Do you have a backache?" Immediately you read all the fine print, even if it is a whole page, because of promises of relief if you buy such-and-such a medicine. If the stimulus is great enough, the interest will be there.

Lack of attention indicates insufficient stimulus. One of the chief causes of inattention is lack of interest. If your prospect is not closely following what you say, perhaps your product is not very useful to him. Or if the prospect genuinely needs the product, you have not made your explanation and presentation clear and interesting enough so that he is alerted to his needs. Vary your approach. If he does not need your product, you are at fault because you did not qualify him; that is, you did not determine if he could use it.

Another reason for lack of attention is worry or preoccupation. Something may have come up that demands his attention, and your visit is simply taking up his time. It is pointless in such cases to waste your time and irritate him. He will want nothing more than to get the interview over so that he can dismiss you courteously. As long as the time is inauspicious and your presentation is doomed to be ineffective, leave gracefully and arrange to see him again.

Talk Too Little

Some prospects talk very little. Occasionally, a skillful buyer will remain silent to test the ability of the salesman. If he wants to get rid of you quickly, he may try the silent treatment to see how long you can last. Sometimes, however, your silent partner may simply be a slow thinker who expresses himself slowly. At other times, he might not understand the proposition, or he might not be interested enough.

Some people are hard to get acquainted with; they make friends slowly; maintain a reserve. But we cannot forget that some of those whom you initially thought unfriendly, quiet, and difficult to get close to, have turned out to be charming people, brilliant conversationalists, friendly, and most delightful once you have penetrated their crusty exterior. When you first meet such a prospect and try unsuccessfully to get through, you may erroneously conclude that he is hard to understand, uninteresting, and possibly a grouch. New salesmen are inclined to think that certain of their prospects are odd, but the experienced salesman recognizes that each prospect has a unique makeup. After all, some people eat grilled cheese sandwiches, pickles, and ice cream for breakfast; others eat oatmeal for supper. Some prefer iced coffee, others want it hot. One person puts sugar on tomatoes, another puts salt on them, and a third puts nothing on them; but no one of the three is right or wrong in being different from the other two.

Break through the exterior of the silent person and he will soon start to talk. It may not be much of a conversation as far as you are concerned, but it will be enough for him. Some people hesitate to say anything because they are bashful, shy, or retiring. Once you have won their favor, they will talk to you as much as they will to anyone else. In the meantime, do not be afraid of silent moments.

If you are having difficulty getting responses, ask the prospect a question and then sit silently, waiting for a reply. Few people can sit silent for a full minute. Salesmen using the silent treatment stated they have waited for as long as five minutes, without a word being said. To the waiting salesman, a minute of silence may seem like an eternity. It may seem long to the prospect, too; but on the other hand, it may seem very short, particularly if he is thinking or is preoccupied. Pleasant conversation does not mean a constant barrage of words. Avoid talking so much, so fast, and so constantly that you do not give the prospect a chance. If his feeble attempts to talk are overwhelmed by your loud babbles, he will soon give up and let you talk yourself out of a sale.

Vacillating

Some prospects are scatterbrained. Their attention wanders and their conversation jumps from one topic to another. You cannot pin them down. As long as such conditions continue, your prospects of success are remote. You must confine your scatterbrained friends to your topic. Whenever they stray, make a pleasant remark and then pull them back on the track. After they have made a number of attempts to digress and you have returned them to the presentation, they might stop interjecting pointless subjects and remain silent—either that or follow as you talk.

A vacillating prospect may be headstrong in the beginning and need some guidance. If you can steady him from his wanderings, he may listen to your talk. If you then detect a loss of interest in your presentation, it could be your fault. You might be making a long, involved presentation that is tiring him, that is beyond his understanding, that is boring, or that lacks interest. Maybe he has been sold on your product long before you completed your presentation, and you did not detect your success. While you were extolling various qualities of your product, the listener was interested primarily in one. After you had finished with that one, he lost interest. Had you been sharp enough, you could have detected this and closed.

The prospect who vacillates may need a salesman who is firm, considerate, and reassuring. If you look into the background of a vacillating person, you may discover that people have dominated him or that he has had a series of misfortunes which have upset him. He lacks confidence. If you can give him a steady, well-thought-out presentation, avoid irritation, and refuse to be upset by his flights of fancy, you may find that this individual willingly becomes a listener and a possible customer.

Skeptical

To some people, salesmen are liars, churchgoers are hypocrites, and doctors are avaricious. When the salesman tries to make a point for such a prospect, he becomes skeptical. Possibly an unfortunate situation in his life determined his attitude. Generalizing from one or several experiences, he concludes that he is not going to allow anyone to put anything over on him.

Learn why he is skeptical. Did his original trust of people hurt him? As you try to overcome skepticism, avoid direct contradiction. When repairing a road, a contractor will put up a "closed and detour" sign. Do not admit defeat by acknowledging that your prospect has closed his mind to your proposition; simply acknowledge that he has closed your road of presentation. It is up to you to put up the detour sign and guide him to the destination by another route.

When dealing with a skeptical person unsuccessfully, try leading him by another route. If he is impervious to your regular sales presentation, try another presentation. If talking gets you nowhere, try demonstrating. If he insists on seeing equipment in action, take him to an installation you sold earlier. If a photograph does not work, try various drawings. If you fail to convince him, bring the manager.

Skepticism can be overcome by presenting facts and data truthfully. Quote responsible people. If you have complete faith in your product and the prospect is skeptical, let him use it for a while on a trial basis if your company will allow you. The skeptical person will not stop buying, will not stop trying, will not stop investigating. But he will be cautious and unwilling to accept statements without proof.

Hostile

TV plays introduced many of us to the hostile witness, but salesmen have long known the hostile buyer. If he is a professional buyer, courtesy demands that he give consideration to your presentation even though he may be seeing you because he is compelled to. He must listen to you if you are a reliable supplier because his job demands it. In house-to-house selling, the hostile prospect is the one who does not want to listen to you; he might even close the door in your face. Should you gain entry, however, a skillful sales talk might make him more agreeable.

If a prospect speaks in a hostile way because of maltreatment or because of purchases which did not live up to the statements of the seller, you can agree with him that such occasions do happen. But you can also point out that a minority of salesmen do this. Most firms are honest and are ready to stand behind their product.

If the prospect is angry and talks against products, and salesmen, and selling, let him go on for a while. It will relieve him to talk. After he has quieted down, you can reason with him. If a professional buyer has been wronged, he still will listen to you because it is his job to do so. But he will be wary, particularly if he has had unfortunate transactions with your company.

If a previous salesman has done something wrong, do not condone it; simply say that you are sorry and then go on. Admit the mistake, but point out that all make some errors. If a problem remains to be corrected, you are there to correct it. At the same time, you feel that your product will benefit the prospect, and so it is to his advantage to listen. It is dangerous for a professional buyer to mix personal anger and business frustration. A buyer may carry on business with a firm he dislikes if he feels that it is advantageous to his company.

When selling to a committee, you usually compete with several salesmen to secure the business. It is not likely that you can gain the "yes" from every committee member. Oftentimes there is antagonism among committee members, and perhaps two people will deliberately disagree every time. In this situation, try to line up a majority of the committee in favor of your proposition. When dealing with a school committee, for example, the board will often take the recommendation of the superintendent. If, for some reason or other, you cannot get the recommendation of the superintendent because he favors a competitor, work strongly with board members, and try to secure a majority for your proposition.

Going over the head of a responsible buyer is a dangerous expedient. First, try every approach through normal channels. If, however, after every attempt you meet a "stone wall," and you still feel that you have a chance of getting somewhere through another means, try it. If you need an order that will use your entire productive capacity for six months; if your plant will close because you do not get it; if you find the usual avenue of approach closed; then do not hesitate to try another approach that may be open. A hostile buyer, too, is vulnerable. Those who believe that it is dangerous to circumvent buyers may take comfort in the fact that each year there is a turnover of about 20 percent of the buyers. The next time you come around, the person you could not get along with may be gone. We cannot tell you how to handle each hostile buyer, but we can advise you not to give up too easily.

Competition

Seldom can you avoid competition. As a matter of fact, meeting and overcoming competition strengthens you. Without competition, you soon degenerate to an order-taker, and when hard selling again appears, you will have lost the art.

When making your presentation, do not mention your competition. You want to keep the attention of the prospect on your proposition because you are trying to have him buy your product. Introducing extraneous factors interrupts the smooth, direct flow of thought and puts conflicting ideas into the buyer's mind. Therefore, do not bring competition into the picture when you present your product.

If the prospect refers to your competition, handle that problem in one of several ways. Admit that some competitors make satisfactory products, and then go on with your presentation. Usually it does not pay to knock competition or discuss the other person's products. If you divert attention to the competitor's products, particularly in a derogatory way, it may arouse the buyer's interest. Furthermore, he may not like to have you knock competition because the other salesman is not on hand to defend himself. Your unsportsmanlike action might boomerang.

When a prospect invites a comparison between your product and a competitor's, face the situation and make the comparison. You could use pencil and paper to list your advantages and your competitor's; your disadvantages and his. This is merely a straightforward comparison.

Many highly touted advantages of competing products become inconsequential in use. Even though my competitor's fountain pen may write under water or through butter, when I use a fountain pen, I seldom write under water or through butter. Even though my portable typewriter is strong enough to drive a car over it, I am not in the habit of driving cars over typewriters. Some insurance policies provide fantastic sums of money in case of particular types of accident or death. The catch is, of course, that such accidents happen so rarely that there is not a chance in a million to collect.

If you are attempting to sell a prospect a car and he insists on visiting a competitor for comparison, there is little you can do to prevent him. If you cannot close him immediately, put some obstacles in his path that will be used when he gets to the other dealer. For example, you can list the various outstanding advantages your car has. As he leaves, say, "When you get to the other dealer, find out if his car has the following," then list the features your car has and the competing car does not have. You can be sure that when he gets to the competitor he is going to ask him about all of these advantages that you have named. The competitor may counter with a similar list, but then it becomes a balancing of known qualities which the prospect had never considered.

As a rule, avoid violent criticism. Any buyer will expect you to compare your product with a competitor's, and he will expect you to place yours in a favorable light. He would have little regard for you if you disparaged your product or your firm. He would wonder why you are working for such a firm.

In the big leagues, most baseball players are not all-around players; they are specialists. By the same token, your product may not be a multipurpose product that will serve several purposes equally well. If it is not a specialized product, it will not compete with a specialized product. If you have a multipurpose tool, consider it as such and point out that if the buyer cannot justify a number of special-purpose tools, he will find the multipurpose tool useful.

If you sell specialized equipment, indicate its advantages and point out savings. If a firm has five jobs to perform, a buyer might get a piece of equipment that would perform all five of the jobs satisfactorily but not outstandingly. A little investigation might reveal that of those five jobs, 60 percent of the work was in jobs one and two, and 40 percent in three, four, and five. In this case, it might be desirable to have special equipment for job one and job two, and multipurpose equipment for jobs three, four, and five. Thus, you might save money by buying three machines instead of one. On the other hand, if each job were large enough, it might be worthwhile to have five special machines. If a competitor is selling a large truck which will meet all of the prospect's requirements, you can point out that your truck, though smaller, will meet 90 percent of his needs at a savings of so many dollars a year; for the additional 10 percent, he can hire a truck at a small cost.

When an unethical competitor has preceded you and filled the buyer's mind with distortions, you have a real job to do. When necessary, give competition the attention it needs, but beware of paying too much attention to it. Get the buyer's attention off your competitor's products. Do this as quietly, skillfully, and easily as possible without hurting feelings. You do not have to block out competition entirely; pass over it; ignore it. You know it exists; the buyer knows it exists. As soon as you can, go on to the advantages of your product.

There have been times when each of us has been maltreated. Often, one's first thought is to get revenge. Instead, if we would put as much effort into positive achievement as we would like to put into getting even, we would be farther ahead. Competition is like a bumblebee at a picnic. As the bee buzzes around, it can be irritating and it keeps you on guard; but seldom are you stung. In selling, when competition is present, be alert, be on guard, be watchful, but do not get into a struggle that will hurt the sale.

Questions and Problems

1. Illustrate rational and emotional buying motives. Can a rational buying motive for one person be an emotional buying motive for another person?
2. Can a well-defined goal govern an individual's purchasing?
3. Each of us may see an article in a different way. Explain.
4. Why may environment govern a buyer's perception?
5. What is a customer attitude? How can you use a customer's attitude in selling?

6. How can you be certain you are communicating effectively?
7. Name and discuss several techniques of presentations. Are there ineffective techniques of presentation?
8. What is the most skillful use of suggestions? What methods can a salesman use to bring out suggestions?
9. Illustrate uses of negative suggestions.
10. Why is it necessary to make a customer unhappy?
11. Is it fair to create a problem in a customer's mind if you have no solution for the problem?
12. How much information should a potential customer get?
13. Discuss the advantages and disadvantages of a standard presentation.
14. Why do some salesmen object to the "canned talk"?
15. Show the importance of organizing your presentation.
16. Distinguish between the standard presentation and the prepared presentation. Are not both prepared?
17. Why do sales trainers stress the need for a strong vocabulary?
18. Is there such a thing as talking too fast? Talking too slowly? Can you do both to a single prospect?
19. Selling must be a dialogue, not a monologue. Give reasons why a salesman must watch himself when talking.
20. What is meant by the term "headlining"? Do most people practice it?
21. Why should a sales trainer insist that a salesman rehearse his presentation?
22. Interruptions are common when selling professional buyers. Discuss several ways of handling interruptions advantageously.
23. When interruptions upset your presentation completely, what should you do?
24. Illustrate several ways of holding buyer attention.
25. When a prospect refuses to talk, what steps must you take to get conversation started?
26. Indicate ways of handling a person who cannot make up his mind. Is this trait common?
27. How do you handle the skeptical prospect? Give several approaches.
28. Outline three methods of handling the antagonistic buyer.
29. At what point would you go over the buyer's head? What are the dangers of bypassing the regular buyer?
30. Give several ways of handling competition. Do you ever bring competition in yourself? What is the danger of knocking competition?
31. How do you handle a prospect who comes from a competitor with a mass of misinformation? Can you openly criticize your competitor to such a prospect?
32. Does overcoming competition mean that you have made a sale?

CASES

6-1: GETZ LANDSCAPE SERVICE

Gilbert Getz operates a landscape service in Brownsville, a suburb of Chicago. Most of the people in Brownsville are on the upper-income level, but there are no wealthy people. The wealthy people live in Greensville, another suburb directly north of Brownsville. The two suburbs are separated by the Tiber River.

Mr. Getz started his landscape service five years ago. The first year he maintained lawns, trimmed shrubbery, cut grass, and cleaned yards. The second year he added the service of replacing old lawns and starting new ones for new homes. By the end of the fifth year Getz Landscape Service was well established. It had a reputation for quality work and of keeping its promises. People using Getz Landscape Service remarked that they liked the work, but that it was expensive.

Mr. Roth has just moved into a new $30,000 home. The lot is a half acre with sandy, poor soil. There are three large elm strees and three large maple trees. All the trees are tall and quite old. The maples have large rotten spots in the trunks. There are several holes used by squirrels.

Mr. Getz called Mr. Roth on April 1 and made an appointment with him for the following Friday evening to discuss landscaping his lot.

First interview on Friday evening:

GETZ: Good evening Mr. Roth. I am Gilbert Getz of the Getz Landscape Service. (Shakes hands with Mr. Roth)

ROTH: Glad to meet you Getz. This is my wife, Mabel; my son, Jim; and my daughter, Florence.

GETZ: Happy to meet you, Mrs. Roth. How are you, Jim? Glad to know you, Florence. (Shakes hands with each)

ROTH: Getz, I've been told you do fine landscaping. Is that right?

GETZ: We pride ourselves on our work, Mr. Roth. We put in many of the finest yards in town. I will be glad to show you some of them.

ROTH: That's not necessary, Getz. We've looked at some already, so we know pretty much what we want. This is about what we like. (Roth shows Getz a sketch and explains what he wants. At times Mrs. Roth expresses her views. The children, Jim, seven years old, and Florence, five, lose interest and wander away.)

GETZ: From your information I know about what you have in mind. Let's walk around the yard while you explain what you want. Then I'll take all this information and prepare a sketch and plan.

I can have it ready by next Friday evening. Shall we set an appointment for next Friday at 7 p.m.? (They walk around the yard and talk.)

ROTH: Fine, Getz. See you next Friday.

GETZ: Good night, Mrs. Roth. Good night, Mr. Roth.

Second interview one week later:

GETZ: Good evening, Mr. Roth. Good evening, Mrs. Roth.

MRS. ROTH: Good evening, Mr. Getz.

ROTH: Good evening, Getz. How did you get along?

GETZ: Fine, Mr. Roth. I have the complete plans here. (Shows them the plan.)

ROTH: Tell us about your plan, Getz.

GETZ: You have a beautiful home, Mr. Roth. You and Mrs. Roth must be proud of it.

ROTH: We rather like it. (Getz notes his face lights up, and Mrs. Roth beams.)

GETZ: To go with this home you must have beautiful surroundings—beautiful lawns, attractive shrubbery, lovely flowers, and magnificent shade trees. Your soil is sandy. That gives you excellent drainage, but at the same time the soil is not very good for growing grass. Rather than filling in with four inches of topsoil and seeding the lawn, I propose using a two-inch top layer of rich soil and then sodding with Merion bluegrass. This is a more expensive lawn, but you will have a beautiful, weed-free lawn this summer. If we seed the lawn, it will take most of the summer to get it in shape. (Getz then explains his entire plan of shrubbery, flowers, trees, and care. At the end of an hour they have walked over the premises and discussed various angles.) Getz says: What do you folks think of this plan?

MRS. ROTH: Sounds lovely.

ROTH: Looks like a good plan, Getz. How much does it cost?

GETZ: This is our two-year guaranteed special landscaping service, Mr. Roth. This is the one we have used at many homes in the neighborhood. We guarantee you this beautiful service for $2,400.

ROTH: $2,400! Wow! We only paid $3,000 for the whole lot.

MRS. ROTH: Seems like a lot of money for a lawn. It's only grass.

GETZ: It may seem high, folks, but you are getting not only a grassy lawn, you are getting a two-year landscaping service.

RoTH: A Milton Landscape Service representative was here last evening. He offered to do the job for $800.

GETZ: We give two types of landscaping service, Mr. Roth. For those content with a lesser job, we seed the lawn, plant some shrubbery, and put in five small maple trees on a lot your size for $800. But once your lawn is green, which is usually about 30 days after we finish planting, we get our money. Then the rest is up to you. Some of these lawns turn out well, others give a lot of trouble.

RoTH: I realize, Getz, I won't get the same service for $800 that you give for $2,400, but for $1,600!

GETZ: Let me go over the difference, Mr. Roth. In our master plan for your lawn we will sod the entire lawn with Merion bluegrass sod. Each shrub is carefully chosen to fit a particular spot. Some are evergreens; others are varieties used to give beautiful effects all year long. The flowers are mixed so that they will bloom all summer and autumn. These are not small maple trees. Each tree is a different variety. Two of them are 20 feet tall when we plant them. Those two will be giving shade the second year.

Anything that dies we replace free the first two years. If you continue to use our service after the initial two years, we replace anything that dies no matter how many years later. The way it looks now, your two large maples will have to be removed not later than next year. This we take care of as part of our service. We spray your elm trees each year to protect them.

Actually, the two services cannot be compared. In the low-priced one you get a green lawn plus a few shrubs and trees. In our complete service you have a beautiful home in a woodland setting of trees, shrubs, flowers, and a spacious lawn. For the low-priced service you pay $800 at the end of 30 days. For our service you pay $1,000 at the end of 60 days and only $100 a month for 14 months. The $1,000 partially covers our out-of-pocket costs for sod, shrubs, flowers, trees, and labor. Actually, we earn nothing until the second year. Then if we have to replant the large trees or some expensive shrubs, our costs increase.

Mr. Roth, now is the time for you to act, to decide to have the beautiful surroundings you want. Don't set up a lot of problems this summer with a new lawn and shrubs and trees that must be watched and watered. Let us start next week to give you the beautiful landscaping you and your wife want.

RoTH: Sounds tempting, Getz. But $2,400! What do you think, Mabel?

MRS. RoTH: With new carpeting, drapes, porch furniture—I wonder how we could make ends meet.

RoTH: Tell you what, Getz. Come back tomorrow at 9 in the morning. My wife and I will have to talk this over. Leave your plant with us. See you in the morning. Good night.

Questions and Problems

1. What are Getz's chances of getting the order tomorrow?
2. Where was his presentation weak?
3. Where was his presentation strong?
4. Draw up your own version of the meeting the next morning. Show what more Getz needs in his presentation.

6-2: FASHION MART SHOES

The Fashion Mart Shoestore carries a complete line of women's dresses and casual shoes. The store is located in a middle- to high-income shopping center. The customers are well-dressed. They are very fashion conscious and are willing to spend extra dollars for matching shoe accessories. The annual sales volume for the store is over $120,000.

Mr. Greenberg, the store owner, is proud of his full line of women's shoe accessories such as handbags, hosiery, socks, gloves, and wallets. Many of these items are tie-ins with matching shoes. Normally these accessories account for 20 percent of the total volume. This volume was especially desirable because these accessories are high-markup, low-markdown, and fast-turnover items.

In the past six months, however, these accessories accounted for only 10 percent of total sales. Mr. Greenberg felt that he was losing additional sales because the salesmen were not presenting the accessories in the correct manner to the customer.

In an effort to overcome this sales loss, Mr. Greenberg observed his salesmen on the floor selling to customers to see what was wrong. Here is one sale he overheard. After the salesman had sold the shoes, the following conversation took place:

CUSTOMER: Yes, I think I will take these red patent shoes and those brown casual loafers.

SALESMAN: Fine, they are both nice-looking shoes, and I am sure you will enjoy them. Now, how about a handbag?

CUSTOMER: No, not today. Well, maybe, I'll look at some anyhow.

SALESMAN: Here are a couple of nice ones. They are only $5.99. This red one looks like it may match your shoes.

CUSTOMER: It's not the exact same shade of red though.

SALESMAN: You're right, but the bag is only $5.99.

CUSTOMER: It's not the price. I am more interested in the color that matches my shoes.

SALESMAN: All right, but we are going to have some more bags in next week. Maybe you'll like some of those.

CUSTOMER: Thanks, I'll wait till then.

SALESMAN: You don't need anything in socks or hosiery today, do you?

CUSTOMER: I do need some socks. What type do you have?

SALESMAN: These socks here are both cotton. One is 99¢ a pair, or two pair for $1.87, and the other one is 79¢ a pair, or two pair for $1.50. However, they are both about the same kind of sock.

CUSTOMER: Fine, I'll take two pair of the 79¢ socks. Thank you for your time.

SALESMAN: You're welcome. It's been a pleasure to serve you. Stop in again.

Questions

1. What should Mr. Greenberg do about his salesman's presentation?
2. What additional sales opportunities were missed?

CHAPTER 7

Making Effective
Demonstrations

Anyone who does a lot of fishing knows that most parts of the lake will be barren; there are only certain spots or very narrow areas in the broad expanse of water in which the fish can be found. Once they have been located, the sportsman must use skill and technique to get them to bite. In selling, we find that most people are not interested in our products. Therefore, we must locate the interested few by qualifying them. When we have found the potential buyers, we must then generate interest in our products. The demonstration is one of the outstanding methods of doing this.

THE WHY OF DEMONSTRATIONS

A demonstration is a test-tube picture of the product in action. It captures the interest of the prospect. It shows him what the product will do, how it will perform, and how it will fit his needs. It backs up the salesman's story and makes it concrete. It informs, teaches, shows, and promotes interest. Because it attracts the audience, a demonstration can do in a few minutes what long explanations might take hours to accomplish.

181

Seller's Viewpoint

When a salesman makes his presentation, it is not how much he talks that counts, but how much the prospect believes. A salesman's statements may not ring true and may raise doubts in the prospect's mind. But if the salesman demonstrates the truth of his statement, the prospect will develop greater trust in him.

For a salesman, the demonstration is an aid to further selling effectiveness; it is not a crutch that can be used instead of effective salesmanship. You can do a better selling job by using a variety of aids to pep up the presentation, to make it sparkle, to make it lively, to make it appealing. Consequently, a top-notch demonstration carefully thought out and presented at the proper time enhances the presentation. Never underestimate the strength of an effective demonstration to regain straying attention.

Buyer's Viewpoint

A buyer recognizes that a demonstration is helpful. However adequate descriptions are, they may not convey the entire meaning or the complete perspective that a buyer wants. However descriptive words may be, they still cannot convey the same impression that a machine in operation does. With potential appeal to sight, sound, touch, taste, and smell, the demonstration leads the buyer towards credibility and conviction.

Most potential buyers will not be antagonistic. They will welcome you because they hope that you have something useful for them. They want to know as much as possible before they decide to buy; demonstrations help them make a decision.

TECHNIQUES OF DEMONSTRATIONS

The salesman who forges ahead is the one who leaves no stone unturned. Nothing is too much trouble if it gets orders. Think of demonstrations not as time-consuming nuisances, but as opportunities to increase your effectiveness. Usually, the more you show and demonstrate, the more you sell.

Excellent demonstrations do not just happen—they are planned and rehearsed. A demonstration must be well done, or it should not be done at all. It should be properly projected to the prospect so that it becomes clear, intelligible, and convincing. You cannot afford a sloppy demonstration. To put on impressive demonstrations, use the latest techniques and tools.

Showmanship

When we use the word "showmanship," we immediately think of an actor on a stage who gesticulates and does vocal acrobatics. Sometimes his words flow in a steady stream; sometimes they are halting, jerky; sometimes low, quiet, earnest. Different moods are suggested through word pace and intonation. All of these effects have one end in view—to stir the audience. The wind blows the branch in many directions, and a professional actor's words and movements bend the audience to his will.

Now let us transfer this thought to that salesman who is most adept in acting, the pitchman. Standing in a store or on the street, he will soon gather a crowd about him by what he says, how he says it, and the interest that he arouses. Like the medicine man of yesterday, he can move people emotionally. To avoid monotony, he talks fast, talks slowly, talks loudly, talks softly. He arouses interest, anticipation, challenge, and desire, and his audience breathlessly listens. Above all, he does not allow enthusiasm to diminish before he sells his goods.

Consider the showmanship of a shoeshine boy. As you sit in his chair, he industriously cleans your shoes and polishes them. If you wish, he will carry on conversation with you. Then, as he finishes the job, he will polish rapidly and snap his rag. Actually, what does the snapping of the rag do towards polishing the shoes? It probably does nothing to the shoes but a lot to your mind. Let us say that you have had your shoes shined two days in a row. One day they were shined by an efficient but silent chap who did his work without fanfare or flourish; the next day they were shined by a pleasant person who chatted with you, put a little showmanship into his shining, snapped the rag vigorously, and made you feel important. Which one got the bigger tip? Now let's go one step further with the shoeshine boy.

In Cleveland, there used to be an outstanding shoeshine boy who would apply polish in a thin layer and rub it off, apply a second layer, a third, a fourth, a fifth—as many as were necessary until he had given you a beautifully polished shoe. He thought nothing of spending 15 minutes or more on shining a pair of shoes. He worked so efficiently and thoroughly that you would not think of leaving him with only a quarter for his job. His shine was superior; so, too, were the tips that his customers gave him.

Include Prospect

Frequently, a demonstration includes action that someone must perform. Whenever possible, bring the prospect into the act. If you are demonstrating machinery or equipment, the buyer will be intrigued by moving handles or pushing levers and seeing wheels turn. He will be fascinated by intricate machinery in motion and by specific operations. In the demonstration, the carpenter will try to saw a board; the fisherman may cast with the reel; the housewife operates the vacuum cleaner or sewing machine; the boy will run the toy train; the prospect drives the car; the office manager runs the duplicating machine; the dentist tries the drill; the mechanic uses the set of tools. If possible, have the prospect perform the entire operation. He will see how the product functions, note its efficiency, and understand its advantages.

When it is not feasible for the prospect to participate in the demonstration or use of the product, paint him into your word picture. Even on the sidelines he can be gratified to visualize himself as the main person in the show.

Avoid having a prospect carry on a demonstration which requires skill without which the demonstration can fail. Not only does failure on his part damage the image of the product, but the humiliation can make him lose face. Embarrassed, he will be eager to get rid of you as quickly as possible. A sale will have become impossible.

A delicate situation can arise in demonstrating a piano. Should the salesperson be able to play the piano well? If the potential buyer plays with confidence, he need not feel inadequate if the salesman also plays. Of course, some customers would have little regard for the salesman who performs poorly. If, on the other hand, the salesman is a superb pianist and demonstrates the piano beautifully, he may embarrass the mediocre pianist who wants a piano just for his own pleasure. In that case, the buyer would be unwilling to sit down and try the piano after he had heard a salesman's brilliant performance. In any demonstration, the primary objective is to make the product look good. If the customer is doing the demonstrating, the product should perform well for him. The better the prospect can tie himself in with the product, the greater are the chances of the salesman making the sale.

Preparing in Advance

One cannot say too much about the importance of advance preparation. A new ship is taken on a shakedown cruise to iron out any weaknesses before it is delivered. Some of us are familiar with the many small problems that arise after moving into a new home. Many unexpected situations may arise when making a demonstration. Therefore, prepare by rehearsing your presentation several times. Not only should the product or equipment be in such good condition that it will work as you expect it to, but it must also look new. Most of all, prepare yourself for the demonstration. The correct words of explanation, the appropriate introductions and follow-up make this much like the production of a play. Every part must fall into place if the finished demonstration succeeds.

Orderly Presentation

Some salesmen do not organize their demonstrations. Each demonstration is given in a different way depending on the efficiency of the salesman. Although some variation may be permissible, too much indicates that a salesman has not grouped the essential features of his demonstration.

Develop a strong and a convincing presentation that applies to the situation. A piano demonstration for a beginner would be quite different from a demonstration for an accomplished pianist. In demonstrating a tractor to a farmer who owns flat land, it would be unnecessary to demonstrate hill-climbing capabilities. If you have a general-purpose product and a specialized product for sale, do not use the same demonstrations for both. A demonstration of a fountain pen for one who writes shorthand all day would be quite different from a demonstration for an occasional user. An orderly presentation must be suited to the needs of the prospect through an approach that he can understand and appreciate.

Your attitude toward your product will help to establish the customer's attitude to it. Handle it carefully as if it were valuable; the prospect will likely do the same. Have you ever noticed a choral director leading an audience in singing? He sings the first verse with strength and fervor, and everybody joins him. He lowers his voice for the second verse. The audience does the same. Notice how the leadership of one is instinctively followed

by others. The same is true in your demonstrations. Merchandise
should be handled and displayed in the manner befitting it.
Beautiful gems on a black velvet background are far more
dramatic than when displayed on a plain counter.

When beginning your demonstration, a part will sometimes
stick. Do not angrily push or jerk, but use a gentle motion to
relieve strain. Carelessly handling beautiful objects or marring
your product through indifferent care is a reflection on your
character. The customer shudders to see a fine product abused,
and he will form a poor opinion of the guilty party. After a
demonstration, replace the equipment in its case as carefully as
you took it out. Again, this shows the customer that you value
your product. If you carelessly thrust it into its container, the
customer will notice this carelessness, and his opinion of you will
be lowered even more. Of course, you should not take valuable
time that could be used for selling in packing your equipment.
There is a difference between rapid but careful handling in
storing and carelessly throwing it together.

Specific instructions cannot be given on how to handle your
product when getting it ready for a demonstration. Undoubtedly,
there are several right ways of doing it, and there are certainly
many wrong ways. But why do something inadequately when only
a bit more effort and thought could make it outstanding? You
cannot afford a poor demonstration.

Condition of Product and Equipment

If the demonstration is to take place in a room or locale of
your choice, the surroundings should be appropriate for your
work. Be sure that your stage setting is impressive. Many a weak
play or actor is tolerated because of the impressive scenery.
Do not hesitate to take advantage of every prop that will enhance
the surroundings and add to the necessary effect.

Can you imagine a customer being asked to try a piano that's
out of tune? If your customer is going to use a handsaw, would
you provide a soft pine board or a knotty oak? If he wants to
use a hammer, will you give him soft wood in which to drive a
nail or hard wood in which he will bend nail after nail? If your
prospect is to watch a demonstration, is the room hot or air-
conditioned, well-lighted or dim, fresh or musty? Go into a salon
in which women are trying on fur garments. You will immediately

notice the elegant surroundings, the thick, soft carpets, the comfortable chairs, the well-groomed attendants, and the attractive decor.

If you are putting on a mechanical demonstration, do you have all necessary items? Are they in working order? Are they entirely suitable for the purpose you have in mind? In some demonstrations, it may be necessary to use a makeshift item, but that is uncalled for if you set up properly in advance. If you are using assistants, be sure that they are properly coached to do the right thing at the right time. When you transport your equipment long distances and use it constantly for demonstration purposes, considerable upkeep is needed. If you neglect it, you may be embarrassed to have equipment fail at a very inopportune moment, or it may look shabby when it should be bright and shiny.

Use Language of Prospect

Use language with which the prospect is familiar. Words are your means of communication. They are not ends in themselves, nor should they be used just to demonstrate ability to speak, vocabulary, or brilliance. During the demonstration, you talk in order to explain and clarify so that the prospect will be convinced of his need for your product. Communicate effectively. Use words that your prospect can understand and appreciate.

Sometimes we forget as we go from one prospect to another that one may be highly trained, another poorly trained; one is a technician, the other a layman. To one buyer, technical language is appropriate; to another, standard English is preferable. One buyer may need a detailed explanation, while another will have been schooled in the processes behind your demonstration. A demonstration that proceeds too quickly for one person may be boring to another. That is why you change your style, your approach, and the way you talk to fit the needs of the particular listener.

Check Frequently With Prospect on Effectiveness of Presentation

Is your presentation getting across? Is the buyer following you? Does he understand what you say? Sometimes you can tell how well an individual understands by looking at him, but do not trust that method too far. The best way to know that your message is clear and your demonstration effective is to check now and then to see if the prospect grasps what you say.

Sometimes the demonstration is so fascinating that the objective is missed entirely. Keep the demonstration a device, not an end. When the prospect enjoys it as an end in itself, it is ineffective. To be sure of its effectiveness, use controlled questions that are pertinent to the effects you are attempting to create. For example, when demonstrating a machine, you can say, "Notice how quietly it operates?" for silent operation. "See how smoothly the gears shift," to illustrate freedom of grinding gears. "Feel how cool it runs?" when you are stressing a cool operation. Use searching questions to find out whether or not the prospect understands the fine points.

If a customer is watching a demonstration that is not pertinent to his work or one which he does not understand, little is accomplished. Thus, it would not prove particularly beneficial for a farmer to watch a tractor demonstration on a crop he does not harvest. Many times we get lost in spectacular demonstrations that show how effective the product is in certain unusual applications, and we forget the prospect's particular needs. You may demonstrate to a farmer how a truck will go over rocks and deep-rutted roads without dragging, but the same demonstration would have little interest to a person who buys a truck for city deliveries.

Appeal to all Senses

While a demonstration frequently appeals to sight, do not forget that we have other senses as well. If you can also appeal to hearing, taste, and smell, your demonstration can be much more effective. You would not want to introduce a new wine to a merchant by having him look at it to appreciate the color; of much more significance would be his reaction to its bouquet and taste.

When appealing to the senses, make the demonstration correspond to the product's actual properties. It is only self-deflating to advertise or to demonstrate falsely. To be of any value to you and the buyer, the demonstration must be realistic and credible. Criticisms have been directed toward certain types of advertisements which always show the young, good-looking, happy housewife, the well-behaved children, the happy and attentive husband.

It would often be more effective to give a down-to-earth impression of what life is like to make the appeal realistic. Advertising can also illustrate situations so unrealistic that the prospect realizes such events seldom if ever happen. The housewife knows there is no detergent she can add to her washing that will make very dirty white clothes come out spotlessly clean. She realizes she will have to scrub some spots by hand and also use bleach to get the natural white back. You can go overboard by stressing excessively the good or the bad qualities of something.

Reaching the prospect in as many ways and appeals as possible can insure a better presentation. A parachute jumper usually has an emergency chute as well as his main one. If the first fails to open, the second one should save the jumper. By appealing to a person in a variety of ways, some one of them may be more effective than others. It is quite possible that what you consider the most minor appeal may be the motivating force.

Occasionally, you can use an appeal which is intriguing even though it is not directly connected with the product. Sometimes, a man who sells a product which has no personal appeal to an individual may carry some interesting object which he shows to the customer by way of introduction. It can open the conversation and create interest which can then be turned to the item that is for sale.

Tests

There are so many ways of testing products that one could devise dozens of ways to demonstrate particular features or points. Consider the taste test. You can test a product to see if it is sweet or sour. You can test it to see if it is fresh or old. Your taste tells you if it is too strong or too weak. You can tell if it is cooked enough or not enough. You can tell if it is well-done or rare. Many products have been successful because they have been changed until the taste appeals. On the other hand, tastes are acquired more than they are inherited; thus, a product that we once disliked may be acceptable after we become used to it.

One well-known beverage company which had established itself in the consumer market was forced by law to change its drink's basic ingredients. The new mixture produced a different taste, and sales went down alarmingly. Then a taste expert was called in, and he developed the beverage so that the taste was practically identical to the original one even though the ingredients differed. Sales improved remarkably.

When we speak of taste, we must also consider lack of taste. Some products are better when they have no taste whatsoever. This is particularly true of medicines which may be bitter or sour. Some foods must have their original taste tempered before they appeal. In some liquid products, the vehicle which furnishes the bulk is tasteless. The taste is furnished by the active ingredients.

Adding the right perfume to a product enhances its receptivity. Anyone who has lived or worked near a bakery recalls the delightful odors that permeate the air around it. Anyone living next to a restaurant may remember or can vividly smell delicious foods cooking and the tantalizing aroma. Anyone who has lived in a town which has paper mills or canneries also remembers the revolting odors. The sense of smell can arouse pleasant or revolting associations. Some products (natural gas, for example), are deliberately impregnated with certain materials which make them offensive. Leaks can easily be detected. In other cases, offensive odors are added to discourage youngsters and animals from using the products.

What a tremendous influence the sense of feel has in testing! You feel the roughness of sandpaper, the sharp pricks of briar, the heat of the sun, the coolness of ice. Some of these may be sensations, yet we call them feelings. You can feel the texture of cloth, the smooth skin of an apple. With our hands, we can feel hardness, softness, resistance, resilience, flexibility, a wavy surface, an unyielding surface, a firm object, hard ice, cold ice, slushy ice, dry ice. In each case, the sense of touch has given us a new image and a new association.

Tests that appeal to the eye and to the ear are legion. Testing a musical instrument for tone, testing a car for quietness of operation, testing an electric fan for sound are all illustrative. Even testing a new home or apartment to see if the noise outside is distracting is not uncommon. Many tests are effective because you see them in operation. Often, tests which are simple and easy to make can bring out the outstanding characteristics that appeal to eyes and ears.

Tests can be physical, chemical, and mental. Go into a store and test two lawn chairs. One sells for $5, the other for $10. As you sit in each one, you notice that the $10 one is more springy, has greater resiliency, and has heavier steel components. You can readily see and feel what accounts for the difference in price. Fastness in color can be tested by exposure to the sun and by washing. High-speed tools may be tested under various conditions of use. A drawer in a piece of furniture can be tested for strength by pulling it out partway and standing on it. Resistance of a tabletop to liquor stains and burns can be tested by pouring various types of liquors and placing lighted cigarettes on its surface. The seaworthiness of a small boat can be checked by taking it out on stormy waters. You can try out the beagle hound to see whether or not he can bring a rabbit around. Can the pointer point a bird? Can the retriever bring the bird?

You can test a machine by operating it in a pilot plant. To see if the pumpkin pie is baked, the cook inserts and then withdraws a fork to see if anything adheres to the prongs. You can test for color by comparison with a standard color. When you are demonstrating the margin of safety, point out that it is twice as safe as it needs to be. Demonstrating the strength of cloth, you can point out that it is twice as strong as it needs to be. On the other hand, when using a solution for washing, you can point out that the strength of the cleansing material is just right, neither too strong nor too weak.

Tests should be appropriate for the product. Many of us have seen spectacular tests which have little relationship to the product. It is hard to justify the high price of a particular article even though its construction is unusually good. You might buy one item at $5, and 99 percent of the time it will be adequate. It is questionable whether you would want to pay $10 for an item that is 100 percent adequate. If one item costs $1,000 and a similar one costs $10,000, you might gladly settle for the $1,000 item even though it is only 50 percent accurate, while the other is 90 percent accurate. Increased accuracy might not be worth the increased price. On the other hand, in filling a prescription for medicine, one would be particularly interested in having exact measures.

Tests should not only be appropriate, they should also be sensible. Your product may be suitable and highly accurate under normal conditions of use, but when it is subjected to unusual stress, it might be inadequate. There is an amusing anecdote about a boy who was especially hard on his clothing and toys.

Finally, he was given an unbreakable doll. Immediately, he went outside, got a hammer and smashed the doll; he had proved that it was not unbreakable. Because he wore the seat of his trousers out rapidly, his mother bought him fine, long-wearing corduroy trousers. Of course, they did not last long when he sat down on a revolving grindstone.

Do not expose your product to tests which unnecessarily reveal weaknesses. In one instance, a salesman told a prospect that his firm used cast iron in the construction of their school furniture to give it strength. A competing salesman came along and pointed out that cast iron, after all, is not very good material for making a school desk. To prove it, he hit it with a hammer. The iron broke.

In a demonstration of a water softener it was shown that a small amount of soap in hard water was not nearly as effective as the same amount of soap in soft water. Garden seeds are tested for germination. The most painstaking and carefully conducted tests are those of new pharmaceutical products. Such tests may continue for years before the value or worthlessness of the product is demonstrated. Incidentally, the battery of tests used for various pharmaceuticals can also be valuable selling ammunition when presented to doctors. The reputable firm that has used a long list of tests on a product before its introduction gives confidence to the practicing physician or veterinarian.

Leaving a product at a home, an office, or a factory for a trial is really a testing period. Frequently, however, supervision is needed to carry out the test under suitable conditions for which the product was constructed. Improper testing procedures may do a lot of harm.

Making Intangibles Real

How can you demonstrate intangibles? Most salesmen feel that the best way is to paint word pictures. Many intangibles have some tangible features connected with them. In selling stock, the prospect may be intrigued by an impressively designed certificate. Why else are stock certificates beautifully engraved (as are many other financial documents), unless to promote faith in the corporation? An unusual order blank can be a form of demonstration. As you fill it out, the customer is intrigued to see you put in measurements, draw in designs, or make special alterations. Blueprints and designs may also be used as a dramatic demonstration. Since it is difficult for many people to reason or think in the abstract, try to associate abstractions with some concrete realities. If you are selling fire insurance, take the prospect to a burned home and show him how the insured rebuilt his home from the proceeds of insurance. If you are selling liability insurance on a car and someone is hesitant, you might take him to a customer who has had occasion to use it. If you are selling life insurance, you might call on a widow with several children who has been the beneficiary of a policy you sold. She could give an eloquent testimony of the value of life insurance.

"Take the bus and leave the driving to us," is a type of testing —the slogan type, which is quite descriptive and brings vivid thoughts to mind. Laundries have imaginative ways of portraying advantages in selling diaper service, shirt service, and linen service. They can show the time you save by using their service. They can show the money savings by using their clothing and linens. By using their diaper service, you have no collection of diapers left when the need disappears. Financial institutions selling savings picture contented people enjoying the benefits of a vacation or retirement. In demonstrating a service or an intangible in which no particular product is involved, put the prospect into your word picture so that he can feel a tangible result.

Many people are thing-conscious. Because they fail to respond to abstract ideas, you must translate abstractions into tangible things. Ask any child what God looks like, and probably he will think in terms of some old man or of someone who looks like Santa Claus. When you say that God is a spirit, it becomes very difficult for the child to visualize what a spirit is. The same might be said for many adults. If the product you are selling is something you cannot see, hear, touch, or taste, it helps if you can draw a comparison with something physical.

The main essential of any demonstration technique is to bring the product or service alive for the prospect. It should make him understand its value and show him how its unique qualities fit into his work or leisure. In a sense, the demonstration is a pilot plan of operation for the real thing. The demonstration should give a prospect a taste of what will happen if he buys the product. It should give him an idea of how the product can be used and how it can make life more meaningful or more enjoyable.

TOOLS OF DEMONSTRATION

There are four ingredients of a successful demonstration. You must have a salesman to make the demonstration, a prospect who listens to and watches the demonstration, tools for demonstrating, and the methods of using the tools. Let us consider the various tools and devices available.

Product

The product is the best tool to use in the demonstration. There can be exceptions, of course; when a product is so complicated or technical that it would be better to have other devices that are simpler and more understandable, use them to demonstrate the action. But when an individual sees the product, observes it, studies it closely, sees how it operates, sees strong points, what can be done with it, and what ought not to be done with it, he gains a strong impression of it. Likewise, it becomes easy to bring him into the demonstration because he can actually handle and use the product. His first clumsy attempts will soon be superseded by more skillful ones. Once he buys the product, he will be able to use it because of what he learned during the demonstration. When he sees the care with which his salesman handles the product, he becomes impressed and tends to do likewise when he purchases it. Often, when we get a new item, we are inclined not to read the directions carefully enough, to skip over some portions of the guarantee, to be careless in reading about maintenance provisions. But if all of these factors have been explained in demonstration, the prospect will remember them. When the item is delivered, he will be ready to reread the information so that he knows exactly how it should be handled.

Rarely do you sell the buyer the demonstrator. Both of you know that it may have been subjected to severe strain. It may be slightly worn, or it may have suffered some mistreatment. Although the demonstration is carried out beautifully, the customer wants a new item when he signs the order. There are some exceptions to this, however; if the demonstrator is the last item available, the buyer will get it. If he needs it immediately, he may be obliged to accept it. When there may be a considerable price differential, he may be delighted to settle for the lower-priced demonstrator. Or, on further discussion with the prospect, you may learn that his need for this item is rather small. In that case, you may suggest that he purchase used equipment which will serve him as well as the new and probably at half the price. Many buyers benefit materially in price reductions by taking the demonstrator rather than an unused model.

Model

A model is usually a small imitation of the real thing. It is far easier to demonstrate a large and cumbersome item with a model than it would be to use the item itself. Usually, models are exact copies of the original equipment on a small scale. Demonstrating with models enables you to give the buyer a clear picture of how a machine or other piece of equipment operates and what its characteristics are. He can see it, handle it, and operate it himself; by doing these things, he gains greater confidence in the product and in his ability to use it. Models must be carefully constructed to take the abuse of the demonstration and still function properly time and again.

Today, when miniaturization has become so common in the electronic field, it is difficult to see how a tiny unit functions. In that case, a model can be built on a larger scale than the original to illustrate its functions. In biology, medicine, and related fields, many of the objects and natural phenomena that technicians deal with are so small that it would be impossible to study them intensively if models were not made of them.

Pictures

Excellent information can be passed on through the use of pictures, photographs, and drawings. A series of illustrations can be used to show the entire product, separate features of it, or any number of views from the top, side, bottom, or edges. Pictures can be used to demonstrate the product because they can show a variety of uses of the same object. Since you and your prospects are so familiar with the use of pictures, illustrations of this nature can be highly effective. Most of us who thumb through catalogs have little difficulty in applying the pictures to our daily lives.

Avoid the use of illustrative material which has become soiled, torn, or dog-eared. When illustrations show signs of wear and discoloration, replace them. Usually, there is no great difficulty in obtaining reproductions to bring freshness to your demonstration.

Overlay

The overlay may be used as a series of transparencies in a loose-leaf binder. The first transparency, for example, may represent the base of a machine. After you and your prospect have studied it thoroughly, then put the next overlay over the base. When you fit the second transparency over the first, a significant new part will be added, and its functions can be easily explained. Then put a third overlay on, and a fourth, and a fifth until at last you have the machine completely pictured. This permits you to study any portion of the equipment separately, in conjunction with any other part, or in relation to the entire unit. When a product lends itself to this presentation, it is most effective. Advantages are simple to demonstrate, not too expensive, and reproductions are easily made.

Display Boards

When demonstrating, a salesman is a teacher. Effective teachers frequently use a chalkboard. Most of us are so familiar with this device that no explanation is needed. Salesmen who have learned to use chalkboards effectively may have a decided advantage in demonstrating how a particular machine works or fits into the prospect's needs. Interesting demonstrations can sometimes use magnetic boards on which objects like model automobiles are attached and moved about freely to illustrate particular points. To make an orderly, step-like presentation, fasten a series of pictures or objects on a cork board or a bulletin board. There are other types of display boards such as the one on which you can attach a heavy object by pressing against a special surface, feltboards to which rough-backed illustrations will cling, and others.

Charts

A variety of charts may be used for demonstration purposes. One of the best-known types is the flip chart. This consists of a series of illustrations in which the salesman can start with the first chart and, after describing the items on it, turn it over on an easel to reveal the next chart. He then describes that one, turns it over, and continues through the series. As he explains the charts, he can use the chalkboard as a supplement, and he can pass out models and samples to heighten interest.

A variety of illustrations may be used in charts. Some are carefully made and reproduced to show an exact operation or present information. Some charts may be handmade to suit the needs of the particular demonstration. A handmade series may be varied from time to time as occasion demands. A third type seems to be handmade in a bold fashion, but it is very skillfully constructed. While the chart may seem to be crudely drawn, this is actually not true at all; it is skillfully done to stimulate this impression.

Charts may be constructed on a variety of materials and may be folded, rolled, or assembled in pieces. They may be in black and white or color; they may be large or small, bold or subdued, extravagantly designed or simple. They can be made in any way as long as the purposes of the chart are not forgotten; it should impress and enlighten.

Graphs

Graphs are a particular type of illustration which can convey certain messages. The common graphs are line graphs, bar graphs (both horizontal and vertical), component bar graphs, and pictographs. The last-mentioned graph pictures actual objects for illustrative purposes. To keep symmetry and proportion, graphs are frequently drawn on a grid which may be lightly drawn in and later erased. Charts may be drawn to scale. Charts on semilogarithmic paper are quite descriptive but must be used with caution since the ordinary layman can easily misunderstand them. We mention them here because they are excellent ways for demonstrating particular ideas when you are dealing with people who are well-versed in sales techniques. Care should be used in constructing and interpreting graphs. They can be tremendously effective, but they also can deceive the customer.

Posters

Posters usually are a series of pictures or illustrations either on soft paper or on stiff board. They are often made in a series and can be shown one after the other; even better, they can be set up in array, side by side, one above the other, or in some such arrangement so that the whole group, taken together, conveys one impression. Using posters all displayed at once, the salesman can go from one to the other as he carries out his demonstration.

The salesman who has a large number of posters available can use them all to convey a message, or he can select certain ones to bring out vivid impressions or convey precise ideas. He is able to segment his presentation by dwelling on certain posters and omitting others.

Kits

"Kit" refers to a number of illustrations and devices which may be used in a demonstration. A kit might be a group of specimens, objects, or samples. It can be a combination of objects and printed matter. It may be samples plus cutaway models. A man who sells canned soups may have several thermos bottles of various soups which the customer can taste. If he sells juices, he can have several thermos bottles of different juices available. A salesman can have a first-aid kit as a sample. The salesman with cleaning fluids and brushes would have small bottles of fluids, soaps, and detergents together with assorted brushes. This material could be used to demonstrate in the buyer's home, office, or factory. The imaginative salesman should be able to think up many types of kits or many products which he might have in a kit to carry the message of his product.

A "kit" often refers to the item itself and not just a sample or miniature model. Think, for example, of the tool kit, fishing kit, medicine kit, and the vacuum cleaner kit which consists of the vacuum cleaner plus its attachments. Another use of the kit refers to partially assembled components which the buyer puts together. This is the case with radio kits, television kits, toy automobile and airplane kits, sailboat kits and, now, even an electric organ kit.

Portfolios

A portfolio is a case that resembles a large book cover. It might be a paper folder or one made of more durable material. It can be small or large. If you wish to create a good impression, you might have one made of beautiful leather or, if that is too expensive, plastic. The man who sells advertising can use a portfolio to carry illustrations of subject matter. He may include a variety of advertising materials and pictures and, perhaps, even premium suggestions. The portfolio is useful in showing previous advertising campaigns, and it is convenient in selling intangibles.

The insurance man, for example, will find it most helpful as he gives vivid descriptions of the various plans he has available. The salesman of securities finds a portfolio an excellent means of assisting him in presenting his material. The individual selling cemetery lots may find a portfolio of color illustrations quite helpful.

Catalog

A catalog is usually considered more of a reference volume than a tool for demonstration. Yet, a catalog can be an excellent demonstration tool. A large catalog is an impressive means of demonstrating the size of your assortment and the volume of items you carry. It gives you readily available illustrations and descriptions of most of the items, and you can immediately turn to the right page. Catalogs can be large or small, loose-leaf, or bound. In constructing a catalog, use a standard size such as 8½ by 11 inches. If you leave supplements with a prospect, he will be able to file them more easily than if your loose-leaf is an odd size. The catalog, like any other tool of demonstration, should be clean, current, and accessible.

Samples

Samples are one of the best ways of demonstrating a product. Samples of food give the prospect an excellent idea of quality, taste, size, and color. Samples of laboratory equipment are used to indicate table construction, corner construction, gluing construction, acid-resistant construction, types of material used, and how the product will react under use. The house-to-house salesman finds samples one of the best ways to introduce a product. Proof exists that if a prospect has been sampled once, he is more likely to buy that product than if the appeals are directed only through advertising. Giving merchandise on a trial basis is really sampling. Over a period of time, the prospect can determine what the article will do for him. Many samples are small amounts of the product which the prospect can use. Other samples merely illustrate the actual product. For example, a calendar salesman leaves a sample calendar which shows how your advertisement would appear if you bought his calendars to pass out to your customers. Previews of movies are samples as are book reviews and outlines.

Visual and Sound Aids

Motion pictures, slides, projectors, phonographs, tape recorders, and other audio-visual devices are useful in conducting demonstrations. The motion picture is a continuous demonstration and represents the best visual aid available. Skilled actors can dramatize and carry out impressive techniques. Slides are particularly useful because the rate of presentation can be controlled. If a slide demonstration is accompanied by a tape recording or a phonograph record, the slide must be changed as indicated by the words on the sound track. Many times, however, salesmen use slides and furnish the explanations themselves. In that case, they can go as rapidly or as slowly as the situation warrants and can vary the length of time for each slide. Additional explanations can be used to clear up particularly knotty points.

The variety of projectors available for slides, charts, graphs, and printed material is a great aid to the salesman. The availability of slide projectors, opaque projectors, micro-projectors, overhead projectors, and the use of walls, screens, and even tiny screens carried by the salesman in a box, permit enough variety to meet specific needs.

The problems of using visual and sound aids require careful attention. You can give demonstrations by using standard-size components; you can enlarge or shrink the size of them. A variety of presentations can be used to demonstrate uses under particular conditions. The addition of color has made visual aids far more effective. Every year new and improved demonstration equipment is introduced. There is a wide variety of small self-contained kits which the salesman may choose in preparing his material and in making the demonstration. Previously dependent on power or electricity at the prospect's office or home, the salesman now has been freed of this obligation by using transistorized equipment, thus increasing the demonstration's flexibility of place and time. Every salesman should explore possibilities of using these various types of equipment.

HANDLING A DEMONSTRATION

To get the most out of a demonstration, be sure that you handle it properly. Attention to detail in advance insures a far better demonstration. A superior demonstration can increase sales; a weak one can decrease them.

Product Features

Your product usually has a number of features superior to those of competing products. All these features, however, will not lend themselves well to demonstration. Some are so unimportant that demonstration of them is not warranted. Others are of such a nature that a demonstration will not be convincing. That leaves, then, only a few features—perhaps one, two, or three which merit demonstrating.

A carefully worked out presentation proceeds step by step toward an ultimate goal. If only one feature is to be demonstrated, it might be well to use it and then try to close immediately. If more than one feature is to be demonstrated, you might demonstrate one immediately after the other; or, you may intersperse feature demonstrations throughout the presentation. If the presentation is long, it is often best to interweave demonstrations to hold interest.

If it is difficult for you to interest the prospect, a carefully worked out demonstration may help. You should neither use selling ammunition wastefully (you might run out before the sale is finished), nor should you give so grudgingly that your talk drags on only to have the prospect terminate the interview long before you have used your best arguments. If you are too slow, you may not even get a chance to make a demonstration; or, if you do get the chance, you might have bored the prospect into inattentiveness.

Particular features of your product which may be interesting to one prospect may have little appeal to another. Thus, there is no need to demonstrate the high-speed potential of a car to an older person who drives conservatively. Neither is it necessary to demonstrate the tremendous get-up and go of a powerful outboard motor that is used primarily for water skiing to one who is solely interested in fishing. The small farmer is not much interested in knowing that three, or four, or five plows can be pulled by a tractor if he is concerned essentially with the motor's economical operation. In other words, demonstrating features which have little or no application to the prospect is wasteful. It is difficult for a salesman not to demonstrate all outstanding features of his product. Yet, he must refrain from doing so if some features have little application for the individual. The buyer's interest, not the salesman's, must always be foremost.

An Aid in Convincing Prospects

Carefully handled demonstrations help to convince prospects. When demonstrating before a group of buyers or a committee, the interchange of opinions among the buying group and the information volunteered by the salesman as he conducts his demonstration provide an interesting, informative conversation that develops depth of understanding for each member of the group. Questions arise and are answered. New ideas are evoked which focus on the product in new ways.

One might compare a demonstration before a group of people to a many-faceted diamond. As the diamond is rotated, each facet sparkles and emits a glow. In a demonstration, each member contributes either by his knowledge or lack of it. Try this procedure: First, make a demonstration to a member of a committee and record all the questions he asks. Repeat the process with each member of the buying group, recording the information that is requested and the questions which arise. Finally, repeat the demonstration again to the entire group. Up to this time, no member of the group has seen the demonstration more than once. It may be old and repetitious to you, but to the buying group it will merely be a second going-over. Notice how many new questions arise because of the interplay among the group. Take another group which is buying a similar product under similar conditions. This group has never had a demonstration. Record all the questions the members ask. Then compare this information with the information you received from questioning and demonstrating before the members of the first group. Notice the vast difference in effect and results. A large number of people who are thing-oriented understand concrete illustrations but have difficulty grasping abstract ideas. Such people find that demonstrations are compatible with their line of thinking and that demonstrations help to convince them of the merits of the product.

An Interest Device

Have you ever gone hunting? If you have, you know that you can walk through fields and woods and see nothing. You can pass innumerable kinds of game but, if they sit motionless, you pass by them without seeing. But let one move a fraction of an inch. Instantly, your eye is riveted to him, and you are ready to shoot. Whether hunted by man or other animals, most animals escape with their lives because they remain motionless and go undetected. Think of this when conducting a demonstration. When you tell your story, you are painting a word picture without action. The listener may be following you, but he will not hear all that you say. If he is vitally interested, he could get 90 percent of what you say; if he is partially interested, half of what you say might register. If he is only casually interested, it is likely that 75 percent of your conversation is wasted.

Careful observation during your presentation will reveal this lack of interest. If, when interest wanes, you can bring in an interesting demonstration, you will notice at once that the attention of the individual becomes riveted to what you do. From minor attention he develops strong attention coupled with interest. The demonstration adds action to words. It is something different; it tells him something he has not known and has never seen. His attention is glued to what you are doing. If it carries sufficient interest, he will follow you throughout. Not only will he follow you, but soon he will ask questions. His hands will reach out to participate. Hand him the control; he will seize it eagerly; under your direction, he can manipulate it effectively.

For the first time, he has become a part of the sales picture—a vital, dynamic, useful, necessary part. He feels it, and he does his best to make the demonstration a success. To him, it is no longer a demonstration. It becomes the real thing—the real operation of a particular piece of equipment—an operation he is guiding successfully. He has chained himself willingly to a series of events which should culminate with a successful conclusion as he demonstrates the worth of the product. The prospect becomes emotionally involved. With an unrestrained air of enthusiasm, he is caught up in the contagion of the moment. Both of you are sweeping forward in a successful venture. He cannot fail because you have arranged the demonstration so that it is bound to succeed. This is not an artificial situation. The prospect is using the product as it ought to function for him in his work, enabling him to perform better, to be more successful, and to achieve greater satisfaction.

Entertaining

If the product that you are demonstrating lends itself to entertainment, be sure to use this feature to the utmost. In demonstrating a musical instrument, it is far better to play a selection that is interesting to the customer than to play a series of notes and chords. Successful music teachers today start their pupils on simple songs to arouse their students' interest. Because dance lessons can be monotonous hard work, dance instructors lighten the series of lessons by having group dancing. This adds recreation to work, and it allows the individuals to practice what they have learned.

When demonstrating features of a game, try to have individuals participate in it. After a cooking or sewing demonstration, the ladies in the audience are often entertained with a luncheon, style show, or music. In conducting a group demonstration, the clever salesman can so involve the people that they have a delightful time. Possibly, one reason why the home or party demonstration is successful in selling housewives is that it furnishes an evening of entertainment. It may be the housewife's only opportunity to get out that week. She has fun and food, and the total cost is the purchase price of one or two items which she can take home.

Do Not Let the Demonstration Drag

Timing is important in making your presentation and demonstration. When timing your demonstration for an individual, set your pace so that he follows you readily. In timing for a group, it becomes more difficult to determine how fast to go. Timing also depends on how important each individual of the group is in the buying picture. Unless you feel that certain people reacting slowly are relatively unimportant, it is wise to go slowly enough so that these people get a fairly good grasp of your demonstration. The average individual will detect a bit of dragging, but it will not bother him too much. A few may become bored, yet they will get the message.

You can point out before making your demonstration that it has been your experience that in any group there are always some who grasp what you say and do faster than others, but that the ones who grasp information readily in one part have difficulty understanding another part. Consequently, to be sure that you are not offending anyone, you probably will go a little more slowly than necessary so that all will be able to grasp what you are saying. This is merely an easy way of telling those who catch on quickly that you want your demonstration to apply to everyone in the group.

Many times, the speed of a demonstration is determined by the equipment. In that case, the speed of operation is determined in advance and is beyond your control during the demonstration itself. Your only control is to repeat it. If you sense that you are boring some and it is not within your power to speed up, heighten interest by introducing additional interesting observations. Many of you remember that in grade school some students seemed hardly ever to study and yet they got their lessons; others worked all the time and still did not get their lessons. In high school, the same was true—some worked very little or hardly at all and they got by. Others were plodding along learning with difficulty. But those who went on to college soon found that there was enough material in any course to challenge the ability of any student. There was always so much additional material available, so much additional reading to do, and so many interesting areas to explore that no matter how bright the student, he could still keep busy learning more and more about the subject.

You can have on hand interesting sets of facts or figures, illustrative material, and a mass of helpful data that will keep the rapid learner busy. Then the slowest member will have time enough to grasp your demonstration, and the rapid learner will gain much additional information without being bored.

Before making a demonstration, you can explain to the group what is about to transpire, what are the main events, and what some of the less significant ones will be. You hope that the one who is slow will grasp the main effects; others can occupy themselves not only with the main effects, but with as many side effects as they can. Preparing in advance will enable you to provide sufficient information during the demonstration to hold the interest of all the persons, whatever their range of ability.

Do Not Let the Demonstration Substitute for Good Selling

Some men put talcum powder on their faces so that they do not have to shave twice in one day. Some people use powder or perfume instead of taking a bath. Some people think that cramming for tests is a substitute for regular study. All of us recognize the many makeshifts that are used in every phase of life. We resent such behavior because we know that substitutes are seldom as satisfactory as the real things. There is nothing wrong with using talcum powder after shaving, or powder or perfume after bathing, but it is totally inadequate to use them to cover sins of omission. The salesman who substitutes devices, gadgets, tricks, and hocus-pocus for top-notch selling will be disappointed. If he thinks that a good demonstration will make a sale, he is wrong. If he thinks that a good demonstration will help to make a sale, he is right.

Although the sales presentation with its various techniques, ideas, and interests may result in a brilliant performance, we should never overlook the powers of an effective demonstration. In many cases, the demonstration is the dominating influence. It is the clincher that makes the sale. Many times, the sale could not be made without a demonstration.

In most instances, depending on the demonstration alone to make the sale is dangerous. The skillful golfer has a bag full of clubs. Each club has a specific purpose, and no outstanding golfer would depend on one club for his different shots. If you were to ask him which clubs to use, he probably would make a number of suggestions. After he saw you play, he certainly could make additional ones. In the end he would say, "Use the club that serves you best in any particular situation." The demonstration is like a particular golf club. Most salesmen find that it has a specific place and a specific use. Yet, that does not mean that you cannot change its use or experiment with it or occasionally substitute it for another sales tool as the golfer might substitute one club for another under particular circumstances. This indicates versatility, open-mindedness, ability to assess a particular situation, creativeness at the moment, and often expediency.

A final word on the demonstration—learn to use it brilliantly. Make your product come alive, stand out in the buyer's mind, and kindle his enthusiasm. In a demonstration, you can be dynamic because you are doing several things at once. You have a chance to show yourself at your best. You have a chance to shine as an individual; be spirited, eager, authoritative, confident. Here is a chance for you to master the situation, to control the interview, to dominate the group, and to show your strength. You can dazzle the intellect by painting vivid word pictures while your hands carry on the work of the demonstration. If the prospect participates, you can tie him to it so firmly, so graciously, so commandingly, so realistically, that—at the end—there is only one appropriate path to follow: he must purchase the product.

QUESTIONS AND PROBLEMS

1. What is an effective demonstration? What do you seek to accomplish by a demonstration?
2. When is a demonstration an effective selling tool? Are there any dangers in using demonstrations?
3. Show how a demonstration can convince a buyer that he needs your product.
4. Is there a difference between showmanship and enthusiasm in making a demonstration?
5. When you tie the prospect in with the demonstration, the results can be spectacular. Describe what happens to the prospect in this situation.
6. What are the dangers of using the prospect in a demonstration?
7. Is it essential that you plan your demonstration?
8. Why is it important to inspect your product and equipment carefully before a demonstration?
9. Why is it important to describe the demonstration in the language of the prospect?
10. The demonstration should be meaningful in the eyes of the prospect. How is this approach frequently violated?
11. Are all five senses equally important in appealing to a buyer? If not, why do we bother diversifying appeals?
12. Describe ten ways of using tests in demonstrating.
13. A test may be spectacular but not convincing. Why?
14. Why do salesmen use tests that expose weaknesses of their product?
15. How can a demonstration lend reality to the sale of an intangible?
16. Show how you can illustrate an abstract principle by a concrete demonstration.
17. Demonstrations are conducted with real objects. In most situations the product itself is the best object to use. Why?
18. Under what conditions would you not use the product in demonstrating?
19. What is a model? What are the advantages of using a model in demonstration?
20. Describe the proper use of pictures in a demonstration.
21. Illustrate effective uses of the overlay.

22. Describe the use of display boards in conveying a sales message.
23. Explain the use of charts in a demonstration. How may effective charts be constructed?
24. Describe some of the advantages and some of the dangers involved in the use of graphs.
25. How can posters be used effectively?
26. Illustrate a number of ways of using kits. What are some of the dangers of using kits?
27. Portfolios are used by some salesmen to convey messages. In what type of selling are they useful?
28. What are the advantages of using catalogs in demonstrating? Is a catalog really a demonstration tool?
29. Elaborate on the use of samples as a demonstration tool. Illustrate several approaches.
30. Discuss the uses of visual and sound equipment in demonstrations. Point out one effective use of each type of equipment.
31. Unless a demonstration is interesting it has little effect. Why is the interest factor of the prospect so vital?
32. Why is it desirable to introduce the element of entertainment in a demonstration?
33. The speed of the demonstration must suit the audience. If there are several prospects, how can you set your speed to accommodate all of them?
34. What is the danger in depending too heavily on a good demonstration?
35. Why is it imperative to handle a demonstration skillfully?

CASES

7-1: WINOTAN SCHOOL BOARD

The members of the Winotan School Board had just seated themselves in the boardroom at 8 p.m. Tom Carter of the Visuo Company had just arrived to give a demonstration of a Visuo Model No. 21 projector.

A month before, Tom had called on the school superintendent, Anton Fraser, to sell his new projector. Mr. Fraser showed interest and followed carefully Tom's presentation. Tom offered a demonstration to Fraser at that time, but Fraser declined. He told Tom he had seen the projector in use previously and liked it. Since this projector sold for $550, Mr. Fraser was hesitant about placing an order until the School Board had seen it and were willing to approve its purchase. If the Board found the projector satisfactory, they probably would order two. Mr. Fraser arranged to have Tom demonstrate the projector to the Board members a month later at 8 p.m.

Tom had finished his last call at 5:30 in Pierson, a town ten miles from Winotan. Since his demonstration was at eight that evening, Tom decided on a leisurely dinner at Halfmoon House, a well-known restaurant on the outskirts of Pierson. He drove to the restaurant and sat down to dinner at 6 p.m. At 7 p.m. he left the restaurant to drive to Winotan. When he got to his car, he saw he had a flat tire. Fortunately, there was a gasoline station a block away, and Tom was able to get a man to repair his tire. Unfortunately, his spare was flat so he couldn't just change tires. By the time his tire was repaired, it was 7:30. Tom drove hurriedly to Winotan. On the way, he was held up at a railroad crossing by a long freight train. Tom managed to get to the meeting just at eight.

Mr. Fraser introduced Tom Carter to the School Board members. He explained that Mr. Carter was a salesman for the Visuo Company. Mr. Fraser mentioned that since they had discussed various projectors at several meetings, he had invited Mr. Carter to demonstrate his projector this evening. Then, turning to Tom, Mr. Fraser said, "The meeting is yours, Mr. Carter."

Mr. Carter thanked Superintendent Fraser and the Board for permitting him to give the demonstration. Then he spent 15 minutes explaining his projector to the Board. He mentioned several unusual features of his machine which made it far superior to any other machine on the market. After his presentation, he asked the Board's indulgence while he set up his equipment. Since he had hurried in at the last minute, he had not even unloaded his equipment.

Tom went out to his car and brought in his equipment. He looked around the room and saw that he would have to place his projector in the back of the room. He looked around for a suitable table for his projector but found none. So he asked Mr. Fraser if he could borrow a table. Obligingly, Mr. Fraser went looking for a table accompanied by Tom. They found a suitable table in a room down the corridor. The two carried the table back, and Tom set up his projector.

Schools usually have projector screens either on the walls or on tripods. Tom had never had any trouble getting one before, so he had not brought his own along. Unfortunately, there was no screen in the boardroom; Tom asked Mr. Fraser if he could locate a screen. The two of them went to the equipment room. Fortunately, Mr. Fraser had a key to the room. Tom found a suitable screen. He returned to the boardroom and set up the screen in the front of the room. Finally, Tom was ready to begin.

He looked for the wall receptacle to plug in the cord. Most rooms have receptacles in both the front and back of the room. But in this room there was none in the rear. Since Tom did not have an extension cord long enough to reach the front, he was forced to ask Mr. Fraser for one. Visibly irritated, Mr. Fraser went to the equipment room and came back with an extension cord. Finally, Tom was ready for the demonstration. It was now 8:45 p.m.

Tom switched on his machine and began his demonstration. He showed several slides, explaining features as he demonstrated. The machine brought out each slide beautifully, too well in fact because some of the slides were dirty, and the dirt showed up clearly. Tom apologized for the dirty slides. He said he had used them the night before and had not had time to clean them.

The tension created by the difficulties of setting up the equipment had eased, and except for some dirty slides, everything was going smoothly.

Finally Tom said, "I have reserved a few outstanding slides to demonstrate two particular features of this machine which are unique." Then he attached a piece of equipment and turned on the projector. It lit up for a moment and then went out. A tube had blown out. Hurriedly, Tom took off the top of the machine and removed the tube. Then he reached for the spare tube. It was not in the case. "Sorry, folks, I'll have to step out to the car a moment to get another tube."

Tom dashed out to the car, rummaged around in a bag, and soon found the other tube. He hurried in, inserted the tube, closed the machine, and snapped the switch. Nothing happened. Then Tom remembered. Last night he had burned out a tube and had used the spare. He had dropped the old tube in the bag, fully intending to stop at a store to get a new tube the next morning. But his morning had been busy with appointments, and he had forgotten to get a new tube.

Questions

1. What should Tom do now?
2. How many mistakes did Tom make?
3. How can you meet unexpected contingencies?
4. Can Tom make the sale?

7-2: THE GREEN CROSS SALES CASE

A state-wide Green Cross plan was organized in 1939. Since that time, it has grown to a dominant position in the field of hospitalization insurance. In 1955, slightly more than 50 percent of the residents of the state were covered by Green Cross. Virtually all of the insured subscribed through their place of employment, i.e., they had group coverage. In the early 1950's, commercial insurance companies began to aggressively sell hospitalization insurance, usually as part of a complete insurance package which included group life, accident and health, and hospital-medical coverage. The commercial insurance companies had successfully penetrated the field to the point where in 1964, Green Cross and the commercial insurance companies each provided hospitalization for about 40 percent of the state population.

In an attempt to check declining enrollment, Green Cross sought to become much more sensitive to the needs of the market. The organization became more marketing oriented. It added a Market Research Department, a Market Planning function, strengthened Advertising and Public Relations, but more important, strengthened its sales organization.

The Sales Division had approximately 20 field offices throughout the state, each with a District Manager and three or four salesmen. The districts were grouped into three regions, with each district manager reporting to one of the three regional managers. The regional managers in turn reported to the general sales manager.

Bob Harrison, a sales representative in one of the outstate offices, reviewed his prospect list and found that new contract negotiations were to be held at a local tool and die plant. The workers bargained independently of the Tool and Die Association and thus had considerable latitude in their negotiations.

The Apex Tool and Die Company employed approximately 100 union workers. The union had group hospitalization through a local insurance agent. The insurance had been in effect for five years, and the benefits and rates had remained relatively constant over that period of time. The monthly premiums were fully paid for by the company, as given below.

$ 5.20   Single person
12.50   Two persons
17.26   Full family

The coverage, by Green Cross standards, was quite inferior. It simply had not kept up with increasing hospital charges. In their most popular package, Green Cross provided many more benefits, but at a cost considerably more than that of the competition. Green Cross policy encouraged promotion of its top coverage in order to provide the highest level of protection to the greatest number of people.

Harrison decided to approach union leadership with his top package just prior to the commencement of contract negotiations. Harrison's problem, as he saw it, was to sell the union on including Green Cross as part of their contract demands. Green Cross hospitalization was priced as follows:

$ 5.75   Single person
15.25   Two persons
21.52   Full family

Harrison arranged with the union president to address the membership at one of their regular evening meetings. The union committee fitted Harrison in at the end of its regular business meeting which was to last about two hours. In organizing his presentation, he decided on an approach similar to those he had given in the past to management.

When time arrived for Harrison's presentation, he passed out copies of the contract to each person at the meeting. He was anxious to demonstrate that he had a good program to offer and no "small print" to hide. He asked the audience to follow him through the contract as he read and explained each passage. During this time, he became a little disturbed at the lack of careful attention being given and the general noise and restlessness.

After 45 minutes, Harrison finished with this portion of his presentation. He tried to encourage some questions, but there were none asked. For the final portion of his presentation, he talked at some length about the cost of the program and how it actually was a fair price, considering what they would be getting. In total, the talk lasted one hour and 15 minutes. Upon completion, he was thanked by the president and was told he would be notified of their decision in the near future. One week later he was informed that his proposal had been rejected by the membership in preference for their existing hospitalization program. The union later successfully negotiated for a 15-cent per hour increase for its membership.

Questions

1. Was it appropriate for Harrison to make a presentation to the union similar to the one he had frequently made to management?
2. Was reviewing the contract an effective way of involving the membership?
3. Do you think the talk should have stressed cost as much as it did? If not, what should have been stressed and how?
4. What appeals could have been made to the union to redirect a portion of the 15-cent per hour increase toward offsetting the increased cost of Green Cross?

CHAPTER 8

Meeting Objections and Sales Resistance

Everyone fears something, and no one should simply equate fear and cowardice. Without fear, we would not survive. If you have driven through our western states, you may have come upon a fool hen. This is a grouse, a game bird, which exhibits little alertness or fear. It will sit in the middle of the road and let you run over it without trying to escape. How it survives as a species is a mystery.

Properly used, fear is a protective device as well as a stimulant for action. Excessive fear breeds timidity; lack of fear leads to foolhardiness and, perhaps, destruction. The salesman who is afraid of objections should overcome such fears if he is adequately prepared to meet his customer. Rather than fear objections, welcome them as signs of interest that indicate progress in the sale.

REASONS FOR OBJECTIONS

Customers have various reasons for objections. The prospect, for example, may not understand what you are saying. He may be unfamiliar with the product, and it may be a mystery to him. What might be relatively simple to you can be quite complex

213

to him. What might be ordinary to you can be unusual to him. Objections may indicate the need for further explanation. Although the prospect may be genuinely interested, he may not understand your product's functions. In that case, how could he fit your item to his needs?

Many people who buy regularly develop buying habits. Any approach which does not fit into their patterns is discomfiting. In a sense, what you are saying, demonstrating, showing, or explaining does not quite register because it is pitched in a different key. Suddenly, you find that you are singing in C major while your listener expects you to use F. Even though you are near his expectations, dissonance rather than harmony characterizes your rendition. Somehow, you must transpose your approach if the buyer is to appreciate and understand your product. He is not likely to change his key. If you want to make the sale, learn to sing along with the buyer.

PROBLEMS WITH OBJECTIONS

An objection is an obstacle that stands in our way and prevents us from successfully concluding the sale. To remove objections, we must understand them.

Are They Real?

Is your prospect's objection real, or is it merely an excuse? If it is a sincere objection, you must handle it one way; if it is merely an excuse, you can handle it in a casual fashion or brush it aside. Many people raise excuses to see how easily you can be stopped or how readily you can be thrown off the track. Maybe they are trying to get rid of you. Perhaps their minds are on something else and they want to be alone. You may, at the moment, be little more to them than a talkative nuisance. To change such attitudes, make your presentation so lively and interesting that it overcomes prejudice and causes the prospect to listen. When you achieve this, you can brush aside excuses.

What Should Salesmen's Attitudes Be?

Whether the objection is real or trumped up, at no time can the salesman's attitude be disinterested or disparaging. The salesman must be pleasant, sympathetic, and interested; he should adjust himself to the mood of the buyer. He indicates that the prospect's ideas are wise, his statements perceptive, his actions carefully planned. Prospects resent a salesman's careless or flippant attitude that shows little consideration or respect.

Observe, if you will, how a young lady can fasten her attention on a young man and listen awestruck as he talks. She never seems to be impatient or incredulous; she always inflates his ego by excluding others from the conversation. If a salesman gives similar attention to his customers, they will react as favorably toward him as the young man will toward the girl. Bounce good off a wall and good returns; bounce evil off a wall and evil returns. Bounce interest, attention, and consideration onto a prospect, and he will bounce them back to you. On the other hand, bounce disrespect, lack of consideration, and indifference, and he will return the disfavor. Even when you are probing the prospect to discover how genuine his objections are, remain sincere. Lack of sincerity will soon be noticed.

When Should an Objection Be Handled?

In timing the answer to an objection, at least three possibilities arise. The first would be to answer the objection immediately but not abruptly. You might pause for a moment or two, rephrase the question, ask a question or two of your own, and then give the proper answer. A second approach is to recognize the objection. Say that you appreciate his bringing it up but that you expect to answer it a little later in your presentation. A third method would be to ignore it because you feel that it is not genuine, that he might forget it, or that you will answer it more effectively later. In this case, go on with your presentation or demonstration without directly answering the question. Only if the prospect repeats the objection will you answer it. If it crops up a second time, it shows that the question is still in his mind. Then, most of what you are saying does not penetrate because your prospect is so busy thinking about his objection he does not have time to hear what you are saying. The sooner you handle such a problem, the better off both of you will be.

When Objections Do Not Apply

Occasionally during a presentation, irrelevant material creeps in, and objections are raised which apply neither to your product nor to your presentation. Often you will have no ready answer for such an objection. As far as you are concerned, no answer is called for; even if you do respond, you might hurt yourself. Your best procedure is to sidestep issues in politics, religion, or some local issue. It is far better for you to let the prospect talk about such a subject himself. Then if he questions you about your position on the matter, agree that certain possibilities exist and let it go at that.

You are an expert on the product that you sell, but in other areas you are only an amateur. You cannot be well versed on all questions that arouse your prospect. If he corners you, say: "Frankly, Mr. Edding, this is a local proposition, and I must confess I really don't know enough about it to voice an opinion"; or, "Mr. Edding, what you are saying indicates that you know far more about the proposition than I could possibly know." Then continue your presentation.

Preventing an Objection

A salesman soon learns that a pattern of objections develops during the course of a presentation. With experience he can tell at almost what exact moment particular objections are going to be raised. Since an objection is an interruption, there are times when he would prefer to answer them later. To avoid early standard objections, he can incorporate answers in his presentation to prevent these objections from arising. For example, a prospect may object to the color of the container. You anticipate this by saying, "Mr. Edding, our glass container is brown instead of clear. This brown prevents chemical action which weakens the solution." "Mr. Edding, the surface of our product is rough instead of smooth. We have found that a rough exterior helps the user to get a firm grip." "Mr. Edding, the color of our numbers may be different from those you have been using. Our experience shows that often these numbers must be read in partial darkness. When we hold our numbers in a darkened area, they glow so that you can see them easily."

Hidden Objections

Hidden objections are difficult to uncover. A prospect's objections may be superficial and may hide the significant problems. As you struggle with such a situation, seemingly getting nowhere, you soon realize that the objection is superficial and that something prevents the prospect from making a decision. Hidden objections may be ones that would embarrass the prospect if they were known. For example, he may not be earning enough to buy easily, or the operation of a piece of equipment may seem too complicated for him to master it. He may want to buy the product, but because he knows his social group might be critical, he hesitates to buy.

When the prospect suggests that you return later, or that you leave your literature, or that he is not in the market now, he might not be authorized to buy.

Hidden objections (or at least one major objection) must be uncovered and handled before you get anywhere. You can use several methods to uncover hidden objections. Start to pack your equipment and casually say, "Apparently, Mr. Edding, there is some reason why you don't want to buy today, or there is something I have omitted. If you would just mention it, maybe we could clear up the problem." Or say, "Since the proposition does not appeal to you now, we will get together sometime in the future. Would you mind telling me why you were not interested today?" He might let his guard down and give you the real reason, and you could swing back into your sales pitch and try to close him. Or you might say, "Mr. Edding, I've laid all my cards on the table, but they didn't seem to make the right combination. Apparently, there is something missing that I haven't been able to supply. What is it?" A perfectly frank approach sometimes brings out a hidden objection. Or list a number of outstanding objections and say, "Certainly one of these prevents you from buying today. Would you mind telling me which one?" If necessary, list the objections on a piece of paper.

If you suspect that the major reason might sound silly, say, "Mr. Edding, objections may be trivial, or they may seem so small that a buyer would hesitate to mention them to a salesman; but what may seem small to one person looms large to another. If there is any problem that concerns you and you feel it would look small in the eyes of someone else, don't hesitate to mention it." The major objection is the one that appears large to the prospect, not to others. If you can get on common ground and discover where the problem lies, you can go ahead easily. Do not diminish the importance of the prospect. He must never feel that you look upon him as unimportant.

Understanding Objections

Have you ever noticed how often people have misunderstandings, get into arguments, become offended, upset, angry? Later, a little investigation often reveals that it all sprang out of a misinterpretation. The people did not understand what the speaker meant, or the speaker's meaning was not clear. Time and again, you will hear two people arguing, and you find out later that there was a very small division between them. They were not discussing the same topic, the identical application, or the precise test used.

When a prospect gives an objection, be sure that you understand it. Before you answer, repeat it, or pause to think carefully. If you and the prospect are not on the same track, the answer might be objectionable. You may be answering a question that he never asked. You may be trying to refute an objection that was never raised. Avoid meaningless replies. What seems to be a long time to you may be a relatively short time to someone else.

When a prospect tells you to meet him at a certain place, be on time. Do not fail to meet him because of poorly defined terms. To meet at noon might be twelve o'clock for one person and one o'clock for another. When you're meeting for dinner, know whether your customer is thinking of six p.m. or noon. Two people may be dining in a restaurant; one says to the other, "I do not like the ice cream here." This surprises the other person who knows the ice cream in this restaurant is the finest. Upon further questioning, he learns that it is not the quality but the small variety that is objectionable.

When a prospect says, "I don't like the color of the garment," he may not be objecting to the red color but the intensity of the red. If it were a different shade, it might not be objectionable.

The author recalls one instance in which a friend was considering purchasing a painting. He spent considerable time looking at it and pondering, but he could not make up his mind. The proprietor of the store tried to close the sale by lowering the price slightly. In this case, the difference in price was inconsequential; the real problem was that the shades and colors might not harmonize with his room. Since the picture was 1,500 miles from home, it could not be returned. Consequently, it was rejected because of the fear that it would not fit the room's decor.

If you are having particular difficulty with an objection, you might stop and say to the prospect, "Mr. Edding, I wonder if we are talking about the same thing. Let's check to see if we understand one another." Or say, "Mr. Edding, it seems that we may be talking at cross-purposes. Perhaps I don't understand your viewpoint. Let's compare notes right now."

Magnifying Objection

Neither belittle nor magnify an objection. If you belittle it, you hurt the prospect's feelings; if you magnify, you erect a stumbling block which may be impossible to move. Many an objection, given too much attention, raises barriers which were originally insignificant. You can raise an imaginary barrier so high that you cannot knock it down.

To handle an objection properly, take it in stride; in the course of conversation, make the logical explanation. An objection ought not be a high wall to stop you, but rather a hurdle to take in stride in your presentation. If a number of objections are raised normally in a presentation, you take them as a runner meets a variety of hurdles. Some objections are minor and will be low hurdles; some objections are major and will be high hurdles. You need different degrees of effort to overcome them, but do not let them stop you. Another way to avoid objections that might be magnified out of proportion is to prevent them by refashioning your sales presentation so that most objections are answered before the prospect names them.

To meet objections satisfactorily, know what objections may arise so that you may have convincing answers ready. Preparation, perspiration, practice—how these three words echo and reecho in the ears of the salesman. Yet, most salesmen do not heed them. They practice them insufficiently, giving inadequate attention to disciplines that should be mastered. As a result, objections which should be taken in stride become obstacles that are overcome with great difficulty. Unless you are willing to prepare to meet objections, prepare adequate answers and practice giving them convincingly and interestingly, selling over objections will be a problem. The sooner you make up your mind to master the art of overcoming objections, the sooner you will have a stronger presentation and the sooner you will be able to call your salesmanship adequate.

TECHNIQUES OF HANDLING OBJECTIONS

Employing effective techniques in handling objections will help to overcome any difficulty that arises between the salesman and the prospect. If you understand the objection, you can answer it.

Pass Over

If the objection appears trivial or insincere, the salesman might ignore it and go on with his presentation. Even if it is important, he may still go on without specifically acknowledging it. In the latter case, you might agree that the prospect has raised a legitimate objection, but indicate that you will answer it later in the presentation. Or say, "Mr. Edding, that is an excellent question you have raised; however, I think you will find that it fits very well into my presentation at a later point," and then go on. If it is important and you ignore it, your prospect will cling to it and bring it up again. During this period, most of what you are saying will fall on deaf ears because your customer will be thinking about the question. To assure the prospect that you will handle the objection later, you might even jot it down. Both of you can then forget it for the time being because he knows it will be easily recalled.

Point-Blank Denial

A point-blank denial is a dangerous one and should be used sparingly. A person objects to being told bluntly that he is wrong. An awkward situation develops when the prospect is put on the spot. Even if he is proved wrong, he is not going to admit it gracefully and then buy. He has been exposed and put into an unhappy position.

Instead of saying, "You're absolutely wrong on that, Mr. Edding," you might say, "Mr. Edding, some authorities feel that ours is the better approach to this situation." Or say, "Our previous experiences indicate that the following result occurs." Instead of saying, "I don't see, Mr. Edding, how you can reach this conclusion when facts clearly demonstrate the opposite," you might say, "Mr. Edding, I can understand how you reached your conclusion; yet, a close study of the facts by experts has revealed that a somewhat different approach would be more suitable."

By all means, avoid any angry response. A statement may arouse you because you know that it is absolutely wrong. If you must use direct denial, either push it aside deliberately as you would push aside any obstacle in your way, or move the obstacle more gently. You can pound a stone away with a fierce thrust, or you can roll a stone away with a firm movement. Both approaches can be direct and to the point, but the latter is more acceptable. No one likes to be contradicted abruptly and roughly.

"Yes—But" Method

The "yes—but" method uses the indirect denial, which is more palatable to the prospect than the point-blank denial. Seldom does a prospect make a statement or raise an objection that does not have some elements of truth in it, though basically it may be unsound or essentially false. That is why the level-headed individual may have difficulty in countering arguments and suggestions of dictators who lead people astray with half-truths.

In selling, recognition of partial truths is useful in meeting objections. By acknowledging the truth in a statement, you do not offend the speaker. By countering the false part of an objection, you can also open up a new theme. Thus, if the prospect says, "Your car is so heavy it takes a lot of gasoline to run it," you can reply, "Mr. Edding, it is true that some people who must do a lot of stop-and-start driving in cities have found this car is not as economical as others; but once you get the car rolling, the amount of gasoline used is no greater than any other car. And the additional comfort of the heavier car on long trips such as you will take will be important." Have facts handy. Know that a six-cylinder car will give you seventeen miles to the gallon, while an eight will average sixteen. Be able to compare mileage, horsepower, and weight with other makes.

To the farmer who says, "Your smaller trees won't bear as much fruit as these large ones," you reply, "It's true that each tree doesn't bear as much fruit. Yet, farmers who have orchards of both sizes of trees find that the yield per acre is about the same since you have more smaller trees than you do larger ones. The advantage of the smaller tree is that you can prune it more easily and pick the fruit more easily." To another objection, you might reply: "Mr. Edding, you say this picnic table is too heavy to carry. That may be true for a husband and wife. But our experience shows these tables are used primarily for group picnics. On such occasions, several men are present, and moving the table is no problem." Still another objection might be answered: "You say, Mr. Edding, that the straight-back chair looks and feels uncomfortable. That may be true for some people. Yet, many of our customers have stated that they need a straight-back chair in the house. They feel so comfortable in it after sitting in a lounge chair that this one should be in every home."

Notice in this indirect denial approach that we do not always say "yes-but." That is the technique, but we vary the approach by using a number of similar words that carry the same meaning. This should be considered more of a graceful transition denial approach that should easily lead from the prospect's statement to yours without antagonizing.

Use Objections as a Sales Advantage

The alert salesman frequently turns an objection into a sales advantage by rearranging words or stating the objection in a little different way. To the prospect who says, "Your shoes won't last as long as others I have seen," the salesman replies, "That may be true, but ours are inexpensive. That enables you to have two pairs instead of one, and so you can have new shoes more often." Or to the objection, "I can't afford such a large house," the salesman replies, "With your large family, Mr. Edding, you can't afford not to have a large house. A smaller one would cramp you, make you uncomfortable, and interfere with your work. Here you can have your own room or study in which you will not be disturbed."

To the customer who says, "It's a nice suit, but I can't afford it; it's too expensive," the salesman replies, "Mr. Edding, that's the reason why you should have this suit. It looks good on you, and your type of work demands an immaculate appearance. You can't afford not to look your best." "You say you can't afford those large shade trees, Mr. Garden, but you need shade trees immediately. Now is the time to enjoy the shade, when your home is new, not in ten years when small trees grow up. These trees will give you shade now and for the rest of your life."

Take the very objection of the prospect and point out how it can be an advantage to him. If a prospect complains about the high price, you can point out how long it will last, that it will not need replacement, or that its style is outstanding. If the prospect says that the product is flimsy, say: "Because of the lower cost, you can replace it easily and have the advantage of a new product more often."

If the prospect objects and you answer "Why?" he is forced to do some thinking before answering. If his is a legitimate objection, his answer will be helpful to your sales. If his objection is trivial, his reply will reflect insincerity. Then you will know what type of follow-up to use. A series of probing questions that follow one answer after the other may be beneficial to both the salesman and the prospect. It forces the prospect to give careful thought to his problem and why he thinks that your product is unacceptable. He is compelled to focus his attention on his own problem; and when he answers questions, he may reveal some of the things that face him. This, in turn, may lead to greater revelation and possibly a substantial order.

If the prospect says, "I can't buy this now," answer "Why?" He might say, "Not only do we have an inventory in the store now but also stock in our warehouse which we have to sell before buying any more. As a matter of fact, we've gotten a little careless and have been ordering stock and have been putting it on the shelves directly, leaving the old warehouse stock intact. It's six months old now, and we must get it on the store shelves." This would give you the opportunity to point out how he can put up a special display or run a special sale. Not only would he sell a lot of this item, but to do so he would bring out his entire warehouse stock and supplement it with new stock for a big show. This would necessitate a large order immediately to supplement the stock already on hand.

Another buyer might say, "No, I don't think I need any more at present." Further questioning reveals that he is considering dropping your line and replacing it with a competitor's. The buyer feels that sales of your product have been slow and the new product of the competitor seems to be moving better. This information is priceless. Not only does it give you an opportunity to resell your product, but it may also open the eyes of your company to the fact that it needs to do more research and development on the present product to bring it up to date. A prospect's objections inform you of what your customer knows or what is bothering him.

Naming Balancing Advantages

Naming balancing advantages, also known as the compensatory method, takes disadvantages or objections and turns them into advantages. If a product incorporates a feature to which someone might object, there usually can be a counterbalancing reason given to offset the objection. Notice the following: "This equipment is too heavy." "It is heavy, Mr. Gorden, but that makes it stronger." "This material is too dark." "It is dark, Mrs. Green, but it won't show spots." "This color doesn't seem so sharp." "It's true, Mrs. Brown, but that enables you to wear the hat with many kinds of clothes." "This car seems so short." "Because of its compactness, Mr. George, it enables you to get through traffic easily and to park readily." "This house seems so far away from town." "That's why it's quiet around here, Mr. Flanders. It's away from people." "This package seems too gaudy." "That may be true in your office, Mr. Nelson, but put it on a supermarket shelf and you will see how it stands out among competing products."

The same birds that try to eat the spring seeds also eat the insects that devour the plants that come from the seeds that you planted in the spring. Seldom do you find any product wholly good or wholly bad. Time and again, we find through research that products which have been considered useless have real value.

TYPES OF OBJECTIONS AND HOW TO HANDLE THEM

If you sell for a period of time, you will hear many types of objections. The more of these you can catalog and develop answers for, the better off you will be. If you have ready-made answers for objections, you can concentrate on problems of the moment: presentation, the necessity of talking over noise, the necessity for observing certain conditions. Many factors will demand your attention. If you anticipate objections and have adequate answers, you can proceed smoothly and with assurance.

Decided Not to Buy a Product

There can be many reasons why a buyer decides not to take on your product. Maybe yours is a new item. Not long ago, a supermarket operator mentioned that in one year his firm had been exposed to 3,800 new items, most of which were rejected. He had found over the years that whether or not he added a particular item did not seem to make much difference. Because his chain sold thousands of items, adding or dropping one was not important. Even if the chain made a mistake by not handling a specific item, this could be corrected by adding it later.

If a customer decides not to buy, your job is to find out why. If you ask him frankly, he may give you the answer. If he objects that it is not advantageous for him to buy, quote a case like his in which the reaction was similar, but when the other man bought, the results were outstanding. If you cannot uncover the real reason for not buying, you might ask as you leave, "Was there something, Mr. Frederick, I said or left unsaid that made you decide not to buy?" If he replies to this question, he will give you another opening to continue your presentation.

If you sense a possibility for reopening the presentation, you may digress into some general conversation as if preparing to leave and then adroitly swing back to the original topic and begin your presentation in another vein. By this time, you may have thought of another idea, or he may have changed somewhat in the interim. With the new approach, it can become an entirely new presentation, and he may see it in a different light and buy. Timing is important. What a man would do one day, he might consider foolish the next day.

Too Many Lines

Too many lines is a frequent complaint, and all too often a just one. On the shelf of a small grocery store, you see six or eight brands of coffee when two would be sufficient; in a small haberdashery, you see two lines of belts when one would be sufficient. Walk into a machine shop, and you may see several little-used special-purpose machines that could be replaced by one general machine which would be adequate for all needs.

If the shoe dealer tells you that he already has an excellent line of winter overshoes and needs no more, with a little probing you might discover that he has an expensive line of rubber footwear. Then say, "Don't you think, Mr. Tree, that overshoe sales would increase if you also had an inexpensive line? Many people use overshoes infrequently and prefer the lighter, inexpensive ones." If a store has several lines and you wish to introduce yours, the buyer will say that he does not need another one. Then point out that by introducing your wider line, he can eliminate four of his present lines. Instead of five, he can end up with two by adding yours. He adds yours and drops four.

If a customer complains that you do not have enough variety, point out that your styles last year after year without becoming outmoded. If a storekeeper is reluctant to take on your line, point out the rapid turnover with a high profit margin. Show that sales and profits per linear foot of space are much greater with your line than with any other. He says that he cannot carry your machines because he would have to carry an additional stock of parts. Indicate that he need not carry parts for your machines because he can order them directly from the factory and get fast service. Be sure to stress the advantages of your line.

No Demand for Product

Drug salesmen frequently find that there is no quick demand for their new products. When they introduce a drug to physicians, they want pharmacists to stock the drug so that prescriptions can be filled at once. But they hear, "I'll wait; there is plenty of time. Wait until the prescription comes in, and then I'll get your product." Even more will you get resistance in putting a new product on the shelf. The druggist will say, "There is no demand for it; no one has asked for it; it won't sell." To counter such statements, indicate how this product can be sold. Use illustrations of other dealers who have successfully introduced your product. If the dealer stocks it, install eye-catching displays to stimulate sales.

If your item is used in manufacturing, offer to send a free trial amount for comparison with products now used. You can hardly expect a manufacturer to accept your product without giving it a thorough trial. If he is to incorporate your material into his product, he must have confidence in its reliability, dura-bility, performance, and safety. If your product is new, you will probably have some advertising or sales promotion to go along with it. Even if there is no demand now, demand will be generated as soon as advertising appears. A major company such as Procter and Gamble has little difficulty in getting a merchant to stock a new product. The merchant knows that the company will support a new product with promotion and advertising.

Product Does Not Fit

When the prospect says that your product does not fit, ask him why your product is so different from similar ones manufactured by others. Why won't it work for him? If he is a retailer, why won't his customers buy it? If your product is more expensive or cheaper than the one he handles, agree and say, "I'm sure, Mr. Prospect, that there are many people living here who would appreciate a product at our price and quality. Seldom will one brand satisfy everyone's demands in an area." Often, the real answer to the prospect's objection is that you have not completely sold him, and it is up to you to do a better selling job so that he can see the value. If a significant problem in construction is revealed, it might be possible to make a slight alteration in your product to enhance the appeal in a particular area. This might be justified if one group of people would like a slight modification; undoubtedly, the modified product would appeal to many others.

Present Product Satisfactory

Many people are content to stay with merchandise they are presently using because change upsets the present procedures. Doing something different or doing the same thing in a slightly different way requires additional effort. Why bother to change when everything seems satisfactory? That would be the attitude of the prospect who is satisfied with present merchandise.

You can agree with a prospect that many of the items he handles are undoubtedly quite satisfactory and that it might seem unreasonable to change. However, he recognizes there is a steady stream of new products as well as old products that are being modified in sundry ways. Ask him to look at his stock and see how many of the same kinds of merchandise he had five years ago. When he thinks about it, he will be surprised to note changes. Those who are slow to change miss excellent opportunities to get in on something new, something better, something that will move more rapidly and prove more profitable. Business is filled with illustrations of how a present-day product has been outmoded by a new product that performs the same function a better way. Some of you may remember when automobiles had the water heat indicator atop the radiator on front of the car. This has long since been replaced by a device which gives the heat indication on the dashboard. In congested city areas in which snow removal has been a problem, heated pipes are laid in sidewalks to melt the snow as fast as it falls.

No enterprising manufacturer can ignore a new material. Cheaper substitutes or better substitutes are being developed; if they are not incorporated into the product, they will soon force the manufacturer to a weaker sales position. At one time, carpeting was made wholly of wool. When wool was in short supply, the prices skyrocketed; manufacturers began experimenting with synthetics and other materials. Now carpets are made of a variety of materials, only one of which is wool. In the automobile market, there is a constant struggle among suppliers of steel, aluminum, magnesium, plastics, zinc, copper, precious metals, and paper. When a new item can be substituted to do a job better or more cheaply than the present one, complacency becomes dangerous. Any alert salesman can show the value of new ideas, new materials, or new products.

Most buyers want to check a product before placing an order. Without a trial order or trying the product in advance, a purchasing agent must know that your product will perform successfully. Such assurance can be given through testimonials, guarantees, and demonstrations. Few salesmen are willing to guarantee that their product will work successfully as a component of another product without a proper trial, not only in the manufacturing process but in use. Failure could be damaging to the manufacturer using the product and disastrous to its producer. For example, you have an item made from magnesium, formerly made from another metal. If this item is joined to another, a reaction may be set up that disintegrates the magnesium, which in some instances is a sacrificial metal. If you are confident that your product will perform satisfactorily for the prospective purchaser or retailer, prepare another more convincing presentation. If the prospect says, "I want to check on it further," ask him, "What would you like to check? If you tell me, maybe I can help you." This may uncover the hidden objection which you can handle easily.

Friend Disappointed with Product

Imagine selling an item house to house and having a housewife say, "I don't want it. A friend of mine bought it, and she was disappointed." How do you feel when a purchasing agent tells you, "We don't want it. I talked with a friend at lunch yesterday, and he said he bought some and it didn't work." Or how do you feel when the druggist says, "I don't think I'll put it in. We druggists had our regular meeting last night, and one said he stocked your product and it didn't go over at all." These are samples of replies which indicate that users have found your product faulty. Perhaps it was not designed to meet their needs, or poor results came from improper use.

One way to handle an objection is to ask the person to tell you who was disappointed. Tell the customer that you would like to correct the problem. If a housewife refuses to give the name, you may assume that this is a trumped-up excuse and that you need to sell harder. If the objection is sincere, your willingness to correct the problem will impress the prospect. If the prospect happens to know the problem, you can explain how it might arise and how to avoid it. By following instructions carefully, she might never face that problem with your product.

A Cheaper Product Will Do As Well

If you hear that "a cheaper product will do as well," you have not qualified your prospect carefully enough. For example, the ordinary individual doing some painting in his home need not have as expensive a paintbrush as a professional painter. The new piano player does not have to practice on the most expensive piano. As a matter of fact, he would be unable to appreciate its fine qualities until he had gained considerable skill. However, this excuse about the adequacy of a cheaper product is often manufactured rather than real. A beautiful piano in a home may not only produce better music, but it also lends more elegance to the interior than would be achieved with a cheaper instrument. No salesman of sterling silver flatware would suggest that the dimestore variety of tableware could not be used for eating purposes. Nor is it likely that the car salesman selling the $5,000 car will indicate that you will have much more trouble-free operation from this car than you would from one selling at $3,000. Both cars might give comparable trouble-free operation, but there would be many other features that would not be alike.

For a good illustration, compare restaurants. You can go to a number of restaurants and for $1 to $5 eat a meal that will satisfy hunger. If you weigh the amount of food received in each restaurant, there will be little difference. But what about the other features? At the restaurant where you get a top-notch dollar meal, you will find noise, smells, perhaps dirt, bare tables, sloppy waitresses, and the food, although adequate, may not be very appetizing. For five dollars you get delicious food served by competent waiters in attractive surroundings. If you ate dinner alone, you might choose the restaurant with the dollar meals. But if you were entertaining friends, you would choose one of the better restaurants with higher prices because a good meal consists of more than food alone.

Do not jump to conclusions. Never assume, because you are calling at a poor home, that the family may not buy a beautiful painting. When calling on a particular store, do not assume that you cannot sell an expensive product. Often, people in moderate circumstances will have an expensive flair in one direction. People living in poor neighborhoods may own expensive cars. People living in low-income areas will often buy the highest-priced liquor. All of us, whether in the home, in the store, or in the factory, have prestige symbols. We could be in the market for one very high-priced product although our other purchases would not be at the same level. Many times, the prospect may find a cheaper product satisfactory. But in too many cases, he continues to buy it because some salesman is not showing him the greater advantages he would have from the better product.

Can't Buy Everything

The objection that a man "can't buy everything" frequently is given to salesmen who talk to wholesalers and retailers. These buyers must reject numerous items because they do not have room for them, they do not think that your item complements their regular lines, or for a number of other reasons. It would be impossible for them to begin to buy all products that they are asked to consider. And yet, many do buy items they had not planned to acquire because some thoughtful salesman has pointed out opportunities or developed methods which permit them to handle these items satisfactorily and profitably. You may agree with the prospect that he cannot buy everything, but also point out that he cannot afford to miss some item like your product. Then show him why.

Do you see the importance of creative ideas in helping the buyer? If you are selling to a retailer, getting the order should be the smallest part of your job. You have not finished your work until you help him move the merchandise to the consumer. The most important job you have is to help the retailer become successful. If you can show how your product will contribute to his success, he should not hesitate to buy.

Think It Over

Find out why the buyer wants to "think it over." You can say, "Mr. Redding, I appreciate your wanting to think this proposition over, but I fail to see how waiting can benefit you. In a situation like yours, you will be losing a wonderful opportunity by delaying. Somewhere, I failed to give the complete information. If you tell me what you'd like to think over, perhaps I can give you the data you need to make your decision."

When the objection is an excuse, brush it aside and continue with your selling. Bring up vital points to close the sale. You might say, "Mr. Redding, I appreciate your desire to think it over, but we've had many instances in which other people have done the same thing. Later, they've come back, bought, and were sorry that they waited. Usually, the reason for delay is some slight difference which can be cleared up readily if we know what it is." Either way, whether dealing with an excuse or a legitimate objection, try to uncover the client's reasoning and cope with it immediately. Then make the close.

Satisfied with Present Source of Supply

Some buyers are loyal to salesmen and are reluctant to make changes. Yet, professional buyers are dependent on their skill and ability in buying to hold their jobs. Say, when you encounter this objection, "Mr. Gordon, I appreciate the loyalty you are showing, yet this loyalty may be dangerous to you. You may be deliberately overlooking opportunities or closing your eyes to developments which are taking place. No one firm has a monopoly on all ideas or the best products. As an enterprising businessman, you just can't afford to pass up new opportunities."

Many new firms have grown rapidly because they have capitalized on new ideas and improvements that appeal to the consumer. Older companies have been afforded the same opportunities but may have passed them by. With a little study, you will be able to develop many examples in which companies have refused to make changes that consumers wanted. As a result, they remained small, struggling firms, or they went bankrupt because they became unresponsive to changing demands.

The salesman selling house to house should not encounter much resistance because housewives are intrigued by new, sparkling, efficient products. Even a salesman selling baked goods house to house must have a changing assortment of items that appeal to the housewife. Not only does he need such standard items as bread, but he also needs new and different pastries.

Not Interested

All of us have used the "not interested" excuse during our lives and all salesmen have heard it. The salesman's response should be "Why?" or "Why aren't you interested?" The prospect's reply will enable you to launch into your presentation again, to stress more plus values, more interesting facts, more selling points. The buyer probably is not interested because you have not marshalled enough facts to strike a responsive chord. Somewhere along the way, if you make a proper presentation, there must be some point that will attract him. If you hear the same objection again, ask yourself: "Is he uninterested because I'm not interesting enough?" Maybe the fault is in you, not in what you sell. Paint word pictures about your product that appeal to the buyer.

When a real estate salesman describes the summer cottage, the husband sees a small building nestling among the pine trees. In front of the cottage, tiny waves gently roll on the white sand beach. He pictures himself lying in a hammock, the wind gently sighing in the trees. In the cool of the evening, he will be out fishing. Dusk will surround him. Fish will break the lake's surface as they feed. All this and more he sees as he exclaims to the salesman, "Yes, we want it." The wife pictures a small dark building with hurricane lamps, wood stove, and round tub and washboard. She can see the flies everywhere, mosquitoes buzzing around, sand on the floor, and children's damp clothes scattered around. She pictures dark, dreary, rainy days when the family huddles inside. All are irritable with nothing to do. All this and more she sees as she exclaims to the salesman, "Not interested."

Talk It Over With Someone

"First, I must talk it over with my wife, my husband, my partner, my friend." What a common objection, and how often it comes up. An appeal to ego sometimes is successful in overcoming it. A husband makes many purchases which he does not talk over with his wife. The wife makes many purchases which she does not talk over with her husband. Many a businessman making important purchases would never dream of talking them over with his partner. Often, then, this excuse is merely a stall. Usually, it arises in major purchases involving considerable sums of money.

One way to overcome this excuse is to dwell on the confidence that the other person has in your customer. He has trusted him with many things before, and he can be certain that he will be trusted now. If it is a major purchase, try to make it look minor. Instead of talking about the total purchase price, talk about payments in terms of months, weeks, days. You might say to the housewife, "Do you have pennies around the house? How many do you think?" She'll admit that she has pennies around the house. "Can you find 25?" Perhaps she'll say, "Oh, I wouldn't doubt it." You then say, "That's not very much, is it?" and she'll agree. Then say, "You need only 25 pennies a day, and we'll move this new refrigerator into your house. Your husband would not object. He knows you will have better protection for your food and that you will not have the trouble that you have been having with your old refrigerator."

To the factory owner who says, "I can't afford $10,000 for the machine," you might say, "How much is the present equipment costing you now?" He might reply, "Nothing, I've got it all paid for." Then you show him that because of breakdowns, repairs, delays, and slow operation, the production of the new machine would be 50 percent greater than the old one. You might say, "Mr. Green, in wages alone, our new machine will save $10 a day—that's $50 a week—$200 a month—$2,400 a year. Let me show you some of the additional savings." And soon you come up with a grand total of $4,000 a year. "Over a period of five years, Mr. Green, you save $20,000 by buying the new machine. I understand you have charge of production in your firm, and your partner handles sales. He's gone a month. Probably, each time you've consulted him, he's ended up by saying, 'Well, I leave it up to you.' And wisely so. Don't you think when he comes back and you tell him about this new machine, he'll say, 'Well done, Jack,' or 'That was a good move on your part.'" Talking it over with someone else indicates that a man lacks confidence. Try to reassure him.

Can't Afford It

May I tell a personal story? When I was in college, I read a well-known insurance company's advertisement on how to retire at the age of 65 with an adequate income. I had always had the idea that one should protect his future by setting aside something during his working years. I filled out the coupon and mailed it for further information. Imagine my surprise when, a week later, a well-dressed gentleman came to see me and introduced himself as a representative of this insurance company. I was flabbergasted. Here was I, a college student, working my way through school, in the backyard of an Ann Arbor home beating a rug. I was in old working clothes, pounding away. This, by the way, was in the depression of the 1930's.

The representative said that he had come in response to my inquiry to see how he could help me. I do not recall the words of our conversation. I pointed out to him, however, that all I wanted was information. I was working my way through college. I had no money; I had no idea of buying insurance of any kind. I could hardly make ends meet as it was. He was a fine, understanding gentleman. He said he appreciated my position, left his card, and said that I should call him when I was in the market later on.

That same evening I bought a $5,000 policy from an agent representing another firm. I could not afford it; I did not have any money; I was not interested. Yet, I bought it. Why? I was borrowing money from people who had no security or protection except my promise. I needed to protect these people, and I bought a policy with life protection, with an income in case of disability, and with a retirement provision. I still have the policy and am glad I took it out then. The second agent qualified me. He discovered my immediate need and convinced me not to put it off. The first salesman observed the immediate situation and concluded I was not ready to buy. The second salesman studied the entire situation and showed how I could meet my need at once. Yes, when the prospect says, "I can't afford it," how often can you answer, "You can't afford to be without it." There are many ways of working out programs which will enable the buyer to afford what you are selling.

Our Business Is Different

You will hear this objection frequently: "My business is different;" "My situation is different;" "My problems are different." If this were true, the salesman's job would be impossible. Most of us soon learn that problems of business firms are not so different as management often thinks.

In handling a prospect who has given this objection, ask him to explain why he thinks his business is different. It will please him to think that you recognize the individuality of his business. As soon as he explains his position, devise answers to show that your product will help him. Be careful not to reply too soon. Pause a bit as if thinking. This will give him greater confidence. Then, stimulate the sale by giving an example of how someone else in a similar position used your product successfully.

Does Not Like Your Firm

When a buyer says that he does not like your firm, or your president, find out exactly what he means. If he says that your firm does not live up to its promises, find out exactly where it failed. Then tell him that you will do all in your power to correct whatever is wrong. If he has some personal gripe against one of the firm's officers, point out that your relationship is a business one and that you are selling a product that will help him. Get his mind off personalities and on your product's advantages.

Even though your firm may have some unsavory characters in important positions, do not agree that they are disreputable. You do not gain by criticizing your firm, its employees, or its product. If you have no regard for those with whom you work, quit. If you criticize your firm, the buyer will be convinced that he is correct, and he will have little regard for you if you work for such people. Either way you look at it, your criticism of your firm or product will be harmful. If the buyer intends to use the product himself, concentrate on it and get his attention away from individuals and personalities. Sell your product's uses, guarantees, price, value, delivery. Use positive ammunition to overcome unpleasant associations.

Does Not Buy From Strangers

Housewives often say that they do not buy from strangers. A housewife may be impressed with your product, but because she has heard of many instances in which people have been defrauded by house-to-house salesmen, she may hesitate to buy. Or it may be that she has been defrauded by a salesman. Under these circumstances, if you have made sales to satisfied customers within the area, mention such sales as examples. Tell her that when she goes to the grocery store, she buys many products that she knows little about. Many salesmen carry identification and credentials which lend credit to their firms and their products.

If a professional buyer raises the same objection, you can easily refer him to one of the standard rating books or other accessible financial data which rate your firm. In most instances, this is a weak excuse and should be treated as such.

Does Not Believe You

Some of your statements may seem so farfetched that a prospect will not believe you. When this situation arises, go through your presentation carefully again. Go slowly, add more illustrations, feed in testimonials, cite examples, try to give information which he can check if he wants to.

If possible, demonstrate your product. Perhaps you can give the prospect a sample which he can test for quality and dura-bility. Suggest the type of test which will best demonstrate the quality of your product. If you test it for him in his presence, be sure that he understands what you have done and knows why it is meaningful.

If your prospect shows disbelief, try the "order book influence." If you can open your order book and show sales to people in the community, to neighbors, or to influential people, the prospect will gain confidence. This method is especially effective in a small town where the banker, the mayor, the car dealer, and other businessmen have given you signed orders.

Service Unsatisfactory

If the prospect says that your service is unsatisfactory, ask him why. On what does he base his claim? Do not argue with him. If he does not have valid criticism, he will evade the issue.

Then go on with your presentation. If he quotes one or more valid instances, acknowledge the possibility that such instances have, unknown to you, occurred. Point out, however, that such is not your firm's policy. Whenever such unfortunate incidents do occur, tell him you are glad to hear about them because that enables you to tell your firm so it can avoid such things in the future. Show him you appreciate his information, and then sell your product.

If at any time he discovers unsatisfactory service, he should tell you; and you will make amends immediately. He knows that any firm has problems, that difficulties arise, and that misunderstandings are bound to occur. But when you indicate that such provocations must be rare because you had not heard of them previously and that you are ready to correct them at any time, he will be more inclined to listen to you.

PRICE OBJECTIONS

Price objections are usually important enough to handle separately. Since price objections are the chief stumbling blocks for many salesmen, careful study should be made to see how these objections can be overcome.

Handling Price Objections Early

When presenting your product to a prospect, the question of price may arise early. Sometimes, you will give the price immediately; other times, avoid it as long as possible. If he insists on getting a price, say, "I will give it to you as soon as I have presented this particular point." If your product has a particularly high price which would shock the prospective customer, you might mention it early to give him the shock at once. Then as your presentation progresses, you will be able to show the qualities, advantages, and features that make your product such a good value.

Higher Price Expectation

If you are selling a product that is new to the prospect, he may have no idea of what the price will be. Then you might build up a high price expectation by the way you present the material. As you explain what you have, how it operates, what its features are, and how customers appreciate its use, you can interject the statement, "Would ten dollars sound too high for this product?" When you have gone far enough to impress the customer that the price might be ten dollars, you finally add, "And as an introductory price, we are giving customers our special rate of three units for $25."

If it is a relatively expensive product, you might say, "Would you think a thousand dollars would be too much for it?" Later you could say, "This product which some customers say is worth a $1,000 is now selling for $795." Many of us have no idea about prices when we encounter a new product or request a service that we have not used before. If the salesman mentions a price, we fix it in our minds as the price that he is asking. Then, if he quotes a lower price, we are pleased.

Built-in Quality

Two items side by side may look alike, yet one can sell for three dollars and the other for five dollars. The customer wonders why. While a product may be priced out of line, you will usually find that there is a reason for the difference in price between two similar products. If you have any doubt about this, go to a clothing store and try on a suit for $60, another for $90, and a third for $150. The most expensive one may not wear any longer, but as soon as you put it on, you know that there is a difference. As you look in a mirror, you look different.

In more expensive products, you sell additional qualities, not only the basic requirement. In ordering steaks, you might go into one restaurant and buy one for a dollar. In the next restaurant you pay two dollars. Both steaks are the same size; very likely, both have the same food value. Perhaps the cheaper one may even have more food value, and undoubtedly it will give your jaws more exercise. The cheap one would be relatively tough, the expensive one tender. One time, a friend walked into a music store and asked a salesman the difference between two brands of pianos on the floor. The salesman replied, "One hundred dollars." Such poor preparation by a salesman is not uncommon. A little observation revealed that the more expensive piano had far more beautiful cabinet work and had features that the cheaper one did not have. Salesmen are careless or prone to overlook many additional qualities of their product which might be appreciated by a customer.

Profit

Price is neither high nor low; it is a relative factor. Price is not high if the dealer can sell merchandise at a profit. But price is high if the dealer cannot sell the merchandise at a profit. Presumably, if the price were lower, the merchandise would sell. Many a customer does not hesitate to pay a higher price when he sees value. Frequently, merchandise which sells at a higher price returns a better profit. Therefore, dwell on the word *profit*. Use illustrations. Take pencil and paper and figure profit for the dealer.

Dealers have become so obsessed with gross margin that they fail to consider turnover. More and more, we are coming to recognize that gross margin is only one profit factor. Oftentimes, selling a product with a low gross margin but with a rapid turnover makes a much larger total profit than one with high margin and slow turnover. With a bit of thought, you can uncover many opportunities for a dealer to handle your product profitably.

Small Unit Payment

Many salesmen sell merchandise with high price tags. The real estate man deals in thousands of dollars; the car salesman deals in thousands of dollars; furniture salesmen deal in hundreds of dollars. When you notice a customer hesitating because of the magnitude of the price, break it down into smaller units. Suggest a small amount down, plus easy monthly payments over three years. The cost per day will not be large when you analyze it.

What holds true for the consumer may also be true for the manufacturer. When you say $10,000, $25,000, or $50,000 to a manufacturer, the price might stagger him. But when this overall price is presented in terms of years of use with monthly payments over a period of years, the cost seems lower even though the final total is greater. Just as distance is covered one step at a time and a job is completed one unit at a time, so may a large sum of money be paid over a period of time by breaking payments into manageable units.

Adjusting Price

A salesman may have considerable leeway in quoting prices. As a matter of fact, price may have many components. There may be a cash price, a time price, different discounts if paid within certain periods, special quantity allowances, rebates for performance, special dating, and many other permissible deviations. Sometimes, you are allowed to meet legitimate competitor prices. Avoid getting entangled with typical price hounds who always insist on a better price than anyone else. Once you give into them, there will be a perpetual price battle. Some salesmen become known as price men. If your product is priced right in the beginning, you should be able to justify your price.

Special Discount

In the course of your day's work, you will meet buyers who insist on special discounts. If the price has not been announced, a salesman occasionally increases his original price and then gives discounts which bring it back to the regular price. If a piece of equipment has extra parts, some of these may be removed and the base equipment sold at a lower price. Once the sale is made, you may try to increase it by adding features which were originally omitted.

Introductory prices will sometimes feature special discounts which permit better prices to customers. Special allowances are sometimes given for large quantities, old models, or special occasions. Legitimate price concessions can be made in such a way that the list price is not lowered. A lower price may be offered because added expensive features are included which customarily are sold at reduced prices. If the customer wants a special discount and you cannot give it, tell him that your firm does not permit price deviations. You may have found, however, that customers have been willing to pay the regular price because of the added advantages of your product. While this customer does not get any immediate reduction in price, in the long run he actually does because the product is better, the results are superior, and more profitable sales can be made at retail.

Prestige

People may object strenuously to paying the asking price, but will often leave one store, go to another, and pay a higher price for a similar item that has a different brand. At times, the brand name alone is sufficient to command a higher price. People who are economy-minded in one area think nothing of spending liberally in a different area. For instance, one traveling man who was allowed a certain amount of money for food each day patronized cheap restaurants for several days in a row so that he could save up enough money to go to a fine restaurant and order a costly meal. One man may drive an old car and wear shoddy clothes but have the finest fishing rod money can buy. Some people buy expensive shoes; others wear expensive hats. Anyone going along the water's edge and seeing the small boats with the giant outboards attached realizes that the latter are prestige items. People will scrimp and save in many ways so that they can belong to a country club and, when there, spend freely.

This desire for prestige is common at all levels of income. By elevating a low-income person's sights so that he may appear superior to others, you can sell him a $20 item instead of a $10 one; the middle-income person, a $30 item instead of a $15 one; and the wealthy individual will not hesitate to pay $100, although he might get an equally satisfactory product for $50. In each case, the lower-priced item is not equally desirable because it does not have the prestige value of the higher-priced one. We may go to discount houses or stores featuring low prices to get a particular gift; but when we package it, we put it in a box which bears an image of high quality and price.

Comparison

Very often, the difference in price between two items is caused by closer attention to detail in manufacture or greater care in finishing. Sometimes, this is hard to demonstrate because the difference is so slight. Frequently, slight improvements add significantly to the cost. In using comparisons, one can bring out the frequency of use. You buy a chair for $25 and use it every day; at the same time, the end table for which you pay $25 seems to have very little use except in an ornamental way. A lawn mower is used weekly throughout the summer while a lawn sweeper costing as much may be used only a few times. A woman buys a dress for $30 and wears it many times. On the other hand, she will buy a formal gown for the same price and wear it once. These few illustrations indicate how difficult it is to say that a price is too high. It is too high only in relation to the value or the pleasure it gives or does not give. If a salesman spends $100 on entertainment for a customer and loses the job, the boss says, "You spend too much." If, however, he spends $100 and gets the job, the boss says, "That was money well spent." You can buy a loaf of bread for the price you pay for a piece of pie in a restaurant. Yet, people still buy pie in restaurants. Think of a variety of comparisons to use in handling objections.

Frequent Calls

A salesman expects to make several calls on the industrial buyer or the professional buyer before he makes sales. Close relationships and friendships are not cemented overnight. If you have trouble selling a retail buyer because he thinks your line is too expensive and you cannot convince him the first or second time that he should stock it, do not give up. Continue to call. Each time you call, discuss some new reason for his stocking your product. Eventually, he will hear so much about it that he will try it. Also, on repeat calls you will meet the buyer in different moods. One day he might be much more receptive than on another day. Buyers change, and the buyer who would not give you a break may be replaced by one who will like your product. On every call, make a sincere effort to give the buyer something worthwhile to think about and, perhaps, to try. Just a series of monotonous, repeat calls on the same buyer is boring to him and time-wasting for you.

Some Common Price Objections

During a year, you will hear many price objections and many reasons for thinking the price is too high. What are some of these?

Too High. This common objection arises from a variety of causes. Sometimes your product is higher-priced than competing products. The price may be greater than the prospect expects to pay, or the prospect might not be able to afford it. Occasionally, you find some people have blundered and are not financially able to buy your items. These people should be eliminated as pleasantly and as rapidly as possible.

If the price is only slightly too high for the prospect, you may not have much trouble in explaining the difference to him. A slight difference can be justified by availability, selection, services offered, convenience, and many other considerations. Sometimes, prices advance rapidly beyond our control, and a potential buyer might not have caught up with that fact. When he shops around, he soon learns that prices have changed. Prices of gasoline during price wars between filling stations may change ten cents a gallon overnight. If an impending shortage of a product appears to be imminent, it is not unusual to have the price skyrocket.

If a customer resists you because he thinks the price is too high, add values one after the other to justify the price. Not long ago, the writer bought a pound of cookies in a store. The clerk took a large number of cookies in her hands and put them on the scale. Then she kept adding two or three cookies at a time until the pointer approached one pound. Finally, she added only one cookie at a time until the pointer indicated the desired weight. She was selling a pound of cookies for a specific price, and she was adding cookies until she had justified that cost. The same is true with your customer. He sees a price tag or hears a price quotation. At first he thinks the price far overbalances the value. Then you start piling on value, adding up qualities, giving comparisons, showing special features, demonstrating particular advantages. Soon you have piled up so much that the pointer swings over the agreed amount and the customer feels that he is getting full value if not more. Whether this should be cookies on a scale or ideas in a discussion, the result is the same. Purchases are not made until the buyer is convinced that value warrants the price.

Other Firms Cheaper. No matter how hard you try, no matter how low you set your price, you will always find some competitor who will sell cheaper. Price competition has always been with us and probably always will be. Price competition has healthy aspects because it forces high-cost firms to lower their prices and to discover new economies. Some firms are willing to cut prices severely and try to operate on smaller margins, or they will take advantage of innocent buyers by charging them exorbitant prices, while others get extremely low ones.

When you meet price competition, stress value, services, reputation, guarantees, delivery dates, durability, trouble-free operation, safety. Even on competitive bids, many buyers do not take the lowest bid because they consider factors other than cost. If the buyer likes you, he may give you an order at a higher price. He justifies his action because of certain factors not covered by price. If he does not like you, he does not dwell on those factors, and you lose the order. Many times, firms have obtained orders on low bids, have substituted inferior materials, and have gotten away with it. Such occasions remind you that you cannot win them all. Some salesmen are extremely price conscious and seem to think everything hinges on price. If they cannot be low, they do not know how to sell.

How many of us buy clothing and shoes primarily on price! We may buy a new car on price, but by the time we have added extras, price has gone out the window. When a person rents a store, the rent is high or low only in relation to sales. The salesman who earns $15,000 yearly and makes $50,000 a year for his firm is much cheaper than the salesman who earns $8,000 a year and makes $15,000 for the firm. We frequently hear the saying that "All things being the same, prices should be equal." Yet, it is rare that all things are equal. Qualities may vary, deliveries may be fast or slow, installation may be prompt or otherwise. There can be so many variations that the alert salesman will often demonstrate that his seemingly high price will, in the end, be lower. You do not buy clothes, machines, equipment; you buy satisfaction.

Goods Don't Carry Enough Profit. The objection that goods do not carry enough profit is being seriously shaken today. Rapid turnover, lower inventory, narrow lines, specialized goods, branded items, and a host of other features tend to wipe out the gross margin factor as the important one. For example, an unknown product with a wide profit margin may not be nearly as profitable as a well-known branded item, highly advertised, with a narrow profit margin. The latter may outsell the former ten to one with the net result that the latter is far more profitable. Wholesalers, retailers, and even salesmen for manufacturers must depend more on volume of sales for profit than on the wide margin commonly received.

At one time, a gross margin of one third was common in the grocery business. Today, 20 percent margin is the usual profit. Few car dealers are able to secure their gross margin on sales of new cars. Many give substantial discount off list even before bargaining starts. Some types of merchandise require more sales effort than others, and businessmen must be taught that extra effort is required to move certain types of products. People buy fire insurance but must be sold life insurance. They buy staple foods but often must be sold certain fancy foods. They buy gasoline and oil for the car but must be sold on car washes, grease jobs, and minor upkeep. A young couple will buy a new home but must be sold aluminum doors and windows. They will seed their lawns but can be sold sodding. Aggressive merchandising, on whatever plane, results in larger or more frequent sales.

Profit should be secured on large dollar sales rather than a large gross margin on a few sales. The advertising and sales promotion activities of your firm are important for increased profits. Merchants who tie in with cooperative advertising get the entire benefit of the sales efforts of the firm. When dealing with merchants who focus on particular margins or amounts of profits, it is necessary to give them a picture of the overall operations. It is not how much you make on a particular day, or in one week, or in one season, but the year's operation that counts.

Wait for Price to Come Down. When you hear this objection, bring up instances in which other people did the same thing only to have the price go up. People who have waited to buy lots have often watched the price rise. Others who used this excuse found all the desirable homes and lots were snapped up, and the ones remaining at lower prices were much less desirable. Most of us who patronize end-of-season sales for reduced prices find soiled, torn merchandise that is not the color we are looking for, not the style we hope to get, and usually not our size. So-called "bait prices," in which a few prices are low, get people into a store. Once there, you find the stock depleted or your size sold out. Then the salesman tries desperately to switch you to some higher-priced item.

One way to attack the lower-price objection is to show that while one is waiting, he is depriving himself of the pleasure of using the item. People have been known to wait for years for a price to come down. By the time they are able to buy it at the lower price, they do not have much use for it. Christmas cards sell at half price the week after Christmas, but they will clutter up closets for a year before you use them. Flowers in a corsage on Friday night may sell for three dollars. The next day, unsold corsages may be hawked on the street for 25 cents, and the flowers still go begging.

Another approach found useful is to indicate that this price will prevail for a short time. After that, it is subject to change.

This puts pressure on the prospect to buy now. Competitive prices are not on a one-way street. Many assume they must inevitably come down, but actually they can go up just as easily. One consideration to mention is that when a price comes down, the quality often goes down with it. Paint a vivid word picture of the losses involved during the waiting period—losses in pleasure, comfort, safety, security—all are costs of waiting. Many times, by waiting you can avoid buying the service or product and thus avoid the price altogether. Thus, you can put off buying fire insurance, or car insurance; and if you wait long enough, you will not have to buy it at all. But think of the sacrifice, worry, and danger involved. Demonstrate to your customer that waiting for the price to come down is not a method of buying cheaper because the worry and loss of use more than make up for the difference in price.

QUESTIONS AND PROBLEMS

1. Why does a salesman fear objections when they arise during a demonstration?
2. Many salesmen welcome objections during a sale. How do you justify this attitude?
3. When a customer objects strongly, the salesman may be using wrong tactics. Explain.
4. Salesmen handle objections at different times during a sale, and each salesman may feel one time is better than another. Why?
5. Are there advantages in anticipating objections? Disadvantages?
6. Many sales are never made because the salesman did not discover the hidden objection. Yet, some exploratory probing might well have uncovered it. Why are salesmen often careless in this stage of selling?
7. A common fault between salesmen and their customers is lack of effective communication. How would you eliminate this weakness?
8. Sometimes, dwelling on an objection magnifies it all out of proportion to its importance. If such a situation occurs, is it the fault of the salesman or the customer?
9. A customer asks a question the salesman thinks does not apply to the sale. How should the salesman handle it?
10. No one likes to be completely wrong, yet a salesman will often have such a customer. Faced with a statement that is wholly wrong, when should a salesman (a) deny it point-blank? (b) use the "yes—but" method?

11. Illustrate several ways of using objections as sales advantages.

12. Seldom do you find a product without disadvantages or a product without advantages. How can obviously inferior products be sold in competition with better products?

13. The store owner may well recognize that your service would be satisfactory, but his present service is adequate and lower in price than yours. Now, what must you do to sell your service?

14. A new item seldom sells itself. In proposing a new item to a druggist, what must you do to convince him to stock it?

15. Why is it necessary to have products in a variety of price ranges and with different appeals?

16. Why must a manufacturer be alert to product changes? Can this help you to introduce a new product to take the place of a staple product?

17. How can you sell a high-quality product in an area where a cheaper product dominates?

18. "I don't doubt your product is all right, but I just can't buy everything that comes along." How do you overcome this objection?

19. How can you overcome buyer loyalty to a competitor?

20. A person who appears to be not interested may be quite interested in your product. Is this a contradiction in fact?

21. When a prospect says he has "to talk it over" with someone, the salesman failed to qualify the prospect. True or untrue?

22. You have spent considerable time and effort in developing a program for a manufacturer. He has been interested all the way until you draw up final plans and give him a price of $100,000. He says, "That's more than my profit for the whole year. I just couldn't begin to afford it." You then go over the plans again and notice that your approach has been too ambitious, but you do see a strong possibility of success if the manufacturer will expand in a way you will show him. There is considerable risk involved, but if it turns out successfully, the manufacturer will increase his income substantially. If it fails, the manufacturer will be unable to pay off the equipment he is to buy from you; and likely you will lose your job. Your company knows the time and effort you have already put on this job. Should you tell them of the planning error you made and ask their advice, or should you boldly carry out your original plan?

23. When a prospect says he cannot afford to buy your product, he may have several meanings in mind. List several possible meanings.

24. Everyone likes to think he is different, his problems are different, his business is different. Is this usually true? Give several examples to justify your answer.

25. In a business situation, is there room for personal dislikes so that you refuse to do business with one another? Is there a place you draw the line?

26. How can you overcome disbelief in the mind of the prospect?

27. What steps should a salesman take to handle a problem of unsatisfactory service? What should he do if the customer is at fault?

28. When price is high, should it be mentioned early in the presentation or at the end? How may circumstances vary your answer?

29. Many people misunderstand quality. Why? Does a low price justify low quality?

30. Cost is relative, not absolute. Explain. Is this true for all buyers?

31. When is it permissible to change your price to a buyer? To what extent is it fair to have a varying price structure for your customers?

32. Is a salesman justified in selling an item to a customer when he does not feel the customer can afford it?

33. How often should a salesman call on a buyer?

34. Evaluate this true statement: "I don't want a salesman to call on me too often, but I do want him available in a hurry when I telephone for him."

35. Describe how you would handle the following:
    (a) "Your price is too high."
    (b) "I can get it cheaper."
    (c) "Your markup is too small."
    (d) "I'll wait until the price comes down."

36. Many retailers have failed because they did not control inventory. The dealer you are now visiting is loaded with unsold merchandise, much of it dusty and old. As you survey the stock, you notice many duplicating brands similar in price and quality. In your particular line of products, he already is stocking similar merchandise of three well-known companies. Just to persuade him to put yours in would push him to bankruptcy faster. What must you do to get him to add your line of products?

37. How can you overcome inertia of people? Why bother to change? You are introducing a new service but find great difficulty in getting people to change their way of life to incorporate your service. Yet, once people become accustomed to your service, they like it and would not go back to their old ways. Outline a procedure to sell your service. Although you would like to use a free-trial period, your company does not permit this approach.

38. One of the most challenging problems facing a salesman is to overcome the influence of a disappointed customer. You are

entering a neighborhood to sell a device to housewives. As you begin selling, you soon discover the housewives are antagonistic. You find out that one lady bought this device and couldn't make it operate. She is thoroughly disgusted and has poisoned the minds of neighbors. You have been assigned this territory and must spend one month here selling. What must you do to succeed in this territory?

Charmaine Loves Me!

CASES

8-1: PETERSON HOME SALES COMPANY

Alfred Jones had just completed the demonstration for his vacuum cleaner. Carefully, he had gone over the outstanding features. Step by step, he had shown the advantage of the water bath to catch dirt and had shown its superiority over bag-type cleaners. Using an ordinary vacuum cleaner of a well-known brand, he had cleaned the carpet. Then following with his own, he showed how much dirt his machine picked up from a supposedly clean carpet. Each accessory was used in an effective way to bring out its advantages and importance to the housewife.

During the demonstration, conversation had been easy and informal. There appeared to be no tension or hostility. Both Mr. and Mrs. Ring had asked a number of questions which were answered to their apparent satisfaction. From time to time in the demonstration Mrs. Ring had operated the machine and several times tried attachments on jobs she picked herself.

To be sure of making an effective demonstration, Jones had chosen his prospect carefully. He felt certain there would be no financial problem in paying for the cleaner even though it might be considered expensive. He had made the appointment a week in advance at the convenience of Mr. and Mrs. Ring, who stated that 7 o'clock Monday evening was satisfactory. Even the children, Barbara, a sophomore in high school, and Jim, in junior high, were interested spectators in the demonstration and took their turns in operating the equipment.

In the step-by-step approach he had been using successfully, Jones brought out his order pad and began filling it in, asking Mrs. Ring which attachments she thought were necessary at this time. Mr. Ring spoke up and said that before they made any purchase, he would like to think about it. Skillfully, Jones conducted the conversation to try to get Mr. Ring to commit himself as to what he wanted to think about, or what had Jones failed to tell him.

After about five minutes of this approach, Jones detected signs of irritation. Realizing that he would lose the sale if he persisted, he agreed that it would be wise not to act immediately. He did, however, get permission to call back the following Monday evening for the Rings' decision. He then gathered his equipment and in a spirit of cordiality bid the family good evening.

When Jones got home that evening, he tried to analyze why he didn't make the sale. Everything appeared favorable. There were no loose ends in the presentation. The "think it over" statement was either stalling by Mr. Ring, or there was some real reason which had not been answered satisfactorily. Making this sale will mean a commission of $50 for Jones, so he intends to do everything possible to close the sale next Monday evening.

Questions

1. Did Jones make mistakes in his presentation?
2. Was the "think it over" reply genuine?
3. Was the close handled properly?
4. What preparation is necessary for the following Monday evening?

8-2: RELIABLE CALCULATOR COMPANY

The Reliable Calculator Company has been in business for years, and its products have a good reputation. About one year ago Reliable introduced its printing calculator; since then, its sales have increased so rapidly that presently it is challenging the company's standard calculator for the lead in sales. Since the profit margin on the printing calculators is considerably higher than on the standard calculator, the company's salesmen have been urged to push the new calculator.

John Fraley has recently come to work for the Reliable Calculator Company as a salesman. This is Fraley's first job since graduating from college. The only prior experience he had in selling came from working part-time in a men's clothing store while attending school. After joining Reliable, he has undergone training in salesmanship and has spent one week at the manufacturing plant studying the company's products. He has also spent time accompanying experienced salesmen on their calls to observe their sales techniques. For the past three months, Fraley has been calling on prospects by himself. His sales, however, have been disappointing.

Following are excerpts from some of Fraley's sales calls:

Interview 1

This sales call was made on a small manufacturing firm with approximately 200 employees. As we listen, Fraley is talking to the purchasing agent, Mr. Cardwell.

FRALEY: You've probably heard about our new printing calculator, the Reliable Deluxe.

CARDWELL: No, can't say that I have.

FRALEY: Well, we introduced it a few months ago, and it is making the old-style calculators obsolete.

CARDWELL: We only have a couple of calculators in the place, so I'm not too familiar with them. What's a printing calculator?

FRALEY: A printing calculator does everything the old-style calculators do with the added feature that it prints all the figures.

CARDWELL: That sounds pretty good. How much are they?

FRALEY: Only $995.

CARDWELL: Only! That's pretty expensive for a calculator.

FRALEY: But this is a printing calculator.

CARDWELL: That's still too much money. The last two calculators I bought cost $500 each. They were used, but they work just fine. I bought two of them for the price of one of yours.

FRALEY: That sounds like a good price. What kind are they?

CARDWELL: Bronson.

FRALEY: When did you buy them?

CARDWELL: About seven or eight months ago.

FRALEY: Had any trouble with them?

CARDWELL: No, they're working just fine.

FRALEY: That's good. Oftentimes, you have problems with used equipment. Now, with our calculator it is easier to check back on your figures because you have a record on the tape just like an adding machine.

CARDWELL: Sorry, we don't need any calculators now. Say, do you carry adding machines? I sure could use another adding machine.

FRALEY: No, we don't, but you could use our calculator not only for adding and subtracting but also for multiplying and dividing, you know.

CARDWELL: I know, but that would cost too much. All I need is an adding machine. But leave me some literature on your machine, and if the need ever arises, I'll give you a call. Okay?

FRALEY: Okay. Sorry you can't use a calculator today. Here's a brochure describing our calculator, and here's my card. Be sure to give me a call when you need a calculator.

Interview 2

In this sequence, Fraley is calling on a large accounting firm which employs about 150 accountants and clerical workers. Fraley has just finished explaining the features of the calculator to Mr. Devore, the buyer.

FRALEY: And so you see, Mr. Devore, the advantages the Reliable Deluxe has over old-style calculators.

DEVORE: Your talk sounds good, but I hope you've improved the quality of your machines.

FRALEY: Why did you say that?

DEVORE: Well, about five years ago we bought twenty of your calculators, and several of them have broken down.

FRALEY: I'm sorry to hear that. Our machines are quality made. Consequently, we seldom have trouble with them. Maybe the machines were abused or something. Sometimes the employees can be rough.

DEVORE: I'm sure our employees aren't hard on the machines. Besides, the Bronsons and Nationals we have don't give us trouble. I wonder about your quality. The service we got on your machines wasn't very good either. It took the serviceman two or three days to show up. During that time two girls had no calculators. That costs us money, you know, when we have to wait like that. Can't you people improve your service? It makes it hard to do business with you.

FRALEY: Well, those things happen occasionally. That was before my time, anyway. We're trying to improve our service all the time, but we can't always get the service department to cooperate. They've got their problems, too. But you won't have any problems with this printing calculator.

DEVORE: That's not what I heard. I heard that these printing calculators are nothing but trouble.

FRALEY: What do you mean, trouble?

DEVORE: They're always breaking down, the tape gets stuck, etc.

FRALEY: That's not right, we don't have any trouble with our machines. One of our competitors, maybe.

DEVORE: No, it wasn't one of your competitors. Bronson seems to have a real good printing calculator on the market now. I'd like to see theirs before I make any decisions. Besides, theirs doesn't cost as much as yours.

FRALEY: I want you to be satisfied with your choice, but no one makes a better calculator than we do. Granted theirs does sell for a few dollars less than ours, but this difference in price is really insignificant when you compare the two machines. We use nothing but the best materials in our calculators which, together with the fine workmanship employed in their manufacture, enables us to offer you the finest calculator on the market today. Why don't you buy four or five to begin with? See for yourself how much better they are than what you are now using. Once you have satisfied yourself, I'm sure you will want to replace all your present machines with Reliables.

DEVORE: No, I'm not going to buy any more Reliables until you people improve your service and the quality of your calculators.

FRALEY: I guess I can't convince you by talking, Mr. Devore, so here's what I'd like to do. Let me leave one of our new Reliable Deluxes with you for a week for you to try out. After you've used it for a while, you'll see that what I'm talking about makes sense. **That's fair enough, isn't it?**

DEVORE: Well, I'll use your machine for a week, but I won't promise anything.

Interview 3

In this sequence, Fraley is calling on another small manufacturing company with about 100 employees. Fraley has asked the receptionist if the buyer is in. She has just called the buyer.

RECEPTIONIST: I'm sorry, Mr. Fraley, but Mr. Ames cannot see you today.

FRALEY: Did he say when he would be able to see me?

RECEPTIONIST: No, but he did say that we don't need any new calculators now.

FRALEY: That's too bad. I'll try again some other day. Good-bye.

Interview 4

In this sequence, Fraley is calling on a small engineering firm. As we listen, Fraley has just finished describing the new calculator to Mr. Stalker, the engineer who doubles as office manager for the firm.

STALKER: That sounds like a real nice machine you have, Mr. Fraley. How much is it?

FRALEY: This calculator sells for $995.

STALKER: Wow! That's a lot of money. We're just a small company, and we can't afford to spend that much money for a calculator.

FRALEY: That's not so much. Rather than looking at it as an expense, consider it an investment. You do a lot of work with figures on your job, and you must be accurate. Right?

STALKER: Right, but . . .

FRALEY: If you make a mistake in your figures, it could throw the whole job off, couldn't it? And this could cost your firm a lot of money, couldn't it?

STALKER: It sure could.

FRALEY: To help insure against this happening, you need the Reliable Deluxe in your office. With all the figures right in front of you on the tape, your likelihood of making errors is greatly reduced. The cost of this calculator is actually quite modest when compared to the money you will save.

STALKER: You're making it sound like we have a lot of mistakes here.

FRALEY: No, that's not what I meant at all.

STALKER: Okay, I like your calculator, but before making a purchase of this size, I have to talk it over with the boss. He's out of town this week, but as soon as he comes back, I'll talk it over with him and let you know.

FRALEY: That sounds fair enough to me. Tell you what—in the meantime I'll leave this machine for you to use until your boss returns.

This way, you'll have a better idea of how the calculator works, and you can demonstrate it to him. Then you'll give me a call when you've had a chance to see him?

STALKER: Yes, I will. Thanks for leaving the machine.

Question

Comment on Fraley's sales presentations and his ability in overcoming sales objections. Can he improve in this area?

CHAPTER 9

Closing the Sale

We can compare selling to a dramatic production. The background is set up, characters introduced, data given, demonstrations made, objections answered, and a climax is reached.

CLOSING IMPORTANT TO BOTH SALESMAN AND BUYER

If the preceding steps have been properly carried out, you have convinced the buyer that he needs your product. Actually, several products could probably meet his need; it is your job to convince him to buy yours! Your firm is the best source for the product; you have the exact item that he wants. It will fill his requirements better than any other. Now you must convince him that the price is right. He must not feel that your price is exorbitant, but that the price is reasonable, and that it is better than he can get anywhere else. Then comes the final step. He has been convinced that he needs the product, that a particular product will fill his needs, that you have the ideal source for it, and that the price is right. Now you must convince him that this is the time to buy it. Closing is the time of decision.

Feelings of Salesman Approaching Close

Picture yourself as the salesman who is ready to close. You have been working hard. You have finished an excellent demon-

255

stration. Your presentation has been outstanding. You are certain that the prospect needs your product. You know that your price is as good as any. Now comes the time to get him to say yes. This is when you show whether or not you are a salesman. If the sale is of any size, every salesman will be apprehensive, for he does not know how the buyer will react. The buyer facing him now seems to be a bit different. What will he finally do? One can liken this moment to that of the fisherman when he reels his bait past the hiding place of the bass. Will he bite? Or the quarterback who has called a pass play. Will it click? In each case, you have done your best. What will happen?

Feelings of Buyer as Close Approaches

Put yourself on the other side of the desk. The buyer has a problem; he must get the right merchandise at the right price. Picture the department store buyer of dresses. Are the dresses the right styles, the right colors, the right prices? Will they sell? How many in each size should he order? Is there a better source? Many thoughts crowd into his mind. He is spending someone else's money. Will it work out all right?

If you are a housewife, you begin to consider. "I have done all right with the old one," or "I have done all right without this item. Maybe I can get along without it now. How will I meet the payments? Am I sure I cannot do better? Am I being unduly influenced by a good sales talk? What will my husband say? Can we afford it? Should I look around some more? Should I wait a little longer? If I buy this, I cannot get some of the other things I want."

Both of you sit facing each other. You wonder, "Have I done everything possible to convince this person that he ought to own my product?" The prospect thinks, "Am I sure that I am not being influenced by the salesman rather than the need for the product?" Both of you have your problems. Not only must you handle your own problems, but you must assure the prospect that you are handling *his* problems satisfactorily.

CLOSING PROBLEMS

As you approach the close, you must decide about a number of problems that present themselves to you. There are several possible paths you might take, several alternatives available. Of the several alternatives, which one is best?

When to Close

The other day, a salesman was driving along a well-known Canadian highway. Since it was only partially completed, he had to cross over to another paved highway somewhere along the way. As a matter of fact, there were several well-designated crossover points, all of which seemed to have advantages. Which one should he choose?

A similar situation arises in closing a sale. Let us set at rest once and for all the idea that there is only one time that you can close a sale. Like the crossover points in the highway, one may be better than the others. On any particular day, one may be preferable to another. But they all can be used successfully. The same is true in closing a sale. There may be many opportunities to start your close. The problem is to recognize the *best* time in *each* sale.

Close Early

There are as many examples of salesmen who failed to close early as there are of salesmen who succeeded in closing early. Never forget that the purpose of your presentation, demonstration, and of all your efforts is to close the sale. If you find it unnecessary to go through all of your presentation, be prepared to stop whenever you sense an opportunity to close the sale. Perhaps the prospect had been looking at your particular item for weeks or months before you entered his office; he may have needed you to answer just one more question. The salesman cannot know how well a man has studied products beforehand.

What may be an important purchase for one individual is merely a casual purchase for another. Some will quibble over the difference of a few cents in one item and think nothing of paying many dollars for another. If the person is a repeat buyer who is well acquainted with the product, there need be very little selling. He comes in, asks the price, and buys it. Another person who is a first-time purchaser may consider it very carefully. The amateur house painter will go into the hardware store to buy a cheap paintbrush to paint his house. The professional painter may spend considerable time and study before he buys his paintbrush because it is the tool with which he makes his living. You may drop into a store to buy a fountain pen and choose one that is attractive and writes satisfactorily. A secretary who uses a pen to write shorthand for a living would be much more critical because of the many features that she would want. A buyer of machinery used for close tolerances is highly critical of performance while a buyer for textile machinery would be more lenient in his specifications.

Close Part Way Through

You have completed the early points of your presentation. You notice that the buyer is interested, but you continue your sales talk because you sense that he is not ready to buy. Halfway through, you detect signs that he may be ready to buy. This is the time to attempt a close. Since it may be hard to detect the exact time, try several closes along the way. Otherwise, you may pass up the best time. In taking pictures, how many times have you waited for a better opportunity only to find that the best opportunity has gone? Do not be afraid to put some closes into your presentation relatively early. Certainly, try before you reach the halfway mark. How do you know that an early attempt may not be the real thing?

Close at End of Presentation

When you have made your presentation and demonstration, when you have handled objections and have done whatever you think necessary to clear up any problems or any questions, you *must* close. Many a salesman dawdles around because he does not know exactly what to do and is afraid to close. When we go swimming and the water feels cold, we usually go in slowly and prolong the agony. Finally, we duck under. The same holds true in selling. Eventually, you must make the close. Just as the water does not get warmer by waiting a few minutes, neither will your sale be helped by waiting for something unusual to occur. In fact, waiting may let the prospect cool off so that you will find it harder to close than if you had moved smoothly at the proper time.

Top salesmen are strong closers. You want to be a top salesman. You want to succeed. You want to be outstanding. Well, then, make up your mind; you *must* be a good closer. In almost any activity, you improve by doing. Your closings will improve if you work at them conscientiously. Remember, when you made that plunge into the lake, it did not seem so cold. The same holds true in closing. Once you make the plunge, it is not so difficult after all.

When you are presenting and demonstrating a product to a housewife, or showing a new machine to a professional buyer, or selling a new line to a store buyer, it is probably desirable to go through your entire presentation first. Essentially, you are presenting something new, and it is necessary that the buyer be convinced of the merits of your proposition or product before he acts. Early closing is good for the person who is already well informed or who buys quickly. At any rate, you should attempt to close at the end of your sales presentation. True, there are rare occasions when you put the close off until you make another call when there would seem to be a better opportunity. But many salesmen who defer the close would be far better off if they were to make it during or at the end of the presentation in the first call.

How Many Times Should You Try to Close?

There is no set number of times to try to close. The only universal generalization about it is that salesmen do not try often enough. They give up too easily.

The salesman may use from one to a dozen attempts to close the sale before he either makes the sale or retires. Statistics show that most sales are made after *several* attempts to close. It is not unusual to try four, five, or six times before you close. Some salesmen may try as many as twenty times. Possibly, the sale that is made easily or quickly may be potentially dangerous. If the buyer makes up his mind so easily, he can change it equally fast and cancel the order or bring the purchase back for exchange or refund. As fishermen know, many times they lose fish because they try to hook the fish before they have firmly taken the bait. However, there are times when fish bite greedily. Likewise, there are prospects who will buy on the first close because they really want the product. Thus, you cannot generalize and say that people who are easily sold are hard to keep sold.

Timing the Close

A successful fisherman soon learns to detect when the fish is hooked. Members of each species have different ways of indicating when they are hooked, and different lengths of time are required to do the job. Nevertheless, the experienced fisherman soon learns when and how to land the fish. In selling, the experienced salesman soon recognizes when the individual is ready to buy.

Closing Signs

What are some of the closing signs that indicate that a prospect is ready to buy? Can you identify the time? The answer to the latter question is a qualified "No." The best you can do is to follow identifying signs. If you succeed in your attempt to close, you chose the right time; if you do not succeed, back up and start over again.

When a salesman is making a car presentation and the husband asks the wife what color she likes best, that is a signal to close. When the lady trying on a dress says, "I certainly could use a dress like this," it is a signal to close. When the shoe buyer says, "These shoes certainly would go well with my new dress," close. When the man asks, "How long will it take to deliver this car?" he is ready to buy. "How does your guarantee work?" is a closing indicator. When the real estate man hears, "This is the best-looking house we have seen yet," he moves in to close. "I've been looking for something like this for a long time," and "Could I get it in time for Christmas?" are closing indicators.

Many times, you can tell by a person's actions when he is ready. Many of us who study people soon learn that under particular situations they have certain expressions. Football players review films of opposing players in games to see if there are any mannerisms that tip off what a player will do next. Opponents have discovered that a particular quarterback will place his feet one way when throwing to one receiver and another way for a different receiver. His posture will differ from his preparation to throw a pass and his preparation to hand the ball to a runner. There are many revealing signs that the alert player can detect. The alert salesman soon learns to detect the signs—facial expressions, nervous movements, eye changes, hand movements. Such actions indicate tension or desire which makes the individual ready for closing.

Trial Closes

The trial close is nothing more or less than an attempt to do something. Some people are willing to try more than others. Some try once and give up. Others keep trying but slowly give up. In selling, do not fear trial closes. When you are sharpening a knife, you often test to see if it is sharp enough. When you taste soup, you try it carefully to see if it is too hot. When a housewife cooks, she tastes now and then to check on the seasoning.

This can be the turning point in your selling career if, as you read this, you make up your mind to try to close. Tell yourself, "I am going to try to close; I will try over and over again. When I do not succeed, I will study my failures to see where I went wrong, to see where I can improve. Then, when I have made careful preparation, I will try again. Whenever I fail, I will study and try again." Do this, and you will not fail.

Let me warn you, however, that blind trials may not lead very far. They show that you have perseverance, but what you need in addition is intelligence. Carefully work out trial closes; carefully think out procedures; thoughtfully work out approaches. In athletics, the real contest is preceded by individual workouts and trial scrimmages. In selling, a certain amount of practice must precede the sale. However, when you are going through all of the selling steps, do not forget that the final one and the most important one is the close. You cannot put it off. Instead of tasting the medicine and thinking how bad it is, drink it. You will find that it is not so bad after all. Do not forget: The close is the final part of every sale.

The Third Party

When two people enter a retail store and you notice that one is to do the buying, separate the nonbuyer from the buyer. It is much harder for two people to make a decision than it is for one; it is impossible if one is a bystander. His comments can frustrate the customer so that he will not buy. Show the bystander some other article to divert his attention; if possible, call in another clerk who will show other items of interest.

Sometimes, you cannot separate two individuals in the buying process. Though one may be more important than the other in the actual buying, the more important individual to you is the dominant one. If the daughter wants to buy something but her mother dominates the sale, you may have to please the mother first, and the daughter will follow the mother's advice. If daughter does the buying but mother does the paying, you must please both parties. Yet, both mother and daughter have the same purposes in mind—please the daughter. The greatest single problem facing the mother is money. Once the sale seems imminent, it is your job to show how easily the purchase can be financed.

When selling to a group of people, experienced salesmen find it helpful to call on each individual beforehand and go over details. If possible, try to get a commitment to buy before the meeting at which the decision is to be made. This approach will enable you to size up the various individuals and sense what their feelings are to you.

Handling Yourself

Throughout the sales presentation and during the entire period involved, you must handle yourself properly. Impress the buyer by dwelling on your strengths and avoiding your weaknesses. How is this to be done?

Show Your Strength. Equip yourself with all needed materials and accessories so that when the time to close comes, you do not have to go looking for the product, samples, models, order blanks, or pens. Paint the prospect into the picture so that he feels as if he already owns the product and is enjoying it. Arrange for a private office or some facility where you will not be disturbed and where you can talk closing terms in complete confidence. Even in retail selling, when you cannot have an office, you can make the close a private affair between you and the customer. Then the customer feels that he is getting your entire attention. Act as though closing were a customary procedure. Do not show hesitation, nervousness, or indecision. Convince the buyer that making sales is an ordinary event in your life. It will be if you want to be a success. Be friendly always; be soothing if necessary. This is no time to arouse antagonism.

Avoid Your Weaknesses. Do not apologize for your product, your firm, or your price. Do not apologize for taking the prospect's time. If he is a qualified person who needs your product, you are doing him a favor. Do not put barriers in front of the prospect. If you question his ability to pay, you may stop him. If you question how much he will be able to use your product, you invite him to reconsider. If you point out the dangers involved in using your product, you may scare him away. If you want to use barriers, put them behind the prospect. Thus, you can show him the problems that may arise if he does not buy. You can indicate how his family will suffer if he does not respond favorably. You can demonstrate how his sales will suffer if he does not stock your line.

Do not make promises you know you cannot fulfill. They will show up later to haunt you. Do not get boxed in with a "no" answer. Do not cry on your prospect's shoulder, telling him your troubles, lack of sales, or other problems. Do not show nervousness; you might frighten away your prospect. Do not expect a "no" answer. If you do, customers will soon sense that something is wrong.

Do not betray confidences. It is so easy to want to talk too much and to pass along a juicy bit of scandal. Though the prospect may enjoy what you are saying, he is also thinking, "If he talks about others to me, I am sure he must talk about me to others in the same way."

METHODS OF CLOSING

A number of closing methods may be used. As the occasion demands, you can use one or more methods until the sale is made. There is no one best method. Start out by using the most effective one that you know. If unsuccessful, try a second close with another approach.

Assume Prospect Will Buy

Assume the prospect will buy. You have made the presentation, the demonstration has been completed, objections have been answered, and choice has been narrowed. At this point, the next logical step would be to make out the order or to settle on some minor details. "Will Thursday of this week be all right for installing your furnace?" "We'll have the house ready for you in two weeks." "We agreed you wanted a policy that gives you protection as well as retirement income, didn't we?" "We'll put on the whitewall tires and have the car ready for you tomorrow afternoon." "You can register for the course tonight and make a down payment of $5, with the remainder payable the first night of the class." These are positive statements that are just one step removed from signing the order.

While you are talking, you can be drawing up the contract or agreement or filling out the order so that it is ready for the buyer's signature. Handled properly, the buyer will not feel forced; he will simply feel that you are reaching a natural conclusion for a pleasant experience. Do not hesitate using the direct close because it is too bold. It is used successfully on many occasions.

People act in predictable ways. Why? Because we have habits or customs. Through repetition we establish habits. We dress in a certain way, eat in a certain way, and sleep in a certain way. Thus, we may sleep on our stomach, our back, on the left side, or on the right side. But most of us do prefer sleeping in one particular position. At home when dinner is announced, we assume that the members of the family will sit down at the table. When it is time to go to bed at night, we assume people go to bed. When we stop at the filling station, the attendant says, "Fill 'er up?" He does not ask, "Do you want gasoline?" but rather, "How much?" In similar fashion, you can assume the prospect will buy.

Summarizing Product Advantages

After a lengthy presentation, it is not likely that the prospect will remember all the points. Therefore, it would be wise to summarize them at the end as a part of your close. Perhaps you brought out points that were not applicable to the prospect. When you summarize, concentrate on those points pertinent to the prospect and omit the ones which do not apply.

Do not become too formal or too stiff in your summarization. Do not talk as if you are hammering your arguments home point by point. Summarize in a pleasant, cordial way that invites agreement as you go along. "Mr. Gordon, we agreed, didn't we, that you wanted a big house? We agreed that you wanted sliding closet doors. The hardwood floors were the ones you liked. You wanted a full basement that could be converted into a recreation room. You wanted a double garage attached to the house. The lot has a number of trees for shade. The house is on a street where there is little traffic." Notice how we are recalling important features one by one. If any particular feature was unusually appealing, stress that a little harder. The review and summarization of points rapidly outline the outstanding features of the product and enables the buyer to see clearly and quickly the overall perspective.

As soon as these important points have been planted in his mind, try to close. Introduce the assumptive close by asking him when he can get together with the owner to work out the financial details. Or, request a deposit as a binder for the agreement. If your presentation has been well done, your prospect should have become so interested that he is ready to buy. Summarizing merely gives the clinching data that firms up the prospect's resolve to buy.

Ask for the Order

One of the bluntest ways of closing is to ask for the order. The bluntness may be tempered, however, by the skill with which you phrase your question. Seldom would the salesman ask, "Will you buy?" Rather, he would make the approach less directly by asking when the prospect would prefer delivery, how he would like to handle the financial terms, or how many cases of the product he would like. Note that all the closes have much in common. This is understandable since they all are leading to the same objective. But the way questions are used, and the strength with which they are asked often is the influencing factor and is one of the determining methods in picking your close.

You may say, "Mr. Gordon, I know that in our discussion you have been in full accord with my statements, and that we have agreed on respective points along the way. Finally, we have agreed that this product would fit into your line of merchandise. As I write up the order, will you give me the quantities, sizes, and colors?"

Notice the directness in the following: "Mr. Swanson, we have completed our demonstration. You have driven the tractor, and have seen how it performs. You have agreed that it has many fine features that would be useful to you. We have agreed on the amount of trade-in for your old tractor. Now, tell me how much of a down payment you would like to make, and we can draw up the papers."

This appeal can be used in a dress shop. "Madam, we have carefully gone over the features of several of the gowns as you tried them on. The one you now have on seems to meet your needs better than any of the others. It is unquestionably the type of gown you will want to wear Monday night when you preside over the meeting. It enhances your natural grace and posture and will make you outstanding that evening. The only minor problem is that the left sleeve is a bit too full. I will call the head of our alteration department so that she can see the slight change needed. Then we can have it ready for you in plenty of time."

Speaking to a purchasing agent, you say, "Mr. Boone, you have seen how this equipment performs. Your chief engineer has seen it in action and feels it will be quite satisfactory. The man who operated it in your factory was enthusiastic about it. Sending in your order today will enable us to deliver this machine in a month. A few days after installation, you will be turning out parts more accurately, faster, and at a lower cost than you have ever done before. As I write up the order, will you tell me which accessories you would like to have?"

Make the Product Unique

One lady from Pittsburgh and another from Cincinnati appeared at a New Year's Eve Country Club Dance in eastern Ohio, wearing identical dresses. Both were horrified that the dresses which cost so much and were supposed to be an exclusive in each city could be duplicated so easily. One lady had bought the only dress of its kind in Pittsburgh while the other lady had bought the only dress of its kind in Cincinnati. By chance, both ladies happened to be at the same party. The dresses were expensive; the ladies were chagrined.

Many people want unique products. People flock to buy something new. Each year when the new models of cars come out, certain people want to be the first to buy. Some vacuum cleaners are sold not on their main features but on their accessories. In addition to cleaning the carpeting, these vacuum cleaners will perform a dozen other jobs. Seldom does the lady stop to think how often she might need them for the other jobs. Many beautiful homes are equipped with the latest appliances and equipment to make entertaining easy. Yet, the homeowner will do most of the entertaining away from home.

Prestige is important. If you are the only one, the first one, or one of the few in the community to possess a product, you feel gratified. You hear the saleslady say, "Madam, this dress was made for you." She flatters you and implies that no one else could wear it so well. The real estate salesman can say, "Mrs. Gordon, I've been watching as you went through the home. When you were in the kitchen, I noticed how eagerly you checked everything. I can truthfully say I've never seen a situation where a person looked so much at home. Already you have made it seem homelike."

You say to a distributor, "Mr. Wadsworth, before approaching you, we made a careful study of all the distributors in the city because we want only one person to represent us. You have noted that we have some unique features about our product. We feel that every sales organization could not handle our product successfully. Having studied your sales organization, we feel that it has the qualities that could put this product over in your territory. What is so different between your salesmen and salesmen in other firms? There are several differences, but the outstanding one is the way that you have taught your salesmen to demonstrate. Anyone who will demonstrate the unique features of our product properly will have no trouble in selling it." If you have an exclusive patent, an original design, or some unusual feature, capitalize on it to influence buyers.

Closing on Single Objection

You have made your presentation, demonstration, and are leading up to the close, but you find an obstacle remaining. The couple buying carpeting like the material and the texture; they approve of everything but the shade, which is not quite what they want. The new car buyer had his heart set on a dark blue shade and yours is light blue. The man tries on the new gray suit, likes it, but he wants a blue one. The husband and wife have gone through the house with a California redwood exterior. The wife is ready to buy now, but the husband still has his mind set on a brick house. The buyer had wanted a one-story warehouse, and the one you are showing him is two stories. Outside of that, it meets all his specifications. As far as can be determined, there is only one obstacle in each instance. If that particular point were satisfactorily cleared up, there would be no hesitation in buying. To reinforce this idea, ask the prospect in each situation if this is his only objection. If this objection were removed, would he buy?

Once having gained his affirmation, the skillful salesman can work to demolish the objection. Point out that the "obstacle" is an advantage or that the feature will do no harm, or that it is not easy to get a similar product with as many desirable features. Any product will not have everything we want. In this situation, the strong features more than offset what appears to be a disadvantage. In one instance, a woman entered a shoestore to buy playshoes and dress shoes for the summer. The salesman readily sold her the playshoes; but since he did not have the summer dress shoes in her size, he convinced her that she would be equally pleased by buying early fall shoes. After all, June is not far from September. The salesman need not worry about doing a disservice when overcoming an objection. Most objections are minor. The customer benefits more by having the product than by doing without it because of some inconsequential weakness.

Using Choice

The next time you have an opportunity, watch a skillful salesman using the "choice" method in selling shoes or clothing. After showing a woman several pairs of shoes, the salesman tries to detect which one seems to attract her most. Then, quietly, he will start removing shoes in which she shows little interest. Finally, he is down to two pairs, or three at the most. These are the ones she finds most attractive, most comfortable, most desirable. So, it becomes a matter of picking one. She is not distracted by a multitude of offerings and is able to concentrate more easily. When a man looks through a suit rack, he finds that most of them are unacceptable. Finally, he narrows down to two and then one.

Watch a department store salesman selling appliances. Usually, he will have several brands and several kinds within each brand. Since he is not particularly concerned which brand a customer chooses, he narrows the choice to a couple which seem to appeal. Finally, he will say, "You will notice that both of these have very fine features. It just becomes a matter of personal preference. You can't go wrong on either. Shall we deliver the X or the Y stove?" Book salesmen find it easier to sell by saying, "Would you like the regular binding or the deluxe?" This close is a natural one since the prospect has been brought along throughout the presentation and must now decide. You are trying to make the decision easy.

While this method is applicable to personal buying, it can also be useful with industrial equipment. You will have different sizes and horsepower in the motors. There are special features which can be readily added. Many products are sold in combinations so that the buyer can have the entire package at once or buy it piecemeal by getting the main unit first and then adding elements as he needs and can afford them. Whatever the buying decision of the prospect, the alternatives are such that the salesman wins. He has presented two or more possible choices from which the prospect may choose. To say "no" requires much more effort at this juncture. When the need exists and a convincing presentation has been made, the logical decision is to choose the best alternative.

Notice how easily specific examples can be used. In selling hats: "Would you want the wide brim or the narrow brim?" In selling shoes: "Do you prefer the black or the brown ones?" In selling gloves: "Which do you prefer, the lined or the unlined ones?" In selling mosquito repellent: "Would you like the stick or the liquid?" In selling soap flakes: "Will the regular or the economy size prove most convenient?" In selling lamps: "Which one appeals the most, the one with the side adjustment or the one that adjusts vertically?" In selling insurance: "Would the monthly payment or the semiannual payment be preferable?" In selling casting rods: "Which one feels better, the five-foot or the six-foot rod?" In selling bedroom furniture: "Which will look better in your home, the mahogany or the walnut?" In selling machines: "Would you want the standard or the rugged model?" In selling trees: "Do you prefer the maple or the birch?"

Closing on a Detail

You are ready for the close. Everything has been going smoothly, and you feel that the prospect is ready to buy. You sense that he is nearly ready to say "yes." But you need one more effort to nudge him over, so you casually bring in one more suggestion as an incidental feature. Yet, both of you recognize that it really means that he has bought. The actual item may be unimportant but one that you would ask about only when you feel he has just about made up his mind. You say, "Mr. Farmer, we have now gone through what this machine will do for you, how it is made, and what you can expect of it. You will notice it comes equipped with two styles of levers. Which one of these do you prefer?" "This fur jacket flatters you, Mrs. Kline. If you will tell us where you want the additional loop and button, we'll put them on and deliver the jacket tomorrow." "If you tell us when you want this machine installed, we'll have an operator there to assist you the first day."

As you think of any specific product or service you are selling, your mind soon becomes filled with details, small advantages, and minor decisions which can be suggested to make the buyer act. These details are transitional. They take the individual from a passive listener stage, through an interested prospect stage, to an active buying position. Nowhere do we suggest that you stop abruptly and start again. Rather, in each case there is a normal transition. Just as a train moves from the main track to a switch, so your presentation moves into the close in a natural termination, signalling you have reached your destination.

Telling a Story—Emotional Close

Many of our actions are motivated by emotions. Love and hate, fear and jealously are basic traits that contribute to human motivations and actions. Since emotions are so fundamental in the human makeup, it is logical to use them in selling.

Many people fail to move or perform unless motivated by emotional conflict or desire. Regulating our lives in so many ways, emotions can be put to work to bring about a desirable close. In selling protective articles or services, you may recall stories or situations in which people have suffered because they failed to act soon enough. If you are a tire salesman, you ought to know of situations in which people have been killed because of smooth tires that could not stop the car. Or, you may know of cars that have been thrown off the road by blowouts of badly worn tires. A shoe salesman can casually refer to men who caught the flu because they went out without rubbers on a rainy day. Most of us have seen the slogan "How close do you get?" Then follows an advertisement for a deodorant, a mouthwash, or some other personal product which might make the individual more appealing. Emotions are often more significant than the intellect. Notice how the constant pressure of a son or daughter will cause a parent to give in. All of us have seen how constant pressure from husband or wife causes the other partner finally to explode. Many of us will spend when we ought not to spend because we hate to admit that we do not have the money. Some parents will mortgage their future to give a beautiful wedding for a daughter. When arranging for a funeral, nothing is too good for the dear departed. From birth to death, our lives consist of a series of emotional complexes, ranging from weak and subdued to very strong. They are always present in some form and can be aroused by the salesman's proper touch.

Be prepared to accept resentment from some prospects when you are using this type of close. They sense what you are doing and they object. Granted, this is a negative approach. Because you have probably failed to close with other words, you turn to this one. When using the emotional closing method, be sure that you have informed the prospect thoroughly about your product, what it will do, and what it will offer so that once he accepts, there are no bothersome details to clutter up the close. He knows what your proposition is; he is partially convinced that he should buy; he can see the merits of it; but he is not thoroughly convinced. Hopefully, the emotional close will convince him to buy.

Standing Room Only

Many people want that which they cannot get. The harder it is to get, the more they strive for it. Being aware of this human frailty, an alert salesman can adopt it in his close by putting obstacles in the way of the buyer. The salesman can try to scare him off. When you challenge the buyer in that way, his interest is aroused, his tenacity asserts itself, and his bulldog persistence sets to work. "No one is going to stop me from getting this," he thinks. "If it's that hard to get, I'd better buy it now." "If I'm the only one in town getting this offer, maybe I'd better snap it up."

If ten items will supply the usual needs of a group of individuals, and if they know that these articles are available, they will show no haste in securing them. Nor will they willingly pay the going price. Should these people find out that eleven items instead of ten are available, they will recognize that there is a surplus, and they will be slow to buy. Even if the price goes down, they will probably not act because they know many are left. On the other hand, if these same people discover that ten items are needed and that only nine are available, they panic. If the seller holds off, the price may skyrocket and the buyers gladly offer a much higher price, even though being deprived of the article would cause little inconvenience.

In periods of short supply, frightened people have pushed up prices. In normal times, these shortages seldom develop; in abnormal instances, such as war or disaster, shortages may develop at any moment. Consequently, you may find opportunities when this particular approach is useful, since you can honestly tell the customer that you have only one left or that you do not know when you can get delivery on another. Or, if he wants it on time for a certain event, he had better get it now. If you are sincere and later events prove that you were right, people will gain confidence in you. If, however, this is merely a scare technique to get action, people will soon discover you, and sales will suffer. This method would not be considered the normal one to use under many circumstances; it is not to be used as frequently as other methods that we have discussed. Rather, it is a method for special occasions when the time is appropriate and the statements you make are truthful and can be verified. Buyers who have unwittingly been misled by this method will resent it, and they will not forget. Others who have followed your advice and succeeded in getting merchandise they need badly will be happy that you gave them the opportunity.

Special Deal

Buyers are always looking for a special deal, a better discount, a larger portion, or better delivery dates; they want something extra over the regular deal. Introductory offers to stores are often made with a free deal attached. "Buy twelve cases and get one free," is a common incentive. An introductory discount is likewise quite common.

A combination offer or a tie-in offer appears to give advantages to the buyer. Think of the pitchman. We have all seen him selling a gadget in the dime store, on the fairgrounds, or at the carnival. After his pitch and demonstration, he makes the offer. Not only does he sell the original article, but adds to it until he has a package all for the price of the original article. In this way, the buyer seems to be getting something for nothing, and he goes for it.

Many magazines use the special deal to get subscriptions. "Send in your subscription now and get this free book." "If you send in the check with your order, we will pay the postage." "This offer good for thirty days only. After that, we return to our regular price." Embroider into your offer special inducements and advantages which enrich it in the eyes of the potential customer, and he will eagerly purchase. Unfortunately, many buyers have learned that if they hold out long enough, they can get special concessions or inducements that other buyers do not receive. In price-cutting and discounting, it is not uncommon for the astute buyer to get a better bargain than the one who buys without bickering. Many have learned that you never know how far you can go until you have tried.

The price-haggling tactic may be worthwhile for buyers, but salesmen soon find out about such prospects. When salesmen know what to expect, they can prepare accordingly. Many times, they approach the price-cutter with a special price so that they can "give in" when the buyer becomes insistent. In that way, they seemingly reduce their price without actually doing so. What they may have done is to start with a higher price and come down to the regular price to suit the buyer who insists on having some concession.

When the bargaining gets hard, many salesmen may be tempted to offer a personal attraction to the buyer, or the buyer may ask for something from the salesman. This may appear harmless, but it is the beginning of bribery. Salesmen who rely on buying their customers rather than selling their products to the customers soon find that they are driving down a rocky road. Once you have whetted the appetite of the unscrupulous buyer, his demands are insatiable. The salesman finds that other salesmen who bid against him are using the same tactics. Finally, the whole corrupt procedure is exposed. The buyer loses his job, and the salesman who participated in the activity loses his job. Those who build on the sure foundations of value, quality, service, honesty, and integrity, find—as the years go by—that selling becomes easier, customers become more friendly, the job becomes more pleasant.

Trial Order

A salesman with a new product for industry must have his product proved in use. Seldom will a purchasing agent switch from a satisfactory product to an unknown one, even though the price appears advantageous, unless he is assured that the new product will perform as well as or better than the old one. At the same time, the purchasing agent does not dare to let opportunities go by. Therefore, he may be willing to give you a trial order to see how your new product works in his situation.

The trial order is used to introduce a new line in a store. The buyer may be reluctant to purchase a large quantity until he sees how it sells. The danger of buying too small a quantity, of course, is that it will be placed on a shelf and no one will push it. The product does not get the exposure it should have, and the sales people do not feature it. Many times, an otherwise perfectly good product fails because of lack of promotion. Notice the immense promotion put behind a new consumer product by a national manufacturer. It is brought to the attention of potential customers through mass media, and it is successfully marketed. That is why a store buyer is willing to take on a product from such a firm but would hesitate to buy a similar product from a smaller or unknown firm, even though both products might be equally satisfactory. When a housewife wants a trial order, be sure she gets enough to give the product a fair trial. There have been instances in which the trial order was either too small or too large, though the latter situation is rather unusual because of the initial cost. When offered a trial order, is the customer really interested in finding out how your material works, or is he just trying to get rid of you? Should the latter be true, try again for a regular order.

Reopening the Sale

When you have tried several closes and have been unsuccessful, prepare to leave. (This does not indicate you have given up!) As you prepare to depart, review silently and rapidly the various closes you have tried to see whether or not you have left something unsaid or undone that would interest the prospect.

You can always try to reopen the sale by indicating, as an afterthought, that you probably should have covered one portion of the demonstration better, that you failed to give complete information, or that he might be interested in some phase which you have not covered fully. In none of these suggestions are you repeating yourself; you are simply trying to present all of the information that you have available. Offer him something new, something additional, something appealing.

Although you could return some other time, you may never find the individual in his present frame of mind again. You may sense that he is almost convinced; should you come back later, you would have to repeat a lot of the spadework. This may be the time to ask if you have omitted anything, if you have failed to make yourself clear, if there is any problem bothering him. As this casual conversation goes on, some clue may be dropped which will enable you to reopen the sale on another theme. A quick-thinking salesman finds many opportunities to introduce material which may again quicken the buyer's interest and lead to a sale.

TERMINATING THE INTERVIEW

In every selling presentation, there comes an end. It is time for you to wind up your call. Either you have made the sale or you have not. Whichever way it turned out, do not linger. The buyer will probably want you to leave so that he can go back to his other activities.

Resell

Do not leave abruptly. The buyer has been agreeable and considerate; he has given you his attention, and he has given or will give you money in the future. Be courteous and leave him with some reassuring words. In no way should you convey the idea that you got the better of him. Reassure him that he has made a wise decision which will help his firm in the future.

Tell the housewife that the product will add pleasure to her housekeeping. Point out to the young couple how the acquisition of a new home will mean much in their lives. Tell them that making the right start, such as they have made today, will lead to a happier future. When a customer has decided to buy, he feels that he has done the right thing. He is proud of himself. Fan that pride into a glow of satisfaction. Impress upon him the soundness of his decision.

Leaving

When you have completed your call, leave. After the sale, there might be a tendency to relax and spend some time in general conversation. What a salesman forgets is that the individual has given him courteous attention for a prolonged period. He has taken time and concentration which that individual might have used elsewhere. Now that the interview is over, the buyer wants to get back to his other activities.

In taking leave, the salesman should not be abrupt or hurried, but neither should he linger. He should act in a calm, collected way; in a business-like manner he should assemble his equipment; in a sentence or two he should resell as has been previously explained. Then, he should leave. Lingering may give the buyer an opportunity to reconsider or to wonder if he acted wisely. If the buyer should have a change of heart, it is easy to cancel the order as long as the salesman is still present. All of us are familiar with people who say that they must leave and then keep talking on and on, never quite making the break. As a host, we have stood courteously talking with such people out in the cold, waiting for them to start their car or to be off. Do not be guilty of such an exit. Make a few brief, courteous remarks and then leave promptly.

When You Do Not Close, Leave the Door Open

As a final suggestion, do not let yourself get "no'd" out of the office. This becomes so final that your chance of getting back is rather slim. If you perceive that the sale is not progressing well and that chances of closing are slim, try to exit gracefully, closing with an agreement for a return call at a later time. Set a specific time for the return visit. In itself, that move indicates that he has sufficient interest to see you again.

It is wise to make the second call if you have met constant interruptions or the buyer has been preoccupied. If your talk is not registering, it is no use to go on. Better try another time when you think your chances are better. Sometimes, more than two calls may be necessary. In each case, arrange your calls so that others may follow if deemed advisable. This means that at each call you should have something new, fresh, worthwhile, and specifically applicable to the buyer. Do not expect him to listen patiently if you drag out old material that he has already heard. He gave you another chance because he expected you to give him something new or different. You may find it advantageous to bring the boss or another salesman along with you on a call-back to create fresh interest.

SELF-APPRAISAL

In the preceding five chapters, you have covered the steps that go into making a sale. The material has not been arbitrarily chosen by the author, nor is it the product of any one individual. Rather, this information has been developed by many successful salesmen who, through years of experience, have discovered workable methods.

What you have read is not theory. It is a series of practical, applied, commonsense approaches to the task of selling. We know that they work because they have been tested repeatedly. The sensible approach is to profit from the knowledge and experiences of others. Learn as much as you can from them. Use methods that they have found successful. Refine them to meet your particular needs. Apply them constantly.

When you first try some of the suggestions, they may not work well. Before you condemn them, see if you are using them effectively; then, ask yourself if you are choosing the best methods for each situation. Of the many methods and approaches that you have been given, some will be better adapted to particular needs than others. Like any tools, these methods must be used properly for the greatest benefit. Challenge yourself now to become an outstanding salesman by preparing yourself, and by carrying out the selling task with tools that have been successfully used by many others. Do not think *you* or *your product* or *your firm* is different. Basic principles remain the same. Modifications may be necessary to make them directly applicable, but the fundamentals remain. Always remember that you sell people.

THE TREE OF ACCOMPLISHMENT

This is a portrayal of the steps involved in making a sale and the preparation demanded of the salesman to successfully complete a sale. Study the steps of the sale. Learn how to make each step effective. Practice each step until it becomes a part of your selling process. You must learn and perform so well that each step blends smoothly and almost unconsciously into the next step. We segment the sale into these steps for instructional purposes. In applied selling, all steps are blended and used almost instinctively in the correct pattern and with sufficient intensity to meet the particular selling situation facing the salesman.

As a background to effective selling, our selling tree must have a strong, live, developing root structure to nourish the salesman's efforts. This root system must be fortified, extended, strengthened, and fed to keep it vigorous in supporting the sales effort.

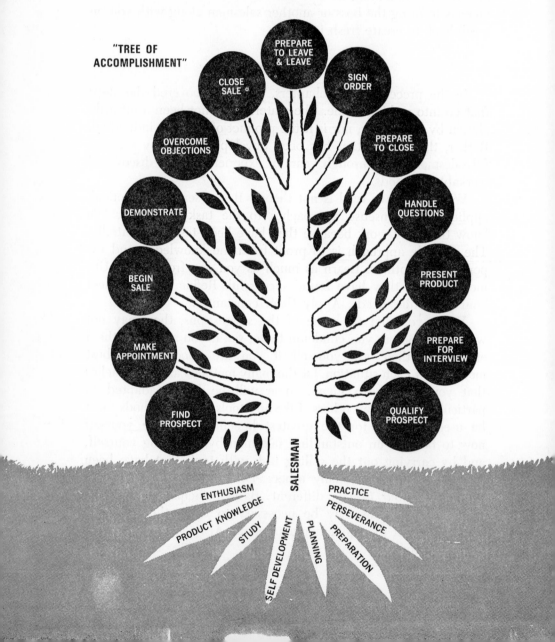

"TREE OF ACCOMPLISHMENT"

PREPARE TO LEAVE & LEAVE

CLOSE SALE

SIGN ORDER

OVERCOME OBJECTIONS

PREPARE TO CLOSE

DEMONSTRATE

HANDLE QUESTIONS

BEGIN SALE

PRESENT PRODUCT

MAKE APPOINTMENT

PREPARE FOR INTERVIEW

FIND PROSPECT

QUALIFY PROSPECT

SALESMAN

ENTHUSIASM

PRODUCT KNOWLEDGE

STUDY

SELF DEVELOPMENT

PLANNING

PREPARATION

PERSEVERANCE

PRACTICE

QUESTIONS AND PROBLEMS

1. Describe the feelings of a salesman as he approaches the close.
2. What are buyer reactions to the close?
3. Is there a proper time to close? Are there many proper times to close?
4. How long should the close be delayed?
5. What are some buyer signals which indicate an immediate close? Are these signals sometimes false? Can a salesman misread closing signals?
6. When is the close inevitable? Are there ever times when you close your presentation without trying for the sale?
7. Is there a limit to the number of times you try to close? Explain, using illustrations.
8. Does each customer have a special time for closing, or are there general indications that may be used to signal an attempt to close?
9. What is the difference between a "trial" close and the "real" close?
10. Why is the third party an obstacle during the close?
11. What procedure can be used in retail selling to handle the third party?
12. It just seems common sense to emphasize your strong points and avoid your weak points. Why, then, is it necessary to caution a salesman on these topics?
13. Give several approaches of the "assuming to buy" technique.
14. What are the merits of summarizing your product's advantages?
15. Why do many salesmen find difficulty in asking for the order?
16. Many people will buy a product that they believe is different. What appeal are you using in such a sale?
17. Is the prospect close to buying if you have narrowed him to a single objection?
18. Illustrate several ways of using choice as a method to close sales. Must all alternatives be positive?
19. When can you base an effective close on some detail of a product or service?
20. What are the advantages and dangers of an emotional close?
21. Are emotions important in the lives of customers?
22. Why are people so interested in getting that which is scarce or possibly unavailable?
23. Can you make a bargain price even more attractive?
24. How can you use the special deal approach to increase sales?
25. When should you try for a trial order? Does the trial order have disadvantages?
26. Why is it better to try reopening a sales interview rather than coming back some other time?
27. Should you resell a customer before you leave? What do you accomplish by reselling?

28. Describe the termination of an interview and leaving the buyer.
29. Should you pave the way for a call-back? Support your answer with illustrations.
30. What can be accomplished through self-appraisal?

CASES

9-1: TRENTON DEPARTMENT STORE

Joe Allenby was a salesman in the sporting goods department of one of the larger chain stores located in the city. Spring had arrived, and for the last week the store had been running full-page advertisements on the latest camping equipment. The biggest feature was the many types and sizes of tents. Joe was anticipating a good season for tents. Tent sales returned generous commissions.

Situation 1

One day Allenby was approached by a man interested in a tent. This is the conversation between them:

ALLENBY: Any particular tent in mind, sir?

PROSPECT: No, just as long as it's big enough for myself, my wife, and the three children.

ALLENBY: Well, that shouldn't be too hard. Here is a nice trailer-tent combination, size 15' x 15' for only $389.

PROSPECT: Well, that's a little high. How about something without a trailer?

ALLENBY: Here is a nice wall tent, 20' x 20' for only $190.

PROSPECT: Sure is nice, but I've got a small car, and the price is still a little more than I had in mind.

ALLENBY: Well, you can't buy something for nothing, you know. Besides, this wall tent would be perfect for your family.

PROSPECT: Yes, you're right, but. . . .

ALLENBY: We do have some smaller umbrella-type tents that are cheaper, but you don't get as much room as in the bigger ones. Would you care to see them?

PROSPECT: Okay.

ALLENBY: Here is a 9' x 9' for only $69, and over here is an 11' x 11' for only $90.

PROSPECT: (Walks in both tents and looks at them) Gee, this 11' by 11' tent looks pretty nice, and the price isn't too unreasonable.

ALLENBY: Oh, it's a nice tent, but don't forget it's smaller and with your family, it might be a little crowded.

PROSPECT: I realize that, but the price is more what I had in mind. You see, I don't want to spend too much. It's going to be for our vacations, and we can't afford a lot.

ALLENBY: Well, at least you have the right idea. Camping sure is cheaper than sleeping in a motel every night.

PROSPECT: You can say that again.

ALLENBY: Let me suggest that when you buy a tent, you also buy sleeping bags, air mattresses, a lantern, and stove. These are items every camper should have.

PROSPECT: Yeah, I hadn't thought of that.

ALLENBY: It's still cheaper than sleeping in a motel.

PROSPECT: Yes, well—thanks anyway. I guess I'll look around some more.

ALLENBY: Good-bye, and thank you.

Situation 2

Allenby is on the floor again the next day. He had gone home the previous night a little concerned because he felt he should have sold a tent to the gentleman the previous day. He resolved not to make the same mistake again. A middle-aged couple approached him:

WOMAN: That's a nice-looking tent over there. (Pointing to the trailer-tent combination)

MAN: Yeah.

WOMAN: Do you think you would like something like that?

MAN: I don't know.

ALLENBY: How do you do. May I help you?

MAN: Yes, we're sort of interested in buying a tent, just for the two of us.

ALLENBY: Any particular model or price range in mind?

MAN: We don't know exactly. Just as long as we like it, I guess. We've never gone camping before.

ALLENBY: Well, here is a nice trailer-tent combination, 15' x 15' for only $389. Plenty of room, and easy to put up. Do you want to charge it or pay cash?

MAN: Wow! I didn't realize they cost so much. Let's see what else you have.

WOMAN: I think it's a real nice tent. What would the payments be?

ALLENBY: I wouldn't worry about the payments right now. They won't be much, and if you like the tent, you won't mind making them.

WOMAN: Do you have any idea what they would be?

ALLENBY: Well, for one year, roughly $35 to $40 a month.

WOMAN: Oh.

ALLENBY: (Turning to the man) Now, over here we have this wall tent, which is 20' x 20' for only $190. This is a more permanent type tent. I believe it would be a little large for the two of you. Besides, it takes longer and is a little harder to put up than the trailer-tent combination.

MAN: How much harder?

ALLENBY: Well, it's just that the trailer-tent combination is so much **easier** to put up.

MAN: How much easier?

ALLENBY: Well, I don't know exactly, since I've never really checked it out.

MAN: How long does it take to put it up?

ALLENBY: About 15 minutes. I would put it up for you, but I haven't read the instructions yet, so I really don't know how. The night crew put this model up. I know you would like the combination though. It's a better tent all around, has a heavier gauge canvas, and you're off the ground, which is nice, especially when it rains.

WOMAN: (Turning to husband) I like the fact that we will be off the ground, don't you?

MAN: Yes, but I'm the one who has to put it up, no matter how easy it is; besides, I really don't know if I want to drag that trailer all around.

ALLENBY: The tent is a real good buy, sir, and it's perfect for the two of you. You can charge it and take it home with you today.

MAN: What are the prices of those tents over there?

ALLENBY: Those are umbrella outside suspension tents. One is 9' x 9' for only $69, and the other is 11' x 11' for $90. They're nice, but they are the type of tent you want if you're going to travel a lot and spend only one or two nights at one spot. They're a little harder to put up. I believe a middle-aged couple like you would be happier with the trailer-tent combination. It seems like every middle-aged couple is buying the combination, and we haven't had any complaints yet.

MAN: Do you mean to say that just because I'm middle-aged I can't put up one of these umbrella tents?

ALLENBY: Oh, no sir, it's just that you're not getting any younger, you know, and the trailer-tent combination is much easier to erect.

WOMAN: Maybe the salesman is right, dear. I like the trailer-tent, and the payments don't seem too bad.

ALLENBY: Well, think it over while I take care of this customer. I'll be right back. Excuse me.

MAN: Okay.

ALLENBY: (Returning) Well, have you made up your mind?

MAN: No, I think we will look around some more. I believe the other department store is offering the same type tent for $20 less, and we want to go look at it.

ALLENBY: Okay, thanks for calling.

Questions

1. Appraise Allenby's handling of the sales.
2. At what point did he attempt to close the sales?
3. How would you have handled the closes?
4. Evaluate Allenby's closing methods and problems.

9-2: FORCEFUL SELLING COUNSELORS, INC.

Situation 1

Phil Griffin is talking to a woman customer in a shoestore. He has sold her a pair of playshoes and is trying to sell her a pair of black pumps for fall wear.

The customer originally came in to inquire about a pair of dress shoes she saw in the window of the store. As she entered the store, she was attracted by a rack of playshoes. She inquired for one particular pair. Phil brought her the pair and tried them on. She liked them and bought the playshoes. Then she inquired about the shoes she had seen in the window.

Phil went back to get the shoes she asked for but found they did not have her size in stock. The time was early July. Many sizes of this particular shoe were sold out, and they were not reordering since the fall shoes had already started to come in. Phil decided to show the customer some of the early fall styles. He explained that they were out of stock of the model in the window, but he did have the early fall styles. The customer wavered somewhat because she felt she should have another pair of summer shoes. But she also showed interest in the fall styles which she tried on.

Question

Develop a dialogue presentation of a close between Phil Griffin and his customer.

Situation 2

Wilbur Hackett watched Mr. Stiles as he walked around the store in a new pair of shoes. Mr. Stiles had been a customer of Wilbur's for three years. Each time he came in he insisted on a particular brand of shoes. Mr. Stiles said that the reason he insisted on this brand was that they were comfortable. Before, he had used other brands that hurt his feet.

The Hackett Shoe Store had recently added another fine brand of shoes. This supplemented their present line at a higher price level. Wilbur was anxious to get his customers to use this new brand. They were finer and better shoes and retailed at prices higher than any other brand presently sold by Hackett. This meant a higher profit on each sale. The shoes were of top quality and had a national reputation.

At the insistence of Wilbur Hackett, Mr. Stiles put on a pair of this new brand of shoe. The outward appearance of the shoes was excellent. Quality was evident, both inside and outside the shoe. As in any new shoe, there was a stiffness which made them not as comfortable as the old shoes Mr. Stiles wore. Yet, even his old shoes had been somewhat uncomfortable when they were new.

Several times in the past twenty-five years, Mr. Stiles had been persuaded to try other brands of shoes. Each time, he had been dissatisfied. He had vowed that from now on he would do no more experimenting. But Wilbur Hackett assured him this new brand would not hurt his feet and would be more comfortable in time than the brand he had been wearing. Finally, Wilbur assured Mr. Stiles that if after wearing them a month he was in any way dissatisfied, he could return them and his money would be refunded. Mr. Stiles appeared impressed but still wavered.

Question

How can Wilbur Hackett close the sale?

Situation 3

Arthur Kniffin, was trying to sell a customer a well-known brand of insulated hunting boots for $12.95. The customer had just come from a store down the street where they sold imported insulated hunting boots for $6.95. He had tried on these boots at the other store but thought they were sort of clumsy. Yet, he didn't see $6 difference between the two pairs.

Arthur showed him the construction of the boots he sold. He explained the durability features. He cited the brand name as one that had been reliable for over fifty years. He talked comfort, lightness, toughness, and other features his boots were noted for. Yet, it was hard to explain the price difference merely by citing quality features. What Arthur realized was that the customer was comparing prices, and even the higher quality, which the customer admitted, could not justify the higher price. Two things were evident to Arthur: (1) the customer was not satisfied with the boots in the other store; and (2) even though the boots he had on now satisfied him, the price was out of line. Clearly, Arthur must try closing on other features or on other appeals.

Question

How can Arthur Kniffin handle the close successfully?

9-3: VERICLEAN LAUNDRY CO.

Allen Friend entered the office and asked the receptionist if he could see Mr. Jones. It was 2:35 p.m., and Allen was on his way to the office when he decided to call on Mr. Jones of the Vericlean Laundry Co. on a "nothing-to-lose" basis. He had last talked with Mr. Jones about five months ago, and he had his doubts about ever establishing his company's product lines.

He worked for a nationally known chemical company selling to industrial accounts only. The product lines consisted of laundry, specialty, and industrial chemicals, which were of superior quality. The company's prices were higher than those of the rest of the industry, but price concessions were made according to the total weight of each order. Three price ranges were offered—under 5,000 pounds, minimum 5,000 pounds, and carload minimum 30,000 pounds. The latter price was by far the best of the three groups offered. The products were quite heavy, and the company Allen was calling on, the Vericlean Laundry Co., a large midwestern organization, would have no problem meeting the carload requirements. According to past usage figures supplied by Mr. Jones, the company's total volume exceeded 50,000 pounds a month. In addition to the pricing system, Allen's company offered other price concessions to firms willing to be distributors or willing to combine their orders with those of other firms in the same area.

Allen's company had spent considerable money in printing various brochures, leaflets, and booklets which the salesmen could supply customers. These publications gave instructions on how to use the products as well as explanations of the various advantages. The company also furnished samples for trial demonstrations. These demonstrations were time consuming and expensive to the customer and required his cooperation since his machines were tied up in the demonstrations. In the laundry trade it always meant isolating the trial batches of clothes in order to determine the results.

Allen was thinking of ways to open the interview when the receptionist informed him that Mr. Jones was ready to see him. He entered the office and was greeted by a seemingly tired Mr. Jones. (He thought to himself that he should not stay long.) He inquired about certain products and Mr. Jones informed him that they were well satisfied with the products they were presently using. In fact, he could not see any difference between Allen's products and his competitor's. Allen told him he did not think his competitor could match his product. He then detailed the many advantages of using his company's products. Jones asked him if he had any literature he could read as he had thrown away the previous literature. Allen did not have literature on all his products but gave Jones what he had. Jones told Allen that one of the main objections his company had was the high cost. He did not know if there was any real difference between Allen's products and the ones they were now using. He then inquired if it would be possible to have some kind of trial demonstration set up.

Allen informed him that a trial demonstration, on a large basis, actually is inconvenient and takes a considerable amount of time. If Jones was willing to put up with the break in schedule, Allen would be more than willing to arrange for a demonstration. "If I can't make it," Allen said, "I'll have one of our other men handle it."

Allen had a few one-pound samples with him that he normally carried. He persuaded Jones to let him use the company's laboratory facilities in order to give him a fast 15-minute demonstration of the superior qualities of two products he thought the laundry would use. The demonstration did not seem to impress Jones. Therefore, Allen left the remaining samples and suggested that the laundry chemists run longer tests, as they would have more time.

Returning to Mr. Jones' office, Allen reviewed the advantages of his company's products. Jones told him he thought the prices were too high. Allen told him he would not mind paying a little more after he found out how good the products were. He continued to expound on the advantages of his products and gave Jones some more literature he found while looking through his briefcase. Jones' secretary interrupted their meeting with the reminder to Mr. Jones that he only had five minutes to sign his letters before the last mail pickup at 4:45. Allen apologized for staying so long but expressed the feeling that it was well worth the time to make the demonstration. He then shook hands with Mr. Jones and left the office.

Questions

1. Evaluate Allen's approach.
2. Where and when did he attempt to close the sale?
3. What steps should he take to close the sale?

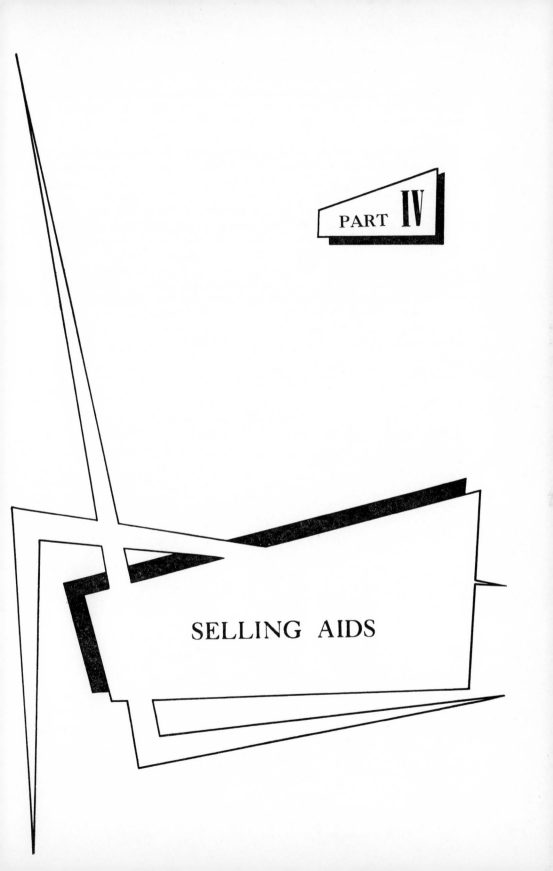

PART IV

SELLING AIDS

CHAPTER 10

Sales Building

The sale has been completed, and you have left the buyer's office. You review the sale. What might have been done better? How could the sale have been increased? How could better-quality merchandise have been sold? How could your presentation have been more persuasive and the sales results greater? If you left the customer with only a token sale or none at all, what could you have done better? Let us sit down together and consider what improvements could have been made.

WHAT YOU CAN DO AS A SALESMAN

First, consider those areas of salesmanship that affect you. What can you do to make yourself more valuable, helpful, interesting, and satisfying?

What to Do—What to Avoid

Go over the steps of the sale to see where you were strong and where you were weak. Study each detail of your presentation and evaluate it critically. Tape a presentation, and play it back to yourself to see how you sound to others. Did you present your product in terms of the needs of the customer? As you talked, were you thinking of yourself or of him? Were the suggested applications interesting to him?

If you were to do the presentation over, what changes would you make? What did you do or say that you wished you had not? Did you discuss topics not relevant to your sale? Did you venture into subjects that could have led to an argument? Did your talk stray from the purpose at hand? Did you talk too much? Could you detect that your prospect became weary once or twice when you belabored a point? Did you interrupt or cut him off when he was talking? Was the presentation too one-sided? Did he buy from you because he really wanted to or because he had to have some merchandise? Will he welcome you on your next call? This is the time to analyze what you said to see where you could improve and what you should avoid in the future.

Study

The progressive salesman finds better ways to do things. He looks for new methods, new devices, new opportunities, and new approaches to substitute for what he has done before or to supplement it. He reads sales books, industry magazines, and business magazines. He studies techniques employed by successful salesmen. He searches exhaustively for new information.

Think

The successful salesman is the thinking salesman. He reviews to see where he has failed, what he has done wrong, what he has omitted. He rehearses his pattern of action, his procedures, his behavior. If he senses that he has offended a customer, he analyzes his weakness. Beyond that, he is not content to continue without improvement. He tries to develop new methods and unique approaches. He continually tries to do his job better and to become more convincing.

Enough cannot be said for the importance of serious thinking. Once you concentrate on your job, ideas begin to come, and you develop new procedures. Taken together, they can eventually lead to a much better presentation than your previous ones.

Plan

A salesman's planning should take several forms. He should plan a variety of presentations suitable for the needs of his many customers. He should cover his territory without waste of time or repetitive backtracking. He should plan his time so that he spends the most valuable parts of the day with his customers. He should do his paperwork in the evening or at nonproductive sales hours. His personal activities should not interfere with his working hours.

As he goes along, he will find important areas of planning. Inevitably, when one develops a number of plans, some will interfere with others. It is up to each salesman to organize his routine so that plans dovetail rather than clash. Some plans must be modified to fit in with others. Some plans must be staggered for different time periods. Activities must be cataloged in order of urgency and time allotted in proportion to their importance. The salesman cannot afford to let days go by and work in a hit-or-miss fashion that results in too few hits and too many misses.

To be meaningful, plans must be in writing. Merely thinking about them and keeping them in one's head means that they can easily be forgotten or sections of them can be omitted if time seems pressing. The mere fact that you write them and try to arrange them in an orderly fashion will stress their significance. Arrange them in order of importance and weigh the value of each. If you faithfully follow a pattern, you will develop sound habits that become a part of you.

Train

The successful salesman is always learning something new. His training continues in a two-pronged fashion—one prong follows those activities which increase his knowledge, broaden his perspective, and develop his creativity. The other prong is the retraining one. It is a refresher in which he goes over material he has once learned but now forgotten through disuse or misuse. Valuable information can easily be forgotten in the press of everyday activity. It is almost like driving on a smooth tire; it functions well enough, but it would be dangerous to trust it too long. In selling, we become so forgetful and so careless that it is necessary to retread ourselves.

Sell in Broader Terms

The successful salesman must think up ways to build sales, to get new customers, and to find new avenues of approach. He should think of selling in broader terms than merely making a sale. He must think of the market of tomorrow. He must plan to change procedures, to incorporate new and better methods. The products he sells today may be outdated tomorrow. To continue successful selling, he may have to change products or shift emphasis. Does he follow the development of the suburban market, the change in people's living habits, the development of new likes and dislikes in purchasing? Is he aware of market segmentation—the Negro market, the teenage market, the senior citizen market, the women's market, the men's market, the market for recreational items? Markets nonexistent today may command much of the consumer's income in the next few years.

Is the salesman aware of studies on consumers? Does he know what motivates customers and how to persuade them? Does he take advantage of the multiplicity of sales aids available? Does he use them effectively? Does he experiment with them, and is he willing to try new methods which will eventually supplant the present ones?

The salesman who is content to keep on going in his usual rut will soon regret his carelessness. If his work consists of mechanical order-taking, he will be supplanted by catalogs and self-service, which are cheaper and equally effective. If he fails to develop into an effective, dynamic, creative, aggressive salesman, there will be no room for him. The only selling jobs worthwhile will be filled by the new breed of salesman. You cannot be content with things as they are; you cannot expect your job to continue as it has in the past.

Quota

Salesmen are becoming more familiar with quotas. Many are now working under quotas which require them to accomplish prescribed results. Thus, you may have a sales quota, a product quota, an expense quota, a product mix quota, and other quotas which may fit your particular area. A sales quota can be given as a certain number of dollars or units of products each month, quarter, or year. An expense quota may be expressed as a percentage of sales but usually is given as a certain number of dollars per week or specific daily allowances for food, lodging, and incidentals. A product mix quota is used when a salesman has several products. He is expected to sell each product in his line in total quantities indicated by quotas. Some salesmen have quotas for collecting accounts, for setting up displays, and for training wholesale salesmen. In each case, your firm is introducing a measuring stick. How well do you perform against a standard?

Each year firms become more proficient in setting attainable quotas that have been developed scientifically, not picked out of thin air. As these quotas become more accurate, salesmen are expected to fulfill them. Quotas are guidelines of performance; they are measuring devices that keep you and your boss informed about your progress. If you perform well, do not fear quotas. If you are a shirker, a quota will spotlight you. Whatever your present situation is, accept quotas as guidelines for a successful performance.

Territory Analysis

Through territory analysis, employers can study a territory to see how effectively it is being handled and how sales compare with potential. If your firm does not stress territory analysis, you have greater latitude to do your own study. If it makes partial studies, you still have the opportunity to explore areas that your superiors are neglecting.

Your territory is your gold mine. From it you must extract sales to pay your salary and expenses and to contribute to the company's overhead. If you work your territory carefully, intelligently, and persistently, you will find the reward greater than you ever dreamed. By using the most up-to-date methods, you can double or triple your productive capacity. You may be startled by how much potential exists in your territory once you begin to uncover all the gold that lies there.

Contests

Some firms use contests extensively. More contests are being developed in which each salesman is rewarded according to his sales record. A contest should stimulate, should arouse enthusiasm, and should encourage better performance.

Enter into the spirit of the contest with enthusiasm and zeal. Here is a chance to distinguish yourself. Your company is going out of its way to make selling easier and more profitable for you and for it. It is good sense to take advantage of these contests and to do as well as you can. Perform well, and win material rewards and admiration of company executives. A contest is a sales builder to spur you on to greater efforts, to make you more successful, and to instill in you the desire to excel. To be successful, a contest must be rewarding to three parties—your customer, your firm, and you. Never forget this three-legged stool of achievement.

Conferences

Every year you will attend one or more of your firm's conferences. Some salesmen consider this a waste of time or a recreation period. In too many conferences, salesmen attend with the idea that nothing will be gained; they enter with a defeatist attitude. With this attitude, it is impossible to gain anything. Until such attitudes are changed, employers will be throwing away money on sales personnel.

Firms set up conferences for well-established objectives. They may want to train or retrain salesmen or to introduce new products and new methods. Often, a conference is used to recharge the batteries of enthusiasm.

Conferences carefully planned and executed are rewarding for the wide-awake salesman. He gains a keener perspective of his firm, gets acquainted more intimately with executives, and he learns more about his fellow salesmen. He gathers knowledge of new sales tools and techniques. He has a chance to improve his knowledge, to find answers to perplexing problems, and to develop better sales strategies.

If you participate eagerly in a conference, if you actively try to develop your techniques, learn more about your product and how to handle questions and problems more intelligently, the conference will be a rare opportunity. Here in one group are many people who daily meet and overcome obstacles which may be serious hindrances to you. Use the conference as a positive sales builder to stimulate you to greater success.

Advertising

The wise salesman takes advantage of advertising whenever possible. Whether the advertising is so extensive as to do almost all of the work or whether it merely acts as introduction for the salesman, it is a force that cannot be overlooked. At its weakest, advertising publicly illuminates your product. At its best, advertising makes the sale. As a blocker in the football game clears the way for the runner, so advertising can clear the way for the salesman. To fail to take advantage of this clearance is unforgivable.

Advertising can talk to all customers at once, but a salesman can talk to only one at a time. Advertising conveys a unified message, whereas the salesman may vary his message from customer to customer. Some variation is permissible and even desirable, but all too often variations end up in mediocre presentations. Powerful advertising is dynamic and exciting. It can build integrity and prestige as well as supplement the creative power of the salesman. Advertising is a workhorse that neither tires nor sleeps, that does not change its mind or unexpectedly say the wrong thing

In many cases, various sales promotion devices are instrumental in moving merchandise. Often, a well-developed promotional campaign will be the deciding factor in the dealer's acceptance of your merchandise. He may take your product because your promotional material is good enough to sell it.

Credit

Credit gives a salesman tremendous advantages. In many areas of retailing it is a must because it furnishes an opportunity to close a sale without cash. When a sale has been made, credit can increase the sale as you suggest other items. In business, credit is used almost universally since few firms pay cash for what they buy. By judicious use of credit, you can strengthen the sale, make deliveries earlier, sell more easily, and increase satisfaction.

Credit encourages purchase of capital equipment. It is a convenient and orderly way to meet financial obligations incurred during the operation of a business. It enables the finance officer to handle money obligations over an extended period of time. It is a powerful tool, enabling the buyer to realize immediate production satisfaction without sacrificing financial mobility.

Develop New Business

In the preceding discussion, we have indicated ways in which you can improve. Now let us look at the other side of the sale from the viewpoint of the customer. If the customer is a retailer, his most important task is to keep his present sales and increase them. You will be welcomed by him when you bring in not only new merchandise but also new ideas. If your customer is a manufacturer, he will welcome ideas on how to use material more effectively and, if possible, on how to stretch its use. He will also welcome suggestions about developing other products from your material. If your customer is a farmer, he will be interested in precise applications. If you are selling fertilizer, he will want to know about the right applications for maximum results. If it is a weed killer, he will want to know the exact amounts to use without harming other plants. If you are selling to the housewife, she will want to know how best to use the article or the material. You can explain how your product can give greater value by using it correctly. Notice we are on the customer's side of the fence, and that we look at the product the same way he does.

For a moment, consider some problems and how to handle them. You have just walked into a shoe repair shop. In discussing your supplies the shoe repairman asks, "Well, specifically, how can I use your material to make more sales?" Or you are a seed salesman who has walked into the garden supply center. The manager is already handling a well-known brand of seed. As a matter of fact, he seems quite well stocked. During your presentation he bluntly asks, "How will your seed increase my sales?" Or you are talking to a buyer of women's sweaters in a dress shop. She says, "We bought some on your advice, but we found that they did not sell very well. In fact, our other line outsold them three to one. Now you are back again wanting us to put in new items and, frankly, my question is why?" Or you are calling on a hardware dealer with a new line of paints. He listens to you for a while and then says, "I already have a well-known, well-advertised line of paints which is quite satisfactory. You are asking me to stock yours in addition to what I already have. Why should I?" We could go on giving illustrations, but these are indicative of the problems facing you. Probably, most of the persons in the examples above are already doing a satisfactory business. They may not be particularly interested in stepping up sales. Yet, it is your job to sell your product.

You might say to the hardware dealer, "Mr. Anderson, I know you have a good line of paints. I gather that you are quite successful in your community. Nevertheless, I am sure there are many people in this community who are buying paints elsewhere. The customer you have today may move away or be attracted to some other dealer. The only way that you can maintain your present situation is by finding new customers. There is no such thing as standing still. Either you are progressing by developing new business, or you are sliding backward by being content with what you already have. If you belong to a church or a club, you know that the only way to keep your membership up is by recruiting new people to replace those who drop out. Similarly, you will recruit new customers if you carry our line of paints."

Help Customers Sell

The salesman who calls on retailers has any number of opportunities to be of service. The retailer, standing in his own shop, surrounded by his own merchandise, talking to his regular customers, gets in a rut. Frequently, other businessmen with whom he talks are operating similarly. When he goes to his luncheon club or chamber of commerce meeting, the men there are much like him and are not likely to furnish many new ideas. But you, an outsider, seeing many stores, talking with many retailers, and having information your firm is constantly gathering, should be able to contribute helpful ideas. Suggest a different way to trim store windows, a new way of merchandising, different tie-in sales, a variation in hours of opening and closing, a change to self-service, the use of special holiday promotions, emphasis on some special events—one could name dozens of suggestions that might be useful to a retailer. Quite likely, one or more of these might prove appealing and worthy of trying.

If you are selling janitor service, mention new techniques which might interest prospective users of the service, or combinations of services that can be offered at different periods of the day or night. Speak of relieving the buyer of his cleaning problems. Point out that professional janitorial service uses protective coatings that are more durable than those applied by amateurs.

If you sell supplies to a summer resort operator, mention what others are doing to bring in more people. Tell him how some operators are enticing people back year after year. Mention that some summer resort operators have increased their business by offering a greater number of services and types of entertainment, appealing to a wider range of guests. Many successful operators today provide not only the physical comforts desired by guests but also entertainment. People on vacations lack imagination to develop enjoyable activities on their own and are willing to pay others to develop them.

If you sell hobby supplies and equipment to a dealer, you can give him literature that suggests how to start hobby clubs. Consider garden clubs, for example. Some people join together in a club for general gardening, some have interests in certain flowers, and others have interests in a few vegetables. Many special clubs concentrate on mums, roses, or dahlias. The renewed interest in square dancing furnishes opportunities for selling specialized equipment. Bowling enthusiasts are ready purchasers of sweaters, balls, and shoes. And have you ever met the fisherman who had enough fishing tackle? Each year he buys something. Study your area, and you will be amazed by the number of suggestions that you can make for improvement.

Improve Communications

Improve your communications and you will have fewer misunderstandings. At times, when a sale is made, the buyer has his mind on several things and fails to grasp the conditions involved. Or, in his eagerness, the salesman fails to bring out all conditions that are implicit in the sale. Such situations lead to misunderstandings and unhappiness which someone must clear up lest they remain as festering sores.

In your work you may call on some customers so infrequently that weeks or months might pass between calls. Such lapses of time let your customer forget you or remember someone who came later with a similar proposition. It is inexcusable to let a customer forget you. Modern methods of communication enable you to hold customer attention in various ways without causing resentment. You might, for example, use a satisfactory pretext for writing a letter. Perhaps you have uncovered some new idea or new item which is being featured. Even though your subject matter might not have too great an appeal, at least the customer will remember you. A birthday or anniversary card is always acceptable. A congratulatory note on your customer's receipt of some honor is in order. You can also call on the telephone. After all, phone calls do not take much time, they are relatively inexpensive, and they are a gentle reminder of your presence.

One method of preventing long periods elapsing without contacting a customer is to have some reminder—some call it a tickler file. This is nothing more than a file that brings information to your attention at designated intervals or days. Some use a reminder book to jot down information. Whatever method you use, be sure that the data is so recorded that at regular intervals it will come to your attention.

If a problem arises between your firm and your customer, clear it up by contacting your customer as soon as possible. It is too injurious to let this situation drag. When a customer needs you, your service, your products, but chooses not to deal with you because of past incidents, you both lose. You lose because he does not buy from you. He loses because he cannot sell the material your firm provides. Even if he is stubborn, that does not give you the privilege of the same behavior. You can both stand on your dignity and starve.

Have you ever thought of improving communications when talking with a new customer? Have you ever considered the use of slides, movies, models, and demonstration equipment to convey your message? Have you, in spite of your customer's apparent agreement during your presentation, later found that he neither understood nor agreed? Are you sure that what you say is clear to him? Are you talking his language? Have you repeated your presentation so many times that you have lost its original intent and allowed yourself to drift away to another meaning?

Do you communicate in a variety of ways? Do you use words, actions, deeds—the way you live, your standing in the community, the impression you give your fellow man? Many of us interpret "communications" too narrowly. We forget that voice, although highly important, is only one of many ways through which we transfer ideas.

A salesman of a well-known brand of mints tells this story. One store in Cleveland had little success in moving its mints. The salesman asked for permission to move a table to an aisle near the front of the store. He placed the table in a strategic location and heaped high his rolls of candy. In the course of a week the store had moved large numbers of mints without any special price reduction. In another case, a well-known variety chain featured a brand of toothpaste at a "special price," a reduction from 39¢ to 35¢. The managers filled a window with a display of toothpaste and did remarkably well in selling it. Ironically, within the same block, a drugstore had difficulty in selling the same product (without advertising) at a cut-rate price of 29¢.

Not long ago, an enterprising implement dealer set up a tent show in which manufacturers of farm equipment were invited to display their various machines. Farmers were invited to attend and, of course, they were furnished a free lunch. It proved to be eminently successful. Manufacturers demonstrated their equipment in a number of applications. Farmers were allowed to operate equipment. Movies and slides gave details which were hard to explain with words. Farmers mingled with each other, with factory representatives, and with dealer salesmen. The entire event became an effective means of presentation and selling in an exciting environment with an enthusiastic crowd. A car manufacturer set up a camping show and invited manufacturers of camping equipment to display their wares with his line of cars at a special showing. Thousands of people attended and thereafter associated the camping equipment with the cars in which (and around which) it had been displayed.

Firms selling through the party plan create their own market. Many of their sales are made to people who probably would not have purchased such an item had they not attended the party and become indebted to the hostess. Those who consider this to be pressure selling fail to realize that to many a housewife a party of this nature is an evening's entertainment which costs no more than many other types of entertainment that are purchased outright.

The preceding illustrations indicate ways of getting people into the mood for buying. Carnivals, church fairs, rummage sales, auctions, and other special events quicken the pulse of customers, arouse them emotionally, get them in a receptive mood, and result in sales. When you look at how often people buy because they are determined to buy, and how many more times they are sold because they are emotionally motivated, you recognize the opportunity for creating sales. Even today's supermarket that furnishes the necessities of life employs various strategies to stimulate impulse purchases.

Your job is to be aware of these many opportunities. When you talk with a customer, use appropriate and incisive techniques to undercut his sales resistance. Man has various facets— the physical, the mental, the spiritual, the intellectual. The same individual who is serious-minded and devoted to his work during the day may be quite a different, fun-loving person in the evening. The one carrying on regular weekly activities may have quite a change in the pattern of living on Sunday. Because of these habits and variations, you have numerous opportunities in which to create sales.

Each year individuals get more discretionary income, the money that is not needed for the necessities of life, which may be spent as the individual sees fit. Since he can spend his income either according to a budget or according to whims and desires, some of this income might readily be captured by the alert salesman, the retailer, the one who sells services, the one who sells entertainment, or the one who is soliciting funds for worthy causes. (Many people get as much enjoyment giving money to worthwhile causes as others would get spending it on some self-indulgence, but usually some clergyman sells them on the idea). As an adult, you are readily satisfied with a small Coke, but your young son will compromise with nothing less than a 16-ounce bottle of soft drink and thinks you are crazy because you settle for the smaller bottle at the same price, so he persuades you to get the large bottle which he will finish for you.

Products and services have value only insofar as the individual can enjoy them. He may end his meal in a restaurant with a piece of pie for which he pays a regular price. Were he asked to eat a second piece immediately after the first, he would probably be unwilling to pay for it. As a matter of fact, he might be willing to pay the restaurant owner *not* to make him eat the second piece. This illustrates that a product may be desirable at one moment and repugnant the next.

Sales may be created by convincing a customer that an item which seems to have little appeal because of limited use does have more uses than are first acknowledged. Thus, fire-resistant home construction material can also be helpful in temperature control. Various opportunities present themselves when a salesman thinks in terms of additional uses. The insurance executive sells a man on becoming a part-time salesman hoping he will become a full-time salesman. The pickup truck can be used for vacations by installing a removable trailer body. A stove can be used for cooking and heating. The basement recreation room can be converted to temporary sleeping quarters. If the salesman puts out feelers which cause the buyer to think of new possibilities and applications, the interaction of ideas can develop a third set of possibilities which relate better to specific needs.

Adapting successful methods of others to present situations opens fruitful areas of exploration which can lead to better operation. If you let your imagination have full play, ideas may crop up which apparently have little purpose or little application at first. Tossed around in your mind for a period of time, however, seemingly barren ideas can become fruitful.

Most of you are familiar with the "brainstorming" sessions in which people in a group record whatever ideas may come to mind on a particular subject. Although most of these ideas may be useless, out of a large number of thoughts recorded, one or two will be significant. On several occasions the author asked groups of students to develop ways of handling problems. As one might expect, most of the answers have been routine with no particular merit. But out of a group of such answers, someone usually comes in with a new idea which might work.

Every day new successful ideas are introduced in the business world. Someone thinks of them; they do not come from "thin air." Why not make that someone you? As a matter of fact, that someone must be you sometime or other, or you will not justify your existence as a creative salesman. Every year business is eliminating the salesman who is merely an order taker, yet business has found no means of replacing the truly creative salesman.

WORKING WITH THE CUSTOMER

So far in this chapter, we have dealt with two facets of sales building. The first group of ideas was concerned with the salesman and his firm and how to improve within these areas. Examples of improvements would be wider lines of products, several price lines of products, or greater utility of products. Salesman improvement would be better preparation, improved demonstration techniques, and better planning. The second group of ideas tried to develop business and increase sales for the customer.

Now we are assuming that the customer is a buyer and that he has additional buying potential that is ready to be tapped by some salesman. Why not let this salesman be you?

Price Variations

One of the strongest inducements for buying is the lower price. For example, a retailer wants to buy at the lowest price so that he can make a wider margin of profit or lower his price. The buyer of a manufacturing firm is always interested in getting the best price, so that manufacturing costs will be lowered and the firm can compete successfully. The buyer of services is interested in a better price which will save him money.

Some salesmen sell wholly on price. Buyers soon learn that they can force such salesmen down by haggling and by hard bargaining. These salesmen either reduce their prices to such an extent that there is little profit for the firm, or they are unable to sell and get fired. There are legitimate price variations, but some are not legitimate.[1] We shall concern ourselves with the former.

In business, we have the "list" price. This may be the actual price paid by a buyer, but in most cases it is an artificial price from which discounts can be calculated. We are not talking about a suggested retail price, but a list price which is used by manufacturers who sell to other manufacturers or users. Some buyers are obsessed with the idea of carrying a minimum inventory; consequently, they buy the smallest possible amounts. Usually, this involves a higher price and sometimes higher transportation costs.

You have many price weapons at hand. Quantity buying gives larger discounts and lower prices. Often, large orders will be shipped freight prepaid. Off-season orders are often sold at a lower price. Sometimes, goods slightly damaged are sold in special bargain lots. Many firms have discontinued models which can be purchased advantageously. Style merchandise slightly out of fashion can be picked up cheaply. Holiday merchandise can

---

[1] If one buyer gets a discount and another does not under the same considerations, such a discount is not legitimate and breaks the law. If one buyer gets a quantity discount and another does not, and the discount cannot be justified through a savings in cost, it is not legitimate. If the quantity discount is on such enormous quantities that all buyers save one is eliminated, such a price discrimination is questionable.

be purchased after the holidays and stored, and the total price of the merchandise plus the storage will be less than buying it during or immediately before the next holiday season. A variety of terms to delay the payment date is often used as buying bait. Occasionally, a firm that is hard pressed for business will offer special terms for a limited time to encourage sales to keep their factory going. At times, pricing is used to keep the firm operating and to minimize losses.

One of the simplest devices for price variation is found in baked goods. Today's unsold loaf of bread will be retailed to-morrow morning at half price. It is common to buy fresh fish Saturday evening for half price because the supermarket cannot carry it over the weekend. One retailer bought ten thousand sweaters from a manufacturer who wanted to get rid of his inventory. He paid about half of the usual wholesale price and then sold them retail at the regular wholesale price.

Many price variations are included in special promotion deals. Such price variation would be considered an advertising or pro-motion cost and not a true reduction of price; but whatever you call it, the retailer is able to get the merchandise at a lower price. He can either pass it on to the customer or make it more profitable for himself. Price variations can also be given when services or functions are omitted. It is not uncommon to buy unpainted furniture and finish it at home. It is not uncommon to buy knocked-down equipment and assemble it. It is not uncommon to buy semi-manufactured merchandise and finish the manufactur-ing in your own plant.

On the other hand, some buyers want everything completely finished and ready to go. In numerous instances, by adding the additional features or additional services, you can get a price increase. Though the basic product you sell carries a slim profit margin, the addition of extras may make the sale quite profitable. Since price is such an effective tool, learn to use it intelligently.

Trade-Ins

As soon as we mention trade-ins, one thinks of used cars. In the enormous automobile industry, the trade-in is of particular importance. As a matter of fact, the used car industry itself is enormous and one that many people patronize at one time or another.

When there is a fixed selling price for a new item, the trade-in is frequently used to overcome the price barrier. Usually, one trades an old car for a new one or a newer one. One may trade an old appliance for a new appliance. Old furniture may be traded for new furniture. However, there is no reason why an enterprising salesman might not take some other object in trade for whatever he sells. One could trade a washing machine on a new car. The difficulty in such a deal is that the old merchandise will be hard for you to move. However, the intelligent salesman soons finds channels of distribution—outlets for merchandise in which he could sell old types of equipment satisfactorily.

Salesmen are reluctant to utilize this method because it entails a little more trouble and a little more thought. Unimaginative, conservative, and reluctant to work, they regard trade-ins of different merchandise an unwarranted excursion into unplotted areas. In making such sales, the alert salesman broadens his knowledge of the sales field. He learns that a trade-in gives useful leverage for adjusting the selling price. Oftentimes, he uses a trade-in as a hidden discount.

Do not take a trade-in and then fail to pick up the old object. The buyer feels something is wrong if you give an allowance for a trade-in and then refuse to take it. In industry, valuable machinery can be traded in on new machinery. Equipment no longer usable in one plant can be used elsewhere. Real estate can be traded because a location that may be wholly inadequate for one firm may be quite adequate for another. Recreational equipment is frequently traded in on a different type of equipment, and a ready market is available for the old merchandise. Occasionally, the trade-in can be more valuable than the merchandise that you have sold. In that case, the seller gives his new item plus cash for the old. One example would be in trading an antique piece of furniture for new furniture plus cash. The furniture dealer might have a ready market for the antique. Do not underestimate the possibilities of trades.

Stepping Up Sales

Increasing a sale often spells the difference between profit and loss. Many opportunities arise whereby an original sale may be increased. Most of us know how the new car sale is often stepped up by adding accessories. When a woman buys a new dress, she buys accessories to match. Once a new home is purchased, there is always the addition of garage, landscaping, storm windows, fence, trees, and many other items. A man who buys a shirt is urged to buy neckties. When you buy a pair of shoes in the fall, there can be additional sales of overshoes, slippers, socks, shoe trees. When new carpeting is purchased, there is always the possibility of new drapes. The furniture salesman has a wonderful chance of increasing his sales. To a retailer, one can suggest related items which move well with the basic pieces. Studies in drugstore sales have shown that salesmen who suggest additional items to the druggist also increase their sales.

Most stores featuring open displays invite the customer to participate actively in the buying function. Give customers access to many items, including those which buyers were not even considering when they entered the store. Anyone standing at a checkout register in a store is amazed to see the variety of items brought up by customers. Suggestions may be made skillfully, courteously, and helpfully without arousing antagonism. Many people who disapprove of having additional items forced upon them are happy to listen to a discreet presentation of additional merchandise.

If you try to step up sales from the customer's viewpoint rather than the salesman's, your suggestions will probably be well received. The customer resents sales pressure when he sees no need for the product. However, he will welcome suggestions for additional items which will more adequately take care of his needs. Since quality is a relative term, usually there is opportunity to step up the quality of the purchase. Many times, the customer is intent on buying an item at a certain price. But once he has seen a similar item of higher quality, he recognizes the value and transfers his attention to the better one. The quality item attracts more attention because it looks better, perhaps feels better, works better, lasts longer, gives trouble-free service, and has many other features.

Sometimes it may be to your interest to step down quality if you feel that the individual is buying something far beyond his needs and that something of lesser quality will meet his needs equally well. This may seem shortsighted, but in the long run you can develop trust and lasting relationships.

Many times it is advantageous for the customer to buy in larger quantities. For the dealer, this means a better discount and more adequate inventory, a wider selection, less danger of running out, and a better looking display. For the manufacturer, it may mean eliminating the danger of a breakdown which would force stoppage of operations. For the restaurant, it may mean the difference of serving customers adequately rather than disappointing them.

On a Saturday evening, talk with the manager of a supermarket about the bread he has left over and wants to sell at a reduced price. Usually, this lower price does not disturb him because it is better to have a few loaves of bread left to sell at a reduced price than to run out and have to disappoint customers. If a store gains the reputation of not having stock, customers will stop calling. If a wholesaler runs out of stock frequently, the retailer or the manufacturer will cease to rely on him and turn to a more reliable source. At any level of business activity, therefore, the salesman can point out the dangers of insufficient inventory.

He can stress the cost of buying in small lots and getting the smallest discounts; he can stress the cost of being out and disappointing others; he can stress the cost of lost sales because of lack of variety. If you are to act as a professional salesman looking after the needs of your customers, it is imperative that you sell them the right quality, the right quantity, and the right selection of merchandise. If they are unaware of their needs, it is your job to show them what they ought to have. To do less is to shirk your job.

Reciprocity

Reciprocity means that if firm A buys from us, we must buy from firm A. Reciprocity has many unpleasant features. The one who substitutes reciprocity for quality and service soon finds customer relations deteriorating. Because you put up with reciprocity, you often have to put up with other weaknesses. Reciprocity can be practiced to such an extent that not only do two firms patronize one another, but they put strong pressure on a third firm, or a fourth firm to patronize them because of some tie-up with a customer of theirs. This can be extended to a ludicrous degree.

In many types of industry, reciprocity is widely practiced. If you happen to be selling in such an area, take advantage of reciprocity just as you would use any other sales tool. But recognize it for what it is—a crutch. If you lean on it too heavily, never exercising other sales tools, your crutch might break. When that happens, you have nothing for support. The wise salesman uses it moderately, never forgetting there are more effective ways of selling. He never lets down in his attempts to develop himself and his firm in various ways. Put your best foot forward. Sell on the basis of service, quality, price, delivery, and other concrete attributes. Reciprocity loses its effectiveness when you depend upon it too often. Those who tend to use it exclusively are sorry excuses for salesmen.

Gifts

The saying "Gifts make foolish the hearts of the wise" is familiar. There is a wide range of custom in gift giving. If you are selling to the owner of a plant or store, and he accepts gifts, there is no particular repercussion because he knows what is being done. If, however, you give gifts to an employee, the proprietor may take offense because he feels that the one who accepts gifts may be prejudiced by them when he purchases.

Insofar as possible, we suggest you avoid gift giving which is meant to influence purchasing. Major gifts can be taken as bribes. However, small gifts, token gifts, are often appreciated and are not of sufficient value to influence the buyer except as an act of thoughtfulness. Certainly, a lunch or a dinner is not to be construed as bribery. A small token gift for an anniversary, a Christmas card, or a small Christmas present is not out of place.

While no one can set an absolute limit between a major gift and a token gift, an item costing below $10 should evoke little criticism. Most buyers would not think of a minor gift of this nature as bribery; nor should you think of it in this way. A gift of flowers or candy to the home on an anniversary, or a gift to one ill in the hospital is well considered. Sometimes, a contribution to a buyer's favorite charity is in order. A gift should be a genuine token of friendship, not a reward. Gift giving as a token of thoughtfulness is always appropriate, and it is always in good taste.

Good Deeds

To be well thought of and have a good reputation is an excellent testimonial for any salesman. One who carries honor, prestige, and is admired is in a favorable position. Some people constantly do kind things for others. Even though such people do not advertise their benevolent acts, word gets around. Kindly, thoughtful acts carried out without fanfare, without a demand for recognition, and without expectation of reward raise you in the estimation of your fellowman. Though the things you do may be in your own neighborhood, far away from where your sales activities are carried on, just the mere doing of such things helps you. Your actions change your personality. Instinctively, your customer recognizes your qualities.

If you are afraid that others may regard you as a hypocrite when you do kind things, do not stop. Do them unobtrusively so that even your acquaintances are unaware of what goes on. In the long run, the results will be gratifying, and you will be a better person because of those good works.

Do minor things for your customer. Each may be insignificant in itself, but accumulated, they soon have an effect. The customer may not warm up to you because you have done one or two small favors for him. But over a period of time, there will come a gradual change of attitude, and soon you will become one of his friends and receive preferential treatment.

Keeping Customers Happy

The happy, contented, successful customer is one who can appreciate your effort. This is particularly true if you helped him to achieve his status. Maybe you bought that hard-to-get football ticket, introduced him to the right people at the country club, helped him move some old merchandise, suggested a way to help his children achieve certain goals, aided him in buying a special type of personal equipment at an attractive price.

All of us have a number of problems—some personal, and some connected with our work. From the individual's standpoint, all of them have to be solved; and whoever helps him to solve his problems will be appreciated. You can suggest the right doctor, the right school, the right camping spot, the right vacation place, or the right home purchase. He will be grateful. Of course, there is always the danger that your suggestions may be misconstrued if he follows them and events turn out badly. Remember, however, you are not urging him to act; rather, you simply have an idea or a suggestion that he might want to follow up.

Keep the customer happy by helping him solve his problems in the way he wants them solved. Find out what he thinks the answer should be; if at all possible, try to help him arrive at this happy state of affairs. If you know that he is going to be disappointed, prepare him in advance by indicating disadvantages of the course of action which he would like to take. Then, when the disappointment comes, he may think that he is lucky that he did not follow through. Sometimes it is just as important to prevent him from doing something as it is to help him correct some fault already committed.

Handling Complaints

Complaints should be handled promptly and settlements made as soon as possible. When an adjustment is essential, do it pleasantly at your earliest opportunity. Adjustments made grudgingly and slowly create an unfavorable impression. You still have the inconvenience and expense as if you had done it graciously, but you have not earned the customer's appreciation. Instead, he will feel that he had to wring out of you what was rightfully his.

Many complaints are unjust. You will have customers who are constantly complaining and wanting adjustments. Keep in mind that you must handle such individuals as part of your job.

When your firm does not want to make a minor adjustment or replace a small part, make the adjustment on your own, and pay for it out of your own pocket to avoid a lot of confusion. You are spending a small sum of your own money, but it is money well invested because of the trouble it saves, the disagreeable situation it prevents, and the possibility that it will preserve a valuable customer. If you are caught in a disagreement between firm and customer, you sometimes can salvage the situation by handling it discreetly without bothering your superiors. In doing so, you must not criticize your own firm or boss even though the customer thinks ill of them.

A complaint may arise because the customer wants to "sound off." Do not stop him from talking; let him talk himself out. This will give him relief. When you agree with him and make a proper adjustment, he will be quite happy because he not only got what he wanted but he also convinced you that he was right.

Some individuals must be handled carefully. Professional men such as the doctor, the dentist, and the pharmacist may be critical of some equipment. If the customer feels that the product or instrument is unsatisfactory, the salesman must exercise great care in handling this complaint. Usually, there is no question about making an adjustment, wherever the fault may lie, because the buyer feels that he is not to blame. The seller takes the blame, rightly or not. Your measurements are taken when you accept the blame even though you are not at fault. Although the buyer is at fault, you take the blame and make the adjustment to prevent any unpleasantness. Do not worry if you get stepped on. The other person will probably recognize that he was wrong, or at least partially wrong, and make it up later in increased sales. Life is full of illustrations of wrongs that are never righted. You will grow in stature as you learn to accept some of these situations.

Packaging

Proper packaging is taking on greater importance in the sale of commodities. Gone is the time when inadequate, poorly constructed, inefficient packaging was tolerated. Today, packaging must be functional, correct in size, in body, in protective features, and it must be attractive. When talking to customers, you will learn their likes and dislikes about packaging. Out of these conversations will come new ideas to improve packaging; maybe the sizes are inadequate, the shape of the package may be annoying, or the package may be difficult to open.

By developing a new package, you may be able to introduce a new line to a new group of customers. You may find that your product appeals to a group heretofore untouched. You may develop a lucrative line which has been nonexistent. Packages relegated to the medicine cabinet or the cupboard because they have been strictly utilitarian may be brought out in the open because of their attractiveness. Customers have purchased items because the containers were reusable for other purposes. Many retailers have purchased items and are now using the containers for other purposes. The same may be true of factories where you find original containers retained as receptacles or for purposes quite different from their original uses.

The rapid development of modern packaging calls for regular updating to avoid obsolete packages. At frequent intervals, you must reassess your package to see whether or not improvements can be made to enhance your product and make it more salable. The thinking salesman sees his product on supermarket shelves, in the warehouse of a manufacturer, and on the shelf in a home. He visualizes the package in various environments. Aware of the rapid improvements in packaging, he thinks of new ways by which the present package might be brightened, made more substantial, lighter but stronger, easier to open, or more lasting. There are many ways in which a package can be changed, improved, made more appealing, and be instrumental in selling the product.

Too often, the industrial salesman thinks his product sold to a factory need not be dressed attractively. But he is wrong. There is no need to have drab, unattractive, unimaginative packaging; nor, on the other hand, is it common sense to have expensive packaging which adds to the cost when less expensive, similar packaging will serve. Depending on the end uses of the product, one item might be packaged in different containers for different buyers. Thus, one salesman who sold castor oil in bottles for medicinal purposes was able to increase sales by putting castor oil in gallon cans for use as a lubricant for air-conditioning equipment.

Segmented Market—Young, Old

In today's society, we have a variety of buyers. We have city buyers, suburban buyers, country buyers, farmers; we have youngsters, teens, middle-age, and senior citizens; we have poor, middle class, and wealthy people; we have large families, small families; we have house dwellers, apartment dwellers. In industry, we have a great number of factories which manufacture thousands of items under varying conditions. Some of these plants are large, but most are small. Some plants are equipped with latest mechanical devices, while other plants still use old-fashioned ways.

A rack jobber said that it was difficult to get manufacturers to package for the supermarket. They had to change from old-style boxes of a half dozen, a dozen, or a gross to one or two items in a plastic bag. These manufacturers had grown so accustomed to furnishing soft goods to the regular channel of distribution that they found great difficulty in changing their packaging to meet the new segmented market. One of the best examples of change is in the soft drink market. There the usual bottle has been supplemented by several sizes of containers. Where once one or two sizes were adequate for particular products, we now have several sizes meeting the demands or the imagined demands of buyers. Not only is there a variety of sizes, but there are many new colors, many new combinations, and many new varieties to please the taste. Foods once sweetened with sugar can now be sweetened with several substitutes which furnish no food value.

Television caters to a wide variety of tastes by having many programs at time periods during the day and evening when each should prove most popular. Styles of cars change during the years. The cars popular one year may be obsolete two or three years later. The salesman no longer has one market but many markets made up of a variety of customers with varying requirements. He is catering to demands of the present. This is equally true whether in the home or in industry.

The same item may be packaged in different ways and even called by different names for different markets. Oftentimes, the identical item will have two distinct names and be priced differently, price being determined by the end use. To give one common example, the price the farmer gets for his milk depends upon whether it is to be sold as milk or manufactured into butter.

Stifle Action—Closed Mind

In any group of customers, you will find the individual with a closed mind. He is not interested in anything new until he is forced into it. He wants to stifle all innovation because he is perfectly happy with things as they are and does not wish to be upset by new ideas. Because such a person does not want new-fangled things, continue to sell him the old ones but say, "One of these days the old ones will disappear and you will have to buy the new ones." Actually, the transition can be made without too much difficulty by changing the individual over a period of time. In his opinion, you will not be changing him from the old to the new; you are simply modifying the old so that he is still buying the old equipment with a few minor changes. This can go on step by step until he finally has the new item that is entirely different from the old.

Some people like to speak happily of the old days and the better quality of things made in the past. As a matter of fact, common sense tells us that if the old was better than the new, most customers would still prefer the old. While the old article may have had some advantages over the new, the new one has so many added features as to make the old inadequate.

Your job is to merchandise the product or service your firm furnishes, and to do it in the best possible way. That does not mean applying the same tactics to all, but rather, differentiating your approach to fit the individual customer. Let him see the advantage of what you offer.

Government Sales

Many of you are aware of the tremendous potential of government sales. Yet some salesmen are overlooking opportunities to build their sales by working with government units. The federal government itself is one of the world's largest buyers, and there are well-defined ways outlined on how to approach this business. Contact your local office of the U. S. Department of Commerce for information or your local chamber of commerce. In foreign countries contact the American embassy. States, cities, municipalities, school districts, counties, townships, fire departments, libraries, hospitals—all furnish opportunities for sales. Much of this buying is done on price bids, but much is also given to salesmen who are not necessarily the low bidders but are furnishing the best quality materials. Then, too, numerous orders are given without bidding because each is small. In total, however, they are enormous. While price concessions are often given to governments, their buying volume makes them valuable. Government units, just like large industry, also have need for thousands of items in small quantity. The commissions, bureaus, and committees buy such items a little at a time and pay the same price as any other buyer of a comparable size order.

Questions and Problems

1. Restudy your presentation or a standard presentation and give it with three different approaches that are possible improvements.

2. Make a list of sources of information that can help a salesman. Divide your list into general and specific sources.

3. Give illustrations of sales approaches that have succeeded because they were carefully thought out before being used.

4. Prepare two distinct sales plans for a product.

5. What are the advantages of refresher training?

6. How can self-management overcome excuses for nonperformance?

7. "Salesmen think too narrowly." Amplify this statement indicating how they can overcome this weakness.

8. What are some of the dangers of getting in a rut in selling?

9. Illustrate several types of quotas.

10. Why should salesmen welcome quotas?

11. How can you compare your territory to a gold mine?

12. Why must you take advantage of contests? Can a contest hurt sales?

13. What kinds of information can be secured at conferences?

14. Why is it to the salesman's benefit to coordinate his selling with company advertising?

15. What can advertising do that personal selling cannot do?

16. How useful is credit in selling?

17. The thinking salesman is ever alert to new business. What ways can the salesman use to suggest new business?

18. How can you become your customer's best salesman? Will this help your firm?

19. Name several ways to improve communication. Show how effective selling can be increased by superior communication.

20. How can communication be effective without the use of words?

21. Why is discretionary income (income not used for necessities) important to some salesmen?

22. Show how products may be valuable at one time but shortly thereafter have no value even though the product is unchanged.

23. What is meant by "interaction of ideas?"

24. Why is price such a dominant consideration in buying? Is the price theme often overworked?

25. Why do we consider price as a weapon? Do most salesmen use the price weapon effectively?

26. Name fifteen ways to vary price without changing the established list price.

27. Discuss the use of special promotion deals as a price variant.

28. How can an unprofitable sale of a machine be made profitable?

29. Trace a sale using a trade-in as a lever to secure price variation. Pick one specific product.

30. How should you handle a product received in trade?

31. Explain the use of suggestions for increasing each sale. Illustrate the suggestion method.

32. Explain the operation of reciprocity.

33. Discuss the use of gifts as aids in selling, pointing out advantages and dangers that can arise.

34. How does a fine reputation in home and community aid in selling?

35. What steps can you take in keeping customers happy?

36. Describe the proper ways of handling complaints. How do you handle the unjustified complaint?

37. Give several illustrations of improved packaging that have increased sales.

38. Show how a segmented market can be handled to the benefit of the salesman.

39. How do you sell the customer who lives in the past?

40. Why are sales to government buyers so important? How do you secure government contracts?

CASES

10-1: TREMBLE WHOLESALE COMPANY

The Tremble Wholesale Company marketed a wide variety of products to drugstores, variety stores, cut-rate stores, and almost any other retail outlet that handled their line of merchandise. Since they did not handle pharmaceuticals, they were at a disadvantage in selling to drugstores. Most variety store buying was done at the head offices of the variety store chains. Consequently, Tremble salesmen found their best sales were to cut-rate stores, and stores owned by independent merchants.

Ronald Gillespie represented Tremble Wholesale Company in the Fair Harbor area of northwestern Ohio. His territory comprised six counties. In this territory were several towns under 10,000 population, one city with 20,000 population, and one city with 30,000 population. Ronald covered 50 major accounts once a month and as many smaller accounts as he could. When he lacked time to call personally, Ronald would call smaller accounts on the phone or mail them literature. The response to this type of solicitation was not satisfactory.

There were about a hundred smaller accounts that Ronald called on personally at least every 60 to 90 days. Whenever time permitted, he would call on new stores or on older stores where he had made no previous sales. It seemed clear to Ronald that he would never be able to handle all the small accounts in his territory satisfactorily. When he mentioned this to his sales manager, he was informed that Tremble would not put any more salesmen in the territory. Ronald would have to do his best with his present territory.

Ronald realized he would never be able to handle all the accounts by personal calls. He was aware that there were many business establishments he never contacted. To make himself more effective he would have to supplement his personal efforts.

In his travels Ronald had seen preprinted order forms. The ones he was most familiar with listed items alphabetically by departments. Thus, all stationery items would be grouped together in alphabetical order, all notions would be in one group, toys would be listed in one group, and so on. At the end of the preprinted order form would be a group headed "Miscellaneous," which covered items that fitted into no specific category.

In the preprinted order form, each item would be listed on a line followed by the wholesale cost per unit, per dozen, per gross, or by some common denominator best suited for that item. At the extreme right end of the line would be the suggested retail selling price. Preceding the item at the left margin was a blank where the buyer could insert the quantity desired. The form would look basically as follows:

Quantity	Item	Unit Cost	Unit Cost Dozen	Unit Cost Gross	Total Cost	Suggested Retail
——	Men's combs, assorted colors	.08	.06	.05	——	.10

Ronald discovered that most of the items he sold could be listed in a ten-page booklet 10 inches long by 8 inches wide. The back of the last page would be a ruled blank page on which a buyer could enter his order for those items not listed on previous pages. The front page would spell out the conditions of the sale, such as cash discount, special promotions, and other information. To make up an order, a buyer would only have to go through the booklet and fill in blanks on the left margin. After the order was completed, the buyer would put the booklet into a postage paid envelope especially provided for this purpose. The order would be received, filled, and shipped the next day and could be received by the buyer on the third day. For example, if the buyer would fill in the order and mail it on Monday, Tremble would receive, fill, and ship the order on Tuesday, and the buyer would get delivery on Wednesday. To encourage larger orders, the buyer would be offered one percent discount on all orders over $100. This would be in addition to the two percent cash discount for prompt payment and any other discounts.

This preprinted order booklet would be mailed to reach customers before the beginning of the month. The total cost of this project was estimated at $3.00 per order. This cost was based on preparing and mailing over a thousand booklets each month. It was estimated that orders would be received from one third of the booklets mailed. Since Ronald Gillespie's territory would probably need only 200 booklets each month, it would be necessary to have similar mailings in each of the other nine territories. It was not economically feasible to prepare fewer than 1,000 booklets. As Ronald thought about his idea, he became more enthusiastic. To him it seemed an excellent way of increasing sales at a moderate cost even though this cost would be assigned to sales in each territory.

Question

Outline Ronald Gillespie's approach in selling this idea to:
   a. His sales manager
   b. Top management
   c. Salesmen in other territories

10-2: HERMAN COOLIDGE

The J. B. West Company of Columbus, Ohio, distributed well-known lines of wine over a two-county area. To fill a vacancy caused by the resignation of one of their salesmen, they hired Herman Coolidge, brother of a wine company representative in a nearby state. Up to this time, Herman had sold only one brand of wine in a small territory.

Herman felt that his association with the J. B. West Company would allow him to make better use of his sales abilities and would allow him to do more creative selling. The company recognized the value of Herman's background in the wine business and assigned him to a suburban territory which cut across the various socio-economic groups. There were high-income areas as well as low-income and rural areas in the territory. Each of these areas provided a market for one or more of the lines which the company sold.

Herman spent his first month on the job learning the territory and becoming acquainted with his customers. He also became familiar with the lines he was selling. It did not take long for his sales to reach an average level. No great gains were scored, but sales remained at about the level they had been with his predecessor.

Herman learned about any new wine licenses granted, any new store openings, and any changes in ownership or license suspensions from a monthly newsletter which was sent to all wine wholesalers in the area and which was posted in his company office. He paid calls on new prospects but often found that a competing salesman had already been there and secured prime shelf space for his line, leaving Herman the poorer shelf spaces and a small portion of the customer's purchases.

Since his sales territory was suburban and therefore took time to reach, there were many days that when Herman stopped at the J. B. West office to pick up samples or to speak to his superiors, he would remain there and contact his customers by telephone. He would call and ask if a customer needed anything. If he found the person in charge of buying not in, he would ask the buyer to return his call and then wait for the reply. This occurred quite often when the weather was bad and driving conditions were poor.

Many times, Herman paid a call on a customer to find that a competitor had erected a large, seemingly successful display on the prime shelf space which Herman thought he had locked up. He could not understand why a customer would replace his lines, which were widely known and most successful in the state, with lesser known brands which generally had poorer sales. He felt that large shelf displays were not necessary with successful brands if sales were consistent. It was his opinion that the manufacturer's advertising, good shelf space, and a minimum of point-of-purchase material would keep up sales.

When a problem arose as to unsalable merchandise or the wrong merchandise being sent on an order, the customer presented the problem to his salesman. When Herman was faced with this situation, he would suggest that the customer contact J. B. West's regular complaint department. Occasionally, he would take the information regarding the complaint and then turn it over to the complaint department himself. He felt that any complaints or adjustments could be processed more efficiently by the department which specialized in this service, and that if he were to perform this service for his customers himself, he would only be duplicating effort. The company had no set policy as to complaints and adjustments but set up the regular service to facilitate handling telephone claims.

Now, eight months after he joined J. B. West, Herman Coolidge was happy in his work, and he felt that he was doing a good job for his company. The sales manager for J. B. West was reviewing Herman's sales record at this time and found that although his sales had remained constant, the competitors in Herman's territory were scoring substantial gains. Upon completing his analysis of Herman's performance, the sales manager told him that unless he showed progress in developing his territory to its full potential, his replacement was imminent.

Questions

1. What is a common danger in being content to just maintain present performance equal to past performance?
2. Show where Herman Coolidge has been weak on the job.
3. Present various ways Herman Coolidge might secure his share of the market.

CHAPTER 11

The Second Mile--
A Study in Human Relations

". . . and if anyone forces you to go one mile, go with him two miles." (Matthew 5:41)

These words, spoken more than 1900 years ago, still have the same meaning for humanity because they express a fundamental and universal truth. As our interest in others increases, we develop a greater understanding and appreciation of people.

The salesman who is willing to go the second mile with a customer is the one who understands people. He recognizes that the more ways he can satisfy a customer's many interests, the greater will be his opportunities to sell.

A customer wants the salesman to recognize more than just his immediate business interests. Without infringing on a customer's personal life, the salesman must learn more about him so that he can adjust to the customer's pattern of behavior. From the discerning salesman's depth of understanding and appreciation, he knows when to help, when to give sympathy, or when to remain in the background.

Just as the salesman must consecrate himself to high ideals of living, so must he be willing to consecrate himself to the

321

highest ideal in serving others. This cannot be a half-hearted effort. Rather, it must be a genuine willingness to serve the customer who trustingly gives him his money. Once the salesman recognizes these demands, he will find that sacrifice is involved. A penalty of obedience, discipline, work, and attention will be exacted. He will have to struggle and give his best if he is to climb high on the ladder of successful selling.

In any generation, the quality of the age is reflected in man's attitude towards improvement. One cannot ignore responsibility for improvement. To believe that you are immune from responsibilities is to persuade yourself that you have none. Such an attitude will defeat you in selling. It will doom you to mediocrity and often to failure.

Cultivate human relations. Pay attention to the needs of those about you, and be particularly aware of your customer, your boss, other members of the firm, and business friends.

TOP-LEVEL SELLING

Your future in selling will be determined by the relationship between you and your customer. We know we should remain friendly with customers and should be willing to help, but few of us really appreciate the depth of the relationship nor how far we should go. "The Second Mile" refers to the extent of our willingness and ability to see the other person's side. In pheasant hunting, most of us can put ourselves in the place of the hunter and understand his feelings, but try to put yourself in the place of the pheasant. Startling, isn't it? When you are fishing, do you ever consider what the fish thinks when he has been hooked? Most of us give lip service to our willingness to see the other side of the picture, but how many of us can actually put ourselves in the customer's shoes and learn his likes and dislikes? Nevertheless, that is what you must do. You must go beyond the normal requirements of your job, see farther ahead, and understand the effect of your product or service on the user.

Be Considerate

Be considerate of your customer's feelings. Do not criticize his politics, his religion, his children, or his background. In fact, be wary of any criticism whatsoever, even that of a competitor.

If the customer chooses to be critical and you can agree, well and good. If you do not agree, you need not speak up in opposition but merely make some harmless remark which does not offend him. Even if your feelings are hurt, do not say anything. You are with him to please him, not yourself.

Be considerate of his time. Do not spend useless minutes or perhaps even hours talking about those things which do not affect him. Listen to what he says even though it may not be on a topic that interests you. As soon as possible, turn to the subject behind your call. You are doing him and yourself a favor by staying on the right track. You have a proposition which will be to his benefit. The sooner this sale can be consummated, the better for both of you.

Be considerate of his background. Whatever his level of education, try to fit your presentation to meet his needs. In no way convey an impression of superiority. If you have an honest product or service, you need not feel inferior, and he will not expect you to. Neither talk up to nor down to a person. Talk *directly* to him.

Be considerate of his status in the community. Be aware of his place among his fellowmen, among businessmen of the community, and among his immediate associates. Try to see him as he would like to see himself, alone or in the group. Develop a keen understanding of what he feels are his strong attributes. Above all, gain a perception of what he is striving for, what he really wants, what his goals in life are.

Serve

Everybody wants to be a leader. Nobody wants to be a follower. Try to be a follower as far as your customer is concerned. Be willing to serve him to your fullest extent. In the boss-worker relationship, one must direct and the other must be directed. You should take the position of the worker and willingly follow directions. When a customer asks a favor of you, try to do it. When he asks you to do a job, do it. Even when he requests you to perform a menial task, do it. This is no time to act superior. To be great, first learn to be humble.

Do not confuse this attitude with self-abasement, fear, degradation, or inferiority. You can serve and still retain self-respect.

As a matter of fact, respect increases when others see that you are willing to do things for them. Go even further in service; try to anticipate things that your customer likes, and do them without being asked. He will appreciate your thoughtfulness. As one druggist said about a salesman, "He does so many nice things for me, I just can't refuse an order."

Notice what a gentle, pleasant way of selling this is. A happy relationship is established because you are doing your utmost to serve the interests of your customer. You recognize that the interests of your customer are your interests. Since his well-being is your well-being, it goes without saying that his success will govern your success.

Success is a pyramid that is built upon blocks of service. Just as a pyramid has three sides and a base, so must your service have more than one side or one direction. Mere service in supplying a product is not sufficient. If you are selling a retailer, there may be the service of delivery, the service of display, the service of counsel, the service of sales aids. Yes, when we speak of service, your service figure may be many-sided. The number of sides, four, five, or more, will be determined by the number of services you can perform for your customer. Since most of us deal with a number of customers, the building blocks we use will be different in size and shape because of the variety of customer needs.

Counsel

Most people are ready to listen to counsel, but they must be convinced the counsel is wise. In areas dealing with selling or using your product, you should be able to counsel better than anyone else. All day long you deal with your product in its various phases. You talk with customers about applications and uses. You should be aware of the various ways your product fits into a particular situation.

If the customer has other needs aside from those connected with your product, be reluctant in offering suggestions. Be careful about giving advice because you may not understand the situation. If a customer has a particular problem and he asks your advice, you may not be able to give much help; but you can suggest some source where help is available.

When you cannot answer his question, you tell him where he can get the answer. If you answer questions that are not in your area, then you are an amateur instead of the professional selling your own product. As an amateur, your advice may be dangerous. In areas outside your field, give suggestions, consolation, and sympathy; but do not try to answer questions that you are ill-prepared to handle. By stepping outside your professional competence, you do a disservice to yourself, your company, and above all, to your customer. Be willing to serve—but serve within your capacity.

Give Attention

Have you noticed the close attention of members of a class as they listen to a lecture, the contents of which will appear on the final examination? How well, as a child, you eagerly listened to a story told by your teacher. Notice the breathless interest as the members of an audience listen to a tense scene in a play. In each instance, suspense has been created that demands attention. A skilled speaker can develop situations which will hold others' attention. Since each speaker varies in his ability to get attention, it is often necessary for listeners to supply the attention that a speaker is unsuccessfully eliciting.

If we are to preserve human relations at their best, it is important to give proper attention and respect to customers. When a customer talks, we listen. We do not interrupt. We do not show boredom. Notice how the young lady listens eagerly as her date talks, shows delight when he tells about his successes, and laughs at his corny jokes. Think about people whom you have most enjoyed. Did they not listen to you, pay attention to you, even fuss over you? You liked it, did you not? Your customer is just like you. Pay attention to him when he talks, and he will like you. Laugh when he tells jokes, and he will appreciate you. Fuss over him, and he will love it. Even if you think that you are overdoing it, the customer will be pleased that you think so highly of him. You will be flattering his ego and reinforcing his self-assurance.

No one is so miserable as the one who feels that he can do nothing well. A person who has lost confidence in himself is like a limp rag; you could wipe the floor with him and get no response. Do not get yourself in that position, and do not let a customer get there. Paying attention to a customer is a form of encouragement that indicates your appreciation of who he is, what he says, and how he works. In a few instances, we may become too complimentary, but those occasions are rare. Usually we err by giving too little attention.

Say "Thank You"

A series of "thank you's" make a wonderful foundation on which to construct your road to success. They tend to fill in the holes, cover the rough spots, and smooth the progress road. Think about your own life. How often have you been offended when people said "thank you" too much? Conversely, how often have you thought that you could have been thanked a little more? "Thank you" is a pleasant phrase. Properly used, it conveys a feeling of well-being towards the other person. He is not a mind reader, and he cannot understand what goes through your thoughts; but he does understand when you *say* "thank you."

When do you say "thank you"? Say it as you leave; say it on the telephone; say it in a letter when you express appreciation for the order. How do you say it? Say it with little gifts or acts of thoughtfulness. Say it by the way you act.

Do Not Blame Him for Errors

In the course of business activities, errors crop up. Under normal circumstances, those errors are not the result of mistakes on one side; they result from misunderstandings or things done wrong by both. To pinpoint an error on a customer is hardly judicious. When a problem arises, and an investigation reveals the fault to be the customer's, the diplomatic salesman smooths over the situation. When you or your firm make an error, there is no question about blame. You must accept the blame even though you may try to mitigate it by indicating extenuating circumstances.

When the customer is to blame, tread a wary path. He does not like to be proven wrong. He feels that he is doing you a big favor by giving you an order. If a little problem crops up, why should you blame him for it? Try to improve the situation, and go on from there as you keep good customer relations.

If you try to press home your advantage by proving that he is wrong, you gain little. At best, you can only imply that the error might be his; you never say it directly. If he is at all reasonable, he will catch the drift of the conversation and recognize that he is wrong. If he is willing to admit it, accept the explanation and take corrective action. If he is unwilling to admit it, make the best adjustment you can.

If his error is very costly, it may be necessary to assign the cost to him. Although he may be unhappy, you hope that he will recognize the justice of your position. Even that does not leave a good taste in his mouth, however. Neither are you happy because he has been saddled with additional cost; you have been given extra work because of a troublesome situation.

Errors must not be allowed to go uncorrected. Whether to meet them head on or wait awhile to see what happens depends on present conditions. Often, time will correct the problem. A problem which looms dangerously large at the moment may later be handled by relatively minor adjustments. Do not get excited in the beginning; do not let the problem drag on indefinitely.

When you feel that a customer has committed an error, search your own operations to see how the error could have been prevented. Even though the customer may be at fault, possibly the error could have been prevented if you or your firm had taken sufficient precautionary measures in advance. It is not so important to assign blame as it is to prevent such an error in the future.

CRAVING TO BE APPRECIATED

All of us want to be appreciated. We know the importance of showing appreciation to a child. When a youngster draws a picture of a dog and brings it proudly to his parents, they say, "What a fine dog you drew," and the child goes away happily. Similar experiences can be repeated throughout life. Most of us have a pleasant feeling when others show their appreciation. This expression need not be particularly demonstrative as long as we know the other person appreciates what we have done. Many adults fall apart and feel that life is not worth living because no one appreciates them. All of us crave attention and appreciation.

Notice how cheerful the school youngster is when he shows mother and dad an excellent report card, or some fine project completed in school. He glows with pride when they praise him for his work. In certain areas of the world, wives used to become greatly upset when their husbands failed to beat them or otherwise abuse them because in their society such actions were expressions of appreciation.

Sometimes, salesmen get so self-oriented they forget to be customer-oriented. They forget that they need the buyer's cooperation, and they take their customers for granted. They perfunctorily say "thank you" when they get an order. They take the buyer out to lunch without realizing that such a gesture may not be enough.

Ways of showing appreciation are numerous and take on many forms. Besides the "thank you" or the written note of appreciation, there are other forms which can be impressive. Entertain the customer and, perhaps, his wife (or even the family) at some activity which all appreciate. Or, contribute to his favorite charity. Send an appropriate gift. Visits to the hospital or flowers sent to the hospital during illness often are quite acceptable. If you discover a customer is having trouble, reassuring words over the telephone can be meaningful. Instead of sending him a Christmas greeting, send him a Thanksgiving greeting. This might be remembered even more forcibly because he will get so few of them. If the customer is engaged in club activity, a door prize might be quite acceptable. If he is to give a talk to a group, your attendance might demonstrate appreciation. If he is featured in a local paper, call him and tell him how much you enjoyed reading about him.

SOLVING CUSTOMER PROBLEMS

The area of customer problems is of major importance and it calls for extended treatment. Many salesmen are unaware of the importance of looking at a customer's problems as if they were the salesman's problems. Yet, that is what they are. Unless the customer succeeds in his enterprise, the salesman cannot succeed in his work.

Every customer wants to be more successful. If he operates a store, he wants to know how to sell more at a greater profit. Here the second-mile approach could be an extensive study of his operations to find possible improvements. You may find that his location could be improved. Perhaps he is not stocking the right merchandise for the community. By talking to people in the area, you may discover wants that he is not meeting. Perhaps his hours are not the right ones for the neighborhood.

Your customer will be delighted to see you taking this much interest. Be careful that he does not get the impression you are poking your nose too far into his business. If you can demonstrate how certain changes will increase sales, he will be pleased. Gradually he will share more of his problems with you. Oftentimes, merely discussing these problems will make him aware of new approaches and new methods of handling them.

With a factory buyer, show how your product can serve more purposes, or how he can use less of it, or how he can use it more profitably. Owners of small plants look for new ways to manufacture, new products to make, and new solutions for their problems. By stressing service, you may overcome prejudice that may have developed toward you or your product.

If your price appears high, this, too, can be overcome; be sure that the buyer gets not only the product but also other valuable extras. Instead of saying, "Here it is," and hearing his reply, "And how will I get the most benefit out of it?" say, "Here it is. Now, let's see how we can get the most out of it for you." He will sense the difference at once. You have placed yourself on his side. You are looking at the problem through his eyes. When you complete the sale, you make your profit, but his opportunities and problems begin when your "job" is done. If you think you have completed your work by selling him, you are wrong. Your success will be measured by the degree that you share his job with him.

In going the second mile, you may feel that immediate reward should result. If that is your attitude, you are not properly traveling the second mile. You must concentrate on the added value for the customer. Perhaps the only gain you will realize is to have your customer use a particular purchase satisfactorily; he may never buy again. On the other hand, you may have created a satisfied, steady customer. If you have a regular customer, think of the danger of losing him if you are unwilling to put forth additional effort. Someone else might come along and take him away from you by doing the things you are unwilling to do.

Friendship

Over a period of time you can develop a firm bond of friendship with your customer. Being a genuine friend is important. The customer must know that he can rely on you for assistance, that you will give sympathetic attention and the benefit of your experience, and your genuine interest.

Possibly, you may work together in civic activities or in church activities. Perhaps you can enjoy sports together. You may have interests in common. You may live in the same neighborhood, belong to the same investment club, or you may find that your families may have things in common. Under such conditions, you are in an enviable position as long as you do not take advantage of similar interests and create embarrassing situations. Friendship must be carefully handled and not imposed on. Friendship gives a decided advantage; treat it with the greatest respect and care. This may be one of the finest opportunities you can ever have of going the second mile with a buyer. With friendship comes trust, reliance, dependence, and many other conditions which you must handle carefully. Never take advantage of the other person but treat him as you would like to have him treat you in similar circumstances.

Keep in mind that there are degrees of business and personal friendship. Have each type clearly in mind so that you know how far to go without overstepping bounds of propriety. In no sense need this statement be taken as a degree of insincerity, but rather as an expression of how to show good taste under different situations.

Never forget a customer. If you forget him, he will forget you and forget to give you orders. If you remember, you will serve your customer by seeing that goods are delivered as specified and on time. Remember to make special adjustments that have been agreed upon. Remember special packing. Remember color assortments. Remember special payment schedules.

If you made special agreements with your customer, be sure your firm is aware of them so that it can follow through. If you can include extras, do so even though they were not promised. If you can give special concessions which will benefit him, do so, even though he does not expect it. If you can favor him without hurting others, do it.

Many times you have a choice whether or not to do favors for your customer. Often, favors require additional effort. He will never know if you do not do them. Perhaps he will never find out if you skip him. But if your thoughts run in this fashion, you are not worthy of your customer. You are not going the second mile. You are not thinking of him first and yourself second. You must be willing to sacrifice self for the benefit of others. This sacrifice must be genuine; it must not be made in the hope of getting a reward. If done to get something, it is not likely to be nearly as effective as when you do it because you want to. When one deliberately seeks happiness primarily, it often eludes him. But if he is interested in serving others and doing that which is right, happiness will come his way without trying for it.

In a previous chapter, we have touched upon the importance of remembering birthdays, celebrations, promotions, and events of importance to a customer. These we need not repeat, but here we urge you to go one step further. Anticipate, if possible, the direction of his business. If you can foresee developments that will aid him, mention them. If you see clouds on his business horizon, point them out as possibilities, not as certainties. Tell him about future conferences and meetings that may be beneficial. Introduce him to people who can assist him directly or indirectly. Help him to secure positions of influence. Send him books, magazines, and other literature that will help him.

Provide him with samples of new products. Furnish ideas successfully used by others in his line. If you know of merchandise bargains, tell him. Help him locate particular kinds of machinery. If he is thinking of importing merchandise, suggest sources. Also, warn him of dangers if you know of some. If he wants to go into export business, help him to secure information. Suggest pitfalls to avoid. If he wants help from state governments or the national government, help him to make the proper contact. If he needs special information, help him find the right agency. Many men, for example, in writing to Washington, D. C., would not know the difference between the United States Chamber of Commerce and the United States Department of Commerce. If your customer asks a question you cannot answer, be willing to find someone who can answer it. You can give either a disinterested "no" or an interested "yes" to your customer's request. To the second-mile salesman, there is only one answer.

CUSTOMER FIRST—ILLUSTRATIONS

Examples of going the second mile can be found in any area of selling. When you sell to an institution, such as a hospital or restaurant, the person whom you need to see may have very few hours available for talking. Be considerate of his time, and call on him at whatever time he feels is best. This may be on particular days of the week and during odd hours of the day or night. Such thoughtfulness does much to foster a warm regard for the salesman.

When the customer complains, give courteous attention and consideration and express genuine interest and concern. Insofar as possible, put yourself on the side of the customer to see what would be an equitable solution. Of course, you cannot do an injustice to your own firm if the customer is unreasonable.

When a complaint is registered, we know that a problem exists somewhere. We know someone is unhappy and that an adjustment needs to be made. Since a remedial step is called for, the person who makes the adjustment must do so with as much grace as possible. He must satisfy as fully as possible the complaints of the distressed buyer.

In a ticket office when customers are waiting patiently for admission to a performance, unpleasant situations will arise. Since a disgruntled customer is not particularly pleasant to handle, the seller needs restraint to avoid any discussion that will heighten the tension. Far better, then, to use soothing words and go out of your way as much as possible to quiet the individual.

In service departments of garages, unpleasant remarks are spoken and tensions develop. The service manager-salesman can enhance the prestige of his firm by giving courteous treatment and remaining calm when customers become belligerent. Often, a customer has a just complaint, and the service manager should make every effort to rectify it. When the complaint is unjust, the service manager must find a way to soothe the ruffled feelings and make the customer satisfied even though he will not be happy. In a bus, railroad car, or other public conveyance, occasions arise when tempers flare and sharp words are exchanged. Yet, there are bus drivers and conductors who handle people very well and calm them without fuss. A bellboy may get into an altercation with a hotel guest, but a good bell captain can soon smooth over the situation. He has learned to go far enough with the other person so that he is not only satisfied but pleased.

There is such a thing as going too far with kindness. Can your helpful acts become offensive? Can you embarrass a customer? The answer is yes. But your judgment should tell you how far to go. In some countries, you can go farther than you would in the United States and still be considered proper. With some customers, you can go far and still be in good taste. A person genuinely motivated by a desire to aid another probably will not go too far in extending help. But if he is motivated by a selfish desire to get ahead, his own selfishness may so cloud his vision that he is unable to detect the limit of propriety. He overdoes it —not because he is anxious to serve, but because he wants the order. Going the second mile must be done in sincerity. Distinguish between sincere encouragement and flattery.

How Much to Talk

"Silence is golden" is well worth remembering. When you are trying to be helpful, weigh carefully what you say. Whether you should speak or remain silent depends on the needs of the individual. Sometimes silence is desirable because it gives the buyer time to think, to consider, to reason. It also gives him the opportunity to talk and ask questions. The understanding salesman recognizes that there are appropriate times for each activity. There is a time to talk, to demonstrate, to present, to answer questions. There are times to be forceful, aggressive, quiet, unobtrusive, waiting, sympathetic. At times, the prospect needs the opportunity to reflect, to consider, to weigh, and to make up his mind. Create an atmosphere in which the buyer feels free to make up his own mind. Yet, surround him with such ideas that he will act favorably to your presentation or suggestion. The second-mile approach creates confidence, calmness, agreeableness, and understanding that lead to a successful sale.

RELATIONSHIP TO EMPLOYER

Although your primary job is to please the customer, you must also please your boss. He has worries of his own; he is responsible for sales even more than you. If you fail, he has to take the blame along with you. Do you try to understand your boss? Do you recognize his position? Do you understand the responsibilities facing him? Do you feel the problems looming over his head? He is boss, all right; but whatever his attitude, he is in a more difficult position than you are. Seemingly, he simply tells you and other salesmen what to do and he sees that you do it. Then, if sales are not made, he can blame you.

Actually, his responsibility goes far beyond that. If you fail, he must help you improve your selling or replace you. It is expensive to replace you, and he cannot know that a new salesman will do better. Therefore, he wants you to succeed. His success is measured by your success as well as by the success of your fellow salesmen. When you think of your boss under these conditions, you can be sympathetic to what he is trying to accomplish. His harshness might only be firmness.

Are you willing to go the second mile with your boss? Are your reports clear, understandable, and on time? Do you treat your customers as he would like to have them treated? Do you put in extra hours of selling effort to do a better job? Do you plan your work? Do you keep him informed of all matters that are important in your territory? Do you go to him soon enough when you feel problems are too hard for you to handle alone? Or do you let them drag until you get so hopelessly involved that no one can pull you out?

Are you willing to do small personal favors without thought of remuneration or praise? Do you think of the boss as an individual with family and problems just like you have? When he is trying to pep up the salesmen, do you criticize him for handing out the same old line, or do you appreciate that his job is to think up something to spur you on? Who spurs the boss on? Probably no one. The sales manager must be self-energizing. Do you quibble when the boss wants you to come in on Saturdays for meetings? Do you complain when he asks for a little extra effort? Do you feel that he is trampling on you for his own advancement?

Some salesmen have too many negative thoughts. They feel they are being walked on and worked to death. As a matter of fact, often these feelings have no counterpart in reality. They arise because the salesman views the firm from his perspective only. He does not realize some parts of a business may suffer temporarily or even permanently in order that more important parts succeed. What you must consider is how other members of the firm look at your job. How does your boss look at your job? What does he think your job is? How does he think it should be done? What does he consider a poor job and a good one?

Going the second mile with the boss means more than talking —it means action that will benefit both of you. It means selling successfully against price competition, product competition, delivery competition, and many other kinds of competitive effort. If your job were simple, you would not have it. Your firm would not need you. It could substitute some mechanical device for you or get someone cheaper. If your job has difficult aspects, accept them. You are employed to handle difficult situations.

Learn to be a well-rounded individual who can cope with problems as they arise. Study your work to see where improvements are feasible. As long as you are content to go along in your usual fashion, you are not effectively cooperating with your boss. If you think up new ways of doing things, or attempt to do things better, or make friendly suggestions that have definite value, you are on the right track; you are giving liberally of yourself.

Generosity should become one of your trademarks. Sympathetic consideration should become your characteristic. Begin to share in the responsibilities of your territory, or take more of the burden carried by the boss. Willingly accept your duty of furthering mutual interests. Become a standby, a dependable person, a confident person who can be entrusted with difficult tasks, a loyal person for executing orders, an adventurous person for original thinking, a thoughtful person for consultation. Care for your customers so that the boss need not worry about them. Care for your equipment and keep it in top shape for demonstration. Do not try to make money by padding your expense account. Take care of yourself physically. Your behavior ought not reflect unfavorably on your firm.

Recognize and applaud gentlemanly conduct of customers. Be concerned with social problems. Be honest. Be watchful, not careless; thoughtful, not indifferent; aggressive, not lazy. You have a position to fill, an example to set, and behavior that impresses people. Be level-headed and prudent when you talk to your superior. Show respect without implications of weakness.

Do not nurse grudges against your boss; do not expect him to give you extra attention. Realize that he has many duties to perform. Although at times he may seem to neglect you, his thoughts will probably be on other salesmen's problems. Try to make his work lighter by giving him aid, suggestions, and thoughtful attention. Remember that you are not his only employee.

RELATIONSHIP TO FIRM

Just as you go the second mile with the customer and with your boss, so, too, must you be willing to go the second mile with your firm. Success for one must be measured by success for all.

Since the motivating force is the salesman, you must try to insure success to everyone connected with the enterprise. At times, you will be asked to do things that do not please you. You may feel that superiors are infringing on your prerogatives, asking you to do what should be done by other people, or giving you extra work for which you are ill-prepared. Nevertheless, try, insofar as possible, to fulfill the wishes of the home office.

It does little good to complain either to the customer or to your firm. Both look at the problem from their points of view, and you are the one who must fit in. Remember, your firm is not a wealthy uncle who is willing to support you. If your firm is to prosper, men like you must successfully contribute their time and talents.

Treat your employer as you would wish to be treated if you were the employer and you were reviewing the work of a salesman. Do not begrudge your employer extra effort, additional time, more concentrated attention. Do your part well, and the firm's management will be pleased. In doing your part, supply that little extra, that activity beyond the call of duty, which will show how earnestly you are devoted to your task.

RELATIONSHIP TO OTHERS

If you are sincerely interested in your work and those connected with it, you should also develop equally good family and community relations. Should your home life be shadowed with the worries of disappointments, bickerings, and instability, you can hardly be expected to hide such cares and show only positive traits to the customer or your employer. One element of life inevitably carries over into another. Make your whole life one single unit; become a living part of those fine qualities which are exemplified by every successful salesman.

Life is a totality. You cannot compartmentalize it successfully. Either you are optimistic, cheerful, helpful, kind with unrestrained enthusiasm and the ability to go ahead—or conversely, you are disappointed, chagrined, unhappy, upset. The latter characteristics prevent proper application to your daily work. Just as it is important to take care of your body, it is also important to take care of your mind, your mental health, your spiritual health, and your attitude toward others. Blended in a positive way, your traits will give you the courage to forge ahead to a goal marked "Success." To reach it, put forth the effort. To enjoy success in the future, think positively.

QUESTIONS AND PROBLEMS

1. What is the second-mile philosophy? Illustrate the second-mile attitude in selling.
2. Must a salesmen be willing to sacrifice his interests to the advantage of a customer?
3. Develop a sales situation where the advantages to the customer are greater than the advantages to the salesman.
4. Can a list of advantages to a salesman contain disadvantages to his customer?
5. Describe how a successful sale must be advantageous to both the customer and the salesman.
6. Describe ten different ways of being considerate to customers.
7. Is there danger of confusing service with an inferiority complex?
8. How can we use services as building blocks?
9. What are some of the dangers of giving advice to customers?
10. When you pay close attention to what a customer says, you accomplish two or more objectives. What are these objectives?
11. Too many people show lack of appreciation. Why can an attitude of this nature hurt a salesman?
12. When a customer makes an error, how should you handle the situation? Give illustrations of handling both major and minor errors.
13. Demonstrate methods of customer orientation.
14. What objectives can you accomplish by showing interest in a customer's problems?
15. Distinguish between business and personal friendship. Can you have both in relation to a customer? What is the essential difference between the two?

16. Why is it so important to remember particular events in the lives of customers?
17. When a customer complains, what are you being warned about?
18. How is a customer's complaint similar to fever in a person?
19. Is there much danger of embarrassing a customer with kindness?
20. "There is a time to talk, a time to remain silent." Give several illustrations to demonstrate the importance of this statement.
21. Does the average salesman belittle the contribution of his boss?
22. Should the salesman offer to share some of the sales manager's problems?
23. Can a salesman stimulate his boss with praise?
24. Point out how the problems of the boss are more complex than the problems of the salesman.
25. Describe a generous salesman.
26. What should be the salesman's relationship to his firm?
27. Show how the mature salesman meets his responsibilities to the world in which he lives.

CASES

11-1: SPORTS EQUIPMENT, INC.

Daniel Feenstra is the salesman for Sports Equipment, Inc. in a large western city in the United States. Much of his time is occupied with regular retailers of sporting goods, but increasingly he is giving more attention to industries that promote recreational programs for employees.

One day as he was sitting in his office writing reports, Mr. Feenstra got a telephone call from a buyer at Fedray Industries. Mr. Jolson, the buyer, told Mr. Feenstra they were interested in baseball equipment. Could he come out and discuss this equipment with Mr. Jolson? An appointment was made for 10 a.m. the next day.

When Daniel Feenstra talked with Mr. Jolson the following day, he learned that Fedray Industries intended to expand their employee recreation program. Heretofore, their program had been confined to a few activities for women employees, but now they intended to expand into a variety of outdoor sports. At the moment, they wanted to start softball teams and later perhaps regular baseball teams. Presently they were thinking of intramural teams. Perhaps in the future they might get into some leagues.

Miss Davidson, the company nurse, had been in charge of recreational activities. For the present, Mr. Jolson stated they hoped to keep her in charge of all company recreational activities, even the proposed ball teams. Eventually, they hoped to develop their recreation department to a point where they could employ a full-time director. After giving Mr. Feenstra the above information, Mr. Jolson asked his advice on how to go on.

Daniel Feenstra immediately recognized an opportunity to sell ball equipment. While the original purchases might be small, he foresaw possibilities of golf teams, tennis teams, water sports, and other types of recreation which could make this a large, continuing, lucrative account. It was evident, however, that to get this program started would demand hard work for somebody. And Mr. Feenstra felt that he would be that person. Miss Davidson could fill in with company background, but somebody would have to start the teams. Once interest was aroused, it would be possible to obtain leadership among employees. Then there would be problems of playing fields, scheduling, and equipment. For the present, all Mr. Feenstra would get financially for his efforts would be minor equipment sales. If the sports program developed, much equipment would be purchased; but major purchases would probably be on a bid basis. In the long run, Mr. Feenstra felt that the program would be beneficial to the employees of Fedray Industries, but how much it would benefit him personally was doubtful.

Questions

1. What are the motives for Mr. Feenstra in helping start the ball team?
2. Will Mr. Feenstra benefit personally?
3. Should Mr. Feenstra request that Fedray Industries pay him for his work?
4. How would you fit the "Second Mile" concept into this situation?

11-2: FLORENCE PARKER

Florence Parker operates a dress shop under her own name in a large city in the southeastern part of the United States. Over a period of years, she has developed the business so that it is one of the leading shops. Not only has she carried on skillful merchandising, but also she has developed a public relations program known to most of the women in the city. She is called on an average of once a week to give a style show, a luncheon preview, or some fashion activity. These activities have grown so fast that she employs one woman who spends all her time in this work. In addition, Miss Parker spends at least one fourth of her time on this work.

The special shows are becoming more expensive, and if the activity is to continue, she will have to hire another woman to devote her full time to this work. Also, these shows have cut into Miss Parker's time so much that business is beginning to suffer. The result has been that Miss Parker began to refuse invitations. She declined requests as graciously as possible. She told these people that the requests were so numerous she was unable to meet them. Some she could not decline, such as the ones that came from influential groups of women. Others were repeat performances that she felt she must meet. But she did manage to decline most new requests as well as some repeat requests. She hoped to reduce the number of shows to about twenty-five a year.

One morning as Miss Parker was seated in her office, her secretary told her that three women from the community church in Onego, a small farming village ten miles from town, were in the office to see her. She invited them into her office, seated them comfortably, and began to visit with them informally. After a few minutes, the spokesman of the group told Miss Parker the reason for their visit.

The church had hired a young minister, married, with two children, to be their pastor. Since it was a small church in the country, his salary was not great. During the past month, the minister's wife had given birth to twin boys. Now the minister had four children, his car was old, and his finances were inadequate. To alleviate the financial distress of the minister, the ladies of the church decided to give a dinner on a Saturday evening a month hence. Not only were church members invited, but all members of the community were to be invited. The price of the dinner was to be somewhat higher than usual for this part of the country. But the ladies thought it would be necessary to get a higher price if they were to raise their goal of $500 for the minister's family.

To make the evening more inviting for guests, they expected to put on some fine entertainment. Part of this entertainment they hoped would be a half-hour style show presented by Miss Parker. The ladies told Miss Parker that they were certain she could put on a show for that particular community that would be "exciting."

Miss Parker considered the request silently for several minutes. She saw the difficulties. She could not bring her regular group of models. Some could be used, but many of the men might find it boring. To enliven the style show, she would have to sprinkle in some local talent, some of the ladies from the group. She would have to secure some garments outside her own inventory because she did not carry much of the merchandise that would appeal to this group. She felt the sales that would result from this group would be small. If she were to put on this style show, it would be expensive, time-consuming, and would truly be a gesture of goodwill.

Questions

1. Should Miss Parker give this style show?
2. What are the advantages and disadvantages to Miss Parker in giving this show?
3. Is the "Second Mile" concept involved here?

4. Can you see any long-run advantages for Miss Parker in giving this show?
5. Will Miss Parker be benefited in any other way than through sales if she gives the show?

11-3: UNITED OFFICE FURNITURE COMPANY

The United Office Furniture Company manufactures and sells office equipment throughout the United States. The company's sales organization is divided into regional and district sales offices so that all potential sales areas are covered adequately.

The Syracuse, New York, district office is responsible for the entire state of New York except the metropolitan New York City area. Chester Simmons is the Syracuse district sales manager. His experience with the company has been diversified. He started out with the company 10 years ago as a salesman in the Houston, Texas, district and four years later was promoted to assistant sales manager of that district. After two years in this position, he was recognized by top management as an excellent prospect for district manager. At this time he was assigned to the home office in Chicago, Illinois, for further administrative and sales duties. Last year there was an opening at Syracuse for a district manager; Simmons applied for the position and was accepted.

Mr. Simmons has an excellent sales and administrative background. He feels that in selling office furniture the salesman has to be creative. He must create a desire for the product and then fit his product into the prospective customer's needs. Further, Simmons believes that office equipment items are generally expensive, repeat sales are few, and product knowledge is important.

United Office Furniture Company carries a complete line of office equipment and furniture, such as file cabinets, desks, chairs, filing systems, safes, water coolers, and modular partitions. This gives the salesmen the opportunity to meet most of the office furniture and equipment needs of any company called on.

Until recently, United had always hired salesmen with sales experience in the office equipment and furniture area because of the great importance attached to the product knowledge required of its salesmen. However, in recent years a trend started in the industry toward the hiring of younger, inexperienced salesmen. The reason given for this change in personnel choice was that many concerns had been in a stagnant state for many years, never changing their sales methods or policies. With the innovation of new sales methods and the entry of younger salesmen with drive and ambition, the entire sales force would be stimulated.

In the Syracuse district at this time, three sales positions opened as the result of two retirements and the transfer of one salesman to another area for health reasons. Mr. Simmons had been hesitant about hiring three younger salesmen to fill the vacancies, but pressure from the regional and home offices placed him in a position of finally hiring three young men after intensive interviewing. Two of the men had prior sales experience in related areas on a part-time basis.

After a six-month training program which consisted of a complete orientation to company products, actual sales calls with company salesmen and review of company policies and procedures, the new salesmen were assigned to their own sales areas.

After a short time, Mr. Simmons found that the new salesmen had drive and ambition but seemed to be overly anxious in that they expected immediate results in sales. He was also receiving complaints from the steady customers in these sales areas. United had always prided itself on its personal attention and cooperative attitude toward the customer. Many of the complaints were concerned with the lack of personal attention from the new salesmen. The new salesmen were going into buyers' offices expecting to merely sit down for a few minutes and talk and then write up an order. The customers were not receiving assistance in helping to solve their problems. Neither were they given any new ideas or suggestions in furniture and equipment trends. Some customers felt the new salesmen were obnoxious in their attitudes and were interested only in writing a sale.

Mr. Simmons found that the sales in these areas were down from previous comparative periods, which he attributed to the lack of experience of the new salesmen. He also felt that a great number of these decreased sales were due to the attitude of the salesmen. He held a conference with the salesmen and told them of the customers' complaints and what could be done to handle these complaints. He explained the importance of product knowledge; he dwelled on the creative aspect of selling; he explained the importance of cooperation with the customer to gain his respect and confidence. Simmons was so deeply concerned about the attitude of the new salesmen and the customers' reactions to it that he decided to talk to the regional manager about it. The regional manager reassured Simmons that this was to be expected but to keep in touch with him on any further developments.

When the same situation continued after a short period of time, Simmons was in a quandary as to what action was necessary to resolve this problem.

Questions

1. What are the basic weaknesses involved?
2. Are the salesmen or the company at fault for these problems?
3. What procedures would you initiate to overcome this unsatisfactory situation?

CHAPTER 12

Managing Yourself

The preceding chapter completed the presentation on methods, procedures, and techniques of selling. If you learn and practice what you have studied, you ought to succeed in selling. However, to avoid erratic selling, spotty performance, and insufficient sales volume, you must learn to *manage yourself*. Just as your car must receive care if it is to perform satisfactorily, so must you pay attention to yourself, the human machine, if you expect to perform at a high level.

TWENTY-FOUR HOUR JOB

Successful people live their jobs. The teacher who teaches a few hours a day and then forgets teaching the rest of the time is not a teacher. He is earning some money by going through the motions of teaching. The farmer farms 24 hours a day. He will work late at night to bring in that last load of hay. He will stay up all night with a sick cow. If a piece of equipment breaks during the day, he will stay up late that night repairing it. The doctor is subject to call even when he leaves his office. Through his home phone or his answering service, he can be reached at almost any hour. The minister is subject to call at any hour of the day or night. Very little of his work is done in his office or study in many instances.

You are a salesman 24 hours a day just as the teacher, the doctor, the minister, and the farmer are 24-hour-a-day people. You cannot be a salesman for eight hours and something else the other 16 hours. This is not to say, of course, that anyone could or should work 24 hours. Rather, you should develop a total awareness of your salesman's functions. Always be alert to the opportunities that can help your sales career.

SALESMEN GROW

Your life has many facets. You cannot isolate yourself, nor can you live a narrow, compartmentalized life. Budget your week so that you spend some time with your family at home. You must work to increase in stature on the job and in the community. Life's responsibilities will take an increasing share of energy. Unless you recognize the demands of a well-developed pattern of living and allocate your time for each essential segment, you will discover that progress becomes more difficult. You may not improve each part of your life at the same time, but eventually each part must be given its proper attention.

The importance of each segment of your life can vary from year to year. One year you might teach Sunday school; the next year you could work with boy scouts; during the third and fourth years you might follow high school athletics; finally, your interests are directed to college or elsewhere. As you become well established in a community, civic duties grow. Imperceptibly, life becomes more complex, time becomes more important, and requests for help increase.

As you grow in your job, your work will demand more time, even if the mechanics of the job take less time. As your sphere of influence grows, it will touch more people who, in turn, will make requests you cannot avoid. Often you get so involved you scarcely have any time for yourself, and your work suffers. To avoid getting hopelessly confused and involved, let us study how to *manage yourself*.

PHYSICAL REQUIREMENTS

Your body is a physical machine that must be given proper attention if you are to sell effectively. When this machine malfunctions, sales suffer.

Food

Exercise moderation in food and beverages; eat and drink sensibly and avoid excesses. If you know you may have to drink one or more cups of coffee with customers during the forenoon, go easy on coffee for breakfast. If you have a buyer for lunch, avoid too much food or drink even if the buyer eats twice as much as you. He will not be offended by what you do as long as he can have what he wants. When entertaining either at noon or in the evening and your guests are drinking freely, tell the waiter to bring you some harmless drink. Guests have a wide latitude in what they do, but you cannot afford to lose control of yourself.

Improper eating habits may have little effect on the young man, but age takes its toll and soon the salesman begins to pay greater attention to what he eats. The sooner you give attention to diet, the more slowly are weaknesses likely to develop.

Clothing

Your dress was covered in an earlier chapter. Suffice it to add that not only appearance but also comfort is important. Clothes should be comfortable. Lounging clothes and slippers can make an evening in a hotel much more pleasant. Clothing for protection against inclement weather must be adequate. You cannot afford to get wet, cold, or uncomfortable too often. Frequently we are not dressed properly for all conditions, but we should try to avoid these situations as much as possible. One way to avoid embarrassment is to have duplicate coats, shoes, overshoes, and umbrellas.

Provide extra clothing. Laundries are not always prompt. The cleaner may not have your suit ready when you need it. Accidents happen to clothes. Be prepared with that extra suit, that extra shirt, and the extra shoes.

Rest

Each day you should start out fresh and optimistic. This is impossible if you spent a sleepless night. Avoid evening activities which prevent sleep. Daily demands tire you. Unless you recoup your energies at night, your next day's work will be listless. For some years the young man may abuse his body with insufficient rest, but eventually his body will complain.

Do not cut into your sleep by staying up late in the evening. Do not try to drive home at night when you ought to stay in a hotel. Many a salesman wastes valuable selling time driving home, when he ought to stay in his territory. This is equally true both at night and on weekends.

Do not take long tiresome drives at night if you are permitted to take a plane. Using public transportation often is faster and less tiring than being your own chauffeur. Do not travel Sunday night if you have an important meeting Monday morning. Do not crowd your appointments so that you must rush from one to another. At the same time, do not be afraid of a 4:30 appointment. Many a buyer will stay after 5:00 if your presentation is interesting.

Rest means not only proper night comfort but also proper day comfort. If your day has been hectic, perhaps by 4:00 in the afternoon you will be in no condition to meet another buyer. An irritable salesman is not very efficient. Determine how much rest you need, and discipline yourself to get enough.

Relaxation

Learn to relax. In the midst of your busy daily schedule, you do not use all parts of your mind and body at the same rate. If your selling requires little movement but much mental attention, your mind tires, but your body does not. Physical exercise in the evening may be relaxing. If your day is both physically and mentally exhausting, a quiet evening may be what you need to relax. Sometimes, going out on a brief visit may relieve tension. Playing with the children at home in the evening may be fun for all. The main idea is to get a change in pace, to rest what has worked hard all day and to exercise what has been relatively inactive all day. At times, you may be desperately tired mentally and yet find that you cannot sleep until you become physically tired through some relaxing activity. Some salesmen feel that playing a game such as bowling is wasting time. On the contrary, it may be the best thing a salesman can do because it builds the body to withstand the rigors of the job.

Do not overlook entertainment—movies, plays, concerts—as a means of relaxation. Such activities cannot only be relaxing but also stimulating because you acquire new ideas as you listen and observe. Relaxation should relieve tension, loosen muscles, and induce a restful attitude. It should relieve you so that you have a chance to recharge yourself physically, mentally, and spiritually.

Medical Checkup

Any operating machine develops weak spots in time. Our bodies, like machines, are not immune to weaknesses. Although the body constantly rebuilds itself, there is always the chance that certain parts weaken. To avoid physical breakdown, have medical checkups at regular intervals. Many executives have medical examinations once a year after they have turned thirty. One way to remember to have checkups is to have one on each birthday. How often you should have one may depend on various circumstances best determined by your physician. Most of us have had the experience of neglecting our teeth too long. Finally, the dentist has no recourse but to pull a painful tooth. Many minor ills, caught early, can be overcome with proper attention. Neglected, such weaknesses become incurable.

FINANCIAL STABILITY

The successful salesman manages his finances adequately. Even though he may work on a "pauper to prince" income (or vice versa) by depending on commissions, he must maintain solvency and a reasonably good standard of living.

Earnings

You may be paid in a number of ways—straight salary, commissions, salary and commission, salary and bonus—but however you are paid, in the long run your salary comes from a percentage of sales. Your firm allows a budgeted amount for sales expenses, and your total earnings and expenses cannot exceed this amount. Small variations may occur, but such amounts do not long exceed the budget.

If your earnings are a level amount each period, plan accordingly. Often, salary fluctuations necessitate a different type of planning. When you begin selling, your earnings may be small. As your selling ability grows, your earnings should grow. There is nothing magic about how much you earn. Except for a beginning or training period during which you are a financial liability, your earnings will reflect your worth to your employer.

He balances your performance against your cost. As the balance of selling grows, he willingly puts a greater earnings on the cost balance side. You register your worth on a scale of values for which he pays commensurately.

Beware of earnings that increase in a spectacular fashion. Do not spend them all. You may be lucky. If your earnings increase rapidly, be cautious in spending until time demonstrates whether or not you can maintain such earnings. A steady but slow increase in earning power is usually more typical of selling. Such progress is fairly dependable.

Expenditures—Budgeting

Very often the beginning salesman with a family may find his earnings inadequate. It is so easy to buy beyond your means. This is the time to exercise prudence in spending. In your early selling career you may change jobs. There can be periods of unemployment. This is no time to incur long-term obligations. You are in a period of adjustment—a new job, perhaps a new place to live, and many things to buy—when you should not spend much money.

Budget your income. List essential expenditures and then those expenditures which you would like to make but which are unessential. As your income increases, you can broaden the list. While certain expenditures such as food, clothing, and perhaps a car might head your list of essentials, there can be major deviations in each category. Some families spend twice as much for food as other families. Men's suits are priced from $50 to $150 and up. Women's dresses sell from $10 to over $100. Often, the difference in amount of service between a lower priced garment and a higher priced one is small. The lasting value may be the same in the higher priced garment and the lower priced one, but the higher priced dress can have a different kind of value. The wife of a young salesman may find a suitable dress for $19.95, but the wife of a top executive may find nothing suitable under $99.95.

You can buy some models of popular priced cars for about $2,000. Other models of the same car cost over $4,000. Both will furnish adequate transportation. Many times you may be tempted to buy high quality when a lesser quality would be suitable. Think of your income as a limited source which can decrease, increase, or even disappear temporarily. The wise salesman gives himself a savings cushion. He does not spend all his money nor mortgage his future indefinitely with onerous payments.

Borrowing Money

Interest is paid for the use of money. Whether you borrow money outright or borrow by having a purchase financed, you pay interest. After all, the individual or institution which makes loans must earn a profit to stay in business.

Whenever you buy and do not pay cash, you are borrowing someone else's money. Somebody pays cash, either you or the person lending money. Consequently, when you buy on time, you pay two costs—the merchandise cost and the money cost. Because of the high cost of some items, you will buy on time because it will be impossible to pay cash. To enjoy now the pleasure of owning a house and car, you buy on time. But as soon as you make these purchases, you cannot buy some other thing with the same money. You will have committed yourself to give a specified amount of your income to time payments each month. This is what is meant by "mortgaging your future."

Credit is an admirable way to finance purchases, but like other good things, it can be used and abused. Judiciously used, it permits you to enjoy a fuller life. Improperly used, credit can bring worry, suffering, and ruin. Do not borrow with the hope of paying back with higher future earnings. Plan to pay back on your present earning scale. Wait until future increased earnings materialize before you borrow against them.

Contributions

Contributions should be high on your list of essential spending. Many contributions, though voluntary, go for essential services. Indirectly, they affect your life as much as food, clothing, and shelter. If your shelter takes 25 percent of your income and your food bill another 25 percent, that will leave you with half your income for other purposes.

Because some young people can dodge contributions, they are inclined to shirk their duty. Inasmuch as you use services, you should contribute to their support. Contribute to your church, United Fund, local organizations, and other worthwhile activities.

One young man used the following system. Each time he was paid, the first 10 percent went to his church, the second 10 percent went to savings, and the remainder was used for living expenses. Each time he got a raise, his standard of living increased. He is now an executive who is doing handsomely.

Contributing, like other activities, can be habit-forming. Willingly carrying your share of the load should become a part of you. It gives you the confidence that enables you to progress faster and with greater assurance.

Restrict Spending

The careful salesman restricts his spending. When he buys, he expects to pay. Life consists of a series of advances and reverses. Unexpected expenditures such as medical bills and unforeseen repairs are inevitable. One is wise to restrict spending so that he can accumulate a reserve to meet the unknown. Just as machinery, equipment, and bridges are built with a generous margin for safety, so should you order your life to provide for emergencies.

Many unexpected contingencies can be handled through insurance. Examine your insurance portfolio to see how well you and your family are protected. Substantial immediate protection for your family can be secured through life insurance at a moderate cost. Investigate term life insurance for the greatest protection at the lowest cost; of course, this gives maximum protection without any savings features. Is your car liability insurance adequate? You cannot protect against all contingencies, but you can save yourself much possible grief by a savings account that can handle minor emergencies and assist in handling a major emergency.

TIME ON JOB

You have only a limited number of hours each day to meet customers. Capitalize on each hour.

Selling Time

Studies reveal that many salesmen spend about 2 hours a day facing customers. If they could increase this time by 30 minutes or one more effective call, that would be 250 extra calls a year. Within the past year, salesmen for a well-known firm have had their daily quota of calls raised from 6 to 10. Selling costs are rising so rapidly that more is required of each salesman. If more work cannot be obtained from the sales force, alternative sales approaches—such as heavy advertising with direct catalog selling —are adopted. Salesmen are eliminated when costs become excessive.

Your primary job is to sell. You sell when you face the customer, but most preparatory activities contribute to these important minutes with the prospect. Not only should you use your best selling approaches, but you should be economical with your time. Jealously guard and use every minute of selling time. Increase the minutes of selling time by eliminating unessential activities and postponing others.

One study of wholesale drug salesmen revealed a direct relationship between the number of items ably presented and the sales of such items. The salesman who was content to present 3 items usually sold one or two. The salesman who presented 6 items sold about 3. He sold twice as hard and increased sales one third. The difference between a winner and a loser in a golf tournament may be one stroke. The first place winner has a score of 274; the second place player scores 275. Yet, in the payoff that one stroke means twice as much money for the first as the second place player. The little extra attention to selling time can pay big dividends.

Travel Time

Many salesmen spend too much time traveling. When you use precious selling time for travel, you are wasting your most valuable asset.

Excess travel time can be eliminated by proper routing. Plan your travel in advance each day. Instead of jumping from customer to customer without regard for distance, plan to go in a direct line from one customer to the next by covering the shortest possible distance. Avoid retracing your route and avoid zigzagging. Sometimes your territory permits you to go directly from one customer to another in an orderly route and end up near your starting point. If, however, your customers are in a more or less straight line, it might be well to start with the one farthest away early in the morning and work your way back to the customer nearest your office or home. Do your distance driving before or after selling hours. If you have one long distance between two customers, try to travel during noon hours.

Do not waste valuable selling time by cruising around to find a parking place. To save a 50-cent parking fee, you may spend 10 minutes of your selling time to find a free place in which to park. Ten minutes' selling time is worth at least $3, perhaps $5. Why try to save 50 cents when the time you waste is worth $5? Wise sales managers arrange to have the employer pay for parking.

Report Time

You may be one of those unfortunate salesmen who is flooded with report writing. Most companies insist on some reports. Others have salesmen write innumerable reports which are used infrequently. A good rule for any sales manager is to require only those reports which are read. Every report should have a useful purpose.

In some types of business, sales reports are very important and must be complete and informative. They must be written on time. A salesman mentioned one instance in which he had to fly from Detroit to Pittsburgh to deliver a weekly report. He had neglected to send it to the home office on time.

When you neglect writing your reports for several days, your memory becomes hazy. Details important at the time of the interview are forgotten or improperly reported. Delaying report writing is one way to lose your job. Many a salesman, otherwise adequate, has foundered on his report writing.

Seldom do you write a report immediately after an interview. Your selling hours are too valuable to be wasted on report writing. When you are told to write your reports as soon as possible, that usually means to write them in the evening of the same day of the interviews. If you have time during the day when you must wait for an interview, you might use that time for report writing. As a rule, complete your day's reports before you go to bed. Rarely should you let report writing wait beyond a weekend. Back work inflicts a severe time penalty.

Preparation Time

Time spent in preparation is time well spent. Preparation implies readiness which in turn implies study of your product, organization of your presentation, and assembling the necessary props to insure success when you talk to a prospect. You prepare yourself, you prepare the environment for your presentation, and you prepare your demonstration. Try to think of every possible contingency; try to eliminate every chance for error.

Do not consider preparation time wasted time. If you go into a busy kitchen, you will note how much time is spent in cleaning and washing dishes and arranging materials before the meal is cooked. Innumerable rehearsals are necessary to prepare a play for production. Painstaking detail and preparation are necessary before a missile is launched.

Preparing forces you to study what you will do when you face a prospect. Since you spend little time with the prospect, be certain that you are ready. Set aside enough preparation time so that you will not be short of the necessary data, and that you will not be embarrassed by ignorance.

Visiting Time

You do not need to spend much time visiting. Most salesmen, as a matter of fact, waste their time and their buyer's time in visiting. One of the best wholesale drug salesmen in Ohio wasted no time at all in such small talk as weather, gossip, or stories. He talked business to his customers—customer business. The customer is more interested in hearing you tell him how to improve his business than he is in listening to jokes.

You cannot, however, make a universal statement to fit all buyers. Some like to spend time visiting; others begrudge every minute of small talk. Surveys show that weak salesmen use a lot of visiting time; strong salesmen visit much less. Some salesmen visit for visiting's sake. They visit because they think it is required. It is like some speakers who think every talk must be introduced with a story or joke. Visiting time, like preparation time and presentation time, should have a purpose. No one of these is an end in itself. Each one of these should contribute to the sale.

Occasionally, after 5:00 p.m. when the office is closed and you have finished your business, you may find a buyer who wishes to relax and chat. Do not hurry away if you sense that he wants to talk. This is a particularly good time to get better acquainted because the buyer is asking you to get better acquainted with him. Never pass up this opportunity to cement friendship. Everything you do in the presence of a buyer should contribute to selling. Avoid visiting when you can, but always keep your visiting to a minimum unless you are sure that you need the chit-chat to make the sale.

Wasting Time

There are innumerable ways to fritter away time. Some salesmen never get started in the morning. Precious minutes are lost through puttering, getting ready, and being unable to make decisions. What shall I wear? What equipment will I need today? What customer shall I see first? These and many other questions can crop up in the morning. Most of them can be answered the night before.

Much time is wasted while waiting to see buyers. While waiting in an office lobby you can either work or waste time reading newspapers, current magazines, or idly chattering. Through careful scheduling, however, you could reduce time waste to a small fraction of your time in lobbies or outer waiting rooms. Calling on the buyers at inopportune periods of the day is an inexcusable waste of time. To make this mistake once with a buyer is understandable; to continue making the same mistake is silly.

Do not waste time at lunch. If you eat alone, adjust your schedule to avoid using selling time. If you take a buyer to lunch, he can spend only a limited time with you. Be observant and be guided by his wishes. If he is receptive, discuss selling at lunch. Adjust your lunch period differently each day, if necessary, so that you maximize selling time.

Do not waste time waiting in the office lobby after lunch if you can be the first to see the buyer after lunch. During the day refreshment periods can waste valuable time. You cannot afford such periods unless the buyers want them. Make your closing hours in the afternoon flexible. You need not stop selling at 5:00 p.m. if buyers work later. Tailor your hours to fit theirs.

You do not forget your job at 5:00 p.m., either. In the hotel in the evening you can waste your time by doing nothing of importance, or you can use it efficiently. You can either daydream or think. Some salesmen confuse the two.

You do not have to forget your work on weekends. Even thinking selling subconsciously helps to fix thoughts and ideas. Instead of letting your mind go blank, apply it to some knotty problem. Many salesmen feel that if they give their employer 40 hours a week, they have done their duty; but selling is not a 40-hour-a-week job. If you choose to forget selling after hours, you are wasting time and doing yourself a disservice. You are dissipating time, which is your most precious selling tool. Wasted time is wasted life. Why fritter away the irreplaceable? You either save time by using it wisely, or you waste time by letting it slip by without accomplishment.

IMPROVING YOURSELF MENTALLY

Your physical self is being replaced constantly. New cells replace old ones. Your hair and nails grow. Your body changes shape. Aches and pains come and go. You are changing each minute.

Mental changes go on like physical changes. We may not be aware of mental changes because they may be hard to determine. Mentally, you become a better salesman or a worse one. Probably you can improve mentally to some extent through desirable associations. Merely being with some people may prove beneficial. It is not likely, however, that you will improve yourself much unless you consciously strive to improve.

Plan a pattern of activity to improve yourself mentally. Set aside a "thinking" period each day when you concentrate on specific problems or subject matter. Address your thoughts to chosen areas and do not let thoughts drift aimlessly. Jot down some of your thoughts and ideas and rearrange them in a number of ways to see if you can establish new relationships.

When difficult sales problems crop up, take time to work out solutions and then test them in sales situations. Revise and rework them. See if you can improve solutions which you now consider satisfactory. Do not be content to solve a problem in a weak way if you can approach it brilliantly. Do not be satisfied to be just good enough. Who knows, you may improve so much that you will be promoted to an executive position, or you may change to a more difficult selling job with another firm at a higher level. If you do well at your present selling job, remain discontented.

This feeling may impel you forward to greater achievement, a harder job, and a more rewarding life.

The possibilities of improving yourself mentally are so enormous that you can work at it all your life. You will never reach your pinnacle of mental development. Most salesmen settle for a mental plateau that is low on the achievement scale. No matter how far you push your mental attainments, you still possess unused capacity. At one period in life what you consider peak achievement may later look feeble. Many a salesman immensely proud of his success ten years ago looks today at that period with amused tolerance. Little did he think then how much farther he would progress.

Do not limit your mental improvement too narrowly. Think of your mind as the hub of a wheel with spokes of effort radiating outward. A strong wheel has a number of strong spokes. Develop each of your mental spokes to reflect a well-balanced mind and a multifaceted approach to life's problems. You will not solve sales problems successfully unless you also solve your other problems successfully.

You learn to manage yourself by working at it. The baseball player learns to throw and to catch the ball, to bat, to run bases, and to be in good position to field the ball. You can learn to manage yourself through self-disciplines of salesmanship that will teach you to prosper as a top-level salesman. There is always room at the top for stalwart, well-trained salesmen who are willing to work to hold their position.

IT'S UP TO YOU

Throughout this book we have emphasized the YOU. Each chapter has involved YOU in a definite relationship. We have stressed the importance of YOU in the equation. Now, what YOU will do is up to YOU.

MY IMPROVEMENT SCHEDULE

I EITHER GO FORWARD
　　　　OR
I SLIDE BACKWARD
I CANNOT STAND STILL

DAILY—Time 1 to 2 hours
　1. Follow current events in daily newspapers, on the radio, and television.
　2. Read some worthwhile literature that may improve, educate, and develop me.
　3. Spend some time in real thinking.
　4. Plan tomorrow's work.

WEEKLY—Time 2 to 4 hours
　1. Read weekly business magazines.
　2. Clean up unfinished work.
　3. Make reports current.
　4. Plan next week's work.

MONTHLY—Time 2 to 4 hours
　1. Read monthly business magazines.
　2. Evaluate month's activities.
　3. Participate in some activity with the family or friends.
Monthly activities can be accomplished both during and at the end of the month.

QUARTERLY—Time 8 hours
　1. Analyze quarter's activities.
　2. Plan definite improvement steps for the next quarter.
　3. Assess current economic conditions.
Quarterly activities tend to be concentrated at the end of the quarter.

YEARLY—Time 3 weeks
　1. Attend convention or special meetings.
　2. Take vacation.
　3. Analyze year's performance and compare with some standard.
　4. Develop quotas for coming year.
Yearly activities may be done during the year as well as at the end of the year. Your year need not coincide with a calendar year.

FIVE YEAR—Time as needed
　1. Refresher training.
　2. Realignment of goals.
　3. Long-range planning.

Questions and Problems

1. Prepare a list of jobs that require a 24-hour response. Show the similarities of such jobs. Indicate why the 40-hour-a-week man will not succeed in such jobs. In hiring people for 24-hour jobs, what characteristics would you seek? How does sacrifice fit into this type of job?
2. Outline a pattern of living that will permit a salesman to give his best to his job. Indicate areas that deserve special attention. Describe the many facets of his life that should be developed, and show why this broad development is essential.
3. Draw up a personal budget for a salesman. Suggest an expenditure pattern. Indicate how he must balance income and expenditures. Advance several approaches on handling income increases. Point out alternative savings and investment approaches.
4. Develop a plan for the most efficient use of time. Show how restrictive measures must be instituted to overcome the waste of time. Point out methods of sandwiching in work and activities to use up short periods of time that might be wasted. Indicate how best to use time by listing activities in their order of importance.
5. Make an outline in detail that will stress the improvement factors. Show how the salesman can grow through self-development.

CASES

12-1: ASHBY EQUIPMENT COMPANY

Ashby Equipment Company is a large distributor of machinery and related accessories in Dayton. Ten salesmen travel out of the Dayton office in territories, none of which is more than 300 miles from Dayton. For many years, each man has been permitted to cultivate his territory in his own way. Needless to say, many odd procedures were developed which caused frequent headaches at the home office. But as long as Fred Ashby was president, this situation continued because Mr. Ashby, who started the business as a salesman, believed that each man should be allowed to develop his territory and himself in his own way.

When Fred Ashby retired, his son, Keith, became president. Keith had grown up in the business. As a young man, he had worked in the warehouse. After he finished college, he became a salesman and handled one of the territories for 10 years. When Lester Diamond, the sales manager, retired five years ago, Keith was promoted to sales manager, a position he handled well.

When Keith became president, he promoted Norbert Rowe to sales manager. Norbert had joined the Ashby Equipment Company

five years ago as a salesman and during that time had made re-
markable progress in sales. He also had shown considerable leadership
potential. Of the entire sales force, he was the most likely man to
become sales manager. Some of the older salesmen were firmly
wedded to their territories and were not interested in the job of
sales manager.

Both Keith and Norbert were aware of the loose control of the
sales force. They had often marveled how the firm succeeded with
such chaotic sales control. Therefore, one of the first steps they
decided on was to institute a series of sales reports which would
enable them to know what each salesmen was doing and what was
his pattern of daily activity.

Undoubtedly, the salesmen would resent writing reports and
would resent any control that would interfere with their freedom.
Yet, some of the salesmen were not doing too well, and some sold a
lot of equipment but of a type that gave little profit. The salesmen
thought they were doing well since their dollar volume increased
each year. However, they did not realize that price increases plus
the growth of the total economy should have caused their sales to
increase faster. Several competing firms had shown far more progress
in the past ten years. What the salesmen failed to detect was that
Ashby Equipment Company had long since lost its dominating position in the industry and was now considered a medium-size firm, and
not a challenging leader.

Keith had watched this deteriorating position with alarm for
several years but had been unable to arouse his father who had
retained tight control of all decision making. In the few years
Norbert had been with the firm, he had noticed this gradual worsen-
ing of position. He had maintained a position of leadership in his
territory but recognized that other salesmen in the firm had let
sales in their territories slip.

Keith and Norbert were ambitious to make their firm a leader in
the field again. To do this, there would have to be a shakeup in the
sales force. With the exception of one salesman, all were strong men,
capable of producing more and better sales than they were doing
presently. Therefore, the job was to build up these men by applying
modern methods which would show each man how to get the
existing potential out of his territory. The first step was to develop
controls through reports.

Questions

1. To what extent would reports arouse salesman antagonism?
2. Exactly what reports would you require the first six months?
3. Are there other controls in addition to reports that could be used?
4. Can you outline a positive approach to control that would arouse
   little salesman opposition?

12-2: LINDGREN TRAINING ASSOCIATES

Lindgren Training Associates had been retained by Swanson Mills of Buffalo to develop a sales training program for their 50 salesmen located in territories throughout the United States.

Swanson Mills had changed its name from Swanson Flour Milling Company. The name was changed to reflect the activities of the firm, which now included the production of many food products in addition to flour and feed. The headquarters of Swanson Mills had been in Minneapolis, but five years ago it was moved to Buffalo. This change was dictated by the development of new production facilities in Buffalo, Atlanta, Omaha, and Evansville. Each of the five production facilities concentrated on a limited line of products which were produced in large quantities and shipped to 14 major warehouses in the United States. Since the largest market was in the eastern part of the United States, Buffalo had been selected as the headquarters of sales activities.

Duane Erickson, who represented Lindgren Training Associates on this project, had put in six months of strenuous work in developing a sales training program. The results were satisfactory to Swanson Mills. They asked Mr. Erickson if he or someone could aid in getting the program started. Mr. Erickson assigned Elton Carlson to this task.

One final phase of the training program requested by the sales manager, August Bard, was to develop a self-improvement schedule for each salesman. Also, he wanted a performance appraisal chart that could be used to assess a salesman's performance on a broad scale of activity. These activities would include sales, profits, handling of customers, use of sales aids, following advertising leads, use of demonstrations, and following suggestions of the home office.

Assignment

1. Develop a salesman self-improvement schedule.
2. Draw up a comprehensive performance appraisal chart that can be used to rate salesmen in this firm.

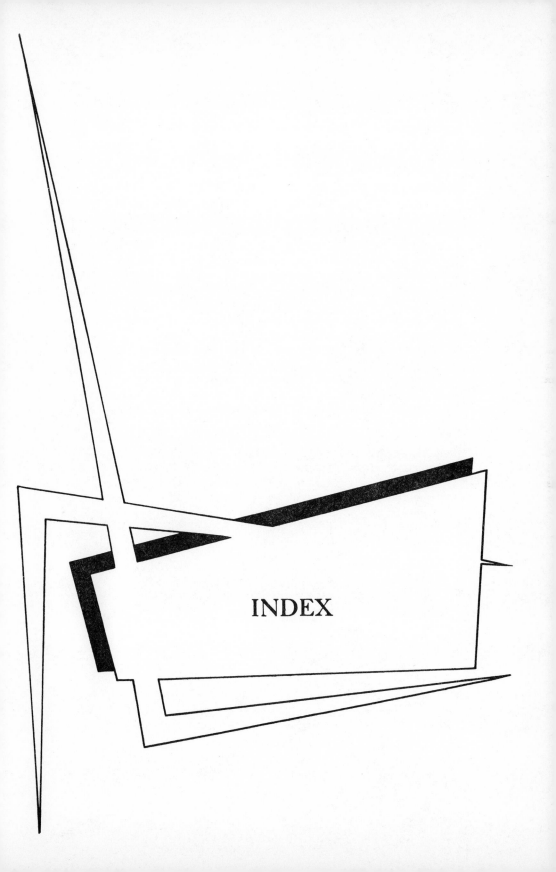

INDEX

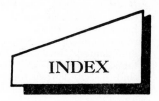

INDEX